CROSSING SIDELINES, CROSSING CULTURES

Sport and Asian Pacific American Cultural Citizenship

SECOND EDITION

Joel Franks

University Press of America,® Inc.
Lanham · Boulder · New York · Toronto · Plymouth, UK

Copyright © 2010 by
University Press of America,® Inc.
4501 Forbes Boulevard
Suite 200
Lanham, Maryland 20706
UPA Acquisitions Department (301) 459-3366

Estover Road
Plymouth PL6 7PY
United Kingdom

Library of Congress Control Number: 2009928793
ISBN: 978-0-7618-4744-1 (paperback : alk. paper)
eISBN: 978-0-7618-4745-8

To my precious scholar-athletes, Kait and Spencer

Contents

Preface

When it is summer, it is basketball camp time for my daughter Kait. At one local camp, the majority of participants seem to possess some kind of Asian Pacific ancestry. Regardless of race, ethnicity, and gender the campers, ranging from eight to sixteen years of age, play hard and usually well. Meanwhile the Asian Pacific participants seem unconcerned that they are breaking down stereotypes many non-Asian Pacific maintain of them. Rather than making accurate no-look passes and hitting jumpers, these Asian Pacific young people should be at computer or gymnastics camps. They should not be crossing over into endeavors dominated so long by non-Asian Pacific people.

This book is not about celebrating sports such as basketball, football, and baseball at the expense of other and often worthier activities. Yet among other things, this book is about people asserting their cultural identities in ways that break down stereotypes. To be sure, learning to master computers and, to a lesser extent, the parallel bars merits respect. And learning how to shoot a three pointer and set a pick, in the long run, may justifiably seem trivial. Indeed, competitive sports in the U.S. can teach our youth lessons that many adults might well question. Competitive sports, however, can strengthen as well as weaken an individual's self-esteem. They can bring people together as well as set them apart. And they have contributed, whether we like it or not, to the development of many cultures. Accordingly Asian Pacific American involvement in sports historically and today ought to demonstrate the flimsiness of the racial and ethnic conventions we entertain. As such, sports deserve our sometimes critical, sometimes celebratory attention.

Researching and writing this book has generally been a joy. In the process, I have learned a great deal and many of my own preconceptions about Asian Pacific people have been dissolved. I have, moreover, drawn inspiration from numerous academic and non-academic scholars in the areas of Asian Pacific American, ethnic, and sports' studies. Some, but not nearly all, of these scholars are cited in this book's endnotes.

Scholars such as Samuel Regalado, George Kirsch, and Larry Gerlach have made substantial comments on at least some of the material included in this book. Meanwhile, I need to acknowledge the library staff people at the University of California, Berkeley, San Jose State University, San Jose Public Library, Stanford University, the National Baseball Hall of Fame, De Anza College, the Bishop Museum, and the University of Hawai'i. Judy Yung, Steve Fugita, Florence Chang, Helen Wong Lum, and Ruth F. Chinn have helped me stay on the right track. More importantly, I need to acknowledge the inspiration of my Sansei wife Cheryl and my hapa or double children, Kait and Spencer.

Joel S. Franks
Cupertino, California
January, 1999

The Second Edition

Since 1999, much has happened in the world of Asian Pacific American sport history. Increasingly, young Americans of Asian Pacific American ancestry have attained high levels of athletic competence in a wide variety of sports. Moreover, my continued research, as well as the research of others, has brought to light experiences that were not or inadequately acknowledged in this book's first edition.

Nevertheless, the basic argument of the book remains critical of the assimilationist perspective on the relationship between sport and Asian Pacific Americans. The concept of cultural citizenship still seems to explain better why Americans of Asian Pacific ancestry have taken up baseball, basketball, football, prize fighting, as well as other sports.

Finally, I should add that my daughter has ended her high school athletic career as a four foot eleven inch point guard in basketball and defender in field hockey. She generally enjoyed her time of maneuvering her small body through the battlefields of high school sports. But she has moved on to college and left the fields and the gyms to her younger brother, Spencer. An eleventh grader, Spencer will hopefully participate in some varsity sport in high school. Yet even if he reminds no one of Steve Nash or Derek Jeter, his mom and dad will no doubt remain just as proud of him as we are of his sister.

Joel Franks
Cupertino, California
September, 2008

Introduction

In the mid-1990s, I attended a symposium on baseball and culture at Cooperstown, New York—the home of the American Baseball Hall of Fame. At one of the lunches held during the symposium, I was asked by another attendee about whether I was going to give a paper. I replied that, indeed, I would deliver a paper on Asian American baseball. My conversation partner responded, "What Asian American baseball?" Sometime after, a Japanese American acquaintance heard about my research in Asian American baseball and started asking me questions about Hideo Nomo, who was then dazzling opponents in his first year with the Los Angeles Dodgers. I felt compelled to remind my acquaintance that my area of research and knowledge was allied with Japanese American baseball and not Japanese baseball. A few years later, my then ten-year-old daughter asked me why there were not any Asians or Asian Americans on her basketball team. My wife who is a third generation Japanese American overheard Kait's question and asked her if she might want to rephrase it. I am, by the way, European American.

The preceding paragraph raises some of the issues that anyone trying to write a book on Asian Pacific American sporting experiences has to confront. First, many Americans, including Asian Pacific Americans who follow sports, seem to assume that Asian Pacific Americans have not played baseball, football, basketball, hockey, or boxed. Granted, some would agree, a few Asian Pacific Americans might hurl their lithe bodies around ice skating rinks or parallel bars, but they do not jam, tackle, or body check. Second, many Americans, including Asian Pacific Americans, consider the experiences of Asian Pacific people as all of one piece. That is, they believe that contemporary professional athletes such as Ichiro Suzuki and Yao Ming can represent Asian Pacific American experiences even though these athletes were born and raised in places and times that differ significantly from the California in which Olympic divers Sammy Lee and Vicki Manalo lived in the 1920s and 1930s. Of course, the experiences of Asian Pacific people with sports have been transnational; they have crisscrossed national borders. But the experiences of an American athlete of Japanese ancestry in the United States has and will differ from the experiences of a native born Japanese citizen in Japan. Finally, the problem of mixed racial and ethnic ancestries is not a small one. Magnificent American athletes claiming Asian Pacific descent such as Tiger Woods, Vicki Manalo, and Herman

Wedemeyer have also possessed non-Asian Pacific ancestry. Should we consider their experiences Asian Pacific American experiences?

Why Asian Pacific Americans and Sports?

One justification for writing a book about Asian Pacific American sporting experiences is that there remains, as the preceding paragraphs suggest, relatively little known about the subject. All in all, the lack of research and writing about Asian Pacific American sporting experiences should not elicit much indignation. There are so many crucial issues that need investigation when it comes to Asian Pacific Americans. Standard texts such as Ronald Takaki's *Strangers from a Different Shore* and Sucheng Chan's *Asian Americans: An Interpretive History* have very little, if anything, to say about Asian Pacific American sporting experiences, but they furnish us with a wealth of valuable information and interpretations regarding the trials and triumphs of Asian Pacific Americans. It seems, therefore, ridiculous to tax scholars such as Takaki and Chan for failing to write about Japanese Hawaiian football and baseball star, Wally Yonamine, when they have done such a fine job addressing anti-Asian immigration laws, the Model Minority Thesis, and Asian Pacific American political activities. [1]

We might, however, now find exploring Asian Pacific American sporting experiences useful since academic and non-academic scholars have performed so much hard groundwork. But we should try to avoid the trap of doing a history that, according to cultural analyst Theodore Gonzalves, "uncritically celebrates the winning of awards, the attainment of social station..." Of course, we ought to remember and celebrate the athletic achievements of individual Asian Pacific Americans. Much of what they accomplished speaks volumes about their courage and endurance, as well as their athletic skills. However, we also need to attend to the anonymous and nearly anonymous Asian Pacific American athletes who will never attain the fame or fortune of a Kristi Yamaguchi, Michael Chang, and Junior Seau. Their experiences, too, helped forge Asian Pacific American ethnic communities, while showing how people have used sports to break down stereotypes and cross the difficult terrain of the cultural borderlands that have separated racial and ethnic groups in the United States. At the same time, we need to keep our minds open to how sports have aided the effort to "raise hierarchies," to quote historian Robert Wiebe. That is, sports even in the relatively democratic atmosphere of the United States have been employed to justify and reinforce racial, ethnic, class, and gender inequalities between Asian Pacific Americans and non-Asian Pacific Americans, as well as among Asian Pacific Americans. [2]

To be sure, many of us consider sports neither important nor particularly enjoyable. Yet even if we do not enjoy soccer or baseball, we should try to recognize the power of sports in the United States and globally. In truth, as pointed out in an earlier paragraph, sports can play an ambivalent role in people's lives. Sports can seemingly liberate participants, even if for a moment, from the bonds of cultural and social conventions. Sports can construct cultural bridges across geographic and social boundaries. Sports are, for many of us, fun to play and watch. Sports can also strengthen divisions among people. They have often proven good investments for those who wish to monopolize racial, ethnic, class, and gender privileges. Sports have, not just recently, but for years, engendered greed and violence.

For whatever reasons, many people of Asian Pacific and non-Asian Pacific have considered sports consequential in their lives and the lives of their family members and friends. This lies at the heart of why we need to examine Asian Pacific American sporting experiences. For through sports, Asian Pacific Americans have been defined and have defined themselves. In short, the cultural citizenship of Asian Pacific Americans has been expressed through sports.

The concept of cultural citizenship emerged in the late 1990s from the work of Latino/a scholars such as Renato Rosaldo, Rina Benmayor, and William Flores. In examining the experiences of Latino/a Americans in cities such as San Jose and Fresno, California, Rosaldo and Flores define cultural citizenship in the following manner: "Cultural citizenship refers to the right to be different (in terms of race, ethnicity, or native language) with respect to the norms of the dominant national community, without compromising one's right to belong, in the sense of the nation-state's democratic processes." Cultural citizenship, therefore, represents the right of people to simultaneously pursue their cultural distinctiveness in the United States and solidify their links to other Americans. Moreover, as a concept cultural citizenship compels us to conceive of racial and ethnic relations in the United States in a more multi-dimensional manner than conventional assimilationist or cultural pluralist perspectives allow. The concept of cultural citizenship finally appears applicable to Asian Pacific Americans historically and today. In the 1920s, San Jose's Japanese Americans supported both community-based baseball and sumo wrestling. In so doing, they asserted their cultural citizenship in the United States—their right to remain unique and yet connected to non-Japanese Americans.[3]

Achieving cultural citizenship has frequently been difficult for Americans of Asian Pacific ancestry due to a complex of factors related significantly to how they have been defined in racial and ethnic terms. During World War II, for example, San Jose's Japanese Americans were unconstitutionally evacuated from their homes to a concentration camp in Heart Mountain, Wyoming. They like, other Asian Pacific Americans before and since, were defined in ethnic and racial terms in such a way that they supposedly posed a threat to their white neighbors.

Accordingly, for Asian Pacific Americans to affirm their cultural citizenship in sports or other endeavors, they have confronted deeply rooted stereotypes, while traversing the cultural borders separating them from other racial and ethnic groups--borders constructed largely out of turbulent mixtures of ethnicity, race, social class, gender, and geopolitics. Sometimes sports eased their journeys. Sometimes sports hindered their journeys.

Sports and Ethnicity

We do not always wish upon ourselves an ethnic label. We often become members of an ethnic group, because those with the power to decide such things declare that we have something significant in common with persons we do not know and may not want to know but inconveniently come from or have parents or ancestors who come from the same part of the world. When we arrive in a country like the United States, we, nevertheless, may gain comfort in living with or near relatives or old friends from our home villages and towns in Southeast China or Northern Mexico. But why would anyone think we have something in common with a person who grew up perhaps hundreds or even thousands of miles away from us simply because they come from China or Mexico? Yet we may consider this imposition of an ethnic group identity not so trying. Indeed, ethnicity may in some ways prove empowering. Bonding with meaningful numbers of people who know something about our native language and traditions could seem worth the trouble. These people could help replenish our cultural roots as we endure in a new and not always very generous society. This business of getting called Polish or Mexican or Chinese American may not have made much sense to us when we crossed into the United States. But it makes better sense now as we still see too many strange faces and too many strange looks in our direction. Thus, for many understandable reasons, we learn to help guard the ethnic borders that we had perhaps little hand in erecting.

For good or bad, therefore, ethnic borders are created so that those in power will think they know better who we are. Ethnic borders are also created so that we will think we know better who we are. To borrow a very ugly term, we can call this the ethnicization process—the process of becoming a member of an ethnic group. This process can harbor both good and bad consequences and those who consciously or unconsciously reinforce the ethnicization process are often inspired by a variety of factors. Moreover, this process may or may not connect to an accurate assessment of an ethnic group's origins and homogeneity.

To see how this ethnicization process relates to the world of sports, let us imagine we have gone back in time to the 1920s to open the sports' section of a daily newspaper in New York City, Chicago, or San Francisco. A column about a Jewish or, as the columnist would probably say then, "Hebrew," boxer, catches our eye. Apparently, this boxer is a leading contender for the lightweight championship of the world and the columnist is extolling his virtues as a prizefighter. Words like "clever," "shrewd," and "tricky" are used to describe this boxer's ability to win bout after bout. Now, very clearly Jewish people have been called worst things than "clever," "shrewd," and "tricky." In fact, the columnist most likely means his words as complimentary and one suspects that the boxer in question would probably read this column with some pride. Yet Jews have long been widely and negatively perceived as predominantly "clever," "shrewd," and even "tricky." Thus, the sports' columnist, willingly or not, reinforces an ethnicization process, which has long characterized Jewish people as possessing certain ambivalently positive or downright negative attributes at the expense of clearly positive attributes--"courage," "strength," and "honesty."

Still on our visit to urban America in the 1920s, we look at a newspaper published for the city's Jewish community. The sports' section in this weekly is typically much smaller than the daily we read earlier, but it has plenty to say about the Jewish contender. It claims no particular love of prize fighting, but the writer still expresses tremendous pride in the boxer's accomplishments, which includes taking on and defeating opponents from all sorts of ethnic groups. This boxer shows America and the world that a Jew could be tough, "could take it and dish it out," according to the newspaper's sportswriter. This Jewish newspaper, too, is aiding the ethnicization process. It is informing readers that if Jewish they have a bond with that prizefighter even though they may have little else in common but their Jewish heritage.

Sports and Gender

While sports can aid the construction of borders separating ethnic groups, they can also aid the construction of borders within ethnic groups. In so doing sports help complicate how we look at ethnicity in America, but also the assertion of cultural citizenship. One obvious, although surmountable, division is that between males and females. We will discuss in chapter one the fact that Asian Pacific American females rarely could claim equal access to recreational sports in their ethnic communities. But we ought to discuss here how assumptions about gender and sports in nineteenth and twentieth century America might have reinforced residual cultural practices among Asian Pacific American and other ethnic groups.

Although non-Asian Pacific commentators can almost luridly overstate the point, Asian Pacific societies have long been highly patriarchal. Women in China, we are often told, suffered through lifetimes of bound feet, if they were not thrown into a river at birth by disgusted parents. Yet in *Unbound Feet*, historian Judy Yung points out new studies that represent Chinese women as experiencing and making a more diverse history. Not all women were passive victims of Chinese patriarchy and not all men commanded their victimization. [4]

It is, nevertheless, safe to say that most Chinese men and women in the nineteenth century would not have expressed any greater joy in seeing their daughters play baseball than their European American contemporaries. Often embattled American Victorian supporters of sports went to great lengths to justify participation in sports when neighbors and friends denounced athletic competitions as generally wasteful of human time and energy, if not sacrilegious. Still, the ideology of manliness helped clear away much of the ideological and spiritual hostility to sports during the nineteenth century. It did so by proclaiming that the ideal citizen of the United States retained an important and a unique blending of characteristics such as independence, courage, and maturity—characteristics widely perceived as foreign to female nature, as well as to the nature of "servile," "childlike" "races" best fit for mindless toil—"races" originating in Africa or Asia. The powerful ideology of manliness conveniently "raised hierarchies," constructed out of a blend of gender, race and class ideologies. It could also justify athletic competition as useful in testing and maintaining manliness--whiteness.

By the end of the nineteenth century, supporters of sports among America's middle and upper classes did not agree totally upon the usefulness of physical exercise for females. Girls and young women, it was often conceded, could engage in physical exercise and perhaps "mild" forms of athletic competition such as the new sport of basketball. As they grew older, however, and entered their childbearing years, some experts warned, women should steer clear of physical exertion. That women of childbearing age were physically exerting themselves as maids in Boston and sugar cane workers in Hawai'i aroused little concern. The prevailing gender ideology tended to dismiss laboring class women of all races and ethnic groups as much too manly.[5]

During America's Progressive Age, one could watch culturally diverse women play basketball with a little more physical ardor than might have been expected in the 1880s. The social construction of gender in America, nevertheless, created more obstacles than it removed to women gaining equal access to recreational or elite, competitive sports. One did not have to be Chinese or Japanese American to enviously watch one's brothers go to the gym or the ball field.

Sports and Class

Classes have divided ethnic groups as they have divided the United States. In tight-knit ethnic communities, familial, kin, and regional ties often softened the sting of class disparity. Your boss might be an uncle or a friend of your parents. Your boss might have given you a job when opportunities for other jobs seemed dim. Your boss might have even furnished you with a place to live. Of course, your boss might have been motivated by self-interest; a need for more labor that would not demand from him or her much in the way of wages, respect, or safe working conditions. Indeed, it would seem ungrateful to forget all that he or she has done for you just because you are paid poorly, often treated contemptuously, and would like a better than even chance to escape a fire engulfing workplace.

Complicating class issues further is that you might instead work for a boss not of your ethnic group, while your cousin might run her or his own business. It is a tossup as to who works harder for very little remuneration. But at least your cousin has some control over the future and perhaps can do well enough eventually to buy a home or finance a daughter's college education.

While class conflict did not always consume Asian Pacific American communities, class boundaries most certainly existed. As historian Valerie Matsumoto points out for financially strapped Japanese Californian farming families, there was little time for recreational sports in the 1910s and 1920s. A child might want to try out for the school team, but practices and games took place after school when work had to be done. As the family settled in and hopefully grew more prosperous, younger brothers and sisters perhaps acquired the freedom to enjoy extracurricular sports and other activities. [6]

In Hawai'i, as we will subsequently explore, working class Asian Pacific Americans could take advantage of the recreational facilities and organizations sponsored in part by sugar and pineapple plantation operators as a way of diverting Hawaiian laborers from militancy. They and their mainland counterparts could also take advantage of recreational facilities and organizations set up by Asian Pacific American and non-Asian Pacific American reformers who believed healthy recreation distracted young working class people from gambling, substance abuse, and prostitution. Nevertheless, whether on the mainland or the Hawai'ian Islands those Asian Pacific Americans who obtained more social and economic privileges most likely claimed more opportunities for athletic participation and the assertion of cultural citizenship.

Sports and Race

The existence of ethnic, gender, and class barriers among Asian Pacific Americans creates a history more complex than most non-Asian Pacific Americans realize. Nevertheless, Asian Pacific Americans have almost uniformly been trailed by what cultural critic Elaine Kim refers to as "racism's traveling eye." In other words, while individual Asian Pacific Americans have slipped through cultural borders they have not easily escaped the glare of institutionalized and personal racism. Asian Pacific Americans have been racialized just as they have been ethnicized and gendered and classed. Indeed, the racialization process has worked in such as way that significant numbers of non-Asian Pacific Americans have failed to recognize the very real and substantial distinctions among people of Asian Pacific ancestry. For historian Ronald Takaki, this has meant that Asian Pacific Americans have been long considered as "strangers" in the United States even when they can trace their ancestry in America back three, four or more generations. Asian Pacific Americans seem to possess a "racial uniform," according to Takaki, which has marked them off from "real Americans." This "racial uniform," in other words, has burdened their efforts to assert their cultural citizenship in the United States.[7]

The term race is used in this book as a historically flexible category that lumps together a group of people based on presumably distinctive and inherent characteristics—often physical, but not necessarily. To say, "people of African ancestry do not have the bodies of good swimmers" is a racial statement. It claims that nature has failed to endow people of African ancestry with the ability to swim well. They can take swimming lessons and practice competitive swimming all they want, but they will not breaststroke or Australian crawl to any Olympic medals.

For a bit, let us return to the 1920s and the sporting pages of urban American newspapers. Such pages were often filled with racial commentaries. For sports' columnist to refer to a Filipino bantamweight as "little" and "brown" did not mean those sports' columnist wanted to insult anyone. Bantamweight prizefighters, after all, are typically smaller than most adult males. And many Filipinos have tended to appear darker skinned than European Americans. The point here is that references to "little, brown" Filipino boxers helped construct a racial barrier between Filipinos who may not always be little and brown and whites who also may not always be large and light-skinned.

In other words, I tend to agree with those scholars who describe race as a social construction rather than a biological reality. For example, sociologists Omi and Winant write:

> The effort must be made to understand race as an unstable and "decentered" complex of social meanings: constantly being transformed by political struggle.... *{R}ace is a concept which signifies and symbolizes social conflicts and interests by referring to different types of human bodies.* Although the concept of race invokes biologically based human characteristics... selection of these particular human features for purposes of racial signification is always and necessarily a social and historical process.[8] (Omi's and Winant's emphasis)

Exotic Otherness or Orientalism

The notion that people of Asian Pacific ancestry represent exotic otherness in historically white dominated societies such as the United States tends to blur the distinctions between national and ethnic categories, on the one hand, and ethnicization and racialization processes, on the other hand. We can find a good example of this in American press descriptions of Japanese athletes participating in Los Angeles's 1932 Summer Olympiad. Historian David Welky points out that Japanese swimmers, in particular, surprised American observers with their ability to win medals. At this time, European Americans too rarely accepted any kind of athletic achievement on the part of people of color without expressing some amount of racial insecurity and a need to somehow devalue that achievement. At this time, as well, Japan represented the only predominantly non-white nation to menace Western European and American global supremacy. Welky, accordingly, writes that Japanese athletic achievements were especially foreboding to white American sports fans. However, Welky maintains that American newspapers "tempered these fears of a Japanese threat by using race and diminutive terms to create an image of tiny and harmless, yet wonderfully exotic people." The American press "drew attention to the fact that the Japanese were from a strange place that only a few Americans had seen. The mysticism of the Orient was a popular theme in the press, and it was understood that the 'sons of the Samurai' from 'the land of the Mikado' were not like us."[9]

Orientalism, according to scholar Edward Said, expresses the "West"'s need to "to deal...with the Orient...by making statements about it, authorizing views of it, describing it, settling it, ruling over it: in short, Orientalism as a Western style for dominating, restructuring, and having authority over the Orient." Orientalist ideology has not always clearly identified the source of Asian Pacific exoticism as cultural or racial. Nor has it always intentionally sought to demean Asian Pacific people. It, however, has claimed that an insuperable barrier endures between the "West" and the "East." Frequently, Orientalism has damned Asian Pacific people as brutal, dishonest, and lecherous. Orientalism has also romanticized Asian Pacific people as wise, spiritual, inventive, and unselfish. Of course, the former form of Orientalism is more likely to lead to My Lai massacres and the latter, more likely and relatively harmlessly, to lead to *Karate Kid* movies. Both forms, however, mask the diversity, the humanity, of Asian Pacific people.[10]

"Primitive" Exoticism

The indigenous people of the Pacific islands, as well, have been viewed by people of European ancestry as exotic, but simple and primitive in their exoticism. Often, indigenous Pacific Islander exoticism has been portrayed as savage. Of course, according to this version of exoticism, the Native Hawaiians would butcher nice white Captain Cook. What else could primitive Pacific Islanders do but display their savagery by cannibalism, head hunting, and running around naked? However, Europeans have often portrayed Pacific Islander exoticism in a seemingly positive light. When people of European ancestry talk about "going native" this has often meant learning how to live simply and happily as supposedly do the native people of the Pacific Islands. This has also meant that when people of Pacific Islander ancestry perform well in aquatic sports, people of European ancestry express little surprise, because indigenous Pacific Islanders ought to swim and dive well in comparison to non-Pacific Islanders.

The Global Perspective

We cannot truly understand the struggles for Asian Pacific American cultural citizenship and Asian Pacific American sporting experiences if we ignore the global context in which these struggles and experiences have occurred. In the first place, Asian Pacific societies have developed their own traditions in athletic competition. Second, these traditions have been influenced by European and American global expansion. Third, these traditions have also influenced sporting traditions among people of European ancestry. Finally, the complex history of Asian Pacific sporting traditions has both aided and harmed the assertion of Asian Pacific American cultural citizenship.

Archeological evidence suggests that sporting activities existed in India and China as far back as 3000 to 4000 years ago. More than 2000 years ago Indians engaged in swimming, wrestling, boxing, javelin, and jumping competitions, as well as various ball games. By around 1000 BC Chinese took up archery and horse riding. By around 500 BC they engaged in soccer.[11]

As in other parts of the world, the development of sports in premodern Asian Pacific societies corresponded with the various ways in which significant numbers of Asian Pacific people lived. Warfare and preparation for warfare combined as an important aspect of life for Asian Pacific people, as for other people around the world. Hence sports such as archery, boxing, wrestling, and javelin throwing made sense in such societies. Asian Pacific societies were also substantially agricultural. The popularity of cockfighting in Southeast Asian societies connects to the long history of agriculture in the area. Asian Pacific people often deeply identified with nearby rivers, lakes, and oceans. Thus surfing harbored significance to Native Hawai'ians that well predated Captain Cook's landfall.

By the 1800s, Europe had grown sufficiently powerful to spread its economic and military influence to Asian Pacific societies. It was, indeed, no coincidence that European empire building corresponded with the growing importance and acceptance of sports in the most geopolitically ambitious European nations. The United Kingdom, in particular, is credited as the incubator of many of our more modern sporting experiences. By the mid-nineteenth century, as Great Britain reinforced its hold on India and defeated the Chinese in the Opium Wars, British cultural leaders frequently extolled sports such as rugby and cricket as crucial nurturers of British military and commercial superiority. That is, rugby and cricket supposedly helped to prepare Britain's future military, political, and economic leaders for the struggle to achieve dominance of the darker skinned, presumably less civilized natives of Asia and the Pacific Islands by providing those leaders with the strength, discipline, courage, and intelligence to shoulder the "white man's burden."

As whites assumed their "burden" in India, China, Hawai'i, and Samoa, they brought their favorite sports with them. Officially, the United States took over the Philippines after the Spanish American War. A Filipino insurgent movement, however, denied the United States easy occupation of the islands for a number of years. As historian Richard Drinnon points out, American colonizers, spurred by the British example, hoped that sports could pacify, if not fully civilize, the people they claimed to believe were their "little brown brothers." Drinnon writes, "Colonial statesmen had carried to the islands polo and trap shooting for themselves and baseball for their new wards, along with soap and toothbrushes for everybody."[12]

Baseball by the end of the nineteenth century was widely considered as the American National Pastime and a reflection and reinforcement of what was best about American society. Interestingly, the United States used baseball to help ease its "white man's burden." At the turn of the twentieth century, Professor Dean Worcester offered scholarly cover for American colonialism in the Philippines. He wrote, "Before the American occupation...the Filipinos had not learned to play...Baseball not only strengthens the muscles of the players, it sharpens the mind." To Worcester, the fact that Filipinos had not discovered the wonders of baseball before American occupation was proof of their unfitness to rule themselves.[13]

By the turn of the century and the American conquest of the Philippines, America's sporting elite as represented by influential institutions such as the American Athletic Union (AAU) had become quite certain of sport's civilizing mission. Proof was found at the St. Louis World Fair in 1904. St. Louis also hosted the 1904 World Olympics and individuals such as James E. Sullivan, head of the AAU, linked the two events with an affair staged at the exposition called Anthropology Days.

The Philippines Reservation was one of the most popular exhibits at the St. Louis Fair. Inhabited by supposedly savage, scantily clad, and tribal Filipinos, the exhibit was organized by the American government and furnished with scholarly backing by prominent anthropologists. Unsurprisingly placed next to a Native American exhibit, the Philippines Reservation, according to historian S.W. Pope, "signaled the arrival of the United States as an imperial power."[14]

In conjunction with the upcoming Olympiad, the AAU's James Sullivan called for the organization of Anthropology Days at the St. Louis Exposition. On August 12 and 13, "natives" from Africa and North America, as well as the

Philippines competed in Olympic events, in addition to contests that supposedly represented their native cultures. A Filipino Igorot, for example, won the "pole climb." However, the "native" athletes, regardless of origins, seemed woeful in comparison to white American Olympic athletes. Pope writes: "The...competitors wore their native costumes—a visible sign of their racial differences—rather than athletic garb. The nativistic spectacle enabled Western spectators to feel morally justified about bringing modern sports and civilization to the emerging Third World."[15]

By the 1910s, the U.S. had apparently worked wonders in the Philippines. Under the headline, "Natives of the Philippines Abandoning Cockfighting for Base Ball," the *Sporting Life* told readers in 1912 that American educators in the Philippines were amazed by the popularity of America's National Pastime among Filipinos. Moreover, baseball "is not only interesting to the boys who play, but is commanding the attention of large crowds who are deserting the cockpits for the diamonds." A similar tone was struck in an article in the May, 1914 edition of *The Playground*. The author was Frank R. White, the Director of the Bureau of Education in Manila. Writing on recreational development in the Philippines, White proudly proclaimed that baseball had passed cockfighting as the sport of preference among Filipinos. He added, "When the natural apathy of a tropical people is taken into consideration, it would seem that extraordinary progress has been made."[16]

Likewise, Fred D. England, the Superintendent of Schools in Manila, wrote to *The Playground* in 1917 that the physical movement crusade had won converts among Filipinos. The crusade had originated in the United States in order to provide healthy recreational alternatives to overwork, on the one hand, and vice and labor radicalism, on the other. A prime target of the crusade were working class young people, generally possessing immigrant backgrounds and presumably needing organized sports to push them toward assimilation. However, as the United States expanded its Pacific Empire, the Organized Play Movement followed the flag to places such as the Philippines. Thus, England declared that Filipinos were excited about sports such as indoor baseball or softball, which was a favorite in the Organized Play Movement. He stated that Filipinos "will turn out by the hundreds to witness a little indoor baseball game between school teams and will shout and yell their heads off."[17]

In 1921, *The Outlook* declared the U.S. mission in the Philippines a success in pointing out that Filipino athletes had won more points in the recent Far Eastern Athletic Games than did Chinese and Japanese athletes. The real victor, according to *The Outlook*, was Elwood Brown, the YMCA's representative to the Philippines as Physical Director. Brown, it would seem, effectively taught Filipinos to play the American way: "Mr. Brown was so instrumental in changing Filipino habits that in the seventh year after his arrival one dealer alone in Manila sold some eleven thousand volley-balls, practically all of them to natives." Americans, moreover, should express pride in Brown's efforts to organize the Far Eastern Athletic Games as a means of bringing Filipino, Chinese, and Japanese people together. Instead of fighting wars, *The Outlook* declared, the three peoples had been peacefully competing with one another in track and field, baseball, volleyball, basketball, swimming and tennis.[18]

Into China, as well, Americans introduced what playground reformers depicted as "Organized Play." Vera Barger, who directed the YWCA's Normal School of Hygiene and Physical Education in Shanghai assumed credit for acquainting Chinese girls to "Western" sports during the early decades of the twentieth century. She announced to *The Playground* that for the first time "Chinese girls," happily trained by her institute would enter the Far Eastern Athletic Games in Shanghai in September, 1921. Indeed, according to the February, 1922 edition of *The Playground*, "a thousand Chinese school girls marching out on an athletic field with bands waving and banners fluttering is a sight to make any spectator thrill." Inspired by Vera Barger, China, according to *The Playground*, had taken a crucial step toward the complete emancipation of its women.[19]

As in the Philippines and China, the sports embraced by Asian Pacific people changed under the influence of white Europeans and North Americans. Significantly, white colonists, along with white Christian missionaries, attacked venerable Asian Pacific pastimes such as cockfighting and surfing. The latter sport, for example, repulsed nineteenth century Anglo American missionaries as immoral since it encouraged the participation of barely dressed surfers of both sexes. Consequently, those missionaries were able to get the Christianized Hawai'ian government to ban surfing for several years.

With or without the help of European and American missionaries and recreation reformers, Asian Pacific people began playing sports nurtured in England and North America. For decades, British colonizers avoided teaching cricket to Asian Indians. By 1900, however, Asian Indians started playing the colonizers' game. During the twentieth century, moreover, the sport became very popular throughout South Central Asia. While Japan avoided European colonization, it could not avoid and, to a significant extent, did not want to avoid European and American cultural influences. The Japanese learned baseball from American teachers in the 1870s. And by the 1900s, baseball had become just as popular in Japan as cricket had become popular in India, Pakistan, and Sri Lanka. In the meantime, other Europeanized and North Americanized sports such as basketball, volleyball, prize fighting, golf, and tennis made inroads among Asian Pacific people. Soccer or association football had, however, achieved greater esteem among Asian Pacific athletes than did American football. Japan established its first national soccer association in 1921, while China forged a similar association three years after.

For much of the twentieth century, Asian Pacific athletes have competed effectively with Europeans and North Americans in "Western" sports. Japanese athletes have performed well on an international level in such sports as baseball, gymnastics, tennis, golf, swimming, and volleyball. China has produced track and field champions, as well as swimming, table tennis and gymnastic stars. The Philippines, as we will explore, has nurtured some of the best prizefighters in the twentieth century. World prize fighting and golf champions have also been native-born Koreans and Thais.

We should also remember that even as Asian Pacific people adopted "Western" sports, they often did so on their own terms. Anthropologists describe the process of fusing cultural practices from distinct cultures as syncretism. The Asian Pacific sports world discloses a great deal of syncretism. According to historian Tony Mason, "Cricket on the subcontinent [of Asia] was able to reinvent itself to fit in with local culture and society. It has its own particular forms and rhythms, including Hindi broadcasts, passionate and noisy crowds, and wickets that have encouraged slow bowling."[20]

Yet while "Western" sports have invaded Asian Pacific societies, Asian Pacific-rooted sports have influenced people of non-Asian Pacific ancestry throughout the world. Surfing obviously exemplifies such a sport, as do the martial arts developed in Japan, China, and Korea. Polo, a popular sport among the elites in the Americas and Europe, most likely originated on Asia's central plains.

Sports have constructed something of a middle ground for Asian Pacific and non-Asian Pacific people on a global basis. For all the justified criticism that they have encouraged, the Olympics have become a medium of exchange for people around the world. One of the great athletic stories of the late 1950s and early 1960s was the heated, yet friendly competition, between African American Rafer Johnson and C.Y.Yang, from Formosa. The two were the greatest all around track and field athletes in the world and they both sought victories in the decathlon competition during the 1960 Summer Olympics held in Rome. What made their competition bittersweet was that Yang attended UCLA along with Johnson and they became track and field teammates, as well as close friends. Johnson ultimately won and Yang finished second.[21]

Elite professional athletes of Asian Pacific ancestry have competed in the United States, while their white, Latino, and African American counterparts have competed in Asia. In the late 1990s and early 2000s major league baseball in North America possessed teams with Japanese and Korean-born ballplayers, while the Los Angeles Sparks of the Women's National Basketball Association had a Chinese player and the Sacramento Monarchs had a Japanese player. And by 2005, a small group of Chinese players, headed by Yao Ming, had made National Basketball Association rosters. By the same token, many fine non-Asian Pacific athletes have competed in Asia. The rosters of Japanese major league baseball teams have consistently included European American, Latino, and African American professionals.

Probably, the most famous use of a sport to inspire Asian and non-Asian interaction was the "ping pong" diplomacy of the early 1970s. By 1971, China sought to achieve friendlier relations with non-communist and anticommunist neighbors, as well as other countries around the world. The United States, which had not recognized the Chinese government since it had assumed a communist guise, allowed the Chinese national table tennis team to tour America. This action propelled the United States toward normalization of diplomatic relations with the Chinese government.

On both sides of the Asian Pacific/non-Asian Pacific divide, sports have, however, been used to justify ethnocentrism and racism. Professional athletes who have not been Japanese citizens or have not possessed unmixed Japanese ancestry such as baseball star Sadaharu Oh have faced discrimination in Japan. At the same time, Asian Pacific born athletes often coped with stereotypes and other varieties of Eurocentricism.

The victories and losses amassed by Asian Pacific athletes over the years have pulled and pushed Americans of Asian Pacific ancestries in different directions. On the one hand, Asian Pacific American publications have long expressed pride in the accomplishments of non-American Asian Pacific athletes. In the 1990s, the Japanese American *Rafu Shimpo* published several articles about Hideo Nomo, when he started wining games for the Los Angeles Dodgers and in the early 1980s, *East/West* often published articles about Chinese and other Asian Pacific athletes. Although these athletes were not Asian Pacific Americans, significant numbers of Asian Pacific American still saw them as people with whom they could identify in a meaningful way. These athletes could strengthen community bonds.

Still, Asian Pacific-based martial artists, baseball players, and table tennis players can make it more difficult for some individual Asian Pacific Americans to assert their cultural citizenship. For these Americans of Asian Pacific ancestry, it might make as much or more sense to identify themselves with the athletic strivings of Peyton Manning or Lisa Leslie as Ichiro Suzuki. They might wish the freedom to use sports to explore cultural terrain light years away from the cultural practices and institutions of their Asian Pacific ancestors. Yet, hopefully, they will also recognize that sports can also connect them to the strivings of decades of Asian Pacific American athletes from whom they and the rest of us can attain comfort and pride.

Racially and Ethnically Mixed Athletes

I will explore the experiences of athletes often identified with more than one racial and/or ethnic group. Whenever possible and appropriate, I will point out the racial and ethnic associations of such athletes as Tiger Woods, Herman Wedemeyer, Johnny Damon, and Vicki Manalo. The experiences of these people show, if nothing else, that if race does matter in sport it poses no insurmountable barrier to athletic achievement. Of course, we could assume that Tiger Woods would be able to hit the golf ball farther and Vicki Manalo would have won more Olympic gold medals if not for their Asian Pacific ancestors. But that would be ridiculous given the fact that superb athletes have existed historically and today among all sorts of racial, ethnic, and national groups.

Sources

Many of the sources used for this book come from newspapers, either produced in the Asian Pacific American communities or by the dominant European American press. Such sources are often tainted by exorbitant ethnic pride, on the one hand, and bigotry, on the other. Nevertheless, they have furnished me with names of individuals and teams, as well as revealing descriptions of Asian Pacific American experiences in sports.

Asian Pacific American newspapers can show how important sports have been to Asian Pacific American communities. While hardly free of sexism, moreover, they have been more likely historically to report on Asian Pacific American female athletes than white-dominated publications. As for the latter, the reader might find him or herself surprised at how often and respectfully the white dominated press has written about Asian Pacific American athletes. Yet the white press has also displayed in subtle and not so subtle forms the way racialization and exoticization has worked in response to athletes of Asian Pacific ancestry.

Organizing the Book

Generally, this book is organized by various sports. The first chapter, however, deals with the crucial issue of Asian Pacific American community development and explores how recreation and sports have interrelated with that development. The second chapter discusses the relationship between Asian Pacific Americans and sports such as prize fighting and wrestling. Baseball is the topic of the third chapter. The fourth chapter takes up American-style football and to a lesser extent, soccer and rugby, while the fifth chapter discusses basketball. The sixth chapter examines aquatic sports such as swimming, diving, and surfing, while the next targets a wide variety of sports such as golf, tennis, gymnastics, ice hockey, volleyball, track and field, and ice-skating. The eighth and concluding chapter uses cross-cultural perspectives to explore in greater depth some of the issues connecting sports to Asian Pacific American cultural citizenship.

In the course of putting together this book, I have made some difficult choices regarding what sports, individuals, and issues to discuss. Very clearly, I have left out of this book many fine Asian Pacific American athletes from the past and the present. I have even more clearly spent more time on some fairly anonymous athletes than very famous Asian Pacific American athletes. I am much less apologetic about doing this than ignoring entirely the experiences of people who need to be discussed. We should know about Michael Chang and Kristi Yamaguchi. However, we also should learn more about relatively anonymous athletes such as Wally Yonamine, Vicki Manalo, Sammy Lee, and Helen Wong Lum—women and men who took on stereotypes, crossed cultural borders, and articulated interesting, poignant, and exciting stories about Asian Pacific American sporting history.

Notes

1. Ronald Takaki, *Strangers from a Different Shore: A History of Asian Americans,* (Boston: Little Brown, 1989); Sucheng Chan, *Asian Americans: An Interpretive History,* (Boston: Twayne, 1991).

2. Theodore S. Gonzalves, "When the Walls Speak a Nation," *Journal of Asian American Studies,* I, (February, 1998), 50; Robert Wiebe, *Self Rule: A Cultural History of American Democracy,* (Chicago: University of Chicago Press, 1995), chapter six.

3. Renato Rosaldo and William V. Flores, "Ideology, Conflict, and Evolving Latino Communities: Cultural Citizenship in San Jose, California," in *Latino Cultural Citizenship*: Claiming *Identity, Space, and Rights,* edited by William V. Flores, and Rina Benmayor, (Boston: Beacon Press, 1997), 57.

4. .Judy Yung, *Unbound Feet: A Social History of Chinese Women in San Francisco,* (Berkeley and Los Angeles: University of California Press, 1995), chapter one.

5. Susan K. Cahn, *Coming on Strong: Gender and Sexuality in Twentieth-Century Women's Sport,* (New York: Free Press, 1994), chapter one.

6. Valerie Matsumoto, *Farming the Home Place: A Japanese American Community in California, 1919-1982,* (Ithaca, New York: Cornell University Press, 1993), chapter two.

7. Elaine Kim, "Preface," *Charlie Chan is Dead: An Anthology of Contemporary Asian American Fiction,* edited by Jessica Hagedorn, (New York: Penguin Books, 1993);. Ronald Takaki, *Strangers,* chapter one.

8. Michael Omi and Howard Winant, *Racial Formation in the United States*: From *the 1960s to the 1990s,* 2nd Edition, (London and New York: Routledge, 1994), 55-56.

9. David B. Welky, "Viking Girls, Mermaids, and Little Brown Men: U.S. Journalism and the 1932 Olympics," *Journal of Sport History,* (Spring, 1997), 24-50.

10. Edward Said, *Orientalism.* (New York: Vintage Books, 1979), 12

11. Kendall Blanchard and Alyce Cheska, *The Anthropology of Sport: An Introduction,* (South Hadley, Massachusetts: Bergin and Garvey Publishers, Inc., 1985), 96.

12. Richard Drinnon, *Facing West: The Metaphysics of Indian Hating and Empire Building,* (New York: Schocken Books, 1991), 347.

13. *Ibid., 300*-301.

14. S.W. Pope, *Patriotic Games: Sporting Traditions in the American Imagination, 1876-1926,* (New York: Oxford University Press, 1997), 42.

15. *Ibid.,* 43.

16. *Sporting Life,* August 10, 1912; Frank R. White, "Recreation Development in the Philippine Islands," *The Playground,* May, 1914.

17. *The Playground,* April, 1917.

18. *The Outlook,* July 27, 1921.

19. *The Playground,* September, 1921 February, 1922.

20. Tony Mason, "Cricket," in *Encyclopedia of World Sport: From Ancient Times to the Present,* I (Santa Barbara, CA: ABC-CLIO), 213.

21. Richard White, *The Middle Ground: Indians, Empires, and Republics in the Great Lakes Region,* 1650-1815, (New York: Cambridge University Press, 1991), x; Peter Levine, *From Ellis Island to Ebbets Field: Sport and the American Jewish Experience,* (New York: Oxford University Press, 1992), 25.

Chapter One: Sports and Asian Pacific American Communities

Imagine, and some of us might not need to imagine very much, a childhood in which after turning five or six one's life is generally focused on going to school and after the day's final school bell rings, working at home or at some factory or shop or restaurant. We experience moments of relatively unsupervised fun, but they are fleeting and often literally stolen from teachers, parents, older siblings, and bosses. For immigrant children and children of immigrants in the United States fun has often ranked as a luxury or a hidden pleasure. To play a game of marbles or merely read a book, comic or otherwise, without interruption by adults was often difficult. There was always something that needed doing—homework, taking a younger sibling to the doctor, or waiting on tables at an uncle's restaurant. However, if that fun entailed playing a sport a child might run into both opposition and encouragement from adults.

Immigrant children and children of immigrants in America have told all sorts of stories about growing up in the United States. Among the most prevalent stories are those detailing the hostility of parents to their children playing sports otherwise popular in America. Joe Dimaggio, the son of Italian immigrants, claimed his father in the 1920s could not understand his sons' attraction to baseball. It was a child's game, according to Papa Dimaggio, diverting the Dimaggio boys from helping in the family's fishing business. Joe should be handling a fishing net, not a baseball bat. Joe, who, according to legend, could not stand the smell of fish, entertained other ideas and learned on the tough streets and playgrounds of San Francisco to become one of the greatest and best paid ballplayers of his time.

Other, less famous immigrant children and children of immigrants, might tell different stories. Lillian Yuen was one of the directors of the only playground in San Francisco's Chinatown. She strongly believed that all Chinatown children, not just the male Chinatown children or the wealthier Chinatown children, should have a chance to play sports. Playing basketball or volleyball, she was convinced, could make them healthier and distract them from less wholesome and potentially criminal ways of having fun. Yuen encouraged young Chinese American youths to visit the playground and take part in volleyball, basketball, and even tennis competitions. Many of these youths grew up to maintain a lifelong love of sports. One of them, Helen Wong Lum became one of the greatest female athletes ever produced in San Francisco. For Chinese American young people, playing a sport was not just a path to enjoyment, but it was also a way to build important relationships beyond one's family and kin. A sociologist might say it was a way to develop and maintain a sense of community.

Defining Community

The word "community" has generally positive connotations in the English language. Nevertheless, as the late Welsh cultural critic Raymond Williams pointed out, community has been defined in various ways. We can first define community as a small, organized society. Second, we can declare that a community consists of those people living in a particular district or neighborhood. Third, we can argue that a community derives from people having something in common. That is, they do not necessarily have to live near one another and know each other personally to forge communal bonds. Using a fourth perspective, we can agree that a community extends beyond the neighborhood and village, but we need to insist that it be composed of people who have a very deeply felt and historically based sense of commonality with one another. Video game players and soap opera fans, in other words, do not form communities, as might immigrants from the same country.

While perceived and used in different ways, community, Williams wrote, is something nearly all of us favor without always quite understanding why:

> Community can be the warmly persuasive word to describe an existing set of relationships or the warmly persuasive word to describe an alternate set of relationships. What is most important, perhaps, is that unlike all other terms of social organization (state, nation, society, etc.) it seems never to be given any positive opposing or distinguishing term. [1]

Sport historians such as Stephen Hardy have recognized the importance of community in their field of study. Hardy, for example, furnishes a helpful and generally open-ended way to think about community:

> [C]ommunity . . . can be viewed in a physical spatial sense, as a locality; in a social sense, as a system; and in a psychological sense, as a state of mind. If its essence is "a sense of belonging" or personal involvement," it can vary in scope from the local street to infinity. Its form can reside in formal systems of interest or informal networks of shared values and common ways of thinking. [2]

In *Habits of the Heart*, sociologist Robert Bellah and his colleagues weigh in on the dialogue over the definition of community by claiming we need to consider real communities as "communities of memory." They explain that any community worthy of the name is "constituted by [its] past." Its members retell stories that construct a collective history that embraces both joyful and painful elements:

> The communities of memory that tie us to the past also turn us toward the future as communities of hope. They carry a context of meaning that can allow us to connect our aspirations for ourselves and those closest to us with the aspirations of a larger whole and see our own efforts as being, in part, contributions to a common good. [3]

To love a particular sport or join an athletic team probably would not constitute involvement in a meaningful community, according to Bellah *et. al.* What seems, nevertheless, apparent is that however seemingly trivial, the feelings and actions inspired by sports link us with people who we consider not only our friends, neighbors, and co-workers, but also to people we might never see and to people for whom sports are anything but trivial. Sports, to borrow from political scientist Benedict Anderson, perhaps can help us invent communities. National and international elites understand this. Indeed, around the time of the Olympics we become quite aware that sports are employed to symbolize both national solidarity and international friendship. In other words, the Olympics encourage Americans to cross racial, gender, class, and regional boundaries and bond with people they do not know and would probably not always like in rooting on American heroes and heroines. Less successfully, however, they inspire Americans to cross national boundaries and recognize a foundation in athletics for global community building. [4]

Asian Pacific Americans and Community

The variety of communities that have developed among the large number of people identified as Asian Pacific Americans ought to strike us as staggering if we agree that people can bond with one another on the basis of the places from which they or their ancestors migrated. And in the case of Asian Pacific people, such places might include China, Japan, Korea, Asian India, Vietnam, the Philippines, and Samoa. And that is just for starters. Not only are there several other Asian Pacific countries not mentioned a few lines earlier, but within the places I have mentioned regional distinctions often prevail and communities in the United States based on such distinctions have emerged. For many people of Asian Pacific ancestry, family and kin have furnished a strong foundation for community. The kind of work Asian Pacific Americans have done has solidified ties among those with similar occupations. Asian Pacific Americans have also bonded with one another on class and gender foundations. Moreover, we need to throw into the mix the not very inconsequential matters of generational, ideolog-ical, and religious influences.

Consequently, the communities developed and supported by Asian Pacific Americans have aided in rendering them far more diverse than many of us who are non-Asian Pacific Americans would assume. Yet despite the important dif-ferences that have existed and continue to exist among Americans of Asian Pa-cific ancestry, sports have helped advance and sustain Asian Pacific American communities. Moreover, sports have encouraged the process of representing those communities to other communities in the United States. They have, in short, affected Asian Pacific American struggles for cultural citizenship.

American Chinatowns and Little Tokyos have nurtured more than their share of athletic organizations. To the inhabitants of these places, as in African American ghettos and Mexican American barrios, community formation clearly has corresponded with geographical boundaries. They have been places in which subaltern peoples of color have been able to exercise their uniqueness--to build their own communities. And historically sports have served in these ethnic en-claves a variety of purposes. To community members, sports have diverted young people from the temptations of the street. Community-based teams and individual athletes have lent community inhabitants at least a semblance of cre-dibility in the eyes of whites and/or the native-born. Sports, at the same time, might well have strengthened ties to the lands from which community-members or their ancestors came. Sports likewise have helped reinforce ethnic communi-ties across significant social and cultural divisions. Sports have even put money, sometimes a great deal of money, in the pockets of at least few community members.

Pre-World War II Asian Pacific American Ethnic Communities and Exclu-sion

Life was typically hard for early Asian Pacific immigrants to the United States. Work filled their days quite nicely. There was little time for sporting di-versions. Such was true for both men and women, but especially the latter whose time away from paid jobs was often spent working without pay for family mem-bers. Nevertheless, until World War II, most first-generation Asian Pacific Americans were males.

Nineteenth and early twentieth century Chinatowns were often called "ba-chelor societies." In them, many men abided an ocean away from their wives and the women who might have become their wives. They were stranded in places like California by restrictive and class-biased national immigration laws and state anti-miscegenation laws. Chinatown stores furnished the social and recreational spaces for male, working class Chinese immigrants. Ronald Takaki writes that "in the backrooms of stores, as the Chinese gathered around the warmth, they challenged each other at chess and checkers, played musical in-struments, listened to the phonograph and read newspapers."[5]

Early Chinese immigrants occasionally found time for the theater. In 1852, the Hong Gook Tong troupe performed the first Chinese play staged in the United States at the American Theater in San Francisco. The Hong Gook Tong consisted of as many as 123 performers. Over ten years later, the *Daily Alta California* described a Chinese theatrical performance in San Francisco in the following manner: "The theatre, of course, was in full blast and such a jargon of sounds, vocal and instrumental, has never before been heard outside of the dominions of Confucius." Despite the patronizing views of the European American press, theatrical performances remained popular in San Francisco's Chinatown. In 1879, a Chinese theater, seating an impressive 2500, was built in California's largest city. [6]

It was a good thing that Chinese theaters existed in nineteenth century San Francisco, because Chinese people were not necessarily welcomed in white-patronized theaters. In 1869, a play called *Formosa* was performed at San Francisco's California Theater. According to the *San Francisco Examiner*, two Chinese men entered one of the private boxes where they sat with two white men. An uproar ensued and the two Chinese audience members were forced to leave. The *Examiner* concluded: "We have simply this to say that these Chinese belong to a race that no caucasian possessed of proper feeling and sensibilities can recognize as his equal."[7]

Holidays also served as a source of entertainment for early Asian Pacific residents of the United States. In 1887, the *San Jose Mercury* reported with some irritability that San Jose's Chinatown celebrated Chinese New Year with explosions and firebombs. San Jose police apparently warned one Quang Toi Woo to desist from setting off firecrackers and then arrested him when he failed to comply. The *San Jose Herald* regarded Chinese New Year celebrations even less tolerantly than the *Mercury*. In 1881, the *Herald* reported that San Jose's city council had permitted the town's Chinese to celebrate the New Year with firecrackers and bombs from 6 AM to 7 PM. "Yet a number of enthusiastic pigtails," the *Herald* declared, "so far forgot their position under a melican man's government as to fire crackers and set up an unearthly din in the still hours of the night."[8]

Several years later, however, the *Mercury* sentimentalized Chinese New Year in a way which anthropologist Renato Rosaldo describes as "imperialist nostalgia." In 1926, the *Mercury* reminded readers of a presumably bygone era when around Chinese New Year European Americans in San Jose found delight in "every almond eyed beauty, courteous, aspiring youth, venerable old person, and excited youngster." Like many white colonials in places like India and the Philippines, the *Mercury,* in other words, seemed to long for the days when the darker skinned "exotics" happily entertained their white superiors. Ignoring the role of racial exclusion in depopulating Chinese San Joseans, the daily blamed the passing of that era and, indeed, the disappearance of San Jose's Chinatown on an impersonal urban development that alone had contracted Chinatown's borders. [9]

On Hawaiian plantations, Ronald Takaki notes, Asian Pacific workers "strove to retain their national identities...They celebrated traditional festivals and recreated...the familiar scenes of the old countries." Japanese workers observed the Buddhist remembrance of the dead, called *Obon*. And on November 3, workers from Japan and Okinawa took the day off to celebrate the emperor's birthday—a practice that decidedly exasperated plantation managers.[10]

For many non-Asian Pacific Americans, some of the ways in which Asian Pacific communities practiced their traditions became spectacles worth seeing. In the late 1800s, whites watched Chinese residents of Monterey County engage in something called "the ring game." According to historian Sandy Lydon, this game was held at the end of an annual celebration, which took place on the second day of the second lunar month. Lydon writes: "The game required a combination of skill, strength, and most of all, luck...The Chinese in California fought for a ring of woven bamboo which was blasted into the air from a great firecracker." The participant who got the ring "would receive the smile of T'u Ti," a god of wealth. [11]

According to Lydon, participants often organized into teams representing the various Monterey County Chinese communities. Consequently, the individual who grabbed the ring honored the team, as well as acquired good fortune. The local European Americans got in on the act. Monterey County newspapers both reported on the "Chinese game" and rooted for the teams representing the closest Chinese community. When the ring game was held at Point Alones, a couple of thousand curious whites showed up to watch. [12]

All sorts of problems related to gambling, substance abuse, and crime beset early Asian Pacific American communities. These problems were not just worrisome to the extent that they harmed people within Asian Pacific American communities. They also helped to represent Asian Pacific Americans in a bad light to already very suspicious non-Asian Pacific Americans, who often quite conveniently forgot about similar problems in their own communities.

Gambling, for example, has long been recognized as a distressing component of early and later Asian Pacific American communities. Sociologist Paul P. C. Siu wrote a classic study called *The Chinese Laundryman*. In this account, Siu noted that "for the Chinese laundryman, gambling is a means of recreation ...is also an expression of the human aleatory impulse of taking a risk and gaining something for nothing."[13]

In the 1930s, another scholar observed that "in certain towns of Northern California, the commercialized gambling of the Chinese is highly organized and constitutes an important part of the business of the community. " Because of its illegality, Chinese gambling establishments were apparently disguised as grocery stores. However, often operators of such establishments did not bother to hide the nature of their businesses. [14]

Sandy Lydon devoted a great deal of attention to Chinese immigrant gambling in California's Monterey Country during the late nineteenth and early twentieth centuries. He insisted: "One of the earliest institutions to form in each of the area's Chinatowns was the gambling hall...Whenever a large group of Chinese laborers congregated, somewhere, somehow, gambling went on. Any event could be bet on, but the most attractive events (and games) revolved around randomness rather than skill. Nothing could substitute for luck" One of the more popular games, according to Lydon, was *Pok Kop Pew*. Here "the bettor attempted to guess which of twenty numbers would be drawn from a pool of eighty."[15]

Another historian, Chris Friday, puts the matter of gambling in a class perspective for Chinese immigrant, as well as other Asian Pacific immigrant, workers. Friday writes that Asian Pacific immigrant workers' "contractors or their foremen ran the games or hired professional gamblers on percentages." For such contractors, workers in debt meant workers more easily controlled. [16]

Japanese immigrants--the Issei--were often depicted as persistent gamblers. Japanese critics themselves complained that Issei gambling was inspired by the pipe dream of quickly striking it rich in the United States, as well as the lack of what the critics considered wholesome recreational outlets in America. What also disturbed these Japanese observers was that Issei gamblers frequented gambling halls owned by Chinese Americans. Indeed, the *Los Angeles Times* reported in the early 1910s that "there are fifteen gambling dens in Chinatown, owned by a company composed of wealthy and representative Chinamen who look upon gambling as a legitimate business."[17]

As far as the U. S. Immigration Commission was concerned in the early 1900s, both Chinese and Japanese immigrants appeared much too fond of gambling. It reported that in Fresno, California, Chinese and Japanese "gambling is so widespread and vice has reached such proportions that they have presented a serious problem to the leading members of these races."[18]

Pre-World War II, Filipino immigrants were stung by reports that they exhausted exorbitant amounts of time and money in gambling halls—especially gambling halls owned by Chinese Americans. Writer and labor activist, Carlos Bulosan explained the attraction of Chinese gambling halls in the 1920s and 1930s to Filipino immigrants. In his classic *America is in the Heart*, Bulosan pointed out that patrons were served free tea in such establishments: "Drinking tea in a Chinese gambling house was something tangible and gratifying, and perhaps it was because of this that most of the Filipino unemployed frequented the place." Buloson, nevertheless, was embittered by what he considered an exploitative relationship between Chinese gambling hall operators and Filipino immigrants. In Stockton, California, according to Bulosan, "the Chinese syndicates, the gambling lords, are sucking the blood of our people. The Pinoys work every day in the fields, but when the season is over their money is in the Chinese vaults."[19]

For many European Americans and Asian Pacific Americans, gambling in Asian Pacific American communities comprised just part of a larger, "vice" problem. Indeed, such communities were widely regarded as "dens of inequities." Gambling halls, as well as opium dens, houses of prostitution, and well-meaning and not so well meaning whites decried pool halls as expressive of "Oriental" decadence. Making matters worse was that Asian Pacific people merchandising vice not only supposedly degraded Americans of Asian Pacific ancestry, but contributed to European American hostility to Asian Pacific immigration. Asian Pacific people were, according to some European Americans, corrupting white youth. After a raid on a Chinese operated opium den in San Jose, the *San Jose Mercury* maintained in 1894 that the establishment was a place "where the Chinese have not been content to have a social smoke among themselves, but have been accustomed to entice [white] lads from 15 to 20 years of age."[20]

Like many other American ethnic and working class communities in the late nineteenth and early twentieth centuries, Asian Pacific American communities were, in fact, not always particularly wholesome. According to historian Sucheng Chan, nineteenth century San Francisco's Chinese community was clearly involved in the "vice industry. " In 1860, she reported, about ten percent of employed Chinese males had jobs related to gambling, opium sales, and prostitution. Prostitutes comprised twenty-three percent of employed Chinese San Franciscans. Chan wrote: "Thus fully one third of the gainfully employed Chinese in the city were engaged in providing recreational vices—an unfortunate fact which gave rise to negative images of the Chinese." Outside of San Francisco, Chan maintained, Chinese often owned businesses connected to gambling, prostitution, or opium. In 1880, sixty-six such enterprises existed, according to the census data, in California's Southern mining region, while 178 operated in the Northern mining region. San Francisco harbored ninety-five Chinese operated businesses associated with "recreation and vice."[21]

As in other ethnic communities, late nineteenth century Chinese merchants and labor contractors considered recreational "vice" as a useful way to profit from poorer, less powerful members of their communities. Chan asserted that in Northern California's "larger towns, these merchants made additional profits by supplying laborers with opium and women (some of whom, after Chinese exclusion, were white) and by running gambling dens."[22]

During the early 1900s, San Jose's Japanese community or *Nihonmachi* consisted substantially of businesses catering to male migrant laborers. Thus, it possessed a number of boarding houses. But it also accommodated pool halls, gambling parlors, and houses of prostitution. Pool halls in early *Nihonmachis* were often constructed with attached barbershops and bathhouses. According to Yuji Ichioka, the Issei could patronize forty-one pool halls in San Francisco, twenty-one in Sacramento, nineteen in Fresno, and thirty-five in Los Angeles in 1909.[23]

Pool was a sport which attracted the participation of working class Japanese and Filipino immigrants. Indeed, for the men who performed hard labor in places like California, the pool hall served multiple purposes. Observers claimed that the game of pool offered relaxation to Asian Pacific laborers. The pool hall itself furnished patrons with a sense of community often absent among migrant workers. For the Issei, Ichioka writes that "in addition to providing the game of pool, pool halls served as a general meeting place for workers to renew old friendships, to exchange work information, and to simply while away leisure time." Filipino immigrants apparently found similar qualities in the pool hall.

When anti-Filipino violence flared in San Jose during January, 1930, inhabitants of San Jose's Filipino community used a Filipino run pool hall, the Manila Pool Hall, as both refuge and meeting place. Indeed, the anti-Filipino ideology in the 1930s frequently denigrated Pinoy laborers as "pool hoodlums."[24]

The patronization of blood sports by Asian Pacific immigrants confirmed in the minds of many European Americans that Asian Pacific people harbored character traits that made it hard for them to assimilate into American society. In 1900, the *San Francisco Chronicle* accused Oakland's Chinese community of regularly staging dog and goat fights before the police terminated such activities. Filipino immigrants frequently put on and patronized cockfights. One Filipina American told scholar Yen Le Espiritu of the cockfights held in pre-World War II Selma, California.

> [T]hey still had their cockfights. The cockfight arena was really the gathering place for all the Filipinos. Even if some didn't like to bet on the cockfights, everybody was there. I remember the women having little stalls, with their little tables filled with individual special delicacies they had cooked. And of course the men who were single at the time were so happy to have Filipino food because they had lived in these barracks, while the families lived in cottages and could prepare their own food. [25]

Filipino laborers in pre-World War II Hawai'i also supported cockfighting. One scholar claimed that cockfighting was "well nigh ubiquitous among the less educated Filipinos in Hawai'i." There were some efforts to legalize cockfighting on the Hawaiian islands, but according to Cariaga, "educated" Filipinos opposed such a move. Children of Filipino immigrants, moreover, supposedly expressed little interest in the controversy one way or another. . [26]

Pastimes such as gambling, pool, and cockfighting may have furnished participants with a sense of community and, in one form or another, attracted European Americans. Still, they drew fire from community-based reformers, as well as whites self-righteously or cynically seeking excuses to ban or restrict Asian Pacific immigration to America. In 1888, the Japanese consul in Hawai'i noted with alarm the enthusiasm in which Japanese sugar cane workers gambled. Indeed, Japanese reformers complained that if American Nikkei wanted to avoid the white hostility faced by Chinese immigrants, they had better take part in recreation considered more suitable by middle class European Americans. By the early decades of the 1900s, however, Organized Play reformers were busy among some Hawaiian youth. In 1920, *The Playground* reported that in Honolulu's working class Palama neighborhood a settlement house had formed a "girls' club with an enrollment of three hundred and fifty" along with a five hundred member boys' club. "The activities of the clubs are gymnasium work, athletics, folk dancing, swinging, and games of many kind." Furthermore, "the Palama Settlement Playground has an average daily attendance of ninety."[27]

Among the people most interested in reforming and, hopefully, controlling Asian Pacific recreation were Hawaiian plantation owners. There were a few overlapping concerns here. First, out of either outraged morality, a desire for a disciplined, productive work force, or both, European American or haole planters frequently sought to discourage gambling and substance abuse among their laborers. Second, despite Hawai'i's enormous dependence upon Asian Pacific labor, anti-Asian Pacific sentiments existed on the islands and planters were always concerned about their ability to represent their workers as hard working, clean-living, albeit perhaps simple-minded, people. A third factor relates to planter concerns regarding labor unrest. Explosive plantation worker strikes during the first two decades of the twentieth century generated a form of welfare capitalism. That is, wealthier employers offered workers recreational facilities such as baseball diamonds and football fields as a way of hopefully diverting them from labor militancy. In 1930, the Hawaiian Pineapple Company constructed a $25,000 gymnasium on Lanai and employed an athletic director. [28]

T. T. Waterman of the Hawaii Sugar Plantation Association pointed out in the 1930s that the "morale" side of providing athletic diversion to Hawaiian workers was important. Spending money on sports equipment would repay employers by reducing turnover and keeping young workers on the plantations. Moreover, plantation sponsored sports would spread "joy to people who did not have much in the way of games back in the lands of their births."[29]

Some Hawaiian workers were, nevertheless, forced to make do when it came to recreation. Cariaga, for example, reported in 1936 that Filipino laborers loved athletics even though their work left them with little time or energy away from the fields. They apparently enjoyed volleyball the most, because the game was relatively easy to set up. They liked baseball, but the sport was too time consuming to learn and play properly and too few plantations had constructed suitable grounds for the game. Despite the limitations of time and lack of money, Jose Rizal Day inspired Filipino workers to celebrate not only a national hero of the Philippines but their love of sport. In the afternoon, Hawaiian Filipinos took part in baseball, volleyball, and basketball. [30]

To be sure, whether on the mainland or the Hawaiian Islands, Asian Pacific American communities were often on their own in terms of recreational sports. Some Asian Pacific Americans hoped that through sports they could express a sense of solidarity with people of their own ethnic backgrounds. In so doing, however, they also seemed to hope that they could represent their communities in the best possible light to a largely antagonistic white society. In places like San Francisco's Chinatown and San Jose's Japantown in the 1910s and 1920s, some community leaders saw the organization of athletic clubs as providing positive alternatives to young men who might otherwise drift toward gambling and drugs.[31]

Asian Pacific community leaders were not unanimous in their approval of recreational sports for community youth. In the early 1900s, Chinese Hawaiian business leaders in Honolulu warmly sponsored the organization of a fine baseball team consisting of players of Chinese ancestry. In the 1920s, however, Chinese American business leaders in Los Angeles largely shunned the idea of sponsoring a Chinese Angeleno nine. As far as many of them were concerned, young men should work rather than play baseball. In the early 1940s, a group of young Filipino immigrants living in San Francisco's Western Addition organized the Mango Athletic Club. In so doing, they hoped that older, more established members of their community would sponsor their competitive athletic teams in basketball, baseball, volleyball, and sandlot football. The community elders refused financial support until the Mango Athletic Club teams started winning games. [32]

Whatever community concern existed over furnishing appropriate recreational outlets for community members, especially youthful community members, females were too often ignored. In San Francisco's Chinatown, the Chinese YMCA and the Yoke Choy club were organized to serve male recreational needs in the 1920s and 1930s. Both organizations, according to historian Judy Yung, excluded Chinese American females. Yet young Chinese American women resolved to patronize the Chinese YWCA, where they could find a social space for leisure reading and piano playing. Open from 10 AM to 10 PM, the Chinese YWCA's recreation center allowed young women to play basketball and badminton. By joining the YWCA, they could also gain access to the swimming pool at the central YWCA in San Francisco, as well as gym classes. St. Mary's Catholic Church in Chinatown, moreover, offered substantial recreational outlets for young Chinese American women. Yung writes, "Chinese girls met there on Friday nights to cook, paint, play the piano, sew or participate in basketball."[33]

Young Chinese American women in the 1920s took the initiative in organizing the Square and Circle Club in San Francisco. This organization furnished leisure activities to members. But just as important, if not more so, it encouraged members to become community activists. For example, the Square and Circle Club pushed hard for extending the hours and improving the lighting in the only Chinatown playground in the city. [34]

If many European Americans believed that sports played an important role in their cultures and that sports could plaster over the differences among them, Asian Pacific Americans often came to the same conclusion. It would be better, many Asian Pacific American community leaders seemed to believe, if Asian Pacific Americans got more attention for playing a game than for getting arrested for gambling or drug possession. It would be better even though many European Americans shortsightedly claimed sovereignty over sports such as baseball and football.

In the 1930s, as second generations matured in Asian Pacific American communities, community-based athletic organizations and leagues blossomed in the midst of the Great Depression. Writing in reference to Japanese Americans in California, historian Samuel Regalado has maintained: "In a period that saw meager wages for some and unemployment for many in the world outside of the playground, Japanese Americans playfields and gymnasiums in the 1930s portrayed anything but a bleak picture. " Female Japanese Americans, too, were encouraged to join community athletic organization. A Japanese American newspaper insisted that in doing so, Japanese American females would become "well and healthy."[35]

As we will explore more in future pages, Japanese Americans interned in first assembly centers and concentration camps by the United States government in World War II used sports such as baseball and basketball to maintain a sense of community under dire circumstances. Males often took the lead in such camp athletics, but as we will find out their daughters, sisters, and wives joined them in their love of sports. While camps eventually included athletic facilities, gymnasiums were not always constructed. Thus, basketball and volleyball had to be cancelled at the Heart Mountain, Wyoming camp because of cold weather. [36]

Yet the development of community sports among Asian Pacific Americans was difficult—especially on the mainland. In the first place, for decades public recreational facilities were often racially segregated. Second, urban Asian Pacific American communities were often too poor and overcrowded to establish adequate recreational facilities on their own, while rural Asian Pacific American communities were often just too poor. Third, depending upon age, gender, and class, Asian Pacific Americans could not all gain equal access to available recreational facilities.

The segregation of recreational facilities was a constant among Asian Pacific Americans growing up in mainland communities before World War II. Chinese American Lee Shew recalled for Connie Young Yu that as an eight-year-old in San Jose in 1917, he was barred from the whites' only swimming pool at the Hotel Vendome. Scholar Karen Leonard reports that children of Punjabi ancestry faced exclusion from swimming pools during the 1930s. [37]

Korean American Olympic diving champion, Sammy Lee, remembered that while growing up in Southern California during the 1930s, he heard remarks such as, "Gee, that Sammy could really be good, but he's not white, so they're not going to let him into some of the private clubs."

> On Mondays, I could swim at Pasadena's Brookside Park because that was so-called International Day, when non-whites were allowed in the pool. Afterward the custodians supposedly drained the pool so the honkies could use it the next day. Even the YMCA didn't want me to train there. The officials said something about my having to have a chest x-ray and clearance from a doctor. My father had a lot of pride and that bothered him. He told me, "We don't have to take that. Don't worry, something will work out. [38]

Vicki Manalo Draves was another Olympic diving champion in the 1940s. Her father was a Filipino, but early in her career, she used her white mother's maiden name of Taylor. She feared she could not practice diving at the pool in San Francisco's famed Fairmont Hotel because of her Filipino ancestry and surname. [39]

Leaders of urban Asian Pacific American communities often expressed concern over the lack of recreational facilities in areas such as San Francisco's overcrowded Chinatown. For decades, only one playground served that Chinatown. In 1941, for example, residents of San Francisco's Chinatown unsuccessfully petitioned the city for a new playground in order to eliminate the problem of "dead end kids" in the community. Even European Americans such as one-time professional baseball player and later executive, Walter Mails, deplored San Francisco's neglect of its Chinese American young people. In 1949, Mails wrote an article for San Francisco's *Chinese Press*. In this article, Mails pointed out that San Francisco's Chinese American community needed more recreational facilities and playing fields. He observed that swimming and basketball were two sports for which Chinese American boys and girls possessed an aptitude and thus they should have more access to basketball courts and swimming pools. [40]

However, many first generation people, as well as older members of the second generation, simply had little time for a leisurely swim or to shoot some hoops. Historian Valerie Matsumoto contends that during the 1920s the older *Nisei* in rural California were too busy helping families become economically stable to worry about athletics. Matsumoto notes that in California's Central Valley, "By the end of the 1930s, the younger Nisei had more opportunities for participation in extracurricular activities, especially athletics. The boys played basketball and baseball and went out for track, although their relatively smaller size prevented them from playing first-string football. "[41]

The boys, as Matsumoto points out, played sports. Asian Pacific American girls, like most American girls, were expected to do other things. As we will later explore, many Asian Pacific American girls and women participated in sports at various levels before and after World War II. But their brothers and male friends were more likely found in high school, recreational, and college basketball and baseball line-ups.

Family, Gender, and Community

For a variety of reasons, early Asian Pacific Americans were disproportionately males, who lived without spouses and children. This was especially so on the mainland. Asian cultures tended to restrict the movement of women, particularly those possessing privileged social and economic backgrounds. If necessary, males migrated, expecting to return home with enough money to at least get them or their families out of debt. If some of those males decided to remain in the lands thousands of miles away from their native homes, then they expected to either return briefly to get married or fetch their wives and children in person or send for them.

Class, however, played a significant role in determining whose spouses would live with them on the mainland or not. Obviously, the Asian Pacific immigrant with more capital could better afford bringing spouses and children with them. Discriminatory immigration laws, furthermore, reflected a substantial class bias. The Chinese Exclusion Law of 1882 barred Chinese immigrant laborers from coming into the U. S. Spouses and children of laboring class origins were excluded as well. At the same time, merchants and other wealthier Chinese immigrants legally escaped immigration restriction. They found it easier, consequently, to get their children passed watchful American immigration authorities. The Gentlemen's Agreement, signed by Japan and the United States in 1908, kept Japanese immigrant laborers from coming into America. Once again, wealthier immigrants faced no such restriction and they, too, were better positioned to form or reconstitute their families.

The politics of race and sex also hindered the development of families in early mainland Asian Pacific American communities. Judy Yung has the following to say about the Page Law, enacted by the U. S. Congress in 1875.

> As economic conditions worsened after the 1873 depression, public sentiment continued to mount against the Chinese. In 1875, Congress stepped in and passed the Page Law forbidding the entry of "Oriental" contract laborers, prostitutes, and criminals. The enforcement process, which involved the stringent screening of women in Hong Kong by the American consul, succeeded in reducing not only the number of prostitutes but also the overall number of Chinese women. [42]

For Japanese immigrants, the picture bride system performed a creative service. The Gentlemen's Agreement may have barred Japanese laborers from coming into the United States, but it did not bar spouses of Japanese immigrant residents from entering American ports. The problem was that if Japanese immigrant laborers living in the United States left for Japan to get married, they could not legally re-enter America. Thanks to the picture bride system, prospective spouses exchanged photographs across the Pacific and marriages were arranged with the immigrant groom *in absentia.* Then the wife migrated to the United States. Accordingly, Japanese immigrants were more likely to live with spouses and offspring than their Chinese immigrant counterparts.

The picture bride system, at the same time, fueled the ire of the anti-Asian movement. This movement, in turn, pressured the United States government to do something about barring picture brides. By 1920, the United States government succeeded in persuading Japan to agree to withhold passports to picture brides destined for America.

Stimulated by growing nativism and racism, the National Origins Act of 1924 slammed the door shut on Japanese migration to the United States. One of the major features of this act was a stipulation that no immigrant ineligible for citizenship was qualified to enter the U. S. Because only immigrants defined as white or black were eligible for American citizenship, Japanese and other Asian people wishing to come to the America were excluded.

Meanwhile, Koreans, much to their dismay, faced similar experiences. To an impressive extent, the problem for Koreans was that they were recognized in the United States as officially Japanese after 1910. This was so, because Japan had turned Korea into a colony. Korean immigrants, therefore, engaged in the picture bride system, but the same immigration laws that confronted the Japanese victimized them as well.

Asian Indians trying to get into the United States also suffered from racially biased immigration laws. In response to the anti-Asian movement, the U. S. Congress enacted a restrictive immigration law in 1917. This banned migration to America from Southern Asia, which encompassed India. In addition, immigrants from French Indochina were barred, as well as those from non-American controlled Pacific Islands.

For awhile, Filipino immigrants in the 1920s were luckier. Because the Philippines was part of the American Empire, the American government recognized Filipinos as United States' nationals, ineligible for citizenship but free to move about the empire. Anti-Filipino sentiment grew in power in the late 1920s and early 1930s. To satisfy the vocal distaste expressed against Filipino immigrants, the U. S. Congress in 1934 enacted the Tydings-McDuffie Act, which substantially barred Filipino migration to the United States.

Like their Chinese and, to a lesser extent, Japanese counterparts, Korean, Asian Indian, and Filipino immigrant males generally faced immediate futures on the American mainland without wives and children. Racist immigration laws, however, comprised only part of the problem. Anti-miscegenation laws in the states in which most Asian Pacific immigrants lived also slowed the development of a second generation of sons and daughters of Asian Pacific ancestry.

These laws, of course, were not always strictly enforced. In California, for example, Asians were barred from marrying people defined as Caucasians. Californians of Mexican ancestry were technically recognized as Caucasians, but Asian Indian males, for example, married Mexican California women with little legal difficulty. Very likely they would have found marrying Californians of Swedish ancestry another matter. [43]

What all this has to do with Asian Pacific American sporting experiences should become clear. While pre-World War I Asian Pacific immigrants made their way into places like Stockton, California, and Salt Lake City, Utah, European immigrants and their offspring also established communities in the United States. They often faced some of the hostility experienced by Asian Pacific people. They, too, were frequently perceived in racist and nativist terms. The National Origins Act of 1924 restricted immigration into the United States from Southern and Eastern Europe. Nevertheless, European immigrants found it much easier to make it passed American immigration authorities than did immigrants from China, Japan, Korea, India, and the Philippines. If they chose to remain in America, they found it much easier to live with spouses from their native villag es, regions, and countries. And, if not, anti-miscegenation laws troubled them little.

A second generation, consequently, more easily emerged from European immigrant communities. In the history of American baseball, prize fighting, and other sports, we can encounter many stories of second generation young people using sports to help them assimilate. For many people living in mid-twentieth century America, the experiences of second generation children such as Joe Dimaggio, Hank Greenberg, Bronko Nagurski, and Rocky Graziano demonstrated that sport possessed egalitarian and democratic impulses. Moreover, such experiences established widely honored traditions of athletic achievement among white ethnic communities.

Where, in comparison, were the Asian Pacific American counterparts to Lou Gehrig, son of German immigrants, Knute Rockne, son of Danish immigrants, and Bob Cousy, son of French immigrants? That such Asian Pacific American athletes did not apparently exist could lead to troublesome conclusions. First, perhaps Asian Pacific American cultures kept Asian Pacific Americans from excelling in sports. Second, Asian Pacific Americans possibly inherited racial traits that kept them from excelling in sports. And, third, culture and race perhaps doubly limited Asian Pacific American sporting endeavors.

Given the widespread anecdotal evidence that many first generation parents, regardless of ethnicity, considered sports a waste of time for their children, we may want to consider the importance of cultural variation carefully. This book, moreover, will hopefully demonstrate that Asian Pacific people have not been racially deficient when it comes to athletics. Therefore, a good answer to why there were no Asian Pacific American counterparts to the aforementioned great second generation American athletes is that perhaps Asian Pacific athletes performed just as competently as white ethnic athletes given how much the forces of racism, nativism, sexism, and class distinctions combined against Asian Pacific Americans.

Hawai'i

In this section we will shift attention from places like California, where the exclusion of Asian Pacific people was enormously popular for decades, to Hawai'i. Unlike California, Hawai'i's earliest white settlers were not men and women of relatively ordinary means, desperate for opportunities that seemingly escaped them in New York or North Carolina. Among Hawai'i's earliest white settlers were men like William Hooper, a New England representative of a firm that owned plantation land in the 1830s. In California, lower middle class and working class white settlers came to perceive Asian Pacific laborers as obstacles to their success. In Hawai'i, middle and upper class white settlers viewed Asian Pacific laborers as vital to haole profit margins.

To be sure, Asian Pacific people found no paradise awaiting them in Hawai'i. They often found brutal and subtle forms of class exploitation. They also found no little amount of racism. They did not, however, find much of an Asian Exclusion movement dogging their futures. For instance, plantation owners generally encouraged Asian Pacific workers to bring along spouses and children. These plantation owners were just partially motivated, if at all, by generosity. They believed that they could stabilize their work force if laborers lived with their families. Since, moreover, spouses and even children could help on the plantation, the haole elite believed the more hands the merrier when it came to filling Hawai'i's labor requirements. And, unlike California, Hawai'i nurtured no militant and largely white supremacist European American labor movement to stand in the planters' way.

Hawai'i, furthermore, endured into the twentieth century with relatively little concern about miscegenation. If a Chinese worker could not find a Chinese spouse, then, perhaps, a Native Hawaiian or a Portuguese person might do. Whether one or both parents or grandparents were Asian, second and third generations of Hawaiians possessing Asian ancestry blossomed during the second third of the twentieth century.

Hawai'i's immigrant generations might have preferred gambling and cock-fighting for recreation, but their children and grandchildren gravitated rather easily toward sports associated with American culture—baseball, American football, basketball, and boxing. Such sports were fun to engage in and watch. They were perceived by community and haole leaders as useful in keeping generally working and lower middle class folks out of trouble, militant trade unionism and dissident political movements. Participants viewed sports as a means of representing community ties to neighbors and other workers. Participants viewed sports as well as a way to distinguish themselves in terms of status and economic conditions. In the 1920s and 1930s, plantation owners were willing to hire competent athletes for relatively decent jobs. Such athletes, in turn, played for teams representing their employers.

Indeed, many fine Asian Hawaiian athletes emerged during the twentieth century. What seems clear, moreover, is that compared to their mainland counterparts, Asian Hawaiian athletes were more successful at competing with and against European American athletes. In so doing, they defied a racialization process that distanced people of Asian Pacific ancestry from athletic achievement in highly competitive, often very physical sports.

One explanation perhaps lies in the demographic dominance of people of Asian ancestry on the Hawaiian Islands. In 1920, for example, about sixty-two percent of Hawai'i's population consisted of people with Asian ancestors. By contrast, people of Asian ancestry comprised just 3. 5% of California's population. High school football and basketball coaches in California could generally thrive without cultivating Chinese and Japanese American athletes. Their Hawaiian counterparts, however, could not uniformly fill their rosters with just haoles.

As for the Native Hawaiians, they were, compared to many indigenous people elsewhere, lucky. Nevertheless, in significant ways, Native Hawaiians shared the fates of other indigenous people who came into contact with European-based cultures in the Americas, the South Pacific, and Africa for the first time. Countless numbers died when they caught diseases brought to the islands by Europeans. Those that did not perish had to work hard at salvaging their cultures and economic independence and frequently failed in the face of determined white missionaries, plantation owners, and their own leaders who were attracted to "Western Ways." Still, Native Hawaiian labor, real or potential, was viewed by the haole elite as too valuable to exterminate. This haole elite, furthermore, was not enthusiastic about attracting to the islands the kind of lower middle class and working class white settlers that too frequently got themselves entangled in genocidal wars against native peoples in other parts of the globe. Nor did that elite wish to compete with rugged white settlers for the islands' resources.

Thus, Native Hawaiians generally survived the initial conquest by white peoples. Significantly, however, they lost control of their land, witnessed the commercialization of some of their venerable cultural practices, and experienced devastating losses of loved ones through diseases that did not exist in Hawai'i prior to Cook. They, moreover, often married Chinese and haoles, as well as other non-native people; thus weakening traditional ties among indigenous Hawaiians. By the same token, the intermarriage of Native Hawaiians and non-native Hawaiians perhaps paradoxically dispersed and broadened the roots of Native Hawaiian cultural practices and institutions. The category of local was developed and extended to people of non-full blooded Hawaiians. The use of pidgin English expressed the cultural bonds nurtured among multicultural, multiethnic plantation workers, as well as reinforced local culture in Hawai'i. Sports as varied as surfing, baseball, and sumo also seemed to sustain this local identity. This is not to say that specific racial and ethnic identities were lost in Hawai'i nor racism and nativism forgotten as tools of oppression. It is to say that the boundaries separating those identities were more blurred. Moreover, that given the impracticality of systematic racial exclusion in Hawai'i, Hawaiian football fields, baseball diamonds, basketball courts, and even golf courses were relatively accessible to Hawaiians of color; a substantial number of whom became superb and relatively famous athletes. [44]

Yet while Native Hawaiians, at first glance, appear to have blended easily into a local culture, some scholars and Native Hawaiian activists urge us to tone down celebrations of Hawai'i as a racial haven. For one thing, Native Hawaiian-based cultural practices such as the hula and, more relevant to us, surfing have been largely stripped of their cultural contexts. Both the hula and surfing were long honored by Native Hawaiians, but in the twentieth century hula dancing and surfing became enmeshed in the efforts of island and mainland commercial interests to romanticize Hawai'i for prospective tourists and represent Native Hawaiians as friendly, child-like, and primitive people. Of course, non-Native Hawaiians should enjoy surfing and appreciate hula dancing, but a number of people of Native Hawaiian ancestry quite understandably have problems with the vast commercialization of these venerable cultural practices. More serious, but related, problems for Native Hawaiians have been poverty, disease, and the continued demographic decline they have suffered throughout the twentieth century. [45]

New Immigrants, New Communities

Since World War II, Asian Pacific America has changed immensely. More liberal immigration laws, combined with the U. S. government's willingness to offer refuge to thousands of Asians fleeing communist-led nations, have expanded and diversified the population of Americans of Asian Pacific ancestry. In particular, this has meant that for the first time in America's history thousands of people from Southeast Asia developed communities in the United States. Moreover, uneven economic developments and political conflict encouraged people from India, Pakistan, Thailand, Indonesia, Malaysia, Sri Lanka, the Philippine Islands, and Korea to seek homes in the United States. Pacific Islanders from Samoa and Guam, likewise, quested for economic advancement in the United States.

These "new immigrants" and their offspring have transplanted sporting practices to the United States, while taking up sports more associated with American culture. For example, Asian Indian and Pakistani immigrants have not surrendered their love of cricket upon arrival in the United States. In the *San Jose Mercury*, T. H. Nhu reported in 1996:

> While the sport may not captivate other Americans, many in the Bay Area's 100,000 member Indo-American community consider it the only real sport around—especially the match between the arch-rivals [India and Pakistan] from the subcontinent. Hundreds of immigrants line up outside of a Fremont theater to watch the match between teams of the same nation... [Cricket] is a national obsession on the subcontinent of India, Pakistan, and Sri Lanka and is wildly popular among the legions of engineers and computer-programmer émigrés. [46]

Takraw, a sport that involves using anything but the hands to keep a ball in the air, is a venerable sport among Southeast Asians and can be seen engaged in by Southeast Asian immigrants in the United States. At the same time, there are plenty of relatively recent Asian Pacific immigrants and their children who play and follow North Americanized sports such as basketball, baseball, ice hockey, and football.

While we can easily generalize too greatly one way or another about the new Asian Pacific American communities, like older Asian Pacific American communities, they too represent a heterogeneous group of people distinguished by national, political, religious, generational, socio-economic, and gender differences. Those who join gyms, Little League teams, and ice skating classes usually are not the people or the children of the people who work in sweatshops or as motel maids. Nor is it likely that the new Asian Pacific American communities encourage female participation in sports substantially more than did older Asian Pacific American communities or, for that matter, any American community. At the same time, female and male high school teams in areas inhabited by the new Asian Pacific American communities will have more than an occasional member who is either a recent Asian Pacific immigrant or refugee or a child of post-1965 Asian Pacific immigrants or refugees.

Cultural Citizenship, Community, and Sports in the Late Twentieth Century

The diversity of Asian Pacific American communities in the late twentieth century has made the struggle for Asian Pacific American cultural citizenship an intriguing process. Older Asian Pacific American communities have still needed to demonstrate they belong in the United States while retaining Asian Pacific roots. Newer Asian Pacific American communities have just started their journeys across cultural borderlands in the United States.

A third generation Japanese American informant told scholar Jere Takahashi how important community sports organizations were for him growing up in the San Francisco Bay Area during the 1960s. Japanese American community sports organizations furnished him with stimulation that came "from competing against other people and meeting people from different areas." These organizations also kept him, as a working class youth, off the streets. [47]

A third generation Chinese American told scholar Mia Tuan that he took part in Asian American sports leagues rather than participate in more mainstream athletic organizations such as Little League baseball. Doing so "provides you with a network of people, Asian American families, kids, and parents in the East Bay. That was during the week too. Families would do everything, so I had contact everywhere."[48]

By 1970, old and new communities of Asian Pacific Americans had converged in places like the San Francisco Bay Area and urban Southern California. Sports, perhaps, have helped connect the people in these communities to one another and non-Asian Pacific American communities. In the early 1970s, the Peninsula Chinese Community Center in Palo Alto organized the first annual Chinese Little Olympics. Among the events established for children of first generation and beyond were contests in basketball free throwing, swimming, football kicking and passing, and sit-ups. Several years later, the "Chinese Little Olympics" was still going strong. In 1981, *East/West* reported that the event attracted 300 participants from as far away as Hawai'i and New York. Organizer Dale Yee remarked, "It is good to see our youth, all of the family, take part. This competition is also a good way to develop self-esteem and confidence. It has so many advantages. It is a healthy family activity. " In Silicon Valley, the *San Jose Mercury* reported that De Anza College served as the site in 1997 of the thirteenth annual Chinese American Athletic Tournament. Approximately 5,000 people showed up to watch and engage in activities such as the martial arts, softball, and table tennis. Meanwhile, Los Angeles's Chinatown hosted an annual New Years' sport tournament. Contests in basketball, volleyball, and table tennis were staged. [49]

In Seattle in the late 1990s, people of Asian ancestry used sports such as basketball to forge a pan-ethnic Asian Pacific community. On its website, the Seattle Asian Sports Club declared its purpose was to "promote self-esteem, discipline, friendship, cooperation, contribution and sportsmanship within and for the Asian community." The club hoped to "to utilize basketball and/or other endeavors as a means of developing skills and continual opportunities for community involvement and contribution." Participating families, the club hoped, would gain "opportunities...to apply the values of self-esteem, discipline, friendship, cooperation, contribution, and sportsmanship in a broad context." At the same time, the Seattle Asian Sports Club hoped to connect to a larger Seattle community. It wanted "to promote openness and awareness within and between-communities of interest on issues of cultural diversity.... to establish a cross-cultural forum/format for awareness and interaction--to provide a working model of cross-cultural self-esteem, discipline, friendship, cooperation, contribution, and sportsmanship. "[50]

Sports have also been used to help solve the social problems facing late twentieth century Asian Pacific American communities. Youth crime in San Francisco's Asian Pacific communities has been exaggerated in the popular media, but it has remained a frustrating problem to community leaders and residents. In 1982, *East/West* reporter Scott Kong explored the effort to prevent Asian Pacific American youth crime in San Francisco by way of table tennis clinics given by Lun Duc, a Vietnamese émigré and champion table tennis player. Kong reported optimistically that Asian Pacific youth seemed attracted to the clinics. [51]

In LaCrosse, Wisconsin, the Southeast Asian Youth Organization (SAYO) allied with a local school district in 2001 to offer volleyball, soccer, and basketball to middle and high school students, many of whom possessed Hmong backgrounds. Tony Yang, who helped create SAYO asserted that the organization diverted working class and poor youth from trouble. He said, "[F]or a lot of Hmong kids, soccer and volleyball are the only sports they can play because size doesn't matter."[52]

Religious institutions such as the Buddhist Church have been important in sponsoring sporting activities aimed at youth. We will explore in subsequent chapters how Asian Pacific American religious organizations have promoted particular sports. But in the 1970s, we should note, the Midwest Buddhist Temple in Chicago formed boys softball and basketball teams which competed in the Chicago Nisei Athletic Association. The temple also sponsored girls' teams in basketball, softball, and volleyball. The temple was involved in bowling and golf tournaments, as well as establishing the Midwest Buddhist Temple Judo Academy. In Salt Lake City, the Young Buddhist Association (YBA), sponsored baseball and basketball squads, while the Bakersfield, California Buddhist

Church supported athletic competition in baseball, basketball, and track and field. [53]

Conclusion

In March, 1973, the Japanese American daily, the *Pacific Citizen*, received a letter from a Japanese American woman protesting a decision made by the Los Angeles School System regarding high school athletics. The school system had decided to do away with B and C teams, which were largely composed of younger and smaller athletes. She feared that such a decision would discourage smaller "Oriental and Mexican" athletes from competing, because they would have to match up against larger athletes. Thus, the Los Angeles School System would deprive those smaller athletes of opportunities to represent their schools in interscholastic competition. [54]

In the early 2000s, the Chinese American Athletic Federation had become the Taiwanese-Chinese American Athletic Federation. Affected by the rift between mainland China and Taiwan, the federation supported an independent Taiwan while the mainland government called for a unified China that would include the Taiwanese. Athletic-minded Chinese Americans in the Bay Area who backed the one-China policy broke off from the federation and established the Northern California Chinese Athletic Federation, which initiated its own Olympic-style annual games. [55]

The responses of athletic-minded Chinese Americans to the controversy have been mixed. Yan Zhao, born on the mainland and an advocate of a unified China, enjoyed competing in table tennis, basketball, and track. She told the *San Jose Mercury* that she felt isolated while competing in events staged by the older federation: "You feel that you're not welcome. It's definitely a shame, though, that the two groups can't get together and hold separate events. " Jay Ni, born in Taiwan, claimed that a majority of Chinese American athletes in the Bay Area "are more interested in playing sports, than in debating politics. " He added, "The kids don't care...They're Chinese-American. They were born here. They just care about the enjoyment and excitement of sports." And Sharon Yu, a member of the Northern California Chinese Athletic Federation, remarked, "We want to show everyone that we're a large community...And that sports is something everyone can enjoy."[56]

In various ways, these Asian Pacific Americans have articulated a key problem connecting cultural citizenship and sports for Asian Pacific Americans, as well as other people of color. Through sports such as baseball, softball, basketball, and football Asian Pacific American can and have shown they belonged; have shown their commonality with each other and non-Asian Pacific Americans. Nevertheless, their experiences in sports have been unique. In part, this is because Asian Pacific athletes have often been smaller than non-Asian Pacific athletes. In part, this is also because Asian Pacific Americans have often been first or second generation, identifying themselves or being identified with Asian

Pacific geopolitics. Moreover, there have been a whole host of other factors, including the historical prevalence of institutional racism in the U. S., which have affected Americans of Asian Pacific ancestry on and off the playing fields.

Notes

1. Raymond Williams, *Keywords: A Vocabulary of Culture and Society,* (New York: Oxford University Press, 1983), 76.

2. Stephen Hardy, *How Boston Played: Sports, Recreation, and Community, 1865-1915,* (Boston: Northeastern University Press, 1982), 21.

3. Robert Bellah, *et. al. Habits of the Heart: Individualism and Commitment in American Life.* (Berkeley and Los Angeles: University of California Press, 1985), 153.

4. Benedict Anderson, *Invented Communities: Reflections on the Origins and Spread of Nationalism,* (London: Verso, 1983).

5. Ronald Takaki, *Strangers,* 128-9.

6. *Ibid.,* 121; *Daily Alta California,* February 17, 1863.

7. *San Francisco Examiner,* September 17, 1869.

8. *San Jose Mercury,* January 29, 1887; San *Jose Herald,* January 29, 1881.

9. Renato Rosaldo, *Culture and Truth: The Remaking of Social Analysis,* (Boston: Beacon Press, 1989), 68-69; *San Jose Mercury,* February 13, 1926.

10. Takaki, *Strangers,* 184-185.

11. Sandy Lydon, *Chinese Gold: The Chinese in the Monterey Bay Region,* (Capitola, CA: Capitola Books, 1985), 328.

12. *Ibid.*

13. Paul P. C. Siu, *The Chinese Laundryman: A Study in Social Isolation,* (New York: New York University Press, 1987).

14. William C. Smith, *Americans in Process: A Study of Our Citizens of Oriental Ancestry,* (Ann Arbor, MI: Edwards Brothers, 1937).

15. Lydon, *Chinese Gold,* 204-205.

16. Chris Friday, *Organizing Asian American Labor: The Pacific Coast Canned-Salmon Industry, 1870-1942,* (Philadelphia: Temple University Press, 1994), 55.

17. *Los Angeles Times,* August 13, 1907.

18. U. S. Immigration Commission, *Reports of the Immigration Commission:* Immigrants *in Industries, Part 25, Japanese and Other Immigrant Races in the Pacific,* (Government Printing Office: Washington, D. C. , 1911), v. 2, 663.

19. Carlos Bulosan, *America is in The Heart,* (Seattle: University of Washington Press, 1973), 116, 118.

20. *San Jose Mercury,* June 12, 1894.

21. Sucheng Chan, *This Bittersweet Soil: The Chinese in California Agriculture, 1870-1910,* (Berkeley and Los Angeles: University of California Press, 1986), chapter two.

22. *Ibid. ,* 144-145.

23. Tim Lukes and Gary Okihiro, Japanese *Legacy: Farming and Community Life in California's Santa Clara Valley,* (California History Center: Cupertino, CA, 1985), 24; Takaki, *Strangers,* 185.

24. Yuji. Ichioka, The *Issei: The World of First Generation Japanese Immigrants,* 1885-1924, (New York: The Free Press, 1988), 89.

25. Yen Le Espiritu, *Filipino American Lives,* (Philadelphia: Temple University Press, 1995), 67.

26. Ramon R. Cariaga *The Filipinos in Hawaii: A Survey of their Economic and Social Conditions Thesis.* University of Hawaii, 1936, 90.

27. Ichioka, *Issei*, 176-179; *The Playground*, November, 1920, 502-504.

28. Takaki, *Strangers*, chapter four; F. K. Katterman, Athletic Director, Athletics and Recreation on Lanai," in Recreation Commission of, City and County of Honolulu, (ed.) *A History of Recreation in Hawaii*, (Honolulu, T. H. : 1936). 47.

29. T. T. Waterman, "Recreation on the Sugar Plantations," in *A History*, 51.

30. Cariaga, *Filipinos in Hawaii*, 89; Maximino R. Velasco, "Native Filipino Sports and Games," in *A History*, 105.

31. Steven Misawa, ed. *Beginnings: Japanese Americans in San Jose*, (San Jose: Japanese American Community Senior Service, 1981), 14.

32. Lisa See, *On Gold Mountain*, (New York: St. Martin's Press, 1995), 156-157; *Philippine News*, January 10-January 16, 1974.

33. Judy Yung, *Unbound Feet*: 148, 151, 152; *Unbound Voices: A Documentary History of Chinese Women in San Francisco*, (Berkeley and Los Angeles: University of California Press, 1999), 351.

34. Yung, *Unbound Feet*, 155.

35. Samuel O. Regalado, "Incarcerated Sport: Nisei Women's Softball and Athletics During Japanese Internment," *Journal of Sport History*, (Fall, 2000), 433, 434.

36. *Ibid.* , 435, 437.

37. Connie Young Yu, *Chinatown San Jose, USA.* (San Jose: Historical Museum Assoc. 1991), 99; Karen Isaksen Leonard, *Making Ethnic Choices: California's Punjabi Mexican Americans*, (Philadelphia: Temple University Press, 1992), 135.

38. Helen Zia and Susan B. Fall, (eds.), *Notable Asian Americans*, (Detroit: Gale Research, 1995), 202.

39. *Ibid*, 72.

40. *California Chinese Press*, February 28, 1941; *Chinese Press*, February 4, 1949.

41. Valerie Matsumoto, *Farming*, 75.

42. Yung, *Unbound Feet*, 32.

43. Leonard, *Making Ethnic Choices*.

44. Elizabeth Buck, *Paradise Remade: The Politics of Culture and History in Hawai'i*: (Philadelphia: Temple University Press, 1993); Jonathan Kay Kamakawio'ole Osorio, *Dismembering Lāhui: A History of the Hawaiian Nation*, (Honolulu: University of Hawai'i Press, 2002).

45. *Ibid*; Haunani-Kay Trask, *From a Native Daughter: Colonialism & Sovereignty in Hawaii*, (Monroe, Maine: Common Courage Press, 1993; Candace Fujikane, "Sweeping Racism under the Rug of 'Censorship': The Controversy over Lois-Ann Yamanaka's *Blu's Hanging*," in *Japanese American Contemporary Experience in Hawai'i*, edited by Jonathan Okamura, (Honolulu: University of Hawai'i Press, 2002).

46. T. H. Nhu, "Indo-American Cricket Fans Chirp Up," *San Jose Mercury*, September 25, 1996; Rob Nixon, "As American As Cricket," www. theatlantic. com, July 2000.

47. Jere Takahashi, *Nisei, Sansei: Shifting Japanese American Identities and Politics*, (Philadelphia: Temple University Press, 1997), 170.

48. Mia Tuan, *Forever Foreign or Honorary Whites: The Asian Ethnic Experience*, (New Brunswick, New Jersey: Rutgers University Press, 1998), 103.

49. *Bridge*, September, October, 1972; *East/West*, January 21, 1981; September 2, 1981; Tracey Kaplan, "Athletes, heritage mingle at Chinese American Tourney," *San Jose Mercury*, August 17, 1997.

50. www. halycon. com, accessed June 9, 1999.

51. *East/West*, August 18, 1982.

52. Anastasia Mercer, "Hmong America Youth Fill Summer Days With Soccer," *Asian Week*, July 13-July 19, 2001.

53. *Buddhist Churches of America*, (Chicago, Il; Norbart, Inc., 1974), 232, 247, 389.

54. *Pacific Citizen*, March 30, 1973.

55. Liza Fernandez, "Politics Shadow Games," *San Jose Mercury*, August 12, 2005.

56. *Ibid.*

Chapter Two: The Ring and the Mat

The Wigwam was a popular "sporting establishment" in San Francisco during the 1880s. It served liquor to a largely, but not exclusively, working class clientele and frequently staged prizefights. While San Francisco achieved a reputation as a socially liberal city in the late nineteenth century, many of its residents understandably condemned prize fighting as a disreputable amusement appealing to the baser instincts of the "lower sorts." At the same time, prize fighting's attractions crossed class and ethnic lines. The participants themselves were typically working class Irish immigrants or sons of Irish immigrants. And the audience shared much that was socially and culturally in common with prizefighters. However, generously sprinkled among the patrons were powerful and often non-Irish American politicians, government officials, and businessmen.

To prizefighting's supporters, the sport symbolized what was best about America in the late 1800s. Even though outlawed in several states, no sport attracted more fans in America than prizefighting. And no sporting figures were more celebrated than professional boxers such as John L. Sullivan and James Corbett. These and other prizefighters signified manliness to many boxing fans. That they were white was significant since manliness was widely perceived by European American males as their own unique attribute. Prizefighters of color such as Peter Jackson won some respect from white Americans. But their success was likely to embarrass white boxing fans since the sight of fallen white boxers at the hands of men like Jackson contested the prevailing racial ideology.[1]

The idea of Chinese prizefighters seemed, at best, worth a chuckle or two to the European American press. And the idea of presenting a match between "the champion Chinese sloggers" or professional boxers seemed worth a dollar or two to the operators of the Wigwam. The two prizefighters were called Ah Fat and Jim Bung in the sporting press. The San Francisco correspondent to the national weekly, *Sporting Life*, expected that the "Chinese heavy weight championship" might prove entertaining, for the participants, presumably unlike many white prize fighters, "haven't learned to hippodrome." That is, if nothing else, the Chinese boxers would put on an honest match. Interestingly, two local African American boxers, June Dennis and Jim Hall, acted as seconds. The *San Francisco Examiner* celebrated the event in racial tones by noting that "{t}he dark-hued did the talking, whites did the laughing, and the copper colored the

fighting." The daily also admitted that "the Celestials" were not very good professional boxers. When they were done, however, "their departure was greeted
with more unbounded enthusiasm than ever received by any of their countrymen
in this state since the Burlingame Treaty."[2]

The Wigwam event recalls a sad chapter in the history of American sports
in which something called "the battle royal" was much too popular among white
American males. The "battle royal" consisted of a group of young black men
placed in a ring before a white male audience. They would fight each other until
one youth remained standing. A "battle royal" is vividly described in Ralph Ellison's classic novel, *The Invisible Man*. The winner was both simultaneously
honored and degraded by his victory. As long as boxers of color fought each
other in such settings the racial boundaries remained firmly in place.[3]

Moreover, the newspaper account of Ah Fat's and Jim Bung's bout can tell
us a great deal about the experiences of Chinese immigrants in late nineteenth
century America. In the first place, the boxers were called "Celestials," a term
which signified to white Americans the other worldliness of Chinese people--
their apparent lack of physical substance. Secondly, the *San Francisco Examiner*
referred to the unpopularity of Chinese immigrants in the United States since the
Burlingame Treaty. Signed between the United States and China in 1868, the
Burlingame Treaty encouraged the movement of Chinese citizens to the United
States. Consequently, one of the primary objectives of the anti-Chinese movement in the United States was to compel the American government to abrogate
that treaty and ban Chinese immigration to America.

We should also note historian Peter Levine's interesting story about the
great Jewish boxer, Benny Leonard. In 1913, Leonard was just beginning a career that would take him to the lightweight championship of the world from
1917 to 1923. On Chinese New Years of 1913, Leonard fought a six round
match in New York City's Chinatown against a boxer named Ah Chung. In reality, Ah Chung was a lad named Rosenberg, who was convinced by the fight's
promoter to allow himself to appear Chinese. The promoter wanted Chinese
New Yorkers to show up, money in hand, at the bout and he believed that by
billing one of the contestants as a "Peking native" and "the only Chinese boxer
in the world," he would pump up attendance.

Rosenberg, AKA Ah Chung, got knocked out for his trouble. He also
failed to fool all of the Chinese New Yorkers at the bout, if he fooled any at all.
At least according to one sportswriter, a Chinese immigrant spectator engaged
Rosenberg in conversation in between rounds: "{O}ur Chinese patron demanded
that the fighter admit he was an impostor. 'You no China boy, you fake,' he
insisted. 'China boy got more sense than to stand up and get licking when he can
iron shirts and collars."[4]

Beyond the crude stereotypes invoked by the sportswriter, this story pits Benny Leonard, a tough Jewish boxer, who defied the venerable stereotype of Jewish men as unmanly and a Chinese boxer, who appeared to defy the stereotype of the equally venerable stereotype of Chinese men as unmanly. Yet as the story unfolds Leonard and even Rosenberg have subverted one stereotype, while the other still shoves Chinese men into a laundry, performing "unmanly" work for whites. Accordingly, however distasteful many of us consider prizefighting, those Asian Pacific men who ventured into prizefighting rings in the first half of the twentieth century undermined powerful stereotypes, while perhaps reinforcing others.

Several months later, Ah Chung was still boxing. He was also still doing a poor job of it. A wire report, published in the *Fort Wayne News*, declared that "Ah Chung, China's representative in the fight ring," refused to complete a bout with Tommy Bresnahan. After three rounds, Ah Chung gave up.[5]

Asian Pacific American Prizefighters

In February, 1899, readers of the *San Francisco Chronicle* learned that "{a} Chinese is to enter the ring at last. Li Hung Foy is his name, and he is in New York at present according to the eastern press. Foy is said to be clever." Foy, the piece in the *Chronicle* went on, was scheduled to fight Tom Cooney in Trenton, New Jersey in March. Both fighters reputedly weighed 154 pounds. As it turned out, Fairview, New York in April, 1899, was the site of a controversial match between Tom Cooney, an African American and Li Hung Foy, described after the bout to *Chronicle* readers as "a Celestial from New York's Chinatown." Referring not very subtly to John Henry folk tales and widely held perceptions of organized Chinatown violence, the *Chronicle* depicted the bout as "a hammer and tong affair with knockdowns in every round." The fight, however, ended in a draw, which provoked unhappy spectators into flinging their beer glasses into the ring.[6]

It is possible that Li Hung Foy, like Ah Chung, was an imposter, boxing in "yellowface." This was not true of Ah Wing, a prizefighter who began to gain notice in California sporting circles in 1900. In April of that year, the *San Francisco Chronicle* announced that at San Francisco's Columbia Club "{t}he band will play 'The Chinese and the Coon' when Ah Wing, the Chinese pugilist and Kid Dobson, the Alligator" enter the ring. In addition to Ah Wing, two black boxers, Henry Lewis and Bob Thompson, would fight one another. But the main event featured Young Peter Jackson, an African American, and Paddy Purcell.[7]

Under the headline, "Why He Deserted The Kitchen for the Roped Arena," the *San Francisco Chronicle* ran a brief article on Ah Wing in late March, 1900.

The article claimed that a famed prizefighting manager named Biddy Bishop had discovered Ah Wing in Auburn, California. The Bishop was then known most prominently as the manager of Young Peter Jackson, who was not only a highly skilled African American boxer but also a boxer who Ah Wing apparently idolized. Ah Wing was described as a cook by trade and had been boxing professionally for two years. The *Chronicle* added that he could play the piano and speak English flawlessly.[8]

Ah Wing seemed to have gotten so much attention that more famous white boxers had become a little anxious. In April, 1900, Kid McGovern, one of the finest lighter weight boxers of his time, announced to the *Los Angeles Evening Express* he desperately wanted to take on Ah Wing. Reflecting some of the more despicable racial attitudes at the time McGovern explained that he did not want "a long-tailed monkey {to} get ahead of him in the eyes of the public."[9]

Ah Wing achieved some success in prize fighting. According to the *Los Angeles Evening Express* in April, 1900, Ah Wing had astonished prize fighting fans. Ah Wing was "rapid and forcible, and posses e{d} plenty of grit and determination." He had just knocked out a boxer named "Handsome" Ed Wiley in two rounds in a bout in Sacramento. In later years, the *San Francisco Chronicle* called Ah Wing "a clever boxer and hard hitter." The daily reminded readers of the manliness prizefighters supposedly harbored, but Chinese males supposedly lacked. It claimed that Ah Wing "possessed...rare gameness, a quality which his race is not generally supposed to exhibit." Moreover, after a bout in 1905, the *Chronicle* enthused: "All hail! Ah Wing!...He last night sent Manual Torres to the land of the nod, scoring one of the cleanest knockouts ever seen in the San Francisco ring."[10]

Eventually, Ah Wing dropped out of sight, only to reappear in a tantalizing story published in the *New York Times* in 1912. A dispatch from Sacramento reported that two "highbinders" wanted to kill Ah Wing, described as "an Americanized Chinaman and one of the most interesting characters in Chinatown." Instead, the two killers mistakenly murdered Willie Wong, a proprietor of a Sacramento restaurant.[11]

Since Ah Wing entered the ring, there have been several other notable Asian Pacific American prizefighters in the twentieth century. The social and legal identities of some of these boxers might seem ambiguous or even mysterious. For example, a legion of the best prizefighters in the lower weight divisions in the 1920s and 1930s came from the Philippines. It is not always very clear as to whether these professional prizefighters ought to be considered Filipino Americans or not. If the latter, we can still recognize them as contributors to Asian Pacific American sporting history given their popularity among Filipino communities in the United States and that they were at that time inhabitants of the American empire and considered U.S. Nationals.

In the 1910s, a prizefighter of Chinese ancestry began to box professionally out of Sacramento. Typical of many of his ring contemporaries, George Lee started his career in preliminary bouts to the main event. Soon, he was a main event boxer himself. According to the *Sacramento Bee*, Lee gained considerable popularity on the East Coast, as well as the American South. The *Bee* maintained that "Lee has met some of the best small boxers in the country and has been an attraction in New York." By 1920, Lee ranked as a contender, although an unsuccessful one, for the bantamweight title.[12]

In 1925, George Lee was no champion, but he was still boxing professionally. On July 1 of that year, the *San Francisco Chronicle* published an article on Lee, accompanied by a photograph showing him in boxing gear and another in "traditional Chinese costume." "George Washington Lee," according to the *Chronicle*, had "strayed from the path of his forefathers" to become "the fighting Chinaman of Sacramento." An *Oakland Tribune* article in 1925 linked Lee with a San Francisco-based prizefighter, Sammy Lee. George Lee by this time had apparently slipped from main event heaven. The *Tribune* described the two Lees, who were apparently not related, as "two little four rounders." Just like George Lee, the San Franciscan was promoted or promoted himself as a representative of the "mysterious Orient." He typically entered the ring wearing "traditional" Chinese attire and a false queue. Sammy Lee, according to the *Tribune*, also played small roles in Hollywood films. Yet he was more than just a showpiece. The *San Francisco Chronicle* called Sammy Lee "the clever local Chinese bantamweight."[13]

Asian Pacific Islander prizefighters were active in Hawai'i during the early decades of the twentieth century. Sam Hop, who was well known in early twentieth Hawaiian sporting circles, boxed professionally. In 1911, Jim Hoao took on George "Slim" Gilmore at Honolulu's Orpheum Theater.[14]

Meanwhile, a few boxers of Japanese ancestry attracted attention in the United States. In 1912, a prizefighter performing under the name of Young Togo was portrayed by the *San Francisco Chronicle* as "the Japanese bantamweight." According to one press account, Young Togo was four-feet ten and 108 pounds. Called the "Yellow Peril" of the ring, he had arrived in San Francisco in 1906. He had no money and no knowledge of English, but he did know "jiu jitsu." Young Togo headed to Los Angeles where he found work teaching Japanese martial arts to wealthy Angelenos. Meanwhile, he learned English and boxing from a fellow named Eddie Robinson. He learned well, winning twenty-seven professional bouts, twenty five by knock out. And supported by "Japanese sports" in places like San Francisco and managed by Eddie Robinson, Young

Togo challenged top bantamweights such as Abe Attell and was capable, according to the *Chronicle*, of taking heavy punishment. A dispatch from San Francisco published in the *Pacific Commercial Advertiser* claimed that Young Togo excited the city's "Japantown". It maintained, "The Japs are liberal patronizers when they have a champion performing for them..." Indeed, "his countrymen" tendered Young Togo a testimonial in San Francisco in June, 1912.[15]

In subsequent years, other boxers of Japanese ancestry fought professionally in the United States. In 1923, the *Sacramento Bee* announced a fight card at the local American Legion hall. Boxing on this card was "Young Mikado, a Japanese," who was scheduled to oppose a prize fighter named "Kid Manila." A Seattle-born Nisei, Jimmie Sakamoto emerged as an all around high school athlete who took up prize fighting in the 1920s. Sakamoto boxed professionally in New York City until blinded in the ring. Sakamoto returned to Seattle where he became an ardent advocate of Japanese American assimilation and a leading member of the time-honored Japanese American Citizens League.[16]

Generally, however, during the 1920s and 1930s, the most prominent prizefighters of Asian Pacific ancestry came from the Philippines. Prizefighters of Filipino parentage proved not only popular among the Filipino immigrants living in the United States, as well as its territories, but they clearly ranked pound for pound among the best professional boxers in the world. The *Cleveland Plain Dealer* reported: "The Filipinos have taken to prize fighting like the proverbial duck to water. They have repeatedly beat the Nordic, the Latin, the Celt, and the Semite in the American realm of pugilism. And in the greater part of the United States their successful efforts have been popular."[17]

Nestor Enriquez, an expert on Filipino sport history, describes the appeal of prizefighting to Filipino young men growing up in the early decades of the twentieth century: "Boxing is our arena. This is where you are matched against your own size. It's also a poor boy's ticket out of obscurity and into the world. A sport that has no economic boundary."[18]

Francisco Guiledo became probably the first prizefighter from the Philippines to capture the sporting world's fancy. Fighting under the name of Young Pancho Villa, he and another Filipino boxer, Klimo Flores, were brought to the United States by a promoter named Frank Churchill, who became a fight manager while serving in the Philippines as a custom house clerk. In announcing Villa's arrival, the *Washington Post* mentioned that he had defeated George Lee in the Philippines. The *Post* piece stated that Villa was outweighed by ten pounds but had decisively defeated the "Celestial." After his arrival, the *Post* observed that Villa was getting bouts because of his "nationality." The daily asserted that Villa was "a novelty in a ring and has proved a gate magnet from his debut here. In addition, he is a scrappy, clever boxer and a hard hitter." Villa, moreover, earned good money, according to sportswriter Arch Ward. For fighting Jimmy Wilde, Villa was paid $75,000 and for taking on Frankie Genarro, he got $65,000 for his troubles. Soon Villa won the flyweight championship of the world, prompting the *Post* to call him "The Little Brown Champion," and then died of blood poisoning from a tooth abscess at the age of twenty-four."[19]

Villa's last fight occurred in Oakland, California. He unsuccessfully defended his title against Canadian flyweight Jimmy McLaren. After the bout ended, Frank Churchill announced that a painful tooth abscess prompted Villa's defeat. Not knowing then that he was delivering something of a eulogy, Churchill declared that Villa was "the gamest little man I ever knew." [20]

Villa and other Filipino prizefighters attracted plenty of patronage from Filipinos living in and around cities like Los Angeles, San Jose, and Honolulu. An important aspect of their appeal to Filipinos in America was their willingness to remain in touch with their biggest fans. Pancho Villa, for example, apparently threw parties for his Filipino supporters. Accordingly, before Villa fought his fatal bout, the *San Francisco Chronicle* predicted that "Filipinos, judging from the way they have been purchasing tickets, will make a big share of the house." Later in 1925, another *San Francisco Chronicle* sportswriter noted, "Filipino fight fans are certainly strong for their own." One Pinoy boxer caught the attention of San Francisco's Filipino fight fans and they would "pack National Hall for his workouts and every bit of good work they heartily applaud." Six years later, the *Los Angeles Times* reported that Filipino boxers had aroused large Filipino followings in Oakland and Stockton, as well as Los Angeles and San Francisco. When Young Tommy defeated Baby Arizmendi in San Francisco, the *Philippines Mail* reported in 1933, "The galleries were crowded with Filipino admirers of Young Tommy, who wildly cheered him throughout the battle."[21]

Filipino American support of Pinoy boxers continued after World War II. The *Philippines Mail* observed in 1946 that many Filipino fans in the San Francisco Bay Area were excited about a match in Oakland between Filipino Star Miasmis and Cuban featherweight, Lorenzo Safora. Filipino American sportswriter, Alex Fabros, noted in 1946 that San Jose's Civic Auditorium held special memories for Filipino fight fans: "The San Jose Civic Auditorium has always been the scene of fistic victories for Filipino boxers in the past." And "Pinoys" in the San Francisco Bay Area "always flocked {there} to witness the unequalled ring abilities of Ceferino Garcia, Speedy Dado, Small Montana, Young Tommy, Little Dado, etc. flash with brilliance." In 1947 the *San Francisco Chronicle* insisted that "{t}here are no more loyal fight fans than Filipinos backing one of their countrymen."[22]

Filipino Hawaiians also backed Pinoy boxers. Filipino Hawaiian, Sal Jacinto, earned about a five hundred dollars a month boxing in Honolulu in the 1930s. He recalled, "Oh plenty Filipinos" watched him fight. "{T}hey always cheer for me. Every time, when the Filipinos, they go, "Sala! Give'me you overhand! Because I was famous for my right overhand."[23]

Filipino fight fans could be harsh critics of Filipino boxers who disappointed them. In 1948, future champion and Hawaiian Filipino, Dado Marino, boxed in Stockton, California. The *Philippines Mail* noted that Pinoys in the area hoped Marino could demonstrate "the Filipino prowess in ring sportsmanship"—hoped he could become another Pancho Villa. However, they were disappointed in Marino's apparent lackluster performance against Mike Bernal. The Hawaiian decisioned his opponent, but Pinoy fight fans thought Marino should have knocked out Bernal. Indeed, many believed that Bernal deserved the decision.[24]

After Villa's untimely death, several Filipino prizefighters competed for the affection of Filipino fight fans. In 1926, Bobby Mars was described by the *San Jose Mercury* as a "game, little Filipino flyweight." Reflecting the prevailing racial labels of the time, the *Mercury* also called Mars a "flashy Malayan." In 1928, Lupe Tenorio, "a Filipino lightweight," won a bout in Cleveland before 9,000 fight fans. Lightweight Rita Punay fought in Los Angeles in 1931. Pancho Villa's brother, "Little Pancho" boxed in the United States, defeating a Korean professional, Joe Teiken, in Oakland in 1933. In the 1930s, Speedy Dado became the bantamweight champion of California. In 1933, Dado was offered an opportunity to fight for the world bantamweight championship in Paris, but refused the trek across the Atlantic, claiming he did not want to leave his family in California for such a long time. A *Los Angeles Times* sportswriter called Dado, "the 'Haviland China' of the Filipinos. He has by far more class, more color, more of everything than any boxer sent here since Pancho Villa of 1921." In 1935, the *Los Angeles Times* dubbed Pablo Dano the "little brown bull of the Philippines." That same year, "Teddy Yocson, San Francisco Filipino" was fighting in Northern California.[25]

Prizefighting did not make life easy for these young men who were often honored as heroes by America's Filipino immigrants. Eddie Muller, the *San Francisco Examiner*'s veteran boxing writer, reported in 1941 on Speedy Dado's decline from boxing's heights. Muller informed readers that Dado was once the most popular of all Filipino prizefighters on the West Coast. He made good money and promised that unlike other Filipino prizefighters, he would not squander his earnings. In 1941, however, Dado was "absolutely broke." Muller maintained that Dado could be spotted selling programs outside of the same Los

Angeles fight clubs in which he "packed ...the rafters when he was a headline performer."[26]

Southern California turned into a center of Filipino American prize fighting. One Filipino American scholar, Benicio Catapusan, pointed out in the early 1930s: "We have in {Los Angeles} a number of Filipino fighters who are making regular appearances in the Olympic Stadium and at the American Legion Stadium in Hollywood...There are about a dozen who are constantly training in the Main Street Gymnasium. The latter may box in 'semi-wind up events' in San Diego or Pismo Beach." Young Nationalista emerged as a veteran of Southern California ring wars. He fought in main events in Hollywood's then famous American Legion Stadium, as well as other prize fighting venues in and around Los Angeles. In 1927, he lost a world bantamweight championship bout to Bud Taylor. In 1932, the *Los Angeles Times* pronounced Young Nationalista as "the ever popular Filipino favorite."[27]

Ceferino Garcia ranked clearly as one of the more successful Filipino boxers based in Los Angeles. After Garcia knocked out an opponent in 1938, the *Los Angeles Times* observed: "All the primitive savagery and fury of the jungle was unleashed by Garcia on his opponent." The *Times* called Garcia the "Filipino bolo puncher" in 1939. Garcia, according to the *Times*, learned this "bolo punch" while cutting sugar cane in the Philippines. Garcia, in short, represented to the *Times* and many of its readers the primitiveness and "cheap labor" of colonial natives. But he was more than a primitive, servile native. In 1939, Garcia defeated the talented Fred Apostoli in Madison Square Garden, thus earning recognition in New York and California as middleweight champion. Fred Kurman of the *Daily Worker* wrote, "Garcia, pride of the Philippine Islands, who swung a bolo knife on a sugar plantation until turning fighter, said he'd get a big kick out of taking the belt back home for the folks to see." One boxing historian has written, "There was an aura of menace about the muscular Filipino with coffee skin and Oriental features, and his left hand was deadly."[28]

Associating Filipino boxers with primitiveness was by no means limited to elite performers such as Garcia. Joe Mendiola was not nearly as successful, but when he boxed in Los Angeles in 1936, the *Los Angeles Times* portrayed him in a similar fashion. Braven Dyer of the *Times* declared, "Joe hails from the Batangas, probably the toughest tribe in the Philippines aside from the Morais, who think nothing of chopping off a head as a daily pastime."[29]

During the 1940s, prizefighters of Filipino ancestry continued to excel. After World War II, Filipino born Rush Dalma fought his way to the world's bantamweight title. Dado Marino was born in Hawai'i and claimed a large following among Filipino Hawaiians. Joe Anzevino, a sportswriter for the *Honolulu Star-Bulletin*, described Marino in 1948 as "the little Brown Doll." Marino, however, was a "little Brown Doll" who also happened to become a world champion at beating others up. In fact, on August 1, 1950, Marino became the first Hawaiian to win a world prizefighting championship. Fighting before 10,763 fans at Honolulu Stadium, Marino won the world flyweight championship. Boxing out of New Orleans, brothers Maxie and Bernard Docusen impressed the boxing world in the late 1940s. They also impressed Anzevino who claimed the Docusens "typify class personalities." The *Honolulu Star-Bulletin* reported that "Oahu's Little Manila is flocking to Napoleon's Gym daily to see classy Maxie Docusen in sparring action." Journalist Carmelo Astilla claimed in a 1998 article in *Filipinas* that the Docusens' popularity crossed racial barriers in their home state of Louisiana. In 1948, Bernard lost to the great Sugar Ray Robinson, who, nevertheless, maintained that the Louisianan was the best boxer he ever faced. Max Docusen promoted ethnic pride across the country in San Francisco, where the *Fil-America Advocate* advertised his upcoming bout at the city's Winterland Arena in the early 1950s. Other Bayou-based Filipino prizefighters in the 1930s and 1940s were Fredy Balbon, Baby Manila, and J.C. Flores. [30]

We have noted the fact that Filipino prizefighters received avid support from the largely working class Filipino communities of California and Hawai'i. It also seems that at least during the years between and after the world wars, Californian and Hawaiian prize fighting promoters were substantially reliant upon the patronage of Filipino fight fans. One scholar reported in the late 1930s that Hawaiian "professional boxing matches depended chiefly upon Filipinos for support. {Filipino fans} came from plantations and all over Honolulu and watch weekly matches in the Honolulu Civic Auditorium." About a decade later, one fight card at the Honolulu Civic Auditorium featured six Filipino prizefighters, three of whom hailed directly from the Philippines. Meanwhile, Catapusan reported that Pinoys helped fill Olympic Auditorium in Los Angeles and Hollywood's American Legion Auditorium. When Filipino prizefighters appeared at these venues to contest boxers of other ethnic groups or nationalities, fear of violence between Pinoy fans and fans identifying with other ethnic groups or nationalities ran high. Catapusan maintained that several fights between fans of Mexican and Filipino ancestries erupted. Yet, he added, nothing resembling a full-scale race riot erupted. Catapusan conceded that prizefighting entertained Pinoys and furnished them with a sense of community, but he worried that it promoted Pinoy gambling and sidetracked Filipinos from work and other more important activities. [31]

Thus, in California, as well as Hawai'i, Filipino support seemed vital to boxing promoters. That support might have appeared all the more crucial during the Great Depression when attracting people and dollars to sporting events was not all that easy. Complicating matters were the discrimination and violence faced by Filipino Californians.

By the end of the 1920s, significant numbers of white Californians became disillusioned with Filipinos who seemed not the docile "little brown brothers" many whites expected to contentedly perform agricultural labor and clean dishes for them. Most Filipino immigrants were young males, taught in Filipino schools that America was a land of freedom. These Pinoys were bewildered to find that that they could not claim the same freedom enjoyed by European Americans. For example, their efforts to date white women aroused hatred and violence. Late in 1929, anti-Filipino violence in Watsonville, California, instigated the shooting death of one Pinoy. From Watsonville, anti-Filipino riots spread throughout the state.

The ill feeling toward Filipino immigrants surfaced in California boxing rings. Early in 1930, the chair of California's Athletic Commission tried to ban Filipino prizefighters from boxing matches staged in the Golden State. He explained that the "presence {of Filipino boxers} was inflaming public opinion." Commissioner Hanlon declared, "Victory of a Filipino over a white boxer with feelings at high pitch, might prove just the spark to ignite a serious occurrence in a crowded fight arena." Despite the fact that the *Los Angeles Times* proclaimed the ban as popular, it ran into opposition from the two Southern California commissioners, who teamed up with a San Francisco commissioner against the Northern California chair. San Francisco's Commissioner Traung protested, "I know of no one with authority to issue such an order except the Governor....Any boxing shows in San Francisco will be heavily guarded, but the Filipino boys are deserving a chance and will not be removed from the cards." Perhaps local boxing promoters not inclined to lose the patronage of Filipino fight fans inspired the Southern California commissioners.[32]

Soon after the division between the athletic commissioners was announced, James Woods, one of the Southern Californians, reversed himself. After claiming opposition to the ban, Woods advised boxing promoters in El Centro to remove Filipino from fight cards. He cited the jailing of a Pinoy in Brawley for "sequestering" a white woman as too inflammatory for promoters to ignore. Nevertheless, bouts between Filipinos and European Americans continued. The *Los Angeles Times* declared that the Hollywood Legion defied the ban by putting Young Carpentero, "a brown brother," on its fight card. According to contemporary social scientist Bruno Lasker, Filipino-white bouts in California eventually "were attended by mixed crowds with the occurrence of little disorder."[33]

Among those Filipino prizefighters caught in the middle of this controversy was a San Jose-based boxer who fought under the name of Eddie Cleveland. The *San Jose Mercury* described Eddie Cleveland as a "little Filipino batt-ler," popular among San Jose's prize fighting fans. In January, 1930, Cleveland won his first main event in San Jose and his professional career seemed on the rise. When, however, the ban was issued Cleveland's manager Norris Lehman got the cold shoulder from California promoters. For awhile Cleveland did not know whether he should move to Mexico or do something else with his life.[34]

A few years later, other controversies arose regarding Filipino prizefighters in California. In May, 1932, Young Corbett defeated Ceferino Garcia in Los Angeles. According to the *San Francisco Chronicle,* "several hundred Filipinos voiced their disapproval of the decision." In September, 1932, Speedy Dado was matched in the Oakland Auditorium against Midge Wolgast, a fine European American boxer. Before the bout took place, newspapers such as the *Sacramento* Bee and the *Oakland Tribune* reported that several thousand handbills were circulated in San Joaquin Valley, an area possessing a high concentration of Filipino migrant workers. These handbills, signed by Kid Lapulapu, claimed the fight promoters in Oakland had been discriminating against Filipino fight fans and fighters. The pseudonym of Kid Lapulapu is interesting in that Filipino le-gend maintains that a native Filipino named Lapulapu killed Magellan, the famed Spanish sea captain. [35]

Kid Lapulapu accused Oakland fight promoters of closing off the cheaper gallery sections to Filipinos; thus forcing them to pay for higher price seats if they wanted to see the bouts. He criticized referees hired by the Oakland promo-ters for making unjust decisions against Filipino prizefighters such as Dado. Lapulapu concluded that Filipinos ought to boycott the Dado-Wolcast fight and that the Oakland promoters' "unAmerican attitude shows prejudice towards Fi-lipinos."[36]

The accused Oakland promoters denied that they entertained any prejudice toward Filipino boxers or fans. In doing so, they made the interesting point that a Filipino boycott would hurt "Filipino boxers more than the management." They also made an unintended admission in the process by stressing that if Fili-pino fight fans did not help fill the Oakland Auditorium's seats they would not feel obliged to showcase Filipino prizefighters in the future. The possibility that prizefighters such as Dado deserved to box regularly because they were very good and not just because they attracted Filipino fight fans was not conceded by Oakland promoters.[37]

A few days before the Dado-Wolgast fight, the *Oakland Tribune* specu-lated that the boycott was failing to gain much support. The daily purported that the proof lay in the intelligence that Filipinos were betting heavily on Dado to win the bout. The *Tribune* also quoted Jesus Cortez, Dado's manager as saying: "We have always been treated well in Oakland." [38]

After the bout was held, *Oakland Tribune* sportswriter, Alan Ward, reported that Wolgast had clearly outpointed Dado and deserved to win. The referee, nevertheless, declared the bout a draw. Ward confessed that "{t}he verdict no doubt softened the ruffled feelings of the hundreds of Filipino fans present who had charged discrimination against their countrymen in bouts here." Indeed, perhaps the boycott had worked after all. The number of Filipinos in attendance was less than expected. And the referee's decision may have reflected a concern that the business of professional boxing in California could not afford to further alienate Filipino fight fans.[39]

A year later, a referee's decision nearly caused a riot among Filipino fight fans in Pismo Beach. Early in his career, the great Henry Armstrong was awarded a victory over Kid Moro. This touched off a disturbance among Moro's supporters. Regretting his decision, the referee added fuel to the fire by calling the bout a draw. Pinoy leaders promised a boycott of fights staged in Pismo Beach. One declared to the press, "We were robbed...by boxing sharks...If they do not treat us fairly there is no use spending nearly a million yearly attending crooked boxing matches."[40]

In April, 1935, Ceferino Garcia lost a decision to Al Manfredo in Sacramento. Fred Pearl, a local promoter wanted the California commission to investigate the fight. Pearl charged that Garcia had been paid off to lose the fight. His proof was that 2000 Filipino fights fans were in the state capital to watch the bout. Yet none apparently showed up by the time the first punches were thrown.[41]

In 1936, a radio broadcast of a fight in Honolulu's Civic Auditorium wound up transmitting the sounds of a riot that erupted after a decision went against a popular Filipino boxer. The *Honolulu Star-Bulletin* dismissed the disturbance by proclaiming that it was inspired by "a couple of so called Filipino leaders who have caused trouble by inciting their countrymen at boxing shows in the past." The vast majority of Filipino fans in attendance were inclined to accept the decision peacefully, until, according to the *Star-Bulletin,* "radical leaders" riled them up. *Star-Bulletin* columnist Don Watson thought that disgruntled gamblers encouraged the minor riot. Rather than heed such troublemakers, Filipino fight fans, Watson advised, should "remember that favorite saying around town, 'Cool head is the main thing.' " The results were some broken chairs and bumped and bruised ushers. Moreover, some Filipino fight fans considered boycotting Civic Auditorium bouts. Indeed, Filipinos in Hilo had decided to stay away from a bout in which a Filipino fighter named Young Gildo was matched against Chuck Delaney.[42]

While prizefighters of Filipino ancestry ranked among the most prominent in the world, from the 1920s through the 1950s, other Asian Pacific ethnic

groups were represented in America's boxing rings. In 1929, a Japanese surnamed boxer, Kimura, faced Angel De La Cruz, a "Filipino" in San Francisco.
One Japanese Hawaiian sportswriter called K.O. Kuratsu the best flyweight in
Hawai' in 1930. During the depression years, Shiku Hashimoto boxed in four
rounders in San Francisco, while a 117 pound Japanese American named Kau-
sau Asasawa fought out of Stockton. In the 1930s and early 1940s, Jack Nishi,
Yosh Mori, Izzy Nono, and Paul Matsumoto boxed in Honolulu. In the early
1940s, the Japanese American newspaper, the *Pacific Citizen*, called "Homicide
Hal" Hoshino "probably the best Nisei boxer to don gloves in recent years." An
Oregon resident, who also boxed out of Seattle, Hoshino was described by the
Pacific Citizen as once "one of the best featherweights in America." In 1941,
Eddie Muller described him as Honolulu's "biggest boxing sensation" and a
"terrific puncher," who had beaten tough opponents such as David Kui Kong
Young. Hoshino's career ended in 1947 after getting knocked out and hospita-
lized in Honolulu by Henry Davis. In 1947, Paul Iguchi and Tom Nakano fought
in Los Angeles. After serving in the famed 442nd in World War II and winning
amateur laurels, Hawaiian Japanese, Tsuneo Maruo fought professionally as a
bantamweight. Robert "The Ripper" Takeshita headlined in places like Honolulu
after World War II. The *Honolulu Star-Bulletin* described Takeshita as "Honolulu's top Nisei junior welterweight." When Takeshita lost to Rudy Gutierrez in
Los Angeles in 1949, about 600 Nisei and Issei were reportedly in attendance.
Other notable post-World War II Hawaiian Nisei boxers were Yasu Yasutake,
Baldwin Okamoto, Richard Asato, James Masuda, Mokey Hanagami, Shigeo
Tengan, and Shangy Tsukano. In the early 1950s, Carl Arakaki was a "popular
club fighter in Southern California, and Tommy Umeda was a 132-pounder who
fought out of Seattle and Los Angeles. Meanwhile, "local Nisei boxer" Fuzzy
Shimada was considered one of the best prizefighters in San Francisco in the
early 1950s.[43]

A number of Korean American prizefighters thrived in the United States.
During the 1930s, a Korean boxer Joe Teiken appeared in American rings.
Dubbed the "Korean Kewpie" by the *Sacramento Bee*, Tei Ken took on such
formidable Filipino opponents as Speedy Dado and Young Tommy. Because
Korea was part of the Japanese empire, Tei Ken's status was often confused. For
example, after losing to "Young Tommy, sturdy Filipino bantamweight," Tei
Ken was called "Japan's leading aspirant for bantamweight honors." Another
prizefighter of Korean ancestry was Umio Gem, depicted in the *Los Angeles
Times* as a "colorful Oriental boxer." Gem's manager was the aforementioned
Jesus or Jessie Cortez, who once told the press that he wanted to take Gem to the
East Coast. However, according to Cortez, "Oriental fighters don't like to go
East…because of the cold weather in winter and the heat in summer." After

World War II, the *Honolulu Star-Bulletin* reported on the doings of Richie Shinn, a "California Korean—popular in Hawaii boxing circles" and Philip Kim, who, in August, 1948, was an "undefeated Korean sensation." In the early 1950s, Kim won a string of fights in Southern California. In 1953, Kim, described in the *San Francisco Chronicle* as "hard-hitting Hawaiian" took on Carmen Fiore for a chance to fight the legendary Kid Gavilan for the world welterweight crown. Unfortunately for Kim, he was on a losing end of a Fiore knock out punch. [44]

In the 1930s, 1940s, and 1950s, a number of Chinese American prizefighters took up where George Lee and Sammy Lee had left off. In the mid-1920s, Harry Soo was a Sacramento-based "Chinese fighter." In 1927, Dick Chang, a "Honolulu Chinaman" fought in California. In 1931, the *Los Angeles Times* called welterweight Ralph Chong "China's contribution to the ring." During the early 1930s, Portland's Ah Wing Lee fought actively in the Pacific Northwest. In the late 1930s, San Francisco's William Wong entered the ring under the name of Young William. "Chinese" Fred Buck boxed in Hawai'i in the 1930s. In October, 1953, Dickie Wong and Richard Choi fought at Honolulu's Civic Auditorium. In 1954, Los Angeles lured the boxing skills of Dickie Wong from Honolulu. In July, 1954, Wong knocked out Gil Chavez at the Hollywood Legion. In 1959, the *Los Angeles Times* claimed that Ward Yee was the "only active Chinese boxer in the U.S." Yee was a bantamweight who had become "one of the trickiest glovemen around."[45]

However, in the late 1930s and into the 1940s, the Chinese Hawaiian, David Kui Kong Young, rated as little less than a boxing sensation. Kui Kong Young became also a source of pride in mainland Chinese American communities, as well as in Hawai'i. When Kui Kong Young was set to take the ring at San Francisco's Dreamland, the *Chinese Digest* called him the "sensational Chinese featherweight." In 1941, the *Chinese News* wondered why Kui Kong Young had not yet earned a chance to fight for a world championship. It cited eminent boxing journalists to support the claim that the Hawaiian harbored world championship skills. For example, Tom Laird of the *San Francisco Daily News* was quoted as writing that Kui Kong Young was "the greatest puncher we've had in the past twenty-five years." To Eddie Muller of the *San Francisco Examiner* Kui Kong Young was a "Chinaman" but also "pound for pound...the best puncher in boxing today." After the World War II, Kui Kong Young was given a chance to fight in a title bout, but lost. [46]

Several other prizefighters of Asian Pacific Islander ancestry are worthy of note. Native Hawaiian Ben Akakuelo was a talented boxer in the 1930s. The decidedly more famous Carl "Bobo" Olson grew up in a working class neighborhood of Honolulu. Part Indigenous Hawaiian, Olson became World Middleweight Champion in the 1950s. For awhile, Olson was considered by many the best boxer in America. However good, Olson was known, fairly or not, as a pri-zefighter with a glass jaw. That is, a good punch to the jaw would knock him out--especially if the legendary Sugar Ray Robinson delivered that good punch. Duke Sabadong came along a little later. In 1956, *Ring Magazine* acclaimed Sabadong as one of the world's most promising heavyweights. The *San Jose Mercury* described Sabadong in 1960 as a "rangy Samoan scrapper" from San Francisco." The next year, the six-foot seven inch Sabadong fought the young Muhammad Ali, who was then Cassius Clay. The bout took place in Las Vegas and the "Hawaiian Giant," as the *San Francisco Examiner* called him, lost a decision to the future champion. The fact that Sabadong constantly fouled his magnificently talented opponent did not help matters. Meanwhile, Ralph Dupas fought his way toward the Junior Middleweight world crown. A follower of Fi-lipino and Filipino American athletes calls Dupas a descendent of the "Manila-men-half-Filipino, half-Mulatto," who have lived in New Orleans for genera-tions. Interestingly, Dupas was temporarily banned from fighting against whites in Louisiana, because he was accused of being an African American and athletic competition between blacks and whites was not allowed. Hailing from Oahu, Paul Fujii won the World Boxing Association (WBA) championship in the 1960s. In 1970, Fujii retired with a record of thirty-four victories and four de-feats. Possessing Irish, English, and Native Hawaiian ancestry, rugged middle-weight Stan Harrington fought some of the toughest boxers in his division in the 1960s. Managed by Ted Kawamura, he beat an aging Sugar Ray Robinson in 1965. Of his thirty-four victories, thirty came by way of knockouts. In recent years, a Samoan David Tu'a has ranked high among the world's heavy-weights.[47]

Thanks to boxers such as Marino and Dupas, enthusiasm for prizefighting remained high among Filipinos in the United States well past the end of World War II. Like the legendary Young Pancho Villa, champion boxer Flash Elorde attracted a transpacific following. In the 1970s, Ben Villaflor won the WBA Junior Lightweight crown. Based in Honolulu, Villaflor was managed by the notable Hawaiian boxing manager Sam Ichinose. Hailing from Waipahu in Ha-wai'i, Brian Viloria was upset in his bid for a boxing gold medal in the 2000 Olympiad. Called the "Hawaiian Punch, Viloria, however, became a successful professional soon thereafter.[48]

Not all professional fights engaged in by Asian Pacific North Americans aroused pride. The provocative Filipino American journalist Emil Guillermo was angered in 1999 by a bout between Margaret MacGregor, a thirty-six year old landscaper from Bremerton, Washington, and Loi Chow, a jockey from Vancouver, British Columbia. The male Chow was defeated by MacGregor and

Guillermo wrote, "No matter how cool Bruce Lee and Chow Yun Far are, in North America the predominant image of the Asian male is still one of computer nerd or bad driver, with the soul of a coolie in ponytail, slight and subservient. It's branded into the culture like the old Bonanza nameplate on the legendary television series."[49]

Amateur Boxers

As amateur boxers, young men of Asian Pacific ancestry were able to represent their communities and, hopefully, achieve a semblance of self-pride. In Honolulu, Abe Konaaihele was a leading amateur in the mid-1930s. The *Chinese Digest* noted in 1935 that Samuel Fooey was a Chinese American flyweight from Red Bluff, California, who participated in a Golden Glove Tournament in Northern California. In 1936, Sammy Lee coached boxing for St. Mary's Athletic Club in San Francisco's Chinatown. The *Chinese Digest* proudly reported that four of Lee's protégés competed in a tournament sponsored by the American Legion for amateur boxers in San Francisco. In 1943, according to the *San Francisco Examiner*, one of the best amateur boxers in the city was Albert Lee, a "Chinese lightweight." Also in 1943, Nisei Frank Tominaga of Firth, Idaho was a bantamweight fighting for AAU (American Amateur Union) championship honors. In 1944, the *Honolulu Advertiser* called Masao Suzuki one of the Territory's finest amateur featherweights. In 1947, when Hawai'i sent a Golden Glove team to the mainland, Yoshi Miyamura, Richard Kikauma, and Frank Kikuyama competed in the 113 pound, 130 pound, and 143 pound divisions respectively. In 1950, Mokey Hanagami was one of Hawai'i's best amateur flyweights. That same year, the *Pacific Citizen* announced that bantamweight Tommy Nozawa won a Golden Gloves novice tournament in Los Angeles and Honolulu's George Masamura boxed as a featherweight in the All-Army boxing championship held at Ft. Bragg. Thirty years later, the *Philippine News* reported on the Boshly brothers, John and James. The two were top Golden Gloves competitors in San Francisco. [50]

In the 1930s, Bob Chan, a top-flight amateur from Chicago, earned attention from Honolulu sportswriter, Loui Leong Hop. Chan, in 1936, was a part of a contingent of Chicago Catholic Youth Organization (CYO) boxers, who had traveled to the islands to face Hawaiian amateurs. Hop maintained that Chan had learned to box in order to survive the tough Chicago neighborhood in which he grew up. Hop wrote, "Of fair complexion and showing no marks for his scraps, one would never suspect Chan to be a boxer...and a good one...in the opinion of Father James C. Carroll, leader of the visiting team." Chan looked more like a "quiet scholar" to Hop than a tough boxer. Chan spoke "perfect English," but he "could rattle his ABCs in Chinese, much to the discomfiture of the writer, whose comprehension of Chan's dialect must be very limited." Chan, Hop asserted, was the only Chinese American participating in CYO tournaments. He had trained to be a chemical engineer but preferred boxing. And he liked his "Chinese cooking." While waiting for the boat to Honolulu in San Francisco, Chan found his way into Chinatown for two square meals before boarding the boat."[51]

Many of the best AAU boxers in the 1940s hailed from Hawaii and possessed Asian Pacific Islander ancestry. At a national meet in 1940, spectators were impressed with the number of fine amateurs from the islands. Among those who shined were Paul Matsuoto, Yasuki Yasutake, Johnny Manalo, and future professional champion, Dado Marino. Indeed, Manalo and Marino faced each other for the 112-pound championship. This marked the first time two Hawaiians had boxed each other for an AAU national title. As it turned out, the bout between the two Hawaiian Filipinos ended in a Manalo victory. In 1946, Hawaiians of Asian Pacific Islander ancestry did well in the national tournament. Yoshi Misamura, David Buna, Baldwin Okamoto, and Walter Chung dominated the 112-pound division, while Tsuneo Maruo did well in the 118-pound division and Robert Takeshita stood out among the 147 pounders. Talented Hawaiian amateurs received top flight advice from local coaches. Hilo's Richard Chinen, a Nisei from Hilo, was one of the most notable. Chinen, for example, coached boxing for the Varsity Victory Volunteers, which included Hawaiian Nisei anxious to bolster Hawaii's defense after the attack on Pearl Harbor.[52]

College and university athletic departments engaged in intercollegiate boxing quite a bit before the 1970s. In 1916, Don G. Lew was called "the only Chinese who has taken up boxing at an American college." Lew boxed for the University of Pennsylvania. Mark Kai-Kee and Yuji Imai boxed for Stanford in the early 1930s. In 1935, Shigeo Nitta boxed for the University of Cal team. When, in 1937, Cal met Stanford, one of the feature bouts pitted Cal's Kai Kim against Stanford's Jack Hato. During the first year of the U.S.'s active participation in World War II, San Jose State College's boxing team was led by a Hawaiian Japanese, Dick Miyagawa. Boxing on the novice team was Japanese American, Lincoln Kimura. Miyagawa, subsequently, headed to the University of Wisconsin after internment. In Madison, he also stood out as a collegiate boxer. Meanwhile, Milton Takashi boxed for the Cal Aggies team from Davis as a 120 pounder. To the north, Jim Yasuda boxed as a 120 pounder for Oregon State. After World War II, Eddie Samira was a "wild swinging Hawaiian" competing for Idaho State. In 1950, Dave Miyagawa boxed for De Paul College, while Harry Harimaki and Mitz Hada competed for Placer Junior College in California. In

February, 1951, Eugene Machida, a standout from Idaho State beat Maoru Ogi of UCLA. During the decade of the 1950s, Phil Ishimaru competed on the University of California, Berkeley squad, as a 125 pounder, while Graf Shintaku and Ed Murakami boxed for Cal Poly. Cyril Okomoto starred on the University of Hawai'i squad and then transferred to Idaho State, where he continued to box. Competing for the College of Idaho was George Nakano. Kim Kanaya and M. Usinoyama competed for San Jose State College. And in the late 1950s one of the better amateur boxers in the country was San Jose State College's T.C. Chung. Meanwhile, Michigan State's varsity boxing team included Choken Maekawa, a 119 pound athlete.[53]

Wrestling and Judo

Through wrestling and other sports associated with physical combat, Asian Pacific Americans have been able to prove themselves individually and connect to the ethnic communities that identified with them. Of course, some of these sports such as sumo wrestling possessed deep Asian roots, while free style wrestling, particularly the frequently loutish professional variety, did not.

In noting the sporting proclivities of Asian immigrants in Hawai'i, scholar Edward Burrows observed in the 1930s that the first generation of Chinese Hawaiians demonstrated some interest in "Chinese boxing." Japanese immigrants in Hawai'i, Burrows maintained, exhibited a great deal of enthusiasm for sports such as sumo, jujitsu, kendo, and foils (fencing). Indeed, hungering for escape from the regimented drudgery of the sugar and pineapple fields during the early 1900s, Japanese Hawaiian workers annually celebrated the Emperor of Japan's birthday. And as mentioned in the previous chapter, plantation discipline consequently dissipated. Moreover, the celebrants practiced the traditional sport of sumo as a means of both honoring the Emperor and enjoying the day's festivities. One former worker recalled that on the Mikado's birthday, "mainly there was sumo...Several young men, usually the good ones, got together at a camp and had Japanese-style sumo matches."[54]

Japanese-based sports such as sumo and kendo seemed to link Japanese immigrants in Hawai'i and the mainland to their cultural backgrounds. Sumo's non-elitist history might well have made the sport particularly appealing to Nikkei working people. As early as the 1880s, the first significant group of Japanese workers in Hawai'i participated in and watched sumo matches. Sumo matches, moreover, were held by Hawaiian Issei for Hawai'i's King Kalakaua in the 1880s.[55]

During the early decades of the twentieth century, Asian Pacific wrestlers attracted support from various people of Asian Pacific ancestry living and working in the United States and its territories. Sumo wrestlers periodically visited Hawai'i from Japan. Interestingly, among these touring athletes was a group of women sumo wrestlers who traveled to Hawai'i in 1911. In 1916, the *Los Angeles Times* publicized a wrestling match set for the Shine Auditorium. The opponents were "Ad Santel, the idol of San Francisco" and "Tarro Miyake, the Japanese jiu-jitsu expert." The daily claimed that Los Angeles's Japanese community was so interested in the match that its members had bought one thousand tickets. Karen Leonard writes that immigrants from India's Punjabi region supported wrestling warmly in the 1920s and 1930s. Punjabi wrestlers toured California's Asian Indian communities and attracted plenty of patronage. During the late 1930s and into the 1940s, a Filipino wrestler named Pantaleon Manlipis performed in Salinas, California. According to the *San Jose Mercury*, Manlipis was particularly popular among Filipino workers: "In Salinas, where he has been a steady performer, Manlipis packed'em in regularly. To his brown-skinned brothers, Manlipis is a man among men." Seven years later, the *San Francisco Chronicle*'s Clyde Giraldo pronounced Manlipis as the largest Filipino athlete in the United States. At 240 pounds, Manlipis was not only large but a "strong wrestler."[56]

Meanwhile, Asian Pacific Americans continued to participate in sumo, judo, and related sports as amateurs. In 1908, Harry Kurisaki and others formed the first judo organization in Honolulu. Three years later, two more judo clubs emerged in Hawai'i--clubs which endured until the 1930s. At this time, a Japanese Hawaiian judo enthusiast named Tetsuo Tachibana complained:

> Judo lacks popularity because it is an indoor sport, giving pleasure mostly to the participants. The niceties of the game, the mental control, the spirit of give and take can be appreciated only by the players themselves. American sports, on the other hand, are more carefree. They are material pleasures, giving enjoyment to the spectators as well as the players.[57]

Hawaiian Japanese, nevertheless, were generally responsible for supporting sports such as judo and sumo. In the 1930s, an organization called Buttokai was devoted to judo, kendo, and kyoda (archery). Edward Burrows reported that in 1937 about 800 members in Honolulu favored judo the most and kyodo the least. Hawaiians also followed and participated in sumo. In 1915, the *Honolulu Star-Bulletin* reported that Hawaiian Japanese awaited news of sumo tournaments in Japan much as American haoles awaited the results of big league baseball games. In 1934, the Oahu Sumo Association was formed with 300 members.[58]

On the mainland, sumo and judo seemed useful as a way of asserting Japanese American ethnicity. In California during the 1920s, a sumo league was formed with teams representing Japanese American communities in San Jose, Fresno, Sacramento, and San Francisco. As in Hawai'i, Japanese Americans in places like San Jose held sumo matches on the Emperor's birthday. Asserting cultural citizenship, they also, however, staged sumo matches on the Fourth of July. In the late 1930s, sumo wrestlers from Japan toured the U.S. under the sponsorship of Japanese American fishing boat operators. During World War II, Japanese American concentration camp internees engaged in sumo tournaments. After World War II, San Jose's Japantown hosted an annual judo tournament held at the Buddhist Temple. A decade later, Shuzo Kato, Kenji Yamada, Dick Yamasaki, and Tats Kojima competed for the Seattle Judo Club.[59]

Asian Pacific Americans have long competed in and coached amateur wrestling. In 1914, "Ten Wanz...a native-born Chinese wrestler" competed for Tufts. In 1936, several Hawaiian Japanese athletes tried out for the U.S. Olympic team, including eighteen year old Eliji Matsumura, a student from the territory's school for the deaf and blind. In 1942, the University of California's wrestling team included three Japanese surnamed competitors—Kibara, Shibata, and Hosokawa. A few weeks before Executive Order 8802 was issued, a wrestling tournament held at San Jose State College included two San Jose State freshmen named Kawata and Inoyue, as well as two high school wrestlers from nearby Campbell High School named Uchiyama and Toyama. In 1950, Joe Kimura of San Francisco State was named outstanding competitor at the Pacific Coast Wrestling championships. Hugh Watanabe of Washington State also participated. Oregon State's Yoshi Kiyokawa was a standout wrestler on the Pacific Coast in 1950. A bit to the east, the University of Utah suited up James Yagi and Robert Mukai in 1950. Ben Ichikawa, Don Suzukawa, Joe Isasi, Robert Fukunaga, Kiyoshi Oshiba, and George Uchida wrestled for San Jose State College in the 1950s, while Los Gatos High School in California suited up wrestlers named Jun Sasaki and Ted Abe. Nearly forty years later, Scott Ozawa competed for El Dorado High School in California's "gold country." And in the early 2000s, Hawaiian Travis Lee won two NCAA titles. The versatile Lee has also mastered judo and Greco-Roman style wrestling. [60]

The Professionals

While much of professional wrestling in North America has long been more show than a competitive sport, it has not always been that way. Early in the twentieth century, professional wrestling was seemingly honest or at least as honest as professional boxing. During the Great Depression, however, professional wrestling promoters shifted dramatically from staging honest sport to less than honest spectacle.

Professional wrestling promoters in places like Los Angeles became avid advertisers of the racial, ethnic, and national differences existing and supposedly existing between participants. In 1925, for example, Jatrinder Gubar was pitched as "the Hindu champion," while wrestling at Dreamland in San Francisco. In 1936, Walter "Sneeze" Achiu was billed as the "Chinese star of Dayton {Ohio}." Four years later, a Ohio newspaper called Achiu "a formidable chap," who once played for football in the 1920s. However, according to this daily, Achiu was a "Hawaiian mat expert." In 1938, the *Los Angeles Times* announced that Lee Yat Wing, who was billed as "the giant Chinese" was scheduled to wrestle. In the mid-1950s, readers of the *Bennington Evening Banner* learned that Prince Maiva, "the barefoot lad from Samoa" was wrestling in Saratoga Springs, New York. Often, however, professional wrestling promoters publicized wrestlers of Asian Pacific ancestry as villains. The results were predictably not always good. For one wrestling show, Nanjo Singh was promoted as an East Indian villain. Excitable fans, consequently, dragged Singh from the ring and beat him. Several years later, Nanjo Singh was wrestling at the Hollywood Legion. The press claimed that his favorite weapon was something called "the cobra hold" and called him the "raging Hindu." [61]

Whether marketed as villains or not, professional wrestlers of Asian Pacific ancestry were often involved in something akin to the "Orientalization" process. Some of these wrestlers may have been willing accomplices of this process. Some may have been exploited by promoters. In any event, followers of professional wrestlers were encouraged to perceive Asian Pacific wrestlers as exotic compared to the questionably more conventional European American wrestlers. This seemed especially true for professional wrestlers billed as Japanese. Two wrestlers of presumed Japanese ancestry were featured on a card at San Francisco's Civic Auditorium in 1936. One of them, Hawaiian and U.S. citizen Tetsura Higami, was promoted as the "Japanese rubber man." Wrestling at Los Angeles's Olympic Auditorium in 1936 was Kimon Kudo, described by the *Los Angeles Times* as "the little Buddha." On the same card was Matsui Hammanaka, billed as "the Jiu Jitsu Star." Hawaiian George Oakaura did not wrestle under his real name on the American mainland after World War II, but performed as the Great Togo. [62]

In 1956, the *San Francisco Chronicle's* Will Connolly wrote about the Togo brothers in one of his columns. Connolly claimed that the Togo brothers were Kibei; a Japanese term applied to people of Japanese ancestry born overseas but educated in Japan. Kizuo and Tosh, according to Connolly, were born in Oregon and their father was a Hood River Valley orchardist. Connolly declared, "{t}he

Togo brothers have a gimmick. They burn incense in the ring in mock deference to their ancestors and toss handfuls of rice to ringsiders."[63]

Building on World War II stereotypes, American professional wrestling often represented wrestlers of Japanese ancestry as not just villains, but villains who were devious and cowardly, taking delight in torturing wrestling's "good guys." Performing in Southern California in 1949, the "Great Togo," according to the *Oxnard Press Courier*, was a "rough Oriental." A wrestler by the name of Mr. Moto was notorious in the 1950s. He was described the by *Press Courier* as the ruthless Mr. Moto.[64]

Kenji Shibuya was an often employed villain the 1960s. Shibuya was born in Utah, but as a youth moved to Los Angeles with his family. Then he headed to Hawai'i. He was good football player, competing in high school and for Hawaiian club teams during the war. After World War II, he joined the University of Hawai'i eleven. Shibuya also took up sumo wrestling. Tetsuo Higami served as Shibuya's early mentor as the Nisei athlete shifted from football to professional wrestling. Once Shibuya gained fame as a professional villain, he was promoted as a master of the allegedly cruel "Japanese claw hold." And while American born, the press referred to him as "Kenji Shibuya of Japan." According to journalist Dennis Akizuki, Shibuya became well known for speaking "in a thick Japanese accent, laugh{ing} mockingly at jeering fans and us{ing} illegal tactics such as throwing salt into the face of his opponent. He would joke that he was sending the 'American dollahs' he was earning back to Japan to buy rice fields."[65]

Well into retirement from the wrestling ring, Shibuya told the press, "I was only interested in making money...What did Shakespeare say. 'All the world's a stage, and we're all actors. Something like that.'" Proud of his Japanese heritage, Shibuya beat up a fellow wrestler for calling him a "Jap." Brian Niya of the Japanese American Museum contends that Shibuya need not apologize for his career.: "I find nothing to criticize these guys about, because it was the only they could have made a living in something related to sports." [66]

Some professional wrestlers managed to escape negative stereotyping, at least for some of their careers. Wrestling in Honolulu in 1919 were Leo Poaha, "Kinjo Ikeda, the Japanese champion," and Frank Kanae, a skilled and versatile Hawaiian athlete. While competing in Salinas, California, Richard Santos was described by the *Philippines Mail* as America's first Filipino wrestler in 1934. Utah's Hoshi Kodiake wrestled professionally in the mid-1930s. Shantu Singh was billed as an Indian wrestler in the 1930s. The *San Francisco Chronicle* described Ghunda Singh in 1936 as a "the big Hindu mastiff." Singh "has plenty of ability and breaks holds with handsprings." The *San Jose Mercury* called Don Sugai "a classy young Nipponese mat star" in 1937. Hsao Tanaka, a Hawaiian

Japanese, wrestled on the islands and the mainland after World War II. Oki Shikama was a very popular Hawaiian Japanese professional. Former football standout and Samoan Hawaiian, Al Lolotai also wrestled professionally after World War II. In June, 1946, he was matched up against Kimon Kudo at Honolulu's Civic Auditorium.[67]

In recent years, Duane Johnson, also known as the Rock, has been the most famous American wrestler of Asian Pacific background. The grandson of Peter Maivia, Johnson played football at the University of Miami before deciding on a career in professional wrestling. Wrestling as Rocky Maivia he rose up the ranks of professional wrestling to become an icon in the late 1990s. As the Rock, he not only found adoring wrestling fans who found him, in turn, wondrously charismatic, but he is presently carving out a film career as perhaps the next Schwarzenegger.[68]

Collegiate Judo and Professional Sumo

What has often given Oriental representations credence to the public has been the very real historical connection between Japan and sports such as judo and sumo. Judo has not been a big-time sport in North America. Judo, however, has been a respected intercollegiate sport in North America. And no college judo program garnered more success than San Jose State's. A major reason has been Yosh Uchida, who served as San Jose State's judo coach for many years. Uchida, a business owner and Japanese American community activist in San Jose, coached San Jose State teams for thirty-five years and coached them to thirty-two NCAA championships. *San Jose Mercury* sports columnist Mark Purdy has called Yosh Uchida "one of San Jose's human treasures."[69]

As mentioned earlier, North Americans of Japanese ancestry have competed in sumo for over one hundred years in Hawai'i and on the mainland. In recent years, however, several Hawaiians have excelled in Japanese sumo wrestling and a few have, in fact, become superstars—albeit, because of their Hawaiian origins—controversial superstars. In the late 1970s, Jesse Kuhaulua emerged as a standout sumo wrestler in Japan. Skillfully wrestling as Takamiyama, Kuhaulua's Hawaiian background aroused a significant amount of bigotry from Japanese sumo followers. Nevertheless, in 1972 the Maui-born Kuhaulua became the first foreign born sumo wrestler to win the Emperor's Cup. More recently, Chad Rowan and Saliva Atisanoe have performed professionally as "Akebono" and "Konishiki" respectively. A 6 foot 8, 462 pound behemoth, Rowan reigned as the prestigious grand champion of sumo and became, in the process, a major celebrity in Japan. Japanese ethnocentricism has also posed a barrier to Rowan's advancement. Still, he became a Japanese citizen in order to

teach sumo in Japan. Even larger, at 640 pounds, Atisanoe became the first foreigner to earn the second highest rank of ozeki. Yet while Rowan eventually
reached the highest, yokozuno rank in 1993, Atisanoe was earlier denied the
opportunity to rise above the ozeki rank. Those who presided over Japan's sumo
destinies claimed at the time that no foreigner possessed the sufficient dignity to
become a yokozono. An angry Atisanoe accused the selection committee of
"racism." Retired along with Rowan, Atisanoe has grown more conciliatory and
into a popular figure in Japan's media circles. Raised on Oahu, Samoan Hawaiian Fiamalu Penitani became in the 1990s a yokozuno as Musahimaru. [70]

Conclusion

There is little purpose in cosmetically treating prizefighting as a professional sport. It embraces a generally ugly past and, if anything, it can look forward to an uglier future. Anyone who knows something about the sport would
almost have to concede that its history is a narrative of appalling violence, mas-
culinity gone berserk, exploited prizefighters, and manipulated fans. Still, there
is something redeemable about prizefighting; something that goes to the heart of
Asian Pacific American sporting experiences.

The men drawn to the prizefighting ring have generally come from op-
pressed and exploited social and cultural groups. They might have surfaced from
hard-pressed Irish American neighborhoods, as did John L. Sullivan. They
might have emerged from colonized Africa, as did Battling Siki in the 1920s.
Their arduous treks into the ring elicit uncomfortable reminders of Battle Royal
participants who beat each other senseless for the amusement of the dominant
white culture. What, after all, did Jim Bung and Ah Fat accomplish? The winner got fifty dollars and both boxers earned ridicule mixed with a bit of respect.

Yet what Mike Marquese writes about black boxers might very well apply
to the cultural citizenship asserted by Asian Pacific American boxers and other
athletes: "The triumphs and tragedies of black boxers, dependent on elite white
power-brokers to make a living in the ring, expected to subordinate themselves
to elite white norms outside the ring, have made black boxing a rich, complex,
living tradition."[71]

For Asian Pacific American boxers such as Ah Wing, the journey into an
America prize fighting arena was a journey across socially constructed boundaries toward cultural citizenship. People of Chinese ancestry living in the United
States faced a racialization process that branded Chinese males as inherently
unmanly. Sadly, perhaps, one of the few social spaces people like Ah Wing
could counter that racialization process was in the prizefighting ring.

Yet as Asian Pacific boxers crossed one racial divide, they could seemingly encounter another. Boxers of Filipino ancestry might prove their courage countless times in the ring. For many European Americans, however, this courage could just as well have been born of the jungle. Just as African Americans were often stereotyped as either docile or savage, the other side of the Filipino as a "little brown brother" was the Filipino as an untamed, instinctual primitive. Moreover, as we will find out with other Asian Pacific American athletes, the relatively small size of these Filipino boxers encouraged constant references from the European American press to them as "little." Consequently, whether individual white sportswriters intended to insult Filipino boxers or not, the affect substantially served to demean the Pinoy prize fighters in order to render them less threatening to white superiority in sports.[72]

Still, the ability of Asian Pacific boxers to achieve respect and fame in the ring became an obvious source of ethnic pride. This appears especially the case among Filipino immigrant communities on the mainland and Hawai'i. For often overworked and underpaid Filipino workers, Cefereino Garcia and Dado Marino glittered as sources of hope and community. At the same time, the admiration Filipino prize fighting fans possessed in Filipino boxers was often manipulated by prizefighting promoters. Yet Filipino boxing fans were not just victims. They could hold their own against prizefighting promoters as in the case of the 1932 boycott. Professional boxing also furnished a few Asian Pacific Americans a crack at entrepreneurship. For example, after ten years of boxing for pay, George Lee retired to work at the California State printing office in Sacramento. Lee, however, also managed prizefighters in the 1930s. After World War II, Shig Takeshita became the only licensed Nisei fight manager on the mainland. In Honolulu in the 1950s, Louie Chou, Bill Kim and Lau Ah Chew were important boxing promoters. More successful, however, were the aforementioned Jessie Cortez, Johnny Samson, Ralph Yempuku, and Sam Ichinose. Based in Los Angeles, Samson brought over to the United States leading Filipino boxers as Young Nationalista and Young Tommy, as well as promoted the fights of American-based boxers such as Eddie Chavez in the Philippines. Involved in many Hawaiian sports enterprises, Yempuku partnered with Ichinose in the 1950s. Ichinose was Dado Marino's Hawaiian-based manager in the 1940s. Ichinose steadfastly promoted Marino on three continents before he could get the Filipino Hawaiian a title shot. Ichinose also suffered frustration when he tried to take three Japanese American boxers, Baldwin Okamoto, Robert Takeshita, and Tsuneshi Maruo to Scotland in 1947. The British boxing authorities refused to let the Nisei fight, claiming they lacked "international repute." Known as "Sad" Sam Ichinose apparently made little money in prizefighting but he did earn a spot in the International Boxing Hall of Fame. Heading up Boxing Enterprises in

Honolulu with Yempuku, Ichinose also carved out something of a political career for himself in Hawai'i as a Republican member of the territorial lower
house. In fact, Ichinose's victorious platform in 1948 declared that if elected, he
would aid Hawaiian youth, fight communism, and help bring statehood to Hawai'i. Ichinose desire to help Hawaiian youth was undoubtedly heartfelt as he
had founded the Japanese American Boys Club in Honolulu in 1935.[73]

Wrestling and other related "combat" sports offered uncertain possibilities,
as well. Wrestling and wrestlers supported ethnic communities. Professional
wrestling in the United States or professional sumo in Japan provided opportunities to some people of Asian Pacific ancestry to gain fame and fortune. Yet we
also can find that professional wrestling in the United States encouraged the
construction of dubious racial and ethnic images, while Japanese sumo followers
could use the sport to express their ethnocentricism against Hawaiian sumo
standouts such as Chad Rowan. For Chad Rowan sumo, however, perhaps offered an opportunity to assert cultural citizenship in Japan.

Asian-based martial arts have, in recent years, enabled Asian Pacific
Americans to become coaches, instructors, and entrepreneurs. We have already
noted San Jose's Yosh Uchida's impressive impact on judo as an intercollegiate
sport. Nisei Mits Kimura, after World War II, became director of the San Francisco Judo Institute. A California state champion, Dave Chow taught judo at the
University of Southern California (USC), University of California, Los Angeles,
(UCLA), as well as to the Los Angeles Police Department. Then there is Ko-
rean-born Jhoon Rhee, who became a widely respected karate master in the
1960s. In the meantime, he founded the Jhoon Rhee Institute in Washington
D.C., which established branches in other parts of the United States. In 1969,
Chinese American Wally Jay coached the Island Judo Jujitsu Club to a team title
in the Pacific AAU Junior Championships. Thirty-five years later, Alex Gong, a
Muai Thai kick boxing champion, operated a popular gym in San Francisco.
Tragically, Gong was murdered after he witnessed a hit and run collision from
his gym. He chased after the culprit, barefoot and wearing boxing trunks and
gloves. Unfortunately, Gong caught up with the suspect two-and-a half blocks
away from the collision. The driver drew a gun and shot Gong at point blank
range. [74]

The U.S. born, Hong Kong-raised Bruce Lee remains, despite his death in
the 1970s, a legend among martial artists. Obviously, the fact that he was able to
parlay his skills in the martial arts into a memorable, albeit brief, film career has
sustained Lee as at least a minor cult figure. To be sure, Lee's influence might
have strengthened the stereotypical ties between Asian Pacific people and martial artistry; might have enhanced Asian Pacific exoticism. Nevertheless, many
remember Lee, as does scholar Darrell Hamamoto, as someone who also defied
the stereotype of Asian Pacific males as unmanly. "For most Asian Americans,"

Hamamoto declares, "Bruce Lee struck a blow against white racism with each high-velocity punched he delivered."[75]

Of course, even if Asian Pacific people met few racial and ethnic barriers in boxing and wrestling, as well as other related sports, their success would have still supported gender barriers. The very point of boxing for culturally diverse Americans is that it has reigned as a "manly" sport, helping immensely in drawing the boundary between what is masculine and what is feminine and serving to make it more difficult for females to assert their cultural citizenship.

Yet women of Asian Pacific American ancestry have competed in boxing, wrestling, and the martial arts. We noted, earlier, the participation of women in sumo. Moreover, in the 1980s, a Chinese San Franciscan named Louise Loo was one of the few women in the United States then engaged in professional boxing. According to an article in *East/West*, Loo fought in the flyweight division as "The Frisco Kid." She claimed that her family had supported her interest in athletics, which also consisted of high school stints in softball and tennis. Another *East/West* article informs readers of the career of Keiko Fakuda. Born in Japan, she learned judo and eventually became a black belt. Upon arrival in the United States, she persistently spread the word about her chosen pastime; teaching judo at Mills College in Oakland, California, as well as San Francisco City College. More recently, Liliko Ogasawara of New Jersey moved across the nation to participate in San Jose State's judo program. In the process, she won four national champions and represented the United States in the 1996 Summer Olympics in Atlanta, Georgia. For Ogasawara, judo furnished something that transcended race, ethnicity, or gender. She was quoted as saying, "It's taught me discipline and to have respect for other people, for my opponents and for my teachers. It's a great way for me to meet people and to travel. It's when you're good at something." In 1999, New York City's Deidre Hamaguchi won national judo honors. In 2000, former San Jose State University standout, Amy Tong, was on the US Olympic judo team. The next year, Stephanie Hata and Sayaka Matsumoto won gold medals at the United States Senior National Judo Championships held at Orlando, Florida.[76]

In the early 2000s, a documentary about female prizefighters garnered excellent reviews. Called "Girlfight," the film's director and screenwriter was Karyn Kusama, a Japanese American. A native of St. Louis and a graduate of New York University, Kusama claimed she had done some boxing herself. She told *Asian Week*, "If we're concerned about boxing being a sport for poor people, poor white people, poor black people, we should start thinking about poverty."[77]

Notes

1. Elliot Gorn, *The Manly Art: Bare-Knuckle Prize Fighting in America*, (Ithaca, NY: Cornell University Press, 1986); Jeffrey Sammons, *Beyond the Ring: The Role of Boxing in American Society*, (Urbana, Ill.: University of Illinois Press, 1988); David K. Wiggins, *Glory Bound: Black Athletes in a White America*, (Syracuse: Syracuse University Press, 1997), chapter three..

2. *Sporting Life*, January 7, 1885; *San Francisco Examiner*, January 27, 1885.

3. Ralph Ellison, *The Invisible Man*, (New York: Random House, 1952).

4. Peter Levine, *Ellis Island*, 144.

5. *Fort Wayne News*, 6 November 1913.

6. *San Francisco Chronicle*, February 26, 1899, April 16, 1899.

7. *Ibid.*, April 7, 1900.

8. *Ibid.*, March 30, 1900.

9. *Los Angeles Evening Express*, April 21, 1900.

10. *Ibid.*, April 5, 1900; *San Francisco Chronicle*, January 15, 1905; January 21, 1905.

11. *New York Times*, 29 March 1912.

12. *Sacramento Bee*, September 1, 1920; April 14,1923.

13. *Oakland Tribune*, August 7, 1925; *San Francisco Chronicle*, July 1, 1925; August 17, 1925.

14. *Pacific Commercial Advertiser*, 7 December 1911; 14 February 1912.

15. *Ibid.*, April 10, 1912; June 7, 1912; *Washington Post*, February 27, 1912; *San Francisco Chronicle*, April 2, 1912; *San Francisco Examiner*, April 2, 1912; *Salt Lake City Herald Republican*, April 5, 1912.

16. *Sacramento Bee*, January 20, 1923; Bill Hosokawa, *Nisei: The Quiet Americans*, (New York: William Morrow and Company, Inc., 1969), 195-197.

17. Quoted in Bruno Lasker, *Filipino Immigration*, (Chicago: University of Chicago Press, 1931), 132.

18. Nestor Palugod Enriquez, Attng Mga Mangalaro; www.pages prodigy.com/NJ/pilipino/sports.html

19. *Washington Post*, March 22, 1922; March 7, 1923; February 8, 1924; *San Jose Mercury*, April 10, 1922; *Philippines Mail*, April 10, 1933; *Chicago Daily Tribune*, November 17, 1934; Peter Bacho, "A Manong's Heart," in *Turning Shadows into Light*, edited by Mayumi Tsutakawa and Alan Chong Law, (Seattle, WA: Young Pines Press, 1982), 38-43; Fred Cordova, *Filipinos: Forgotten Asian Americans*, (Dubuque, Iowa: Kendall/Hunt Publishing Company, 1983), 93-94.

20. *San Francisco Chronicle*, July 5, 1925.

21. *Ibid.*, July 4, 1925; September 3, 1925; *Los Angeles Times*, November 18, 1931; *Philippines Mail*, March 27, 1933.

22. *San Francisco Chronicle*, November 5, 1947; Philippines Mail, July, 1946; August, 1946.

23. Social Science Research Institute, University of Hawai'i, Manoa, *Kalihi: Place of Transition*, I, (Ethnic Studies Oral History Project, 1984), 13.

24. *Philippines Mail*, April, 1948.

25. *San Jose Mercury*, September 3, 1926; September 9, 1926; *Los Angeles Times*, January 18, 1928; January 18, 1931; February 1, 1931; November 16, 1935; *Oakland Tribune*, January 20, 1933; *Philippines Mail*, April 10, 1933; *Sacramento Bee*, June 21, 1935.

26. *San Francisco Examiner*, 2 March 1941.

27. Benicio Catapusan, *The Filipino Occupational and Recreational Activities in Los Angeles*, (Saratoga, CA: R & E Research Associates, 1975), 31; *Los Angeles Times*, November 18, 1932; *Waukeda Daily Freeman*, April 19, 1927.

28. *Los Angeles Times*, June 18, 1938; October 3, 1939; *Daily Worker*, October 4, 1939; Peter Walsh, *Men of Steel: the Lives and Times of Boxing's Middleweight Champions*, (London: Robson Books, LTD., 1992), 97.

29. *Los Angeles Times*, December 2, 1936.

30. *Honolulu Advertiser*, July 1, 1947; *Honolulu Star-Bulletin*, August 23, 1948; July 5, 1948; July 2, 1948; www.alohafame.com; Carmelo Astilla, "Life in the Bayous, " *Filipinas*, October, 1998, pp. 56-59; *Fil-America Advocate*, October 15 1952.

31. Cariago, *Social Conditions*; *Honolulu Star-Bulletin*, November 2, 1948; Catpusan, *Filipino Occupation*, 42-43

32. *Los Angeles Times*, January 31, 1930; February 1, 1930; *San Francisco Examiner*, January 30, 1930.

33. *Los Angeles Times.*, February 1, 1930; Lasker, *Filipino Immigration*, 132;

34. *San Jose Mercury*, January 20, 1930; February 3, 1930.

35. *San Francisco Chronicle*, April 13, 1932; *Oakland Tribune*, September 18, 1932.

36. *Oakland Tribune*, September 18, 1932; *Sacramento Bee*, September 21, 1932.

37. Oakland *Tribune*, September 19, 1932.

38. *Ibid.*, September 20, 1932.

39. *Ibid.*, September 22, 1932.

40. *Philippines Mail*, November 13, 1933.

41. *San Francisco Chronicle*, April 24, 1935.

42. *Honolulu Star-Bulletin*, May 9, 1936; May 11, 1936; May 12, 1936.

43. George Sakamaki, "Japanese Athletes in Hawaii," *Bulletin of the Pan-Pacific Union*, (August, 1931), 12-13; *San Francisco Examiner*, May 3, 1929; June 13, 1937; March 1, 1941; March 5, 1941; *Sacramento* Bee, September 16, 1932; July 14, 1933; June 21, 1935; *Pacific Citizen*, April 29, 1943; July 5, 1947; August 9, 1947; August 16, 1947; October 24, 1947; January 7, 1950; January 14, 1950; March 4, 1950; *Honolulu Star-Bulletin*, May 2, 1936; March 17, 1947; July 5, 1948; July 9, 1948; April 1, 1950; *San Francisco Chronicle*, December 13, 1931; July 12, 1934; December 8, 1953; December 9, 1953; Los Angeles *Times*, July 18, 1938; February 17, 1938; *Oxnard Press Courier*, July 17, 1951.

44. *Sacramento* Bee, September 16, 1932; July 14, 1933; *Philippines Mail*, March 13, 1933; *Honolulu Star-Bulletin*, August 14, 1948; *San Francisco Chronicle*, December 13, 1931; July 12, 1934; *Los Angeles Times*, July 18, 1938; February 17, 1938; *San Francisco Chronicle*, December 5, 1953; December 6, 1953.

45. *San Francisco Chronicle*, January 3, 1925; *Los Angeles Times*, November 20, 1931; November 7, 1959; *Sacramento Bee*, July 1, 1933; *Chinese Digest*, March 1937;

Honolulu Star-Bulletin, May 2, 1936; October 3, 1953; *Los Angeles Sentinel*, July 5, 1954; July 22, 1954.

46. *Chinese Digest*, September 1938; *Chinese World*, November, 1941; *San Francisco Examiner*, January 10, 1938.

47. *Honolulu Star-Bulletin*, May 1, 1956; May 3, 1956; *San Francisco Examiner*, May 1, 1957; June 16, 1961;*San Jose Mercury*, April 17, 1960; Nestor Palugod Enriquez Attng Mga Mangalaro; www.alohafame.com; www.starbulletin.com, September 10, 2000; Arthur K. Powlison, "Report of the Citywide Athletic Association," *Recreation in Hawaii*, 81-82; Barney Nagler, "Archie The Medicine Man," *Sport*, October, 1955;

48. *Philippine News*, January 6-January 12, 1975; January 23-January 29, 1975; January 30, 1975; February 5, 1975; www.starbulletin.com., December 21, 1999; *San Jose Mercury*, September 23, 2000.

49. Emil Guillermo, "Sucker Punch," www.asianweek.com., October 14, 1999.

50. *Chinese Digest*, December 13, 1935; October 30, 1936; *San Francisco Examiner*, December 1, 1943; *Pacific Citizen*, April 1, 1943; February 18, 1950; February 25, 1950; *Honolulu Advertiser*, March 14, 1944; January 31, 1950; *San Francisco Chronicle*, September 18, 1947; Arthur K. Powlison, "Report of the Citywide Athletic Association," 81-82; *Philippine News*, March 15-March 21, 1980.

51. *Honolulu Star-Bulletin*, March 13, 1936.

52. *Ibid.*, April 1, 1948; *Charleston Daily Mail*, April 10, 1940; April 10, 946; Bill King, "Hawaiians Take Titles in A.A.U. Boxing in Boston," *Helena Independent*, April 11, 1940; Frank Odo, *No Sword to Bury: Japanese Americans in Hawai'i During World War II*, (Philadelphia: Temple University Press, 2004), 207.

53. *Fort Wayne News*, February 19, 1917; *Stanford Daily*, February 13, 1931; February 1, 1937; February 2, 1953; *La Torre*, San Jose State College Yearbook, 1942, San Francisco *Examiner*, February 20, 1941; *Honolulu Star-Bulletin*, May 3, 1944, p. 8; San Francisco *Chronicle*, March 16, 1935; February 19, 1953; *San Jose Mercury*, March 6, 1942; February 1, 1955; March 4, 1956; April 21, 1960; *Reno Evening Gazette*, March 1, 1949; *Sacramento Bee*, March 18, 1950; April 6, 1947; *Pacific Citizen*, February 18, 1950; March 11, 1950; February 10, 1951; *Nevada State Journal*, March 28, 1957; April 4, 1957.

54. Edward Burrows, *Hawaiian Americans: An Account of the Mingling of Japanese, Chinese, and Polynesian People*, (New York: Archon Books, 1970), 83; Takaki, *Strangers*, 185.

56. Franklin Odo and Kazubo Sinota, *A Pictorial History of the Japanese in Hawaii, 1885-1924* (Honolulu, HI Bishop Museum Press, 1985), 78; Burrows, *Hawaiian Americans.*, 125; *Los Angeles Times*, April 7, 1916; Karen Leonard, *Ethnic Choices*, 60; *San Jose Mercury*, September 11, 1939; *San Francisco Chronicle*, March 2, 1944; *San Francisco Examiner*, March 4, 1947.

57. Burrows, *Hawaiian Americans*, 195-196.

58. *Ibid.*, 196; *Honolulu Star-Bulletin*, May 3, 1915.

59. Misawa, *Beginnings*, 16; Alison M. Wrynn, "The Recreation and Leisure Pursuits of Japanese Americans in World War II Internment Camps," in *Ethnicity and Sport in North American History and Culture*, George Eisen and David K. Wiggins, (eds.)

(Westport, CT: Greenwood Press, 1994), 124; *Stanford Daily*, February 3, 1937; *San Jose Mercury*, February 5, 1971; *Seattle Post-Intelligencer*, April 18, 1955.

60. *Williamsport Grit*, May 3, 1914; *Honolulu Star-Bulletin*, April 3, 1936; *San Jose Mercury*, March 1, 1942; March 11, 1950; March 10, 1951; *San Francisco Examiner*, March 19, 1950; *Pacific Citizen*, January 28, 1950; February 27, 1950; *San Francisco Chronicle*, February 16, 1956; *Spartan Daily*, February 15, 1956; *Los Gatos Times*, January 20, 1955; *Placer Mountain Democrat*, January 13, 1993; Brian Cazenueve, "College Wrestling," *Sports Illustrated*, March 28, 2005.

61. *San Francisco Chronicle*, September 11, 1925; December 24, 1934; *Charleston Daily Mail*, February 23, 1936; December 22, 1939; *Los Angeles Times*, November 1, 1938; May 28, 1946; *Marion Star*, April 5, 1940; *Bennington Evening Banner*, March 1, 1955.

62. *San Francisco Chronicle*, January 2, 1936; *Los Angeles Times*, November 1, 1936; *Pacific Citizen*, January 14, 1950.

63. *San Francisco Chronicle*, January 16, 1956.

64. *Oxnard Press Courier*, October 27, 1949; November 18, 1952.

65. *San Jose Mercury*, February 4, 1965; August 18, 1965; Dennis Akizuki, "Ex-Ring Heavy Now A Good Guy," November 29, 1999.

66. Akizuki, "Ex-Ring Heavy."

67. *Pacific Commercial Advertiser*, March 4, 1919; *Philippines Mail*, January 29, 1934; *Helena Independent*, *November 16, 1935*; San *Francisco Chronicle*, January 2, 1936; March 15, 1936; *San Jose Mercury*, July 7, 1937; *Honolulu Star-Bulletin*, June 25, 1946; July 5, 1948; October 7, 1948.

68. www.asianweek.com., March 8-March 12, 2002?

69. Carol Jung, "Japantown Project Finds Life," *San Jose Mercury*, July 17, 1996; September 25, 1996.

70. *San Jose Mercury*., May 29, 1996; *Hokubei Mainichi*, September 3, 1977; www.alohafame.com, accessed March 3, 1998; *Honolulu Star-Bulletin*, November 6, 1998; December 21, 1999; *Sports Illustrated*, February 8, 1993.

71. Mike Marquesse, "Sport and Stereotype: From Role Model to Muhammad Ali," *Race and Class*, (April-June, 1995), 3.

72. David B. Welky, "Viking Girls, Mermaids, and Little Brown Men: U.S. Journalism and the 1932 Olympics," *Journal of Sport History*, (Spring, 1997,24-50

73. *Chinese Digest*, December 20, 1935; *Pacific Citizen*, August 9, 1947; February 18, 1950; www. alohafame.com, accessed March 3, 1998; *Honolulu Star-Bulletin*, October 2, 1948; November 3, 1948; *Honolulu Advertiser*, March 8, 1935; March 11, 1935; January 31, 1950; April 17, 1951; *Fil-American Advocate*, March 15, 1953; *Oxnard Press-Courier*, May 24, 1954 .

74. *Los Angeles Times*, January 12, 1964; *Washington Post*, March 24, 1968; *East/West*, September 3, 1969; Bill Lee, "Voices: Lessons of a Slain Kick Boxer," www.asianweek.com, accessed January 30, 2004.

75. Darrell Hamamoto, *Monitored Peril: Asian Americans and the Politics of TV Representation*, (Minneapolis, Minnesota: University of Minnesota Press, 1994), 61.

76. *East/West*, January 20, 1982; November 9, 1983; *San Jose Mercury*, July 14, 1996; September 10, 2000; *Sports Illustrated*, September 14, 1998; Ethen Lieser, "Judo Girls Go For the Gold and Get It," www.asianweek.com, August 13, 2002.

77. *Asian Week*, September 28-October 4, 2000.

Chapter Three: Bats and Balls

Baseball Saved Us won the 1993 Parents' Choice Award. Written by Ken Mochizuki and illustrated by Don Lee, it tells a charming story from the perspective of a Japanese American boy experiencing life in a World War II concentration camp and the return home among a people who generally regarded Japanese Americans with suspicion and, too often, outright hostility.

Before the narration begins, Mochizuki inserts an Author's Note, which briefly introduces youthful readers to the World War II experiences of over one hundred thousand Japanese Americans. Mochizuki writes that the explanation for the internment of West Coast Japanese Americans was that the "U.S. government said…it could not tell who might be loyal to Japan." Mochizuki's note, however, does not mention the decades of racial and ethnic hostility encountered by people of Japanese ancestry in the United States before the Japanese attack on Pearl Harbor. It does wisely explain that "none" of the interned Japanese Americans "were ever proven to be dangerous to America during World War II." Mochizuki adds that "in 1988, the U.S. government admitted that what it did was wrong." The note does not draw attention to the years of hard struggle it took for Japanese American and non-Japanese American activists to wring that apology and reparations from the U.S. government.[1]

One of the major themes of the book itself is that baseball helped Japanese Americans maintain a sense of community among themselves as they lost their homes and endured the concentration camps. Meanwhile, internees' family relations underwent confusing changes. In the camps, parents felt they possessed less control over their children; especially older children. Accordingly, when the young narrator's older brother, Teddy, talked back to his father, "<t>hat's when Dad knew we needed baseball."[2]

The dad, the narrator, and their presumably male friends built baseball fields and bleachers. They sent for equipment such as bats, balls, and gloves, which "arrived in cloth sacks from friends back home." The "moms" were not completely left out of things. They "took the covers off mattresses and used them to make uniforms. They looked almost like the real thing."[3]

The narrator struggled as a ballplayer at first. But playing baseball was a little easier in the camp than at home, because "the kids were the same size as me." Eventually, however, he practically willed himself into knocking a game-winning homer. Inspiring his clutch slugging was the white soldier in the guard tower overlooking the baseball field: "He probably saw the other kids giving me a bad time and thought that I was no good. So I tried to be better because he was looking." When he surprised everyone with his homer, the narrator "looked up at the tower and the man, with a grin on his face, gave me the thumbs-up sign."[4]

Consequently, a second theme is that like youthful Americans of all racial and ethnic backgrounds, the juvenile hero of *Baseball Saved Us* sought self-validation through America's National Pastime. Yet he also, through baseball, sought the validation of the people who put him, his family, and his friends behind barbed-wire fences.

After he and his family left the camp, the narrator learned that "things were bad again when we got home." At school, he found that he "had to eat lunch by myself." He played baseball once more, but he had gotten better in the camp. And "the other guys saw that I was a pretty good player. They started calling me 'Shorty,' but they smiled when they said it." At his first game, the narrator felt nervous. He looked at the crowd and believed that "all these mean eyes were staring at me, wanting me to make mistakes. I dropped the ball that was thrown to me, and I heard people in the crowd yelling 'Jap.' I hadn't heard that word since before I went to Camp—it meant that they hated me."[5]

Lee's illustration shows the red capped young hero, face down, as white spectators apparently yell at him derisively. The narrator heard the crowd 'screaming, "The Jap's no good" and transcended the racial taunts by socking another home run. The last page of the book displays an illustration of his white teammates crowding around and hugging the young hero joyfully.

Baseball Saved Us exhibits the paradoxical relationship that has developed between baseball and Americans who have suffered discrimination in the United States because of their race, ethnicity, gender, or class. On the one hand, the sport, as America's National Pastime, has encouraged culturally diverse Americans to assert their cultural citizenship. It has, that is, offered them a sense of community, self-worth, and connections to other communities of Americans. On the other hand, it has also furnished them with persistent reminders of raised hierarchies in the land of the free--that perhaps baseball has "saved" some people more than others.

Baseball and Asian Pacific American Communities Before 1965

Baseball served early Asian Pacific-based ethnic communities rather well by solidifying them and frequently representing them in a better light to European Americans. Interestingly, baseball has long appealed to many Americans as their "National Pastime," despite the cross cultural, international roots of the sport. As is well known among baseball historians, Americans had introduced the game to Japan in the late nineteenth century. Meanwhile, Koreans and Chinese started to play baseball and after the United States conquered the Philippines in the late 1890s, Filipinos engaged in America's "National Pastime."

Indeed, some Americans in the early twentieth century regarded baseball as such an important way to understand the worthiness of American life that they assessed Asian Pacific peoples in terms of their ability to learn and master the game. Albert G. Spalding has been given considerable credit for popularizing baseball as America's National Pastime. In his book *America's National Game,* the baseball pioneer proudly noted Japan's enthusiasm for the sport by the early twentieth century. He maintained that "the fact is quite in keeping with what we know of the little brown men of the Orient." Baseball, according to Spalding, was a combative sport, embraced by aggressive, competitive, and progressive people. The Japanese, Spalding argued, shared these attributes, at least, with white Americans.[6]

After the United States militarily conquered guerrilla opposition in the Philippines during the early 1900s, it sought to pacify the natives. Many American government officials and missionaries in the Philippines believed that baseball could win the hearts of truculent Filipinos. The Seymours write that during the 1910s, "Major General J. Franklin Bell, in command at Manila, may have been unaware of the scanty uniforms and the bolo threats, for he said baseball had done more to 'civilize' the Filipinos than anything else." Scholar Dean Worchester was a major proponent of baseball's power to solidify American rule in the Philippines. He claimed, "Even the old men have gone wild over the game...It seems strange indeed to see the old Igorote more stolid than the American Indian toss his hat in the air in wild exuberance of a fanatical baseball fan. Legislation failed to regulate cockfighting, moral progress societies accomplished nothing, but since we instituted the American baseball game the cockpit has been deserted." In 1915, the *Washington Post* reported on Filipinos watching occupying U.S. marines playing baseball: "Being of an imitative nature, however, the Filipinos were not contented to stand by and watch. They took delight in aping the ball players, and with the aid of the marines, soon learned the rudiments of the game."[7]

Meanwhile, a team of Filipinos toured the American mainland in 1913. The American press reported that the Filipinos came from different "tribes." Thus, "they are obliged to speak in a tongue other than their own in order to carry on a conversation among themselves." Playing semi-professional and college nines, the Filipino ballplayers lost more often than they won. But they were capable of "putting up a pretty good article of ball." In the San Francisco Bay Area, for example, the Filipinos beat a semi-pro team in Santa Rosa, 8-4.[8]

In the early 1920s, the *Sporting News* feared that Filipinos had lost interest in America's National Pastime. Perhaps, the weekly speculated, Filipinos had also grown tired of American rule and would never be adequately Americanized. But the fault, according to the *Sporting News,* lay at the door step of the American colonial authorities who no longer seemed to understand baseball's power to bridge cultural differences.[9]

Ten years later, however, the *Sporting News* reported Filipino baseball was in good shape. An All-Filipino team had defeated an All-Hawai'i nine in Manila. Reginio Portucion was a pitching hero for Manila's National University and a Philippine Baseball League thrived with teams such as the Manila Cits, McKinley, Mills, Manila, and Cavite. An outfielder named Pablo Chu was one of the league's stars.[10]

In another outpost of the American Empire baseball was used to calm down troublesome Asian Pacific workers. During the first decades of the twentieth century, Hawaiian plantation owners frequently experienced difficulties with their labor forces. The largely Asian Pacific work force sought better pay and working conditions. As a consequence, haole sugar and pineapple plantation owners introduced a form of paternalism into the troubled relationships with their workers. They, thus, tried to implement recreational programs designed to convince workers that their bosses cared about them and that there was no need for them to organize trade unions and strikes. Baseball was, therefore, perceived by haole plantation owners as an excellent way to deflect workers from labor militancy.[11]

Indeed, Hawai'i was probably the site of many of the earliest Asian Pacific community nines on U.S. soil. America's "National Pastime" had been played on the islands since the 1850s. Interestingly, one of the game's great pioneers, Alexander Cartwright, moved to Hawai'i after spending a little time in Gold Rush California. The first box score of a game played in Hawai'i lists names that were both Anglo and Native Hawaiian. In 1890, Kamehameha, a school for Hawaiians of indigenous ancestry, won the Honolulu championship. Nevertheless, in 1899 the *Hawaiian Gazette* complained that Kamehameha ballplayers could hit but they could not field. By 1915, the *Washington Post* purported, baseball had fulfilled its colonial mission. The U.S. military had skillfully helped to propagate the gospel of baseball on the Hawaiians Islands. Indigenous Hawaiians had, according to the *Post,* gratefully accepted the gift of baseball from their colonial rulers: "Childlike and enthusiastic" Native Hawaiians "played the game for all it was worth.... The Hawaiians, it might be mentioned, are possessed of unusual speed and although they play barefooted, run and slide to the bases in a way that would do credit to our own players."[12]

On the mainland, patrician Chinese students living in Hartford, Connecticut took up baseball in Gilded Age America. Members of the Chinese Educational Mission formed a nine called the Orientals and, according to observers such as William Phelps, played the game well. As the United States lurched toward passing the Chinese Exclusion Act, the Chinese government ordered the mission to return home. While waiting in San Francisco for a China-bound steamer in 1881, the Mission nine was challenged by an Oakland baseball club. Wen Bing Chung a Mission student, remembered that "<t>he Oakland men imagined that they were going to have a walk-over with the Chinese. Who had seen Celestials playing baseball?" However, the Chinese nine won, surprising their opponents and the spectators who witnessed a "strange phenomenon—Chinese playing their national ball game and showing the Yankees some of the thrills of the game."[13]

Despite the Chinese Exclusion Act, the Chinese presence in the United States continued to pose a dilemma to American nativism and racism. In 1884, the *Sporting Life* reported that a "California man is trying to teach a lot of Chinamen how to play baseball with a view to organizing a Chinese base ball team." However, the *Sporting Life* assured readers that "he has met with little success thus far and will meet with less in the future." In 1885, the *San Francisco Chronicle* pointed out a multiracial, multiethnic baseball game engaged in by "Spaniards, Dutch, Americans, and Chinese."[14]

The majority of Chinese immigrants living in the United States lacked the patrician background of those young men involved in the Chinese Educational Mission. Most were laborers who in growing numbers by the 1880s inhabited overcrowded "ethnic enclaves" such as San Francisco's Chinatown. There, according to one *San Francisco Chronicle* reporter, interesting games of baseball were played in 1887. *Chronicle* readers were told that on "any Sunday afternoon on Stockton Street one may see a team of rising Mongolians wrestling with the technicalities of the Great American game, while different pawnbrokers, pork butchers, and influential high binders and their wives beam down approvingly from the rickety balconies." The next year, the press noted the existence of two Chinese teams playing in Chicago.[15]

However, as baseball could serve as a possible cultural bridge builder, it could also clearly reinforce barriers between Chinese and non-Chinese Americans. The anti-Chinese movement remained active after the Chinese Exclusion Act. In 1886, anti-Chinese Californians began a statewide boycott of Chinese owned-businesses and non-Chinese owned businesses hiring Chinese or dealing commercially with Chinese in the United States. To publicize the boycott, a group of young men living in Sacramento formed a nine called the Boycotters.[16]

In Hawai'i, ethnic-based teams emerged early. Native Hawaiians, as mentioned earlier, had probably played the game since its introduction to the islands. Early in the 1900s, the Asahi club sprouted out of a nine organized for Japanese Hawaiian youth in Honolulu. Organized by Steere Noda, who also batted over .500 for the team in 1912 and 1913, the Asahis turned into one of the most formidable contingents in Honolulu baseball. The son of plantation workers, Noda became a territorial legislator and influential supporter of Hawaiian sports. At about the same time, an elite Chinese Hawaiian nine was formed in Honolulu by the Chinese Athletic Club. By the 1910s, several Chinese Hawaiian teams existed. In 1912, the Young Chinese Athletics had organized a team that competed against nines such as the Chinese Kahunas. That same year, the Honolulu Cracker Company team won the city's Chinese Triangular League. In 1915, Filipino Hawaiian nines competed in Honolulu and Kauai, while Korean Hawaiians organized teams and leagues.[17]

Very likely, these early Hawaiian nines, as well as many pioneering Asian Pacific teams formed on the mainland, were organized less out of a desire to encourage assimilation into American society through baseball than to keep young men out of gambling and opium halls. In San Jose, California, an Asahi nine was organized in the late 1910s. Mas Akizuki, one of the founders, recalled that he wanted to help provide healthier recreational outlets for Japanese American young men. San Jose's Asahi club received relatively little support from the local *nihonmachi* in the beginning. Yet within a few years, the San Jose Asahis became a consequential community institution. In his own way, Jack Graham of the *San Jose Mercury* tried to compliment the Asahi rooters who customarily showed up at "the Jap diamond." They were the "biggest bunch of rooters...of any team in the city <and> their diamond is probably the best in town and fast games are the rule."[18]

The San Jose Asahi team was not by any means the first Japanese American community nine established on the mainland. Because the Issei were more familiar with baseball than any other first generation immigrant group in the United States during the early decades of the twentieth century, they, unsurprisingly, organized baseball teams wherever they lived in substantial numbers. Among the earliest was the Fuji club, established in San Francisco in 1900. One of the founders of this club was Chiura Obata, an artist and subsequently an art professor at the University of California, Berkeley. In 1909, the *Los Angeles Times* announced that a local "Jap team" would play a "colored" team at Joy Park. It added, "Fans will be treated to an exhibition of the national game by the best talent of the black and brown races." In Seattle, scholar Gail Nomura reports, an Issei nine surfaced around 1904. By 1910, an all-Issei league existed, with some of the teams playing white nines. In 1910, 500 people watched the Mikados, from Seattle, defeat the Columbias from Tacoma for the Issei Pacific Northwest championship. During the 1910s, Seattle had its own Asahi team. Issei Fred Fukuda, later a banker and teacher, organized the nine and subsequently played for and managed the team. According to the *Seattle Post Intelligencer*, the Seattle Asahi players were "a little weak in batting, <but>the little fellows are wonderful fielders, fast, and good runners.[19]

Japanese American teams like the Seattle and San Jose Asahis helped strengthen community solidarity as Issei players gave way to the Nisei. During the 1920s and 1930s, the Issei in Japanese American communities expressed great pride in the baseball played by their children, the Nisei. Baseball historian Jay Feldman quotes Pete Matsui, who competed for a Japanese American nine in Southern California known as the San Fernando Aces. "It was all community-oriented. The communities didn't intermingle like they do now, you see, and the ball club was an important part of community identity, so they really wanted us to do well." Japanese American baseball in Yakima Valley, according to Nomura, "served to bring together the two generations and lessen the generation gap between immigrant fathers and their American-born sons. In baseball, the immigrant fathers could come together with their sons in a shared passion."[20]

Japanese American community nines sprang up throughout the Pacific Coast before World War II. In 1923, the *Sacramento Bee* announced the formation of an "all Japanese baseball league" in Northern California. The league consisted of nines from San Francisco, Oakland, Alameda, San Jose, Sacramento, Isleton, Stockton, and Fresno. Japanese American community nines, moreover, played against and impressed non-Japanese American opponents. The San Jose Asahis, for example, attracted favorable attention from the local European American followers of baseball. The *San Jose Mercury* maintained in 1923 that "the Japanese boys have proved themselves to be thorough sports and are highly spoken of among other teams in the winter league." To the south of San Jose, Japanese Americans in Santa Cruz had organized a nine that played such teams as Watsonville's Filipino Athletic Club in 1933.[21]

California's Central Valley emerged as a hotbed of Japanese American baseball during the 1920s. Marysville's Japanese American community petitioned the city council for help in constructing a second ball park; claiming that one park would not satisfy the needs of European American and Japanese American young people alike. The petitioners, however, assured the council that white youngsters could use the proposed park as well.[22]

The Japanese American Yamato Colony was represented by a ball club which faced Central Valley opponents such as the semi-professional Lodi nine in 1926--a game that the Yamato team lost, 1-0. In Sacramento, a team called the Nippon Cubs played in the city's Municipal Baseball League in 1927. During the Great Depression, the Church Division of Sacramento's Twilight League had clubs called the Japanese Baptists and the Japanese Presbyterians, who played nines representing the First Evangelicals and the Church of Latter Day Saints.[23]

Kenichi Zenimura is widely credited as a pioneer in Japanese American community baseball on the mainland before World War II. Zenimura was born in Hiroshima, Japan in 1900. He, subsequently, migrated to Hawai'i, where he nurtured his baseball skills. In 1920, he moved to Fresno, California. There he labored as a restaurant worker and as an auto mechanic. In 1923, Zenimura managed a team called the Hawaiian All Stars, an all Japanese Hawaiian squad featuring Kenso Nushida, who was described by the *San Francisco Chronicle* as a fifteen years old "diminutive pitcher." The Hawaiian All Stars, the *Chronicle* announced, were all American citizens and spoke English. Their tour of California had been arranged, according to the *Chronicle.* by an unnamed Japanese American newspaper. The players had been offered jobs to remain in Fresno and Stockton after the tour ended. These players apparently supported Zenimura in making Japanese American baseball a lively and competitive affair in California's Central Valley. Later the 1920s, Zenimura helped establish a ten team Nisei league in Fresno, while also playing for the all-Japanese American and formidable Fresno Athletics.[24]

Los Angeles had long furnished a home to Japanese American baseball. Before World War II, the Los Angeles Nippons took on some of the best semi-pro nines in the region. Good enough to earn a try out by the PCL's Los Angeles Angels, Sammy Takahashi was known as a "flashy shortstop" for the Nippons. And while Takahashi did not make the Angels, he did play minor league ball in the Western International League. [25]

Pre-World War II, Japanese American teams regularly played Japanese teams, either in the United States or Japan. The Seattle Nisei made six trips to Japan from 1914 to 1923. Fred Fukada explained his team's objectives: "One is to make our young players understand their mother country more deeply. And the other is to introduce to Japan and also study the current situation of Japanese commerce, which the president of the Seattle Chamber of Commerce strongly recommended." .In 1935, the Tokyo Giants toured the United States as Japan's first professional team. While in the San Francisco Bay Area, the Giants faced the San Jose Asahis. Aided by Russ Hinaga's key hit, the Asahis beat the Japanese professionals, 3-2 in late March.[26]

While Japanese American baseball gets more attention from historians, Chinese American community nines were also prominent on the mainland before World War II. In 1900, the *New York Times* announced that a team of white soldiers would play a Chinese team at a New York City armory. In 1908, the Chicago *Daily Tribune* noted the existence of a talented group of Chinese athletes called the Hip Lungs, competing in the city's 1st Ward League. In 1912, Colusa, California was the site of a Chinese American celebration of the founding of the Chinese Republic. An automobile parade was a feature, as well as a speech made by noted San Francisco journalist and reformer, Ng Poon Chew. Another highlight, however, was a baseball game pitting a picked nine from Colusa's Chinese American population and a team chosen from Colusa's Chinese band. In San Francisco, a baseball team represented the Chinese Athletic Club in 1918. In Los Angeles, the Chinese American Lowa club was formed in the 1920s. In early February, 1923, the team was in first place in The Greater Southern California Baseball Association. The *Los Angeles Times* observed in 1925 that the Los Angeles Chinese beat a nine called the City Merchants, 14-5.

One member of the team recalled that he and his teammates used their speed to rattle opponents. [27]

The Oakland Wa Sung nine ranked as one of the best semi-professional clubs in the Bay Area during the 1930s. Chinese Americans and non-Chinese Americans observed that the Wa Sungs had players capable of performing in the Pacific Coast League, arguably the finest minor league in professional baseball during the 1930s. The team was coached by a pitcher named Al Bowen, who was otherwise known as Lee Gum Hong. Brothers Henry and George Bowen also performed for the Wa Sung nine, as did Al Huey, Lock Kai-Kee, Allie Wong, and Joe Lee.[28]

Filipinos in pre World War II California and elsewhere also fielded baseball teams. For example, in the early 1920s Filipinos in Chicago organized a nine and the Filipino All-Star club participated in San Francisco semi-professional circles in 1926. In the 1930s, Filipino Athletic Clubs in San Francisco and Watsonville, California, supported nines. In depression-ridden Los Angeles, Filipinos organized an Indoor Baseball League with one hundred participants representing the Ilocos Sur Association of America, the Filipino Patriotic Association, Pangasian Youth, La Union Association, the Catholic Filipino Club, Filipino Youth, and the Sons of Cebu.[29]

Ethnic-based community softball teams attracted the participation of Asian Pacific American females during the 1930s. The *Chinese Digest* boasted about an Oakland softball team called The Dragonettes, led by pitching star, Gwen Wong. According to *Chinese Digest* sportswriter, Herbert Eng, Wong was "a left-handed Amazon." The decade, furthermore, witnessed the proliferation of Japanese American female softball teams. In 1935, thirteen such contingents competed in the Southern California Women's Athletic Union. And three years later, the number rose to twenty.[30]

On December 7, 1941, the Los Angeles Nippons were playing a nine representing Paramount Studios. The *Hollywood Reporter* claimed that the "FBI men allowed the game to continue" after the attack on Pearl Harbor was announced. But once Paramount won, 6-3, the agents "then rounded up the Jap contingent." Subsequently, West Coast Japanese Americans, uprooted from their homes and first placed in assembly centers and then dispatched to concentration camps, supported baseball as both a means of joyful diversion and community support. Writing about baseball and other sports in the concentration camps, historian Samuel Regalado claims, "Their freedom impaired, baseball and other recreational activities were major factors in maintaining community cohesion. These activities nurtured cultural camaraderie, competitiveness, and pride." According to Jay Feldman, about thirty-two nines were organized at the Gila, Arizona camp. At Tule Lake, internees removed canvas covers from government issued mattresses and sewed them together for uniforms.[31]

The *Manzanar Free Press*, an internee operated newspaper, revealed a great deal of female softball playing. The young women engaged in softball league with teams named the Twixteens, Zephyrs, Modernaires, Lambdas, and Pickups. "Teddy Bear," who reported on sporting activities for the *Free Press* complained about the softball grounds, which "looks as if a family of gophers made themselves at home." Among the female internees who stood out was Jane "No Hit" Ota, who starred as a pitcher at the Jerome, Arkansas camp. [32]

Undoubtedly, baseball and softball meant a great deal to many of the internees. One of them was Henry Honda, who was a top-notch pitcher for the San Jose Asahis before World War II. Honda was able to attract the interest of the Brooklyn Dodgers, who offered him a tryout when he left the camp. The Dodgers were interested but did not ink Honda to a contract because they knew of his impending military obligations. After the war the Cleveland Indians also expressed a desire to give Honda a contract but he turned it down because of an injured pitching arm. In any event, Honda told the *San Jose Mercury* in 1996 that "<w>hen I think about the camp, the baseball and softball games are what I remember most....It was the only thing that gave us enjoyment."[33]

Japanese Hawaiians by and large did not face internment during World War II. In part, this was because racial and ethnic relations developed differently on the islands than the mainland. Racial and ethnic borders existed and were, in fact, often supported by baseball. Nevertheless, it often seemed easier for Hawaiians to transcend those divisions than, for instance, Californians.

League play had been organized on the islands since the early 1890s. One history of Hawaiian baseball claims, "Fans cheered on their favorites robustly, but the statistics and minute details about each team and player held no interest for them. Attendance was strictly a social pursuit. Each game was followed by a big luau." During the 1910s, a former New York lawyer named J. Ashman Braven created the Honolulu League, with seven, ethnically-based, teams. The Asahis were, of course, the Japanese Hawaiian contingent. Among the other teams were the Chinese Hawaiian Tigers and the Portuguese Hawaiian Braves.[34].

In the 1920s and 1930s Hawaiian ethnic groups supported a plethora of baseball teams. The Asahis remained one of the best teams in Hawai'i. When, however, the United States entered World War II, the lives of all Japanese Hawaiians were shaken. Among the transformations was that the Asahi club underwent a name change to the Athletics. White players, furthermore, were brought on to the team. The Chinese Tigers frequently rivaled the Asahis for baseball supremacy in Honolulu. Possessing indigenous and Chinese ancestry, the talented John Kerr competed for the Chinese Tigers in the 1930s. A skilled pitcher and hitter, Kerr was the first person to hit a home run out of Honolulu Stadium—a 450 foot shot. In 1940, The Chinese Tigers won the Hawaii Baseball League championship. A Hawaiian of indigenous and Chinese descent, Tommy Kaulukukui provided both needed pitching and hitting for the team that were sometimes called the "Mandarins." He also was the assistant team owner. Joining Kaululukui on the Tigers were his brothers Charles, Edward, Joe, and James, as well as Filipino Hawaiian pitcher Crispin Mancao. Korean Hawaiians, meanwhile, had organized a baseball league in the mid-1930s, with teams representing the Korean Athletic Association, the Delta Frats, and Wahiawa. [35]

After the war, the Hawaiian Asahis were revived and once again became a largely all Japanese Hawaiian contingent. In 1951, the team was managed by Takeo "Fats" Nakamura and included the skilled Jyun Hirota and infielder Jimmy Wasa. However, another generally Japanese Hawaiian team called the Rural Red Sox emerged as a powerhouse in the post-World War Hawaiian baseball. The team was managed for several years by Lawrence Kunihisa, a one time HBL shortstop and subsequently a territorial legislator and prominent businessperson. [36]

San Francisco's Chinatown nurtured post-World War II community baseball. In 1945, the *San Francisco Chronicle's* Will Connolly observed, "Chinese boys are going in for baseball in a big way, if only in the spirit of perversity to prove they can eclipse the Japanese heretofore the prime exponent of baseball, outside the continental U.S.A....Chinese should make excellent ballplayers. They are nimble of foot and quick of hand, and unlike the Japanese, grow big enough to hit a ball hard." In the spring of 1946, the *San Francisco Chronicle* noted that "two Chinese baseball teams" played every Sunday at Golden Gate Park. On a Sunday, the *Chronicle* declared one team "got but 2 hits, while their opponents got five, and the youngsters were playing good ball all the way." In 1947, the *San Francisco Examiner's* Carl Reich displayed less appreciation of Chinese American community baseball. Reich wrote, "when <San Francisco's> police department abolished the Chinatown detail there was no thought it would affect the sports world." According to Reich, San Francisco police sergeant, John Dyer, had fathered the Chinese Optimist Club nine, but had not been able to "look after his youthful charges." Apparently only four had shown up for one game and the Chinese Optimist nine had to forfeit a game. The Chinese Optimist ballplayers did not give up on baseball, after all. In 1950, they beat the Napa Optimists, 8-6. [37]

Japanese American community baseball thrived on the American mainland after World War II. In 1947, the *San Jose Mercury* reported on a scheduled game between the San Jose Zebras, a Nisei team, and another Nisei contingent representing the Santa Barbara Athletic Club. During the war, the players on the Santa Barbara Athletic Club nine had competed for the Gila Relocation Center. After the war, they reunited to form the only non-white team in the Southern California Semi-Pro League. In the 1950s, nines such as the San Francisco Nisei Clippers, as well as the Japanese American San Jose Zebras played in the San Francisco Bay Area. In 1951, the Penryn Japanese American Citizens League competed in the Placer-Nevada Baseball League. In Utah, the Japanese American Athletic Union had nines in Honeyville, Syracuse, Murray, Ogden, Davis, Garland, Corrine, and Salt Lake. One of the organization's goal was to promote "good will."[38]

Across the mainland, Asian Pacific American males and females played community softball. In 1947, a Japanese American women's team captured a Minneapolis city championship. Chicago's Filipino American community supported softball in 1953. In 1973, Japanese American female softball teams in California represented businesses such as Sumitomo Bank, Mike's Arco, Salon Suzanne, and Japan Food.[39]

Back in Hawai'i Americans of Japanese Ancestry (AJA) had established flourishing teams and leagues. In 1950, the great Wally Yonamine played for the Waialae nine in Honolulu. Other AJA teams could be found in Moiliili, Kakaako, McCulley, Kalihi, and Kalihi Valley. Les Murakami, who managed an AJA team in Honolulu and coached the University of Hawai'i nine for years said, "When a group of people can last and hold a league together for this many years without major struggles, you know the <AJA> organization is good and the guys are high class."[40]

Other Hawaiian Asian Pacific Islander ethnic groups maintained community baseball and softball leagues. In 1949, the Oahu Filipino Baseball League consisted of teams such as the Young Americans, Hawaii Fil Vets, Wahiawea Fils, Waialuu Filipino Community Club, Filipino Federation of America. That same year, Honolulu's Chinese Baseball League included teams sponsored by local firms such as the Kam Express, Rico Ice Cream, Chinese Amateurs, Chings' Contractors, and Acme Mattress. Community softball teams flourished in Hawai'i, where Korean Hawaiians competed in a softball league in Honolulu in 1951 and Hawaiian Filipinos organized softball leagues on Oahu and Kauai Moreover, the Filipino Federation Alpatio Lapaluma Girls' team competed in the Women's International Invitational Softball League in Honolulu.[41]

Touring Asian Pacific Islander teams from Japan and Hawai'i seemed to help solidify a sense of community among Japanese Americans and Chinese Americans on the mainland during the early decades of the twentieth century. In 1905, a Japanese baseball team representing Waseda University in Tokyo arrived in the United States. This marked the first U.S. tour of a Japanese nine. The games the Waseda club played on the West Coast drew large contingents of Issei fans. When Waseda played the Stanford University nine in San Francisco, the *San Francisco Chronicle* maintained that 2/3 of the 2000 people in attendance were Japanese. The scene, according to the *Chronicle*, was like a "holiday in Hiroshima." Six years later, the Waseda nine made another tour of the United States. While in Salt Lake City, the Japanese students beat the University of Utah team. According to a report published in the *San Francisco Chronicle*, Salt Lake City's Japanese Colony showed up in significant numbers and celebrated the Waseda nine's victory. When, in 1935, the Tokyo Giants arrived in San

Francisco to barnstorm the American mainland, the *Chronicle's* Ed Hughes predicted, "The visitors from Nippon will get enthusiastic support from Japanese of this city and surrounding territory." Indeed, when the Giants played against the San Francisco Missions of the Pacific Coast League Hughes noted "a big outpouring of Japanese to greet the Giants." Eighteen years later, the Tokyo Giants were in California again. The Japanese American citizens of Santa Maria feted the professionals with a barbecue dinner. In Southern California, the Orange County Japanese American Interclub Council presented a traveling Japanese team in 1960 a plaque and two crates of oranges. [42]

In 1912, a team of Chinese Hawaiians ostensibly representing the University of Hawaii came to Sacramento, California to play a couple of the local white teams. Under the headline, "Orientals Await Opening Game," the *Sacramento Bee* reported that Sacramento's Young Chinese Association planned to give "their countrymen" a big reception. All of Chinatown, the *Bee* forecasted, would appear at the game. Even Sacramento's Japanese American community expressed interest in the coming contests, the *Bee* noted. The reason was that the Chinese Hawaiians had previously beaten in Honolulu Japanese teams representing Waseda and Keio Universities. In 1913, the "All-Chinese" defeated a Stanford nine, 7-3. The *San Francisco Chronicle* claimed, "suppers were late on the Stanford campus and in Palo Alto due to culinary celebrations and kitchen fannings over the 'Chinese victory.'" In Los Angeles a year later, the ChineseHawaiians, of whom only a minority actually possessed Chinese ancestry, played the Occidental College nine. On the day of the game, the *Los Angeles Times* crudely predicted, "Every Chinese laundry and vegetable wagon in the city will be out of commission this afternoon." After the game, the *Times* acknowledged that about 150 spectators from Los Angeles's Chinese community cheered the Hawaiians as they beat the mainlanders, 6-4. The Chinese American spectators took the winning nine to the Los Angeles Chinatown, where they treated the ballplayers to a large and festive banquet. [43]

The Stars

For much of the 1900s, the mainland witnessed the impressive performances of several Hawaiian athletes, many of whom possessed blurred racial identities. A number of these athletes were baseball players. Beginning in 1912 and ending in 1916, a group of talented ballplayers often publicized as representing the fictitious Chinese University of Hawai'i toured the American mainland. There, the Hawaiian ballplayers, not all of whom possessed Chinese ancestry, played semi-professional, college, and African American professional nines. In the process, they wound up winning far more often than not.

On their 1912 mainland trip, the Hawaiians won 66, lost 44, and tied 4 games. In 1913, they won 105 games, while losing 38 and tying one. And of the fifty-nine games they played against college and university nines, they won fifty-four. The next year, the Hawaiians won 125 out of 150 games. They also competed against and more than held their own against top flight Hawaiian clubs, as well as visiting nines from the mainland.[44]

Commercial interests in Honolulu's Chinatown and, indeed, Honolulu at large supported the "All-Chinese" team's trek to the mainland in 1912. Hawaiian boosters believed that a Chinese Hawaiian team would effectively promote the islands to prospective mainland tourists and investors. Moreover, Honolulu's Chinese merchants demonstrated more than a bit of class snobbery as well. According to one press report, they hoped that that the team would show mainlanders that "all Chinamen are not laundrymen or cooks" and thereby ease the ability of non-laborers to get into the United States. Thus "every member of the team is a graduate of either an American or a Hawaiian school or college and all speak English, in addition to the four other languages which are commonly heard on the Hawaiian Islands as fluently as they play baseball."[45]

Interestingly, the Hawaiian nine came to the mainland at a time when anti-Asian Pacific sentiments were widespread, especially on the West Coast. A major argument against Asian Pacific immigration on the mainland was that Asian Pacific people lacked the ability to successfully adapt themselves to American culture. Thus, the largely Chinese Hawaiian team's 1912 trek to the mainland attracted attention from the national press, as well as local coverage. Under the headline, "The Chinese Team: The Colorful Visitors from Hawaii Superior to Japs Who Visited in 1911—There General Work Causes Astonishment," an article in the *Sporting Life* compared the Chinese Hawaiian nine favorably to Japan's Waseda University team, which toured the United States in 1911. At the same time, in comparing the Chinese Hawaiian nine to the Waseda club, the *Sporting Life* suggested the foreign nature of the Chinese Hawaiians, even though these players were purportedly born in Hawai'i and were, therefore, American citizens. The article maintained: "In marked contrast to the Japanese, the Chinamen use great judgment, and their plays are daring, their fielders hit well, and they have pitchers, who are almost, if not quite, as good as any college pitcher in the United States." The *Sporting Life* article also expressed some amazement at how American the Chinese Hawaiians seemed. Claiming that they excelled in their command of the most contemporary American slang, the Chinese Hawaiians did more than simply hammer a University of Chicago pitcher in one game: "<T>he Chinese players shouted through large megaphones, 'Everybody's doing it now' and added still more to the demoralization of the Chicago pitcher." A baseball columnist for the *San Francisco Chronicle*, James Nealon, agreed that the "Celestial Combination" played better baseball than the Waseda nine. But his praise was limited. He comforted white Americans who believed baseball skills reflected a racial hierarchy by explaining that "<l>ike all

foreigners who adopt the game, they play mechanically and display little knowledge of the inside game."[46]

According to San Francisco reporter, Abe Kemp, the Chinese Hawaiian
nine was originally organized in Honolulu in 1905. Financially supported by
Chinese merchants in Honolulu, the players in 1912 ranged in age from 18 to 24.
One of the team's biggest stars was Lai Tin, later known as William or Buck
Lai. He also reigned among Hawaiian track and field performers. Ho Sing Hung,
also known as Sing Hung Hoe, was reportedly as good in soccer as in baseball.
Lang Akana was another top player, but he also doubled as a singer known as
"the Hawaiian nightingale." Indeed, the Chinese Hawaiians not only comprised
a baseball team, but at least some joined a glee club that accompanied the nine.[47]

Newspaper reports of the Chinese Hawaiians' tour of 1912 blended respect
with what could also be interpreted as contempt. While in Sacramento, the Chinese Hawaiians took on a local team with Hap Hogan, a manager of the Vernon
Pacific Coast League (PCL) team serving as umpire. Hogan was quoted by the
Los Angeles Times as saying that umpiring was easy: "<I>f a man can umpire a
game in which Chinks are engaged and get away with it without a kick, he
should know something about umpiring." Several weeks later, the Chinese Hawaiian contingent lost to the Fordham University nine. According to the *Sporting Life*, Fordham was "an enigma to the invading Yellow Peril."[48]

With ballplayers of Japanese and Native Hawaiian ancestry on board, the
somewhat less Chinese Hawaiian nine traveled to Southern California in March,
1914. Earlier, they had toured Northern California, where they beat respectable
Stanford University and St. Mary's College nines. The *Los Angeles Times* dispatched mixed signals regarding the Hawaiian ballplayers. In publicizing an
upcoming game between Occidental College and the Hawaiian ballplayers, the
Times published cartoons displaying stereotypical images of "exotic" Chinese
trying to play the white man's game. One cartoon showed European American
players stepping on queues of supposedly Chinese Hawaiian base runners. The
caption read: "A practical way to stop a base stealer." The text, nevertheless,
praised the Asian Hawaiian athletes even though the article's subheadline read:
"The Yellow Peril." The *Times* claimed that as batters, the Hawaiians were hard
to fool, because they used short, choppy swings and they displayed "sensational
base running and perfect fielding." [49]

After the game, a *Times* headline declared that "nine little Chinamen" defeated the Occidental club. An accompanying cartoon again evoked stereotypical images to characterize the Asian Hawaiian ballplayers. But also again the
actual text of the story reporting on the game reveals Asian Hawaiians transcending racial stereotypes. The victorious nine not only won the game, but also
seemed to have a fine time doing so. Hardly queued "exotics," the Hawaiian
ballplayers were expert bench jockeys as they rode the umpire and the opposition persistently. After losing an argument with the umpire, one Hawaiian re

turned to the bench complaining, "Well, for the love of Mike, did you ever see anything to beat that guy? He ought to get a job of blowing safes." When the Occidental catcher tried the hidden ball trick, En Sue Pung, described by the *Times* as "the Ty Cobb of the South Seas" yelled, "I thought that we were going to learn something about baseball by coming across the Pacific Ocean. I didn't expect to see any one try such a bush league trick at least a century old." The *Times* writer claimed that the Hawaiian nine proved "that baseball follows the flag" and that perhaps British poet Rudyard Kipling was wrong—"the East and West had at last met." [50]

The next spring, the even less Chinese Hawaiian team attracted respect and stereotypes as they played games in the San Francisco Bay Area. Now called the Hawaiian Travelers by the Honolulu press, they first upended Stanford, 10-7. Showing aggressiveness on the base paths, the Travelers stole seven bases against the Palo Alto aggregation. The University of California, Berkeley, nine proved more difficult and shut out the Hawaiians. Before the game in Berkeley, the *Oakland Tribune* declared that "the little men of the east are said to be exceptionally strong in the pitching department." One of the prime reasons why such "little men" could do so well was that the Hawaiian nine had recruited "a Manchurian <pitcher> of considerable height and bulk. for the heavy work." The Hawaiians, then, traveled down to Santa Clara Valley to play against the Salt Lake City's Pacific Coast League nine, which was training in San Jose. [51]

The *San Jose Mercury* did all it could to boost the game in advance. A piece published in the daily announced that Nat Strong managed the Hawaiian team's tour. The New York City based Strong was one of the most prominent baseball promoters in the nation. The article reported that the team's biggest star and captain was the aforementioned Lai Tin, who by this time had enticed the interest of the Chicago White Sox and that the team featured pitchers with the last names of Apau and Ako, who was actually Native Hawaiian named Luther Kekoa. "The club," the piece in the *Mercury* proclaimed unblushingly, "is without doubt the greatest drawing card playing baseball in the United States." It went on to reassure readers that the Hawaiian club consisted of gentlemen, capable of playing the equivalent of Minor League mainland baseball. [52]

The San Jose *Mercury* continued to represent the Hawaiian ballplayers as perfectly reputable young men on the day of their game against Salt Lake City. While respectable, the Hawaiian ballplayers were also depicted by the daily as racialized aliens. *Mercury* readers learned that "Uncle Sam is pulling another of his wise old tricks in sending these boys around the country.... Our Uncle is showing off his ability as a developer of races and as a teacher on this baseball trip." Although they seemingly needed America's National Pastime to set them on the path toward the highest levels of civilization, the Hawaiians were "refined gentlemen of the highest type." They reminded the reporter of typical mainland "college boys." "In fact," the article declared, "the most interesting thing about these young fellows is that they are regular—not different, not un-usual." Its author reported that "they speak English, spend many afternoons around the piano, ragtime music and Hawaiian songs are popular with them." One favorite song consisted of the words, "Ring, Ring Hawaii, ring/ Swell the chorus of our song."[53]

A good crowd packed San Jose's Luna Park that March Sunday to watch the Hawaiian Travelers oppose Salt Lake City. The *Los Angeles Times* told Southern Californian readers that Luna Park's "bleachers unmistakably root<ed> for the Chinese to win." Both sides played well and even though the Coast Leaguers eked out a 3-2 victory, the "University of Hawaii showed that they knew the American game." The *San Jose Mercury* revealed that the game did not proceed without incident. Apparently, Lai Tin knocked down Salt Lake City's second baseman while trying to get into second safely. In so doing, the third baseman stirred the crowd and the players. In any event, the *Mercury* reported that the Hawaiians were clever ballplayers, who knew how to play with "the aplomb" of "major leaguers." [54]

As they toured the mainland, the Hawaiian Travelers represented what some important cultural theorists describe as cultural border crossings. Who they were, what they did, and how they were perceived reveal shifting cultural identities and exchanges. For example, several of the players possessed no fixed Chinese or Chinese American identity. In 1914, the *Los Angeles Times* referred to pitcher Foster Hueng, whose real name was Foster Robinson, as a "big half caste." Several of the best players on the Hawaiian team were part-Hawaiian and part-Chinese—players such as Lang Akana and Buck Lai Tin. [55]

Clearly, the Hawaiian Travelers played baseball well. By and large, they succeeded on the basis of team speed, skilled fielding, and good pitching from the likes of Foster Robinson, Luck Yee, and Apau Kau, who pitched a no-hitter against Baylor in 1915 but, subsequently, died in action during World War I. A *Los Angeles Times* reporter pointed out, "I found that none of the Chinese depended much on their hitting. They seemed to have no special desire to make extra-base hits. Their idea of baseball is to get on first base; then get around the rest of the way by speed and skill." In other words, they demonstrated gifts in what baseball experts called then "inside baseball."[56]

As mentioned earlier, the Hawaiian ballplayers crossed racial and ethnic borders to play formidable African American nines such as the Chicago American Giants and the Taylor ABCs, based in Indianapolis. In 1912, however, a mainland wired story reported, "The color line has been drawn in a great many cases but this one may be tied, but not beaten. The Chinese baseball team that came over here with a great reputation was challenged by the Lincoln Giants of New York recently. The answer came back from the yellow boys that they drew the color line and would not mingle." Still, many Chinese Hawaiian ballplayers were quite used to playing against African Americans. On Oahu, black soldiers affiliated with the 25th regiment competed in baseball as well as other sports. And the 25th regiment nine vied with the elite Chinese Hawaiian teams for top spot in Honolulu baseball circles. The *Pacific Commercial Advertiser* described one 1915 game between the 25th and an "All-Chinese" nine as a "battle royal."[57]

In New York City, the Hawaiian Travelers wound up taking on the formidable Lincoln Giants on a regular basis. On September 16, 1915, for example, Chinese Hawaiian pitcher, Apau Kau, shut out the Giants, 5-0, before 7,000. The African American weekly, *New York Age,* claimed "the Orientals played a flashy brand of ball that kept the 7,000 fans on edge from start to finish."[58]

After the talented Chicago American Giants edged the Hawaiians in 1913, 3-2, the African America newspaper, the *Chicago Defender* insisted, "The Giants had easy pickings and played horse with the little men from the University of Hawaii." In 1916, the *Defender* reported that the Hawaiians barely lost 4-3 to the ABC's. The *Defender*, like the European American newspapers, expressed an ethnocentric amazement that the Hawaiians played baseball so well. It claimed that "some of the Chinese act like real ballplayers and there is no doubt that they like the game. They were caught on the bases several times by snappy throws, but appeared to know many of the American tricks."[59]

It was not an easy life for these Hawaiian ballplayers as they crisscrossed the Pacific and the American mainland. In 1914, the team encountered the Chinese Exclusion Law head on as the ballplayers were temporarily waylaid at the Angel Island's immigration detention center in the San Francisco Bay. Apparently, American officials doubted the citizenship of the Hawaiians who had to wait twenty-four hours before they were admitted into the United States. Writing in *Baseball Monthly,* Sing Hung Hoe responded with ambiguity to his encounters with the American mainland. He apparently agreed with many of those who watched the Hawaiians play on the mainland and considered them foreigners despite the fact that those players lived in a U.S. territory and were U.S. citizens. A son of Chinese immigrants, Hoe claimed he tired of some of the hardships of travel endured on the mainland—"eating 'quick order' dinners at crowded railroad stations and 'dog houses'…with many curious eyes staring." Yet Hoe appreciated "the sportsmanlike spirit exhibited by *American* college students and fans. (Italics added) He also declared he admired the speech of a "welcoming college president," who announced, "The Yellow Peril! We have seen it here this evening. That's the only kind of yellow peril that I know. Let Providence give us more of this kind."[60]

Because the Hawaiian Travelers fielded players of non-Chinese descent by 1914, a resentful Honolulu's Chinese community organized a very good team of players possessing Chinese ancestry, some of whom had previously played with the Travelers. In the spring of 1915, this team, sponsored by the Chinese Athletic Union (CAU), headed to Asia to play in China and the Philippines. One of the CAU team's stops was at the Far Eastern Athletic Association games, where it represented China in baseball. Indeed, the Chinese president, Yoan Shi-Kai reportedly donated five hundred dollars to help the Hawaiian team defray expenses for the transoceanic trip. The team was also financially supported by Chinese and non-Chinese Hawaiian business and community leaders who hoped the CAU ballplayers would ably promote Hawaii in East Asia. Among those who played for the CAU were Hoon Ki, a fine pitcher and son of Chinese immigrants and Kan Yen Chun, one of Hawai'i's best catchers and also a son of Chinese immigrants.[61]

The CAU nine played well. It won the Far Eastern Athletic Association championship and then proceeded to Manila. In the Philippines, the Chinese Hawaiian ballplayers impressed the American colonists. A correspondent for the *Manila Times* concluded, "Taken by and large, these Honolulu men are cool and brainy ball tossers. They are still young and there is no doubt but that with a little more experience in the game they will make wonderful players."[62]

One Chinese Hawaiian baseball player discovered racism's command of the cultural borders. In December, 1914, the Portland Beavers of the Pacific Coast League announced the signing of Lang Akana, a son of a Chinese immigrant father and a Native Hawaiian mother. In 1914 and, in fact, until major league baseball expanded to the Pacific Coast, the Pacific Coast League (PCL) was one of the best, if not the best, minor professional league in the United States. Thus, it was no small matter for Akana to lure the attention of Beavers' owner, Walter McCreadie.[63]

Actually, Akana was not the first Hawaiian to gain notice in the PCL. In 1907, the San Francisco Seals opened the season with Hawaiian Barney Joy on their pitching staff. Possessing part-indigenous Hawaiian ancestry, Joy was described in the press as a "husky brown-skinned lad." Joy was expected at the start of the season to not only pitch well, but draw fans curious to see one of America's colonial subjects playing baseball in America. Joy got off to a slow start. An early season illness prompted some of the press to wonder if Joy had the fortitude to pitch in the PCL. But after mid-summer he began to blow away the Seal opposition and, in the process, boost Seal attendance the year after the devastating earthquake. In September, 1907, the Boston Nationals signed Joy to a major league contract.[64]

The Boston Nationals' acquisition of Joy provoked racial controversy. According to a piece in the *Washington Post,* a significant portion of America's baseball world was convinced that Joy was a "colored pitcher"—that "the employment of this negro from Honolulu is like a match in a powder magazine." To be sure, the *Post* pointed out, Joy was racially "Malay" and not a "Negro." Nevertheless, he was as "dark as an Ethiopian" and many wondered if any of his big league teammates would room with the Hawaiian.[65]

It is not entirely clear why Barney Joy failed to officially don a Boston National uniform although perhaps his racial identify presented a quandary to his major league employers. We do know that he remained on the islands after 1907, although he was offered a chance to pitch for Spokane of the Pacific Northwest League in 1912. However, due to some kind of miscommunication between the Spokane management and Joy over transportation to the mainland, the Hawaiian failed to report to the Washington club and Joy never ventured across the Pacific again to play Organized Baseball.[66]

Pitcher John B. "Honolulu Johnnie" Williams made his pitching debut for the Sacramento Solons against the Vernon Tigers in 1911. After the game, Williams was sent down to pitch for the Victoria, B.C.'s professional nine for more seasoning. In 1912, Williams made the Solons on a permanent basis. Referring to his skin color, the *Sacramento Bee* called him "Dusky" Williams. Indeed, Williams did possess Hawaiian ancestry. He was a fairly good pitcher, who, at least, got what baseball lovers describe as a "cup of coffee" in the majors and, in the process, became the first Hawaiian big leaguer.[67]

In the process, however, Williams must have angered a few ballplayers back home when he joined the Detroit Tigers spring training camp in 1914. Like Joy, Williams proved a big attraction to fans and the press. E.A. Batcheldor of the *Detroit Free Press* interviewed Williams, who insisted that Hawaiian baseball was hurt by all of the Japanese and Chinese Hawaiian ballplayers. Williams admitted that many were talented. However, he claimed they were overly sensitive to criticism and were not interested in getting better. Moreover, Williams complained that Chinese and Japanese Hawaiians controlled the islands' labor market.[68]

Unlike Joy and Williams, Akana found it impossible to break into Organized Baseball. Some of the press, however, asserted little doubt that Akana deserved the opportunity. Roscoe Fawcett of the *Portland Oregonian* claimed Akana was a good outfielder. In referring to Akana as half-Native Hawaiian and half-Chinese, Fawcett wrote, "No ballplayer blending half portions of poi and chop suey ever before has embellished a professional diamond." Meanwhile, the *Los Angeles Times'* Henry Carr argued that the management of the Los Angeles PCL franchise should have signed Akana instead. Nevertheless, Akana encountered passionate opposition by many white players on PCL rosters. These players informed Walter McCreadie that Akana's skin was darker than Jack Johnson's and they threatened a boycott if Akana was not released. Johnson, a controversial African American Heavyweight champion, seemed to many European Americans overly enthusiastic about flaunting the color line. And for whites to compare Akana to Johnson echoed a time earlier in Chinese American history when the anti-Chinese movement consistently coupled Chinese with African

Americans. Sadly, McCreadie, while publicly regretting the existence of a color line in Organized Baseball, gave in and released Akana before the Hawaiian could put on a Portland Beaver uniform. Akana, however, survived. A product of a middle class home, Akena carved out a versatile career in Hawai'i as a Protestant minister, member of the Honolulu sheriff's department, and an executive with the Hawaiian Islanders Pacific Coast League team.[69]

Akana's teammate, Lai Tin, was somewhat more fortunate in terms of mainland baseball. He reportedly attracted the attention of the Chicago White Sox for the 1915 season. The *Washington Post* commented that if Lai Tin made the White Sox, "he will enjoy the unique honor of being the first Celestial to play on a National or American League team." Yet no evidence is available that Lai Tin even got a try out from Chicago's South Side club. After the 1916 Travelers' tour of the mainland, Lai Tin decided to remain on the mainland, substantially because he fell in love with a New York City woman by the name of Isabella Reynolds. In 1917, he played for semi-pro ball for the Brooklyn Bushwicks and the Upland nine in the Delaware Valley League. .In 1918, Lai Tin, now known as William Lai, got a try out invitation from the Philadelphia Phillies. He went to training camp with the Phillies and played some exhibition games for Philadelphia's National League entry. Lai played no official major leagues for the Phillies, but wound up playing four years of minor league baseball for Bridgeport of the Eastern League. The *Bridgeport Telegram* greeted Lai's initial appearance in an Eastern League uniform with what it no doubt considered as a compliment: "The chink displayed plenty of pepper and he didn't talk in Hong Kong either." [70]

Describing himself as racially Mongolian to his Philadelphia draft board in 1918, Lai remained with Bridgeport through the 1921 season, even though Ed Walsh, a hall of fame pitcher who managed Bridgeport in 1920 tried to drive the Chinese Hawaiian out of the league. Subsequently, Lai returned to the famed Bushwicks semi-pro club that played out of Brooklyn. At that time, he apparently caught the eye of John McGraw, who put the Hawaiian on the New York Giants spring training roster in 1928. An Associated Press article incorrectly declared when the New York Giants recruited Lai: "For the first time in history of the game, a Hawaiian may cavort about the infield of a major league club next summer." Lai could field, but seemingly could not hit to McGraw's satisfaction and was cut. According to the *New York Times*: "Buck Lai, the Chinaman, shows that he can field with the best of them, but his only claim to hitting prowess is his own assertion that he was the second best batter on the Bushwicks." [71]

Lai did not go quietly. McGraw wanted to send the Hawaiian to a minor league team in Little Rock. However, Lai did not relish the ideal of heading to

Arkansas. Acknowledging a prevailing stereotype about Chinese American male career choices, Lai insisted that he would "go in the laundry business first." Lai stuck around the Giants camp, with no apparent acrimony with McGraw resulting. Subsequently, Lai agreed to go to Newark of the International League.[72]

In the mid-1930s, Buck Lai led a team known of "Hawaiian All-Stars" through the small towns and big cities of the American mainland. When they arrived in Helena, Montana in 1936, the *Helena Independent* informed readers, "The greatest attraction to ever invade the United States will be seen here on Tuesday, May 26, when Buck Lai's Hawaiian All-Stars composed of the best players of the Hawaiian islands and made up of Chinese, Japanese, and Hawaiians."[73]

Two other Hawaiian Travelers, Vernon Ayau and Andy Yamashiro, played minor league baseball on the American mainland. Ayau, a talented shortstop, suited up briefly with the Seattle franchise of the Pacific Northwest League in 1917. Initially, Ayau's signing was treated as a joke by the press in the Pacific Northwest. However, Ayau convinced many that he was a "snappy little shortstop" and "about the fastest thing ever seen on a baseball diamond." Nevertheless, the managers of the Butte and Great Falls nines threatened to boycott Seattle if it kept Ayau on the roster. Seattle, however, wanted to give Ayau a try, hoping that a description of him as a "young Chinese <who> is a hard hitter and clever infielder and is certain of making good in organized baseball" was on the mark. Thus, according to the *Washington Post,* Ayau became "the first Chinese ball player to make his debut in organized baseball." However, Ayau's light hitting spelled doom for his professional career with Seattle, which let him go after a few weeks into the official season. Ayau, however, finished the Pacific Northwest League season with Tacoma.[74]

Across the country, the speedy outfielder and son of Japanese immigrants, Andy Yamashiro played in 1917 under the name of Andy Yim for Gettysburg of the Blue Ridge League. Previously, Yamashiro had played as a Yim for the Hawaiian Travelers. Undoubtedly, the team's management wanted to further the fiction that the Travelers composed an "All-Chinese" team. In any event, he joined former teammate Buck Lai on the Bridgeport team in 1918. Together, they made quite a hit with the *Bridgeport Telegram,* which commented that "the <t>wo Chinamen are l<e>ading players" The daily added that <w>ithout the Chinamen who are playing for Bridgeport the locals would not be in the running and the evidence needs no corroboration. The men with the almond eyes and the yellow skin are very near the entire works for Bridgeport team's in 1918." The next year, Yamashiro surfaced as an outfielder for the Eastern League's Hartford franchise, for which he played nineteen games [75]

Among other early Hawaiians of Asian Pacific descent who performed professionally on the mainland in the early 1900s were Frank Blukoi, a Hawaiian of apparently Filipino ancestry, who performed for the famed All Nations team and the Kansas City Monarchs from 1916 to 1920. A poster for a game between the All Nations' nine and the African American Indianapolis ABC's described Blukoi as "The Giant Hawaiian considered by critics to be the best 2nd baseman outside of Organized Base Ball." Among his teammates were the great Negro League pitchers, John Donaldson and Jose Mendez.[76]

During the early 1930s, Kenso Nushida was a left handed, semiprofessional pitcher in Central California. The Hawaiian born son of Japanese immigrants, he lived in Hawai'i for years and, as mentioned earlier, pitched on such teams as the Japanese Hawaiian All-Stars, which toured mainland communities in 1923. After moving to the mainland, Nushida found work as a farm laborer and store clerk in California's Central Valley. Stockton and continued to compete in a region that brimmed with Japanese American community baseball.[77]

In 1932, minor league baseball franchises were coping, but not always very well, with the Great Depression. Money for many families was too precious to spend on baseball games. The owner of the Sacramento Solons PCL team, Lew Moreing, wanted to put people in the seats of the franchise's ballpark. However, as the long PCL season went on, the Solons languished in mediocrity and attracted few fans.

Moreing, realizing his club was out of the running for a PCL pennant, decided to sign Kenso Nushida late in the summer of 1932. Nushida, Moreing hoped, would attract publicity and fans as a novelty. The fact that some of these fans would come from the Japanese American communities in and around Sacramento and Stockton did not seem to bother Moreing any more than Filipino prize fight fans bothered Great Depression boxing promoters. As it turned out, Nushida did garner Japanese American support in and around Sacramento and other PCL cities. When the Solons played in Los Angeles against the Los Angeles Angels, *Los Angeles Times* reporter Harry Williams noted that "there was a distinct saffron sheen reflected by the crowds and lights, perhaps a third of the crowd of 7,000 being Japanese out to see their countrymen do his stuff." Three large bouquets of chrysanthemums were presented to Nushida "by a pretty little Japanese sheba dolled up in a gay kimono."[78]

With little or no obvious intent on doing harm, therefore, European American press members such as Williams could represent Nushida and other people of Japanese descent as racialized aliens, as physically distinct, exotic, and perhaps not to be taken all that seriously. Interestingly, the 1932 Summer Olympics had just been held in Los Angeles. For the first time, Japan entered a team.

Meanwhile, many Americans and Europeans considered Japan a threat to "western" interests in East Asia and the Pacific. In an article on the American press's coverage of the 1932 Summer Olympics, David Welky points out that U.S. newspapers consistently referred to "little brown men" when depicting Japanese male athletes. Doing so, Welky argues, expressed a way for white Americans to diminish fear of the Japanese by contemplating the Asians' presumed lack of height. Of course, labels such as "diminutive" were not just applied to Japanese and Japanese American athletes by the sporting press. These labels were useful, nevertheless, in asserting consciously or unconsciously the supremacy of frequently larger, white athletes and by extension those who identified themselves as white.[79]

Nushida, consequently, was constantly depicted as singularly small. Indeed, Nushida was short—much closer to five feet than six feet in height. Thus, Harry Williams may not have been deliberately bigoted when he called Nushida the "Tom Thumb of baseball" and joked that "Moreing has a warehouse up in Sacramento said to contain 2,000 tons of rice. Nushida, who is not much bigger than a mouse, can burrow into the rice next winter and live happily until spring." Williams, however, in his own way reinforced the racial borders that had been constructed between people of Asian Pacific and European ancestries.[80]

Admittedly, Nushida was not a great professional pitcher, but he ought to have been considered as more than just a curiosity. One of his teammates, Paul Vinci, claimed Nushida "is one of the smartest pitchers he has ever seen." Nushida apparently commanded good control and a clever assortment of curve balls.[81]

In September, 1932, the PCL Oakland Oaks signed Lee Gum Hong, a pitching star for the Chinese American Wa Sung nine, an outstanding high school pitcher in Oakland, and an employee of the International House near the University of California, Berkeley, campus. Like the Solons, the Oaks were going nowhere in the PCL pennant race and looked forward to any kind of boost in the attendance at their home park. Immediately upon Hong joining the Oaks, Eddie Murphy of the *Oakland Tribune* announced that his pitching debut would take place in Oakland against Nushida and the Solons. Murphy, moreover, claimed that Hong's signing had caused a great deal of rejoicing in San Francisco and Oakland's Chinese American communities.[82]

The Nushida-Hong duel occurred while Japan and China engaged in a violent conflict over Manchuria; a conflict that Americans of Japanese and Chinese descent could not easily ignore and over which they frequently expressed bitter partisanship. Despite the bloodshed resulting from Chinese and Japanese warfare, Nushida's and Hong's PCL employers and the Bay Area sporting press seemed willing to transform an international tragedy into entertainment and profits. A headline to an article written by Eddie Murphy read: "Japan vs. China in a Pitching Duel at the Oakland Coast League Park." Murphy's article announced that local Japanese Americans and Chinese Americans were expected to show up in impressive numbers to see the "first Oriental duel in organized ball." The Wa Sung club, moreover, had purchased one hundred tickets in order to support Hong, who was curiously known in Bay Area bush league circles Al Bowen.[83]

Indeed, Nushida and Hong, as well as some of the people with whom they shared their ethnic experiences seemed willing to allow Asian warfare to become sporting spectacle. Baseball historian, Yoichi Nagata, quotes Hong before he took the mound against Nushida as declaring, "This is a battle of nations. I represent China. Nushida represents Japan. And China shall win."[84]

Eddie Murphy announced that 3,000 fans paid to watch Lee Gum Hong matched against Nushida. Murphy reported that among those in attendance were a notable number of Chinese Americans who "used up a good supply of fireworks in letting " Lee Gum Hong know "that they approved of his work." As it turned out neither pitcher performed well. Nushida tired after a little over four innings, but Lee Gum Hong wound up losing the game, 7-5. Four days later, Nushida and Lee Gum Hong were opposed again in the second game of a double header ending the 1932 season. The Oakland pitcher won this time, 7-1. Interestingly, neither Hong nor Nushida wore PCL uniforms again, although *Honolulu Advertiser* sports columnist William Peet insisted that Nushida did draw well for the Solons.[85]

A few years later, the Sacramento Solons signed another player with a Japanese Hawaiian background. Fumito "Jimmy" Horio had been competing in California semi-professional circles for awhile before going to Sioux Falls, Iowa in 1934. In Iowa, Horio played Class D minor league ball—the lowest level of organized professional baseball at that time. Horio did all right. His batting average was an adequate .282 in 148 games. Horio's next stop was Tokyo, where he joined the newly formed Tokyo Giants. During the spring of 1935, the Tokyo Giants traveled to the U.S. mainland where they played the Solons in a series of games. The Solons were impressed enough with Horio to tender him a contract offer and he joined the PCL club once the Giants ended their tour in June. While finishing the season, Horio rode the bench as a reserve outfielder and did not rejoin the Solons in 1936. [86]

In 1931, the Seals suited up "Prince" Henry Kauhane Oana, a Hawaiian of indigenous and Portuguese ancestry. Oana joined the Seals' organization in 1929. After a brief stint with the San Francisco club, the Seals sent Oana down to the Arizona State League for more seasoning. By 1931, the Hawaiian had become a fixture in the Seal line-up. An outfielder possessing speed and power,

Oana slugged twenty-three home runs and hit an impressive .345 in 1931. The Seals could not have won the Pacific Coast League championship that year without him. Oana played a bit in the major leagues as an outfielder for the Philadelphia Phillies. He even pitched for the Detroit Tigers during World War II. Although he had some good moments, Oana was admittedly not a great major league pitcher for the Tigers. Still in 1946, the "handsome Hawaiian," according to the press, won twenty-three games for the Texas League's Dallas Rebels. What is more the thirty-six year old veteran garnered the Texas League's pitcher of the year award. Subsequently, Oana managed a minor league team in Austin and his last season was with Texarkana of the Big State League in 1951.[87]

Two other Hawaiians attracted interest from American Organized Baseball in the 1930s. In 1933, the St. Louis Cardinals invited Hawaiian Ted Nobriega to its spring training camp. Possessing Portuguese and indigenous descent, Nobriega was called "a genuine Hawaiian ukulele" by the *Sporting News*. Nobriega hoped to stick with the Cardinals as a pitcher but was farmed out by the St. Louis club. In 1935, John Kerr was signed by the Phillies as a pitcher. Nevertheless, in the spring of 1936, Kerr unsuccessfully tried out for the San Francisco Seals.[88]

After World War II, a Filipino American, Bobby Balcena, carved out a noteworthy career in Organized Baseball. Born in San Pedro, California, Balcena was a rarity given the paucity of Filipino females or Pinays living on the U.S. mainland before World War II. In short, both of Balcena's parents were Filipino immigrants.[89]

After a stint in the navy during the waning years of World War II, Balcena was originally signed by the St. Louis Browns of the American League. He started his career with Mexicali of the Sunset League and pushed up the minor league ladder to the Seattle Pilots of the Pacific Coast League. In 1952, fans of the San Antonio Texas League club voted Balcena's the team's most popular player. Meanwhile, the St. Louis Browns moved to Baltimore and became the Orioles and in 1954, the American League franchise invited Balcena to a spring training camp, only to send him down to the minors. Arriving in Seattle in 1955, Balcena had to fight for a permanent job. Called the "Filipino flyer" by the *Seattle Post-Intelligencer's* Paul Rossi, Balcena's bat and speed launched him toward PCL stardom. He also became fan favorite. Seattle's relatively sizable Filipino American population especially latched on to Balcena. Sportswriter Royal Brougham wrote, "Shrill-voiced Filipino fans are noisiest of all sports followers and if you hear an earpiercing whoop at your elbow at the ball park, it will be a dark-skinned rooter cheering for Bob Balcena, the boy with the bolo punch at the plate who is leading the hitters." At 5 ft. 7 and 160 pounds one would not expect Balcena to display much home run punch, but he hit fifteen homers for

Seattle in 1956 and respectably batted in the high .200s. Accordingly, toward the end of the 1956 season, Balcena was called up to play for the Cincinnati Red-legs. The press noted that "Balcena is believed to be the first Filipino to reach the major leagues." Balcena got into seven games, mostly it would seem as a pinch runner or substitute fielder. He got no hits in two official at bats.[90]

Balcena failed to make the Redlegs opening day roster in 1957 and never returned to the major leagues, although he lasted five more years in the minors. Among the franchises he played for was the Hawaii Islanders PCL team. Apparently, the Islanders wanted the veteran outfielder because they hoped he would appeal to potential Filipino Hawaiian customers. Balcena died in the 1990s, virtually unknown as a Filipino American pioneer in professional baseball.[91]

Several players of Asian Pacific Islander ancestry played Organized Baseball after World War II. Hank Matsubu, Jiro Nakamura, and George Fujioka were California Leaguers. Indeed, Matsubu and Nakamura formed the first "all-Nisei" battery in Organized Baseball. Bill Shundo played in the Arizona-Texas League, while Percy Ching appeared for the New Mexico-Texas league.[92]

In 1956, the American mainland press announced that an "astonished baseball world" learned that Brooklyn Dodgers had signed Bill Nishita and assigned the Hawaiian to the Triple A Montreal Royals. The Dodgers had invited Nishita to spring training and he responded with promising pitching performances. Joining Nishita in minor league baseball in the 1950s was Jack Ladro, a Hawaiian of Filipino and Portuguese descent, who played in the New York Yankees chain.[93]

While he did not gain fame in U.S. professional baseball, Hawaiian Nisei, Henry Tadashi "Bozo" Wakabayashi deserves mention. Born on Oahu, Wakabayashi headed eastward in the 1930s to attend Hosei University in Tokyo. At Hosei, Wakabayashi pitched his team to two league championships. In 1936, Wakabayashi joined the professional Hanshin Tigers. He eventually became one of the best pitchers in the as yet youthful Japanese major leagues. After sixteen years, Wakabayashi won 243 games and lost 141, while achieving an impressive E.R.A. of 1.99. Subsequently, Wakabayashi became the first Nisei elected to the Japanese baseball hall of fame.[94]

The second Nisei to receive such an honor was Wally Yonamine. Born on Maui, Yonamine surfaced from World War II as one of the greatest Hawaiian athletes of all time. A son of an Okinawan father and a Japanese mother, Yonamine, as we will explore in the next chapter, was as well an excellent football player, who competed with the San Francisco 49ers in 1947. Meanwhile, Yonamine continued to play ball on various island teams such as the Athletics, which had previously been the Asahis. In February, 1950, Yonamine tried out for the San Francisco Seals. At that time, the Seals' manager was Frank "Lefty" O'Doul, a long-time supporter of developing baseball ties between the United States and Japan.

Joining Yonamine at the Seals spring training camp was Herman Wedemeyer, the most famous Hawaiian athlete since the emergence of the great
swimmer and surfer, Duke Kahanamoku. Possessing mixed ethnic ancestry,
Wedemeyer was an All-American halfback and a fine outfielder at Saint.Mary's
of Moraga, California. He had tried his hand at a pro football career, but that
career was flagging and he decided to give pro baseball a try.[95]

Interestingly, both Yonamine and Wedemeyer were identified in the San
Francisco press as representing a "hang loose" Hawaiian ethnicity. The *San
Francisco Chronicle* declared that "Wedemeyer and Yonamine...reported <to
the Seals' camp> wearing aloha shirts, looking cool and confident as they began
the job of making the varsity." Wedemeyer failed to persuade O'Doul that he
was ready to hit PCL pitching. The magnificent Hawaiian athlete wound up
journeying through the lower levels of the minor leagues in 1950. Yonamine,
according to the *San Francisco News*'s Roger Williams, "impressed O'Doul
with his all around play. Wally really shines with his throwing, fielding, and
hitting." O'Doul "particularly likes his deft sliding ability." Nevertheless, Williams predicted that the Seals would send Yonamine down to the lower divisions
of minor league ball."[96]

According to John Olds, who reported on the Pacific Coast League for the
Sporting News, O'Doul considered Yonamine "one of the most impressive roo-
kies in the camp." Olds claimed that the Seal manager believed "Wally has a
perfect swing and great power." Still, Roger Williams was right. The man Olds
called "the squat Hawaiian-Japanese left-handed hitting outfielder" would not
make the Seals' opening day roster.[97]

Indeed, the Seals sent Yonamine to Salt Lake City of the Pioneer League.
There, he achieved an outstanding .335 batting average, prompting a Brooklyn
Dodger pitcher and one time Pioneer Leaguer to claim in 1953 that the best hitter he ever saw was "Y-A-N-A-M-I-N-I, maybe. He's a Jap." Yonamine, moreover, proved a big hit with the Pioneers' management. Team owner Bert Dunne
hoped that Yonamine could climb up Organized Baseball's ladder at least as far
as the Seals. Cold War America, as well as Yonamine, would benefit: "Wally
Yonamine may prove to be an American 'secret weapon' in the ideological tug-
of-war for Japan...The sight of Wally Yonamine playing for the Seals in a tour
of Japan will prove to the Japanese people that racial democracy works in the
United States."[98]

O'Doul, however, thought Yonamine's chances of making it to the American big leagues were limited because of a relatively weak throwing arm. Yonamine recalled that he was not enthusiastic about making Utah his permanent
baseball home nor spending the rest of his professional career in the American
minor leagues. Lefty O'Doul, fortunately, advised the Tokyo Giants to sign Yonamine. The Giants pursued Yonamine for over a year. They were willing to
offer him a signing bonus of $3000 and $300 a month in addition to room and

board. This was a good salary by Japanese major league standards at the time and the Hawaiian, subsequently, braved the doubts of ethnocentric Japanese baseball fans and joined the Giants in 1951. [99]

Yonamine batted .354 as a Japanese major league rookie in 1951. But at first life was admittedly not easy for the Hawaiian. Yonamine could not speak Japanese and required an interpreter. A diet of Japanese food did not initially sit well with him. Moreover, Yonamine had to overcome dubious and often overtly hostile Japanese baseball supporters, who feared that the American would have a bad influence on Japanese baseball. We should, of course, remember that just six years earlier, Japan was engaged in a bitter war with the United States. The wounds left by the war throughout the Pacific Basin were not easily healed. And unlike American mainlanders, the Japanese were quite willing to extend the category of American to non-haole and even Nisei Hawaiians such as Yonamine. Culture and nationality rather than racial uniform seemed to stigmatize Yonamine in the eyes of many Japanese fans. Indeed, it took a month for the Japanese government to clear Yonamine's entry into Japan in the spring of 1951. [100]

What perhaps made matters worse for Yonamine was that he signed to play for the Tokyo Giants, Japan's oldest and most beloved professional team. Yonamine, in fact, fearlessly confirmed the prejudices of some Japanese baseball supporters by running out sacrifice bunts and knocking down infielders in order to break up double plays. In short, he played in Japan with the aggressiveness and individualism associated with the American style of baseball. Yonamine recognized that at least in the beginning a good many Japanese fans hated him. He remarked in 1953, "They disliked me intensely when I came because I was Nisei and American...The irony was that they grew to really like me because I played like one." [101]

For several years, the left-handed batting and throwing Yonamine roamed center field and as a swift spray hitter led off the Tokyo Giants batting order. Indeed, many still consider Yonamine the best leadoff hitter in Japanese baseball history. Famous teammates such as Sadaharu Oh became his biggest fans. Japan's greatest home run hitter refers to Yonamine as his mentor in baseball. Oh, who once played with Yonamine on the Giants, claims in his autobiography that he still cherishes the autograph given to him as a teen-ager by the Hawaiian. Yonamine, according to Oh, taught him and other Japanese big leaguers the value of aggressive base running, which meant kicking the ball out of the hands of infielders, breaking up double plays, hook sliding, and, in particular, stealing bases. Nevertheless, according to Oh, some Japanese baseball fans took a dim view of Yonamine's combative style of play. [102]

Yonamine's hitting also merited a great deal of scrutiny by Japanese major leaguers. During his playing career, Yonamine won three batting titles in 1954, 1956, and 1957 and retired with a .311 lifetime average. The fact that Yonamine varied his batting stance according to the situation and used the bunt is widely credited with greatly changing the way Japanese batters approached the difficult art of hitting a pitched baseball consistently.[103]

Typically a modest man, Yonamine, according to sportswriter Jerry Izenberg, could not help but think he would transform Japanese baseball in the 1950s. In 1953, he declared:

> I think…I can just about lead this league in doubles and triples for as long as I play. They throw sidearm from the outfield. It's like they are begging me to take an extra base and I do. The pitching? These managers have their guys throwing in the bullpen every day. By the time their turn in the rotation comes along. It's like they are coming off four straight days as a starting pitcher.[104]

While he earned a great deal of respect, popularity and an MVP award in Japan, Yonamine could not wipe away every last vestige of ethnocentricism in Japanese baseball any more than Jackie Robinson totally erased racism in American baseball. In 1961, Yonamine possessed the highest lifetime batting average of anyone in Japanese major league history. This apparently bothered Giant teammate Tetsuharu Kawakami, who was called "The God of Batting." A fervent Japanese nationalist, Kawakami became the Giant manager in 1961 and promptly released Yonamine, who then finished his playing career with the Chunichi Dragons. Sadly, after retiring as a player in 1962, Yonamine's lifetime average had slipped two points below Kawakami's.[105]

Yonamine remained in Japan to coach and manage in the Japanese major leagues. Indeed, Yonamine managed the Chunichi Dragons to the Japanese World Series. In doing so, he became the first non-Japanese citizen to manage a team in the Japanese World Series. What made this pennant particularly sweet was that it was won at the expense of Kawakami's Giants. In 1988, Yonamine retired from Japanese Major League baseball. Subsequently, he earned entrance into the Japanese Baseball Hall of Fame, although the Hawaiian feared that bigotry on the part of Japanese voters kept him from waiting until the second year of eligibility. Throughout a long career in Japanese major league baseball, Yonamine claimed that he returned to Hawai'i after each season. He would look around his old home in Maui and not see what tourists typically see. He would see a place of hard work, rarely rewarded with what it deserved. He would think about cutting sugar for a lifetime and swear he would do better when the next baseball season rolled around. Meanwhile, Yonamine won distinction as both a Hawaiian and Japanese sports hero. In the late 1990s, the Japanese government recognized Yonamine's contributions to Japanese sports with an award, while Governor Ben Cayetano of Hawai'i appointed Yonamine as a special advisor for sports promotion. Yonamine's major assignment was to travel to Japan in order to persuade Japanese major league teams to spring train on the Hawaiian Islands

then suffering from severe economic problems. Paid but a dollar a year, Yonamine declared, "I just want to do something good for Hawaii." [106]

Catcher Jyun Hirota was another versatile athlete from Hawai'i. A fine
football player, Hirota was a backfield star for the University of Hawai'i eleven
after World War II. In the 1950s, Hirota played with Yonamine on the Tokyo
Giants. Baseball historians Nagata and Holway relate a story about a team of
Japanese Major League All-Stars hosting the touring New York Giants. The
New York club was then managed by the famous Leo Durocher, who, while
coaching base runners from third base, decided to just vocally tell runners when
to steal bases rather than hand-signal them. Durocher assumed that none of the
all-stars would understand his commands in English. However, an exasperated
Durocher found the all-star catcher consistently throwing out New York Giant
base runners. But since that catcher was the Hawaiian born Hirota, Durocher
should not have been so surprised. Indeed, Yonamine, as well, was on the team.
Hirota later coached the University of Hawai'i baseball team. [107]

Besides Wakabayashi, Yonomine, and Hirota, other Japanese Americans
competed in professional baseball in Japan. Before World War II, Hawaiian
Japanese such as Yoshio Tanaka and Ted Kameda played in the Japanese big
leagues, as did mainlanders George Matsura and Sammy Takahashi. After
World War II, Bill Nishita, George Fujishige, Andy Miyamoto, Douglas Matsuoka, Dick Kashiwaeda, Howard and Harvey Zenimura, Stan Hashimoto, Fibber
Hirayama, Eddie Takei, and Carlton Hanta became Japanese major leaguers. [108]

In 1959, Fibber Hirayama was the subject of a thoughtful piece written by
Mark Harris for *Sports Illustrated.* A relatively well known writer who has
penned several fine novels concerning major league baseball, Harris traced Hirayama's baseball career from the World War II concentration camps to his
transformative impact on the Hiroshima Carps. Harris depicted Hirayama as a
cultural bridge between the United States and a still wore-torn Japan. He asserted, "In the person of Fibber Hirayama, whose ancestry is Japanese, whose
techniques are American and who contains in fine balance within himself his
double heritage, the humiliated but emerging city of Hiroshima glimpses the
ideal fusion of West with East." Hirayama's aggressiveness and egalitarianism
shaped by mid-twentieth century American culture, Harris seemed to claim,
altered the conservative and authoritarian personality of the Hiroshima Carp
franchise. [109]

A handful of Asian Pacific Americans made it into the American big leagues in the last decades of the twentieth century. Tolia "Tony" Solaita was a
power hitting first baseman in the 1970s for the Kansas City Royals among other teams. Solaita, moreover, spent a year with the Japanese major league Nippon
Ham Fighters. Solaita was born in American Samoa and was tragically murdered there in the early 1980s. After a brilliant career pitching for the University
of Nebraska, Ryan Kurosaki became the first Japanese American to pitch major

league baseball in the United States. In 1975, the graduate of Honolulu's Kalani High School, appeared twelve games in relief for the St. Louis Cardinals. Lenn Sakata is a Honolulu-born Japanese American. After starring for Gonzaga University in Washington, Sakata became a well-respected utility infielder for the Baltimore Orioles. While with the Orioles, Sakata was the first Asian Pacific American to play in the American World Series. In all, Sakata played eleven years in the American League for the New York Yankees and Oakland Athletics, as well as the Orioles. Subsequently, Sakata coached and managed professional baseball in Japan and the U.S. While Sakata managed the California League San Jose Giants in the early 2000s, Ethen Leiser wrote in *Asian Week,* "He's a player's manager with emotions always kept in check. It has to be that way. Otherwise, in this up-and-down world of professional baseball, Sakata's hair might turn Christmas white." Mike Lum was also born in Honolulu. Possessing Japanese ancestry but the adopted son of Chinese Hawaiians, Lum appeared in a big league uniform for several years in the 1960s and 1970s. Lum, subsequently, became a hitting instructor for teams such as the Chicago White Sox. Possessing indigenous Hawaiian ancestry, Milt Wilcox had some fine years as a pitcher in the 1970s and 1980s. Attlee Hammaker was a sometimes very effective left-handed pitcher for the San Francisco Giants in the 1980s. His mother was Japanese and his father was European American. The Hawaiian born Ron Darling first attracted national attention as a pitching star on the Yale University baseball team. There have not been many Yale students who went on to big league stardom. Darling was no superstar, but he pitched several years with the New York Mets in the 1980s and had some fine seasons. He was especially known as a superb athlete who could field his position as well as pitch. Lesser known major leaguers of Asian Pacific Islander descent include Don Wakamatsu who played briefly for the Chicago White Sox in 1991 and, subsequently, coached in the big leagues. [110]

Wendell Kim never played big league baseball, but deserves some attention as the first Korean American to wear a major league uniform. Born in poverty in Honolulu and reputedly abused by his father, boxer Philip Kim, Wendell Kim grew up in a tough Los Angeles neighborhood. His baseball skill attracted major league scouts and he wound up playing several years in the San Francisco Giants minor league organization. Kim later went on to coach and manage Giant-operated minor league clubs, before several years of coaching third base for the San Francisco Giants. After leaving the Giants, he became a third base coach for the Boston Red Sox and the Chicago Cubs. [111]

Laurie Gouthro and Shelly Uwaine also deserve some mention. A fine all around athlete, Gouthro is a Filipino American who starred in softball at Florida Community College and the University of South Florida. Gouthro also became a member of the Colorado Silver Bullets, a professional women's baseball team that toured the United States in the mid-1990s. In 1997, a professional women's baseball league operated on the Pacific Coast. Playing shortstop for the San Jose Spitfires was Hawaiian Shelly Uwaine.[112]

Crossing Foul Lines, Crossing Borders

Asian Pacific American ballplayers showed they could compete with and against some of the best ballplayers around. In 1924, Asahi standout Earl Tagahara was chosen to play for the San Jose All-Stars against the Pittsburgh Pirates, who were then training in San Jose. Jack Graham, a *San Jose Mercury* sportswriter, declared that Tagahara was "the Japanese wiz boy." His "fleetness of foot and sureness cannot be excelled. He is also a terrific pitcher and the populace will be given a chance to see this little lad in action." During the game, Tagahara got one hit out of three at bats, scored a run, and apparently made some fine catches. Three years later, the great Babe Ruth and Lou Gehrig led barnstorming teams into California. While they were in Fresno, they faced a group of local all stars, which included Japanese American players such as Harvey Iwata, Johnny Nakagawa, and Kenichi Zenimura. Just north of San Jose, Russell Hinaga captained and Harry Kuwata took center field for the Milpitas town team in 1930. In the 1930s, Wa Sung luminary Allie Wong performed in an all-star game consisting of some of very good Bay Area professionals, some of whom performed in the PCL and the major leagues.[113]

Since the early 1900s, schools on the American mainland fielded teams with Asian Pacific American players. In 1908, the *Los Angeles Times* noted that Henry Pan Hoe, a "Chinese Baseball Wonder" from Hawai'i captained the Pomona Prep School team. William Achi, a "native of Hawaii," caught for both Stanford and the University of Chicago. A Hawaiian of indigenous ancestry, Jack Desha competed for Harvard in 1911. Raised in Hawai'i, Chor Ou played baseball for Western High School in Washington, D.C., in 1914. In the mid-1910s, Los Angeles High School had a player described by the *Los Angeles Times* as "Sangi...the Japanese...pitcher." A decade later, a young man named Earl Tanaka not only played for Occidental College, but captained the team. One of the Occidental players volunteered the information that "T...may be yellow on the outside...but he is white on the inside." Victor Wong played for Belmont High School in Los Angeles, while George Tong starred at baseball for Lincoln High School in Los Angeles and then suited up for the University of Southern California. A Japanese Hawaiian, Bert Itoga, played for the University of Kansas in the early 1930s. In Southern California, UCLA suited up Otani and Okura in 1931. In the mid-1930s, Kiyoshi Nogami lettered in baseball for the University of California. And shortly before Japanese Americans were evacuated from places like San Jose, Tom Okagai played second base for San Jose High School.[114]

In Arizona during the late 1930s, Bill Kajikawa starred on the Arizona State baseball and football teams. In 1940, Kajikawa coached his alma mater's baseball team. After fighting for the 442nd in World War II, Kajikawa returned stateside to continue to coach the Arizona State baseball team. In 1947, he conducted a baseball school sponsored by the Brooklyn Dodgers.[115]

In New York City, William (Buck) Lai, Jr., became a fine outfielder for Long Island University (LIU) in the late 1930s and early 1940s. The son of the great Chinese Hawaiian player, Lai played on his father's Hawaiian All-Star teams before he headed for LIU. After serving in World War II, Lai ultimately coached the LIU baseball team and wrote a popular instructional book on baseball while coaching and scouting for the Brooklyn Dodger organization. Beyond the baseball diamond, Lai also served LIU as a basketball coach, athletic director, physical education department chair, and provost. In 2001, Lai was chosen for the LIU Sports Hall of Fame.[116]

During World War II, Asian Pacific Americans, including Japanese Americans, played with non-Asian Pacific Americans. Before evacuation, Kay Kiyokawa pitched for Oregon State. Thanks to a Quaker sponsored program, Kiyokawa left the West Coast for the University of Connecticut, for which he played baseball during the war. Keo Nakama, the great Hawaiian swimmer, was also a good ballplayer who played for Ohio State. And in St. Louis, George Shimizu pitched for Washington University.[117]

Like the little hero of *Baseball Saved Us*, Asian Pacific ballplayers competed with and against non-Asian Pacific ballplayers after World War II. In 1946, Tetsu Kaneko played for Inglewood High School in Los Angeles and Shig Tachibana starred as a pitcher for Mountain View High School in the San Francisco Bay Area. In 1947, two San Jose Zebra stars, George Hinaga and Babe Nomura, played with non-Japanese Americans on the Southside Market Nine.[118]

Fresno State College featured talented Asian Pacific American ballplayers after World War II. Fibber Hirayama was a speedy outfielder for Fresno State. When the California nine visited Hawai'i, the five foot three inch outfielder threw out a runner going home from third. Wallace Hirai, a Honolulu sportswriter, claimed that only Joe Dimaggio had made such a throw from the outfield in the twenty-five year history of the Honolulu Stadium. Howard Zenimura was Fibber's Fresno State teammate. Zenimura batted an impressive .412 for the Bulldogs in 1949.[119]

Hawaiian Bill Nishita was just one of several fine Asian Pacific Americans who played high school and college baseball in the 1950s, 1960s, and 1970s. In the early 1950s, Nishita pitched for Santa Rosa Junior College and the University of California, Berkeley, while left-handed Peter Higuchi hurled for the Yale University nine and Tommy Ogaki played for San Jose State. Catching Nishita at Santa Rosa was fellow Japanese Hawaiian, George Fujishige. At USC, Chinese Hawaiian Charley Ane not only starred as a lineman on the football team but also stood out as a pitcher. In Massachusetts, Japanese Hawaiian, Henry Tominaga, was an ace pitcher for Springfield College. In 1956, Maka Tashima played for Coalinga Junior College, which won the Northern California Junior College championship. In the late 1960s, Eugene and Frank Tom suited up for Galileo High School in San Francisco. In 1973, Jack Suguwara starred as a pitcher for George Washington High School in San Francisco. Also in the 1970s, Bob Uemoto was a catcher for Oregon State, David Fukumoto was a catcher for Whittier College in Southern California, and Dave Kitamura starred on the Colorado State University nine as a shortstop. A few years later, Japanese Hawaiian Glen Goya became the first person of his ethnic background to win the Division I batting crown while suiting up for Colorado State. Meanwhile, Bob Shigematsu, a former Fresno State baseball player, became the first Nisei to be named an All-American softball player by the International Softball Congress.[120]

In Hawai'i, Asian Pacific ballplayers did not find it strange to compete with and against players identified with other racial and ethnic groups. In 1908, the *San Jose Mercury* reported that the Diamond Head team consisted of a shortstop named Sing Cong. In 1912, an All-Honolulu team beat an All-Maui nine. Barney Joy pitched for the winners while talented Japanese American standout Andy Yamashiro was stationed in center field. Three years later, an All-Oahu nine defeated the All-Chinese with Lang Akana, Barney Joy, and Andy Yamashiro in the line-up. In indoor baseball, the Palama Settlement House team included in 1914 players such as Hong Chang, Hong Kee, Tom Moriyama, Foo Yan, and Bung Chong.[121]

Over time some of Hawai'i's top clubs consisted of players of diverse racial and ethnic ancestries. There were plantation-sponsored nines that had Native Hawaiians, Japanese Hawaiians, a handful of African Americans, and, according to old time Negro Leaguer, Newt Allen, "quite a few Koreans." While playing in Hawai'i before World War II, Allen and another African American star, "Bullet" Rogan, were apparently offered jobs checking crates for Dole Pineapple if they would but play for the company nine on Saturday and Sunday. Company teams, claimed Allen, would split gate money at season's end. Baseball, therefore, offered little wealth for culturally diverse players in Hawai'i, but it seemed to furnish a chance to climb a few rungs up the economic ladder.[122]

Young Hawaiian women also transcended racial and ethnic borders to play baseball. Eleanor Heavey, a woman of indigenous Hawaiian, English, and Chinese ancestry recalled in the late 1970s that she played "hardball" as a youth living in the working class Kakaako district of Honolulu in the 1920s. On her team were Native Hawaiians, as well as Chinese Hawaiians. She declared that there were about four or five such teams in Kakaako alone.[123]

During and after World War II, baseball continued to furnish opportunities for Hawaiians to cross racial and ethnic lines. The onset of World War II did not

dim Hawaiians' passion for baseball. In 1941, noted correspondent Bob Considine maintained, "There is probably more baseball here per capita than anywhere on the mainland." Hawai'i, Considine wrote, harbored a "bewildering
number of leagues." After the attack on Pearl Harbor, William De Fossett
joined many U.S. servicemen and women stationed on the islands. A former
Negro Leaguer, De Fossett and his brother Joe played on an integrated semi-pro
team representing Aiea, a community on the outskirts of Honolulu. Native Hawaiians, whites, and Japanese Americans played on the team. A haole owned the
club, while a Native Hawaiian managed it. The coach was a Japanese American.
Before, during, and after World War II, Filipino American Crispin Mancao
pitched for a variety of Hawaiian teams, possessing diverse rosters. The largely
Nisei Rural Red Sox was one of the teams that made use of Mancao's services.
In 1961, he pitched briefly for the Hawaii Islanders of the PCL. In 1948, a Hawaiian all-star team was organized to tour the mainland. One of the organizers'
goals was to boost Hawaiian statehood. Everywhere the team went, members
apparently rendered Hawaiian songs and presented leis to their opponents. One
of its stars was Jyun Hirota, but it featured a line-up comprised of players such
as Crispin Mancao, Lefty Higuchi, Larry Kamishima, and Jun Muramoto.
Among the nines it opposed was the Harlem Globetrotters' baseball team. Jun
Muramoto remembered, "It was a dream come true...We played a lot of baseball
in small cities as well as major league parks." About the same time, a Hawaiian
female softball team called the Singapore All-Stars barnstormed the mainland,
while multi-racial, multi-ethnic Hawaiian women played a variation on baseball
called jungle ball.[124]

In the mid-1950s, a culturally diverse team of Hawaiians appeared in Mil-
waukee to represent the Islands in the Global World Series. Larry Kunihisa managed the team, which was comprised of "Cris Mancao, diminutive Hawaiian
pitcher," Sal Kaulukukui, who led the series in RBI's, and Vic Mori, who
slugged two triples.[125]

The University of Hawai'i has been represented by culturally diverse base-
ball and, more recently, female softball teams. The Rainbow baseball nines have
developed fine players over the years, including Tommy and Sal Kaulukukui,
Jyun Hirota, Stan Hashimoto, Colin Tanabe, Eric Tokunaga, Franz Yuen, and
Derek Tatsuno. Paul Ah Yat, whose full name is Paul Anthony Papalekaimanu
Ah Yat starred for the Rainbows before inking a professional contract with the
Pittsburgh Pirates. Tommy Kaulukukui coached the University of Hawai'i nine
as did Toku Tanaka, Jimmy Asato, Dr. Tom Ige, Henry Tominaga, and Jyun
Hirota. Les Murakami coached the University of Hawai'i baseball team for more
than twenty-five years during the last decades of the twentieth century. In 1981,
Murakami won the Lefty Gomez Award for outstanding contributions to amateur baseball. In 1986, the NCAA named him district coach of the year, while
the Western Athletic Conference (WAC) selected Murakami as its coach of the

year in 1987 and 1991. In 1999, the American Baseball Coaches Hall of Fame honored Murakami as a member. [126]

Other Hawaiian universities and colleges have been represented by Asian Pacific American baseball and softball standouts. Joey Estrella, a former University of Hawai'i star of Japanese ancestry, coached for the University of Hawai'i, Hilo, for many years in the late 1900s and early 2000s. Many fine Asian Pacific American athletes played for Estrella—young men such as Lance Suyama, Guy Oshiro, Kaha Wong, Keith Yasui, Lance Fukumitsu, Joe Arakaki, and Eric Tangawa, Hawaii Pacific University has suited up Ben Agbayani, who played major league baseball for the News York Mets, as well as hired Asian Pacific American baseball coaches such as Allen Sato and Pat Kuniyoshi. [127]

Meanwhile, mainland colleges and universities recruited Hawaiian ballplayers. The University of San Francisco (USF), for example, has not been known as a collegiate baseball powerhouse. In the late 1990s, nevertheless, several Hawaiian ballplayers made their way across the Pacific to the USF campus. According to a 1998 article in the *San Francisco Chronicle*, USF's hiring of Chad Konishi as an assistant coach was crucial in forging a Pacific link between USF and the Hawaiian islands. A Hawaiian who pitched for the University of California and subsequently served as an assistant coach for the City College of San Francisco's nine, Konishi recruited fine high school ballplayers such as Greg Omori, Troy Nakamura, and Ryan Yammamoto for USF. According to Nakamura, Konishi's Hawaiian background helped, but also "<t>here's a desire to get off the island and experience Division I baseball." Nakamura later became an assistant coach at USF, where he ran a youth summer baseball camp. [128]

David Nakama also coached in the San Francisco Bay Area in the 1990s and 2000s. A one-time coach of the Hawaii Island Movers, a team of Hawaiian high school and college standouts, Nakama headed up the baseball programs at San Francisco State and Mission Community College in Santa Clara. Nakama also assisted at De Anza College in Cupertino. In the early 2000s, Nakama was an assistant coach for the nationally respected Stanford University baseball team. [129]

The University of Nebraska recruited talented Hawaiian ballplayers in the late 1900s. David Murakami and Bryan Akisada played for the Cornhuskers in the 1960s and 1970s. Ryan Kurosaki became an All-American pitcher for the University of Nebraska in the early 1970s. Danny Kimura, who graduated from Honolulu's Iolani High School, starred at third base and the outfield for the Cornhuskers before transferring back home to the University of Hawai'i. And in the early 2000s, few college pitchers surpassed Kalani High School's Shane Komine in success. Ethen Leiser described Komine in the *Asian Week* in the following manner: "Komine has the ability to snap every ounce of his body into velocity that can reach the mid-90s Komine also mixes in a slider, change-up and curveball to keep hitters honest." Komine started a few games for the Oakland Athletics in 2006.[130]

Catcher Kurt Suzuki headed east to play for California State University, Fullerton, after graduating Wailuku's Baldwin High School. At Cal State Fullerton, Suzuki helped lead an NCAA championship team in 2004, while attaining All-American honors. Suzuki was drafted by the Oakland Athletics and was brought up to be the regular starting catcher for the Athletics in 2007.[131]

In 2006 and 2007, Oregon State won the NCAA championship. Players of Asian Pacific American ancestry proved essential to the Beavers' success. Star shortstop Darwin Barney was subsequently drafted by the Chicago Cubs. Some experts likened his performance to the great New York Yankee shortstop Derek Jeter. Hustling Joey Wong anchored second for Oregon State in 2007, while Mike Lissman proved the Beavers with some power, Jason Ogata served as a designated hitter, and Koa Kahalehoa provided speed in the outfield. [132]

Before and after World War II, Asian Pacific American female athletes also competed on the diamond with and against non-Asian Pacific players. During the 1930s, Alice Hinaga was one of the stars of the Night Ball Association in San Jose. Night Ball combined baseball with softball and Hinaga emerged as a top-notch pitcher for teams such as the Premier Paint Girls. In 1940, Emma Wong received national publicity for her abilities as a pitcher. Called a "Chinese charmer," Wong averaged ten strikeouts a game. Playing for the Kaimuki softball team in Honolulu in 1950 were Mildred Mahaulu, Lilly Kau, and Rose Kaiahu. After World War II, Mary Yee played right field for a softball team representing the Alameda Naval Supply Center. The *Chinese Press* proudly reported on one of her winning hits at a game held at the Oakland Oaks field in 1950. In Honolulu in 1950, the McCulley Makula softball league featured athletes such as Harriet Doi, Dorothy Kamashiro, and Eva Inoyue. In 1951, Dorothy Dung, Charity Tsui, Annette Akana, Gwen Wong, Miriam Wong, Tina Kipi, and May Kaleo competed in Honolulu's Amateur Softball Association. In Colorado and Southern California, Nancy "Skipper" Ito carved out a career as one of the best softball players of all time. A Denver native, Ito played for the Denver Tivolis baseball team, the Bank of Denver softball team, the Bloomer Girls baseball team in New York City, and later starred as catcher for the Orange Lionettes' powerful softball contingent.. In the process, she was named to the National All-Star team thirteen times from 1960 to 1970. In 1982, Ito won a place in the National Softball Hall of Fame in 1982. In the mid-1980s, Lisa Ishikawa stood out as a pitcher for Northwestern University's female softball team. Ishikawa had learned softball in her hometown of Stockton, California. In 1996, Kim Ly Maher, a Vietnamese refugee, played her way onto the American gold medal winning Olympic softball team, after starring for Fresno State. She, subsequently, became an assistant coach for the University of California's powerful softball team. In 1998, Kristy Odamura earned Division II All-American recognition as a shortstop for the University of Hawai'i, Hilo. UCLA's nationally prominent softball team was led in part in the early 2000s by the powerful bat of Samoan American Claire Su'a. Kelly Inoyue-Perez, by the way, was an assistant coach for UCLA. Born in Honolulu, Lovie Jung played a magnificent second base for the University of Arizona and then moved on to the United States Olympic team.[133]

Entrepreneurs, Executives, Scouts, Umpires, and Trainers

While some Chinese athletes showed a passion for playing nineteenth century baseball, in Kansas City a Chinese American laundry operator got involved in the entrepreneurial end of the National Pastime during the 1890s. Quong Fong, interestingly, crossed racial and ethnic boundaries to organize an all-African American nine called Wall's Laundry Grays.[134]

Hawai'i, however, has furnished more opportunities for Asian Pacific people to operate and promote baseball. Sam Hop was one of the men who managed the Chinese Hawaiian touring team during the 1910s. Lang Akana became one of the Hawaii Islanders' early executives. For years before that, however, Akana had owned the Hawaiians, a team that competed in the Hawaii Baseball League. Chinn Ho, another Hawaiian with a lifetime of experiences in the islands' sporting circles, served as president of the Hawaii Islanders.[135]

Japanese Hawaiian Duane Kurisu founded the Hawaii Winter League in the 1990s. The league originally consisted of four teams and was intended to provide experience to young American and Japanese minor league prospects, as well as rehabbing major leaguers. Kurisu hoped that baseball executives in Japan and North America would recognize that Hawai'i was "where the world comes to play baseball." However, the league died because of lack support from major league baseball in America.[136]

In the late 1990s, the New York Yankees hired Kim Ng, a Chinese American woman, as an Assistant General Manager. Ng was put directly in charge of salary negotiations with the players. As a pioneer in terms of gender, ethnicity, and race in major league baseball, Ng urged other Asian Pacific Americans to pursue professional sports management as a career choice. She confessed, however, that "judging from my own family and friends, I don't think that the sports industry is the industry of choice." Ng, subsequently, moved to the Los Angeles Dodgers as Assistant General Manager. While in that capacity, she was subject to racially insensitive remarks by New York Mets scout, Bill Singer., who was consequently fired.[137]

After World War II, American and Japanese major league teams used the services of Asian Pacific American scouts. Tsuneo "Cappy" Harada served professional baseball on both sides of the Pacific in several capacities. In 1965, for example, he helped the San Francisco Giants acquire the services of Japanese southpaw, Masanouri Murakami, who became the first person of his nationality to compete in the American big leagues. Honolulu café owner Ralph Yempuku scouted Hawai'i for major league owner Bill Veeck after World War II. Presently,, Eric Kubota serves under Billy Beane as a supervisor of scouting for the Oakland Athletics.[138]

In 1956, Hank Shimada became the first Asian Pacific American to umpire in American Organized Baseball. The Vacaville native was hired by in the California League. The thirty-two year old Shimada had previously umpired armed service baseball in Europe.[139]

Baseball and The "Racial Uniform"

Yoshi Ishikawa's memoirs of what it was like to live as a Japanese immigrant in the United States during the 1960s yields an interesting account of racial and ethnic constructions and border crossings through baseball. Yoshi had apparently played baseball in Japan before coming to the United States. His Japanese friend, Frankie, urges him to join the high school baseball team if he wants to make American friends: "<Y>ou should play either basubaru or footobaru. Footobaru's not so good for Japanese 'cause you need pawu. But you should do ok at basubaru.' " Indeed, Yoshi takes Frankie's advice and makes the team. When he does well, however, his teammates would say things to him like "you're a great kamikaze" or "you're Vietcong."[140]

For Yoshi, baseball stood as a distinctive site for the blurring of racial, ethnic, and national identities. Clearly, to his teammates all Asians looked alike. Similarly, the relative success of Hideo Nomo in the mid-1990s and later other Asian Pacific born major leaguers such Ichiro Suzuki and Hideki Matsui, evokes an interesting connection between the former Japanese major leaguers, Asian Pacific American communities, and baseball as a builder and transcender of cultural borders. From one perspective, when Nomo starred for the Los Angeles Dodgers, it made little sense to associate his achievements with Japanese Americans, let alone other Asian Pacific Americans, many of whom were third and fourth generation U.S. residents. What they seem to have possessed in common with Nomo and what Yoshi seems to possess in common with Vietnamese people is what Ronald Takaki describes as the Asian "racial uniform," which has historically distinguished Americans of Asian Pacific ancestry from other Americans. Those so labeled might well know that culturally they have very little in common. They might also know that Nomo without a baseball uniform on looks more like a computer "nerd" or a convenience store owner than a major league pitcher to the vast majority of Americans, including perhaps Asian Pacific Americans. Perhaps, Nomo furnished these Asian Pacific Americans with a potent reminder of their distinctiveness. Perhaps, as well, he, and other Asian Pacific major leaguers, have exploded for them those racial and ethnic conven tions that shout a white Texan might blow a fastball pass Barry Bonds, but not someone who looked like Nomo or Korean fireballer Chan Ho Park.

To be sure, the Dodger franchise that hired Nomo and Park has long understood that racial uniforms contain a market value. Certainly, Jackie Robinson was a great ballplayer, but he was also a great ballplayer who could draw African Americans into Brooklyn's Ebbets Field. In Los Angeles, the Dodgers discovered gold in Fernando Valenzuela, an often great pitcher who enticed people of Mexican ancestry into Dodger Stadium to buy Dodger caps and Dodger "dogs." In the 1960s, the Dodgers sponsored "Japan Day" games and kept a section of Dodgers Stadium available for Japanese and Japanese American fans. The Dodgers' continued interest in signing players of Asian Pacific and Latin American backgrounds accords well with Los Angeles's dual image as both a gateway to the Pacific Basin and to South America. In Nomo and Park, the Dodgers acquired the services of talented and marketable young pitchers.

During the 1997 season, for example, the Dodgers linked to the relatively sizable population of Korean Angelenos by staging a Korean American Night, which the franchise publicized by distributing huge Chan Ho Park street banners throughout Los Angeles's Korean American neighborhoods. The Dodgers also built a ticket kiosk where large numbers of Korean Angelenos lived and worked. In 1998, sportswriter Jeff Weinstock quoted Richard Choi of Radio Korea to the effect that in Los Angeles, "When Chan Ho is pitching there are not any customers in Korean restaurants...There are no customers in Korean markets. They're listening to the radio or going to Dodger Stadium. Chan Ho is—what can I say? --he's a big shot now." However, Park did not always welcome the attention he received. In 1997, he complained that because of the close scrutiny of the Korean press and local Korean fans, he had lost his personal freedom to patronize dance clubs and date. According to the *Los Angeles Times*, Park had become concerned about keeping his squeaky clean image before Los Angeles's Korean American community.[141]

The Dodgers, of course, were not the first professional baseball franchise to market racial uniforms. Earlier in this chapter, we discussed how the Oakland Oaks and Sacramento Solons hoped to dig into the pockets of various West Coast Chinese and Japanese American communities. Indeed, the Solons seemingly remained popular among local Japanese Americans for years.[142]

Yoshi Ishikawa recalls the Masanouri Murakami phenomenon. Murakami was the first Japanese professional inked by an American major league franchise when the San Francisco Giants signed the left-handed pitcher in the mid-1960s. Murakami's impact and talent did not match Nomo's. Ishikawa, nevertheless, remembers, "The Japanese community in California went in to a frenzy over Murakami...In the mid-sixties, when Japan was barely mentioned in the American media, Murakami's story would go down in sports history."[143]

While Giants' owner, Horace Stoneham, may have profited from Muraka-mi's appearances in Candlestick Park, Japanese entrepreneurs tried to market racial and ethnic pride in the small city of Lodi during the early 1960s. The Lodi Crushers played in the minor California League and Harold Peterson wrote, "In an area rich in Japanese Americans, the Crushers had a Japanese owner, pro-gram ads for Japan Air Lines…a large box reserved for the Nisei society, a Jap-anese pitcher, and a Japanese night."[144]

During the early 1980s, the Japanese American community in the San Francisco Bay Area expressed considerable support for Atlee Hammaker, who, according to *East/West* journalist Robert Tokunaga, reciprocated. Although the San Francisco Giants had gotten lax in maintaining ties to the considerable num-ber of Japanese Americans living in and around San Francisco, Oakland, and San Jose, the franchise staged a Japanese American Day in July, 1983—a day, by the way, on which Hammaker was scheduled to start. Several years later, the Giants honored Japanese American baseball with a day in 1996.[145]

The emergence of Asian Pacific superstars and stars such as Ichiro Suzuki and Hideki Matsui has not been ignored by Asian Pacific American communi-ties and media. The *Asian Week,* for example, has furnished constant coverage of superb athletes such as Suzuki and Matsui. Richard Lapchick, a sports studies scholar, has pointed out that Asian Pacific major leaguers have helped bridge cultural differences between Asian Pacific American communities and non-Asian Pacific Americans. He writes that Nomo, Park, and Suzuki have pulled "Asian Americans closer to the mainstream by making the love of their team a common interest to share with whites, Latinos, and African Americans."[146]

The relationship between the MLB and Asian Pacific American communi-ties has not always been so positive in post-World War II America. In 1981, an Oakland Athletic catcher was quoted in the press saying that opponent batters were getting "chink hits" off of Athletic pitchers. Accordingly, at least some Asian Pacific Americans in the Bay Area were upset. One letter writer to *East/West* declared, "I don't want an apology. I just want to make sure nothing like that ever happens again." Nearly twenty years later, merchants in Philadel-phia's Chinatown protested the proposed construction of a baseball stadium in their neighborhood.[147]

The emergence of Asian Pacific Islander stars and potential stars has not been welcomed warmly throughout the American baseball world. When Ichiro Suzuki first wore a Seattle Mariner uniform in Oakland in 2000, the dynamic outfielder was pelted with coins and ice. That same year, Chicago Cub prospect, Korean Hee Seop Choi was greeted in Nashville with organ music consisting of "Kung Fu Fighting" and David Bowie's "China Girl."[148]

Cricket

Cricket's popularity among Americans of South Central Asian descent should remind us of the historical variety of ball and bat sports globally and even in America. In ante-bellum America, Philadelphia was the center of America's cricket world. The city was home to a large number of Anglo Americans avid in hoping to keep their favorite team sport alive. Students at nearby Haverford College enjoyed cricket as one of their favorite pastimes.

As America headed for the twenty-first century, Haverford remained true to its love of cricket. However, its coach was Kamran Khan, a former member of the Pakistani national team and later captain of the American national team. Khan started coaching at Haverford in 1973 and in 2000 at least half of his players could trace their backgrounds o the Indian subcontinent.[149]

Moreover, according to journalists Melwani Lavina and Rob Nixon, émigrés from South Central Asia have attempted to fuel cricket's rise as a popular sport in the United States. In 1995, according to Lavina, émigrés from India and Pakistan played cricket in the Midwest as well as Houston, Texas. Lavina reported that the United States Cricket Association was headed by Nazir Khan, a Pakistani based in Philadelphia, and the association's four vice presidents included Jimmy Colabavala, an Indian, who was also the president of the Southern California Cricket Club.[150]

Conclusion

Very clearly, baseball has served as a vehicle of Asian Pacific American cultural citizenship. In recent decades Asian Pacific American community teams continued to exist. In 1974, Southern California Japanese Americans staged the Harry Ota Memorial Baseball tournament. Nines called the Spartans of Gardena, the Kono Hawaii Dolphins, the Reedley JACL, and the Selma Sansei were among those participating. We know that, moreover, Asian Pacific Americans have played baseball and softball beyond their ethnic communities. In the 1996 summer Olympics, Vietnamese American Kim Ly Maher competed on the gold medal winning softball team, while a lefthander from UCLA, Jim Vo Parque, pitched for the Olympic baseball nine. [151]

In the late 1990s and early 2000s, American ballplayers of Asian Pacific ancestry often did well in the North American major leagues. Parque, for example, joined the Chicago White Sox starting rotation in the 1999 season and looked like a future standout until arm troubles sidetracked his career. A Filipino-Samoan from Hawai'i named Benny Agbayani sparkled as a hitter for the New York Mets in 1999 and 2000. Filipino American journalist Emil Guillermo described Agbayani as "<b>uilt low to the ground, with the width of an island sunset. And a heart to match. The guy has no quit." Agbayani drifted out of the

American major leagues and became a prominent slugger for Japan's Lotte Marines in 2004. A Hawaiian Japanese ballplayer, Onan Masaoka, made the Los Angeles Dodgers as a relief pitcher. In the early 2000s, Danny Graves, who possesses Vietnamese ancestry, became one of baseball's better relief pitchers, while Mike Fetters, a Samoan Hawaiian, continued to collect innings as a reliable relief pitcher. In 1986, the Iolani High graduate was drafted out of Pepperdine University. An Hawaiian of indigenous and African American descent, Jerome Williams pitched several fine games as a starter for the San Francisco Giants. Dave Roberts, who possesses African American and Japanese ancestry, is a dynamic outfielder who helped the Red Sox win the World Championship in 2005. And Johnny Damon, an outfielder with a Thai mother, achieved stardom as a lead off hitter for the Kansas City Royals, Oakland Athletics, the Boston Red Sox and most recently the New York Yankees. While serving in Vietnam, Damon's father met his mother. The outfielder grew up in Orlando, Florida, where his dad worked as a security guard and his mother took in sewing and cleaned office buildings. Wearing long hair and a beard, Damon's likeness found itself on tee-shirts in Boston—tee shirts asking, "What would Damon do?" [153]

Certainly, we should not sentimentalize Asian Pacific American strivings in baseball nor should we give way too much to skepticism. Asian Pacific Americans have found, perhaps, that baseball may not have saved them. Still, America's National Pastime might have helped make their frequently bitter experiences more tolerable, their lives more joyful, and their ability to assert their cultural citizenship somewhat fortified. If Mochizuki's book does nothing but remind us that baseball need not belong to any particular race, gender, or class, it has done quite a bit.

Notes

1. Ken Mochizuki, *Baseball Saved Us*, (New York: Scholastic, Inc. 1993), 9.

2. *Ibid.*

3. *Ibid.*

4. *Ibid.*, 11.

5. *Ibid.*, 13, 15.

6. Albert G. Spalding, *America's National Game*, (Lincoln and London: University of Nebraska Press, 1992), 395.

7. Harold Seymour, *Baseball: The People's Game*, (New York: Oxford University Press, 1990), 324; *Honolulu Star-Bulletin*, June 24, 1915; *Washington Post*, August 22, 1915.

8. *Daily Commonwealth*, May 10, 1913; *San Francisco Chronicle*, June 23, 1913; *Coschocton Tribune*, August 23, 1913.

9. *Sporting News*, August 9, 1922.

10. *Ibid.*, April 7, 1932.

11. Ronald Takaki, *Pau Hana: Plantation Life and Labor in Hawai'i, 1835-1920*, (Honolulu: University of Hawai'i Press, 1983); Franklin Odo and Kazubo Sinota, A *Pictorial History of the Japanese in Hawaii, 1885-1924* (Honolulu, HI Bishop Museum Press, 1985), 79.

12. "Pro Baseball in Hawaii," www. maui.net, accessed March 13, 1998; *Hawaiian Gazette,* May 23, 1899; *Washington Post, 22* August 1915; Thomas Kaulukukui, The Development of Competitive Athletics in the Schools of Hawaii, (Thesis (M. Ed.: University of Hawaii, 1941), 18

13. Ruthanne Lum McCunn *Chinese American Portraits: Personal Memories, 1828-1988.* (San Francisco: *San Francisco Chronicle* Books, 1988), 22-23.

14. *Sporting Life,* June 10, 1884; *San Francisco Chronicle*, May 19, 1885.

15. *San Francisco Chronicle,* November 25, 1887; *Washington Post,* September 2, 1888.

16. *Sacramento Bee,* April 15, 1886.

17. National Baseball Hall of Fame and Library Archives, Cooperstown, New York; Odo and Sinota, *Pictorial History,* 79; *Pacific Commercial Advertiser,* July 1, 1912; July 10, 1912; November 4, 1915; *Honolulu Star-Bulletin,* February 15, 1915; September 20, 1915; Arthur Suehiro, *Honolulu Stadium: Where Hawaii Played,* (Honolulu: Watermark Publishing, 1995), 13; Kerry Yo Nakagawa. *Through A Diamond: 100 Years of Japanese American Baseball,* (San Francisco: Rudi Publishing Company, 2001), 6.

18. Misawa, *Beginnings,* 14; *San Jose Mercury,* May 7, 1922.

19. www.majorleaguebaseball.com, accessed February 18, 1997; *Los Angeles Times,* April 14, 1909; Gail M. Nomura, "Beyond the Playing Field: The Significance of Pre-World War II Japanese American Baseball in the Yakima Valley," in *Bearing Dreams, Shaping Visions: Asian Pacific American Perspectives,* edited by Linda A. Revilla, Gail M. Nomura, Shawn Wong, and Shirley Hune, (Pullman, Washington: Washington State University Press, 1993), 16-17.

20. Jay Feldman, "Baseball Behind Barbed Wire," *The National Pastime: A Review of Baseball History,* (no. 12), 37; Nomura, "Beyond," 18.

21. *Sacramento Bee,* April 14, 1923; *San Jose Mercury,* February 3, 1923; *Philippine Mail,* June 26, 1933.

22. *Sacramento Bee,* June 2, 1925.

23. *Ibid.,* March 5, 1927; July 2, 1933; *San Francisco Chronicle,* October 5, 1926.

24. www.majorleaguebaseball.com, accessed April 3, 1998; *San Francisco Chronicle,* February 9, 1923; February 12, 1923.

25. *Los Angeles Times,* January 32, 1938; May 15, 1939; *Pacific Citizen,* September 20, 1947; *Nichi Bei Times,* January 1, 1973.

26. Nakagawa, *Through a Diamond,*.16-17; *San Francisco Chronicle,* March 28, 1935.

27. *New York Times,* May 12, 1900; *Chicago Daily Tribune,* June 26, 1908; *Sacramento Bee,* April 1, 1912; San *Francisco Chronicle,* February 16, 1918; *Los Angeles Times,* February 2, 1913; March 9, 1925. George and Elise Yee, "The 1927 Chinese Ball Team," *Gam San Journal,* (December 1986), p. 3

28. *San Francisco Examiner,* March 6, 1934; *Chinese Digest,* June, 1937; Eve Armentrout Ma and Jeong Hui Ma, *The Chinese of Oakland: Unsung Builders,* (Oakland Chinese History Research Committee, 1982), 4.

29. *Chicago Daily Tribune,* May 15, 1922; San Francisco *Chronicle,* February 13, 1926; *Philippine Mail,* June 26, 1933; *San Francisco Examiner,* June 9, 1935; Catapusan, *Filipino Occupational,* 34.

30. *Chinese Digest,* March, 1938; Regalado, "Incarcerate" 433. Samuel O. Regaldo, "Incarcerated Sport: Nisei Women's Softball and Athletics During Japanese Internment." *Journal of Sport History,* vol. 27. (No. 3 Fall, 2000), 133.

31. Otto Friedrich, *City of Nets, A Portrait of Hollywood in the 1940s,* (New York: Harper & Row, 1986),.102; Sam Regalado, "Sport and Community in California's Japanese American 'Yamato Colony' 1930-1945," *Journal of Sport History* 19 (Summer 1992), 130; Feldman, "Barbed," 38-39.

32. *Manzanar Free Press,* July 22, 1944: www. majorleaguebaseball.com, accessed February 17, 1998.

33. *San Jose Mercury,* July 17, 1996.

34. "Pro Baseball in Hawaii," www. maui.net, accessed January 16, 1998; Frank Ardolino, "The Big Leaguers hit the Beach," *The National Pastime#*16, 1996, 43

35. Gary Okihiro, *Cane Fires: The Anti-Japanese Movement in Hawaii, 1865-1915,* (Philadelphia, PA: Temple University Press, 1991), 193-276.; "Pro Baseball in Hawaii," www.maui.net; *Honolulu Star-Bulletin,* May 2, 1936; September 3, 1940; Suehiro, *Honolulu Stadium,* .32; Cisco, *Hawai'i Sports: History, Facts, & Statistics,* (Honolulu: University of Hawai'i Press, 1999), 30; United States Census Manuscripts, City and County of Honolulu, 1930.

36. *Honolulu Star-Bulletin,* May 12, 1951; February 19, 1998.

37. *San Francisco Chronicle,* September 8, 1945; April 1, 1946; July 31, 1950.

38. *San Francisco Chronicle,* August 1, 1951; *San Francisco Examiner,* November 25, 1947; *San Jose Mercury,* August 15, 1947; August 17, 1947; May 9, 1954; *Pacific Citizen,* March 17, 1951; *Utah Nippo,* April 26, 1950.

39. *Pacific Citizen,* September 3, 1947; *Fil-America Advocate,* January 15, 1953; *Nichi Bei Tiimes,* September 5, 1973.

40. *Hawaii Herald,* January 4, 1951; *Honolulu Star-Bulletin,* February 19, 1998.

41. *Honolulu Star- Bulletin,* July 1, 1948; January 1, 1949; January 7, 1949; December 2, 1949; June 5, 1951; *Hawaii Herald,* February 7, 1950; February 19, 1998; *Fil-America Advocate,* December 15, 1952.

42. *San Francisco Chronicle,* May 3, 1905; May 2, 1911; March 2, 1935; March 3, 1935; *Sporting News,* February 25, 1953; *Santa Ana Register,* July 20, 1960.

43. *Sacramento Bee,* April 5, 1912; *San Francisco Chronicle,* April 1, 1913; Los *Angeles Times,* March 14, 1914; March 15, 1914.

44. Harold Seymour, *Baseball: The People's Game,* (New York: Oxford University Press, 1990), 173; *Los Angeles Times,* March 10, 1914; *Washington Post,* September 28, 1914.

45. *Elyria Evening Telegram,* August 19, 1912.

46. *Sporting Life,* May 11, 1912; *San Francisco Chronicle,* April 7, 1912.

47. *Sporting Life,* April 13, 1912.

48. *Los Angeles Times,* April 9, 1912; *Sporting Life,* June 1, 1912.

49. *Los Angeles Times,* March 10, 1914.

50. *Ibid.,* March 15, 1914.

51. *Ibid.*, March 14, 1915; *San Francisco Chronicle*, March 11, 1915; *Oakland Tribune*, March 10, 1915.

52. *San Jose Mercury*, March 12, 1915.

53. *Ibid.*, March 14, 1915.

54. *Ibid.*, March 15, 1915; *Los Angeles Times*, March 15, 1915.

55. *Los Angeles Times*, March 15, 1914; Rosaldo, *Culture and Truth*; Jose David Saldivar, *Border Matters: Remapping American Cultural Studies*, (Berkeley: University of California Press, 1997); Gloria Anzaldua, *Borderlands/La Frontera: The New Mestiza* (San Francisco: Spinsters/Aunt Lute, 1987); Allen Klein, *Baseball on the Border*; (Princeton, New Jersey: Princeton University Press, 1997); United States Census Manuscripts, City and County of Honolulu, 1900.

56. *Los Angeles Times*, December 15, 1914; *Washington Post*, December 7, 1918.

57. *Decatur Review*, July 29, 1912; *Pacific Commercial Advertiser*, November 17, 1915; November 21, 1915.

58. *New York Age*, September 16, 1915.

59. *Chicago Defender*, October 4, 1913; May 20, 1916.

60. *Pacific Commercial Advertiser*, March 18, 1914; S. Hung. Hoe, "America Invaded By Oriental Foes," *Baseball Monthly*, (March, 1914), p. 68; United States Census Manuscripts, City and County of Honolulu, 1930,

61. *Pacific Commercial Advertiser*, March 10, 1915; March 11, 1915, March 14, 1915; March 25, 1915; April 2, 1915; October 17, 1915; U.S. Census, MS.

62. *Honolulu Star-Bulletin*, May 28, 1915.

63. United States Census Manuscripts, City and County of Honolulu, Hawaii, 1920.

64. *San Francisco Examiner*, April 11, 1907; Sporting *Life*, August 29, 1907; *Washington Post*, September 4, 1907; United States Census Manuscripts, City and County of Honolulu, Hawaii, 1930.

65. *Washington Post*, September 8, 1907.

66. *Oakland Tribune*, March 27, 1912.

67. John E. Spalding, Sacramento *Senators and Solons: Baseball in California's Capital, 1886-1976*, (Manhattan, KS: Ag Press, 1995), 25; *Sacramento Bee*, April 4, 1912; United States. Census Manuscripts, City and County of Honolulu, Hawaii, 1930.

68. *Pacific Commercial Advertiser*, March 18, 1914; March 26, 1914.

69. Alexander Saxton, *The Indispensable Enemy: Labor and the Anti-Chinese Movement in California*, (Berkeley and Los Angeles: University of California Press, 1971); Steven Riess, *Touching Base: Professional Baseball and American Culture in the Progressive Era*, (Westport, Connecticut: Greenwood Press, 1980), 193-194; *Chicago Defender*, January 16, 1915; *Portland Oregonian*, January 19, 1914; January 21, 1914.

70. *Washington Post*, December 3, 1914; March 24, 1918; *Middletown Times Press*, July 21, 1917; *Bridgeport Telegram*, May 20, 1918.

71. August 14, 1920; 1917-1918 Draft Registration Cards, June 5, 1917, Philadelphia, Pennsylvania; *Sporting News*, January 8, 1920; December 16, 1920; *Helena Independent*, January 10, 1928; *New York Times*, March 4, 1928.

72. *New York Times*, March 14, 1928; March 15, 1928.

73. *Helena Independent*, May 24, 1936.

74. *Fort Wayne News*, April 17, 1917; *Fort Wayne Sentinel*, May 18, 1917; *Washington Post*, April 22, 1917; *Sporting News*, May 10, 1916, May 31, 1917; July 5, 1917

75. United States Census Manuscript, City and County of Honolulu, Hawaii, 1930; *Bridgeport Telegram*, May 22, 1918; May 28, 1918; *Sporting News*, January 8, 1920.

76. Janet Bruce, *The Kansas City Monarchs: Champions of Black Baseball*, (Lawrence: KS: University of Kansas Press, 1985), 15; *The National Pastime: A Review of Baseball History*, (Spring: 1986), backpage.

77. Yoichi Nagata, "The First All-Asian Pitching Duel in Organized Baseball: Japan vs. China in the PCL," *Baseball Research Journal*, (no. 21), p. 14; United States Census Manuscripts, Hilo, Hawaii, 1910; United States Department of Labor, Passenger List, "All Aliens Arriving from a foreign port or port of Insular possession, Siberia Maru, Sailing From Honolulu, August 12, 1928.

78. *Los Angeles Times*, September 16, 1932.

79. David B. Welky, "Viking Girls."

80. *Los Angeles Times*, September 16, 1932.

81. *Oakland Tribune*, September 27, 1932.

82. *Ibid.*, September 20, 1932.

83. *Ibid.*, September 28 1932.

84. Nagata, "Pitching Duel," p. 14; *San Francisco Examiner*, September 21, 1932; September 28, 1932; September 29, 1932.

85. *Oakland Tribune*, September 29, 1932; Nagata, "Pitching Duel," p.14; *Honolulu Advertiser*, March 2, 1933.

86. Spalding, *Sacramento*, 84.

87. Paul J. Zingg and Mark D. Medeiros, *Runs, Hits, and an Era: The Pacific Coast League, 1903-58*, (Urbana, Illinois: University of Illinois Press, 1994),. 71. *San Francisco Examiner*, May 2, 1929; *Sporting News*, August 26, 1943; July 19, 1950; *San Jose Mercury*, September 1, 1946; *Honolulu Star-Bulletin*, April 9, 1997; United States. Census Manuscripts, Ewa Plantation, Hawaii, 1920.

88. *Sporting News*, March 23, 1933; *Honolulu Advertiser*, March 31, 1935; November 28, 1935; *San Francisco Chronicle*, March 1, 1936.

89. United States, Census Manuscripts, City and County of Los Angeles, 1930.

90. Emil Guillermo, "Diversity on the Diamond," *Asian Week*, October 3, 1997; *Sporting News*, November 3, 1948; September 10, 1952; *Seattle Post-Intelligencer*, March 6, 1955; April 19, 1955; *Coschocton Tribune*, September 14, 1956.

91. Guillermo, "Diversity;" *Sporting News*, July 5, 1961.

92. Larry Tajiri, "Yonamine of the Bees," *Scene*, (July 1950); *Pacific Citizen*, July 26, 1947; January 28, 1950.

93. *Ames Daily Tribune*, March 30, 1956; Bob Cole, Jr., "4 Hawaii Sandlotters Receiving O.B. Trials," *Sporting News*, May 30, 1956.

94. www.alohafame.com, accessed December 21, 1998.

95. Grantland Rice, "Who is Our Top Athlete," *Sport*, (October, 1946).

96. *San Francisco Chronicle*, February 21, 1950; *San Francisco News*, March 11, 1950; *Honolulu Star-Bulletin*, April 6, 1950.

97. *Sporting News*, March 8, 1950.

98. *Ibid*, May 10, 1950; April 8, 1953; Tajiri, "Yonamine."

99. Jerry Izenberg, "Another Side of the Rising Sun," *New Jersey On-Line*, July 12, 1997; *Hawaii Herald*, February 9, 1950; March 3, 1950; *Honolulu Advertiser*, April 17, 1951.

100. *Honolulu Advertiser*, March 4, 1967; John Saito, "Nisei Inducted Into Japan's Hall of Fame," *Nikkei Northwest*, March 1, 1994.

101. *Ibid*; Center for Labor Education and Research of the College of Continuing Education, University of Hawai'i, "The New Rice and Roses Presents Hawai'i's Plantation Heroes," Video Documentary, (1992); Yoichi Nagata and John Holway, "Japanese Baseball," in *Total Baseball*, edited by John Thorn and Peter Palmer, (New York Warner Books, 1989), 594.

102. *Ibid*; Sadaharu Oh and David Faulkner, *A Zen Way of Baseball*, (New York: Times Books, 1984), 78.

103. *Ibid.*

104. Izenberg, "Another Side."

105. "Wally Yonamine," *Ballplayers*, www.sportline.com, accessed March 16, 1998.

106. *Ibid*; The Center for Labor Education, "Plantation Heroes;" www.hawaii.gov, accessed March 14, 1999; Saito, "Nikkei."

107. Nagata and Holway, "Japanese Baseball," 594; *Honolulu Star-Bulletin*, September 23, 1953; *Blue Book of College Athletics, 1966-1967*, (Cleveland: Akron Engraving Company, 1967), 108

108. *Honolulu Star-Bulletin*, November 9, 1949; *Pacific Citizen*, March 11, 1950; Cole, "4 Sandlotters."

109. Mark Harris," An Outfielder for Hiroshima." *Sports Illustrated*, August 1, 1958, p. 59.

110. *Honolulu Star-Bulletin*, January 29, 1997; Bill Kwon, "Sports Watch," July 29, 2000; Ethen Leiser, "It is Designed to Break Your Heart," *Asian Week*, August 10-August 16, 2000; John Feinstein, "Out and In The Tigers Door," *Washington Post*, October 12, 1984.

111. "Tiger Among Us," *Asian Week*, February 12, 1998-February 18, 1998; Robin Carr, "Happy Days on the Farm," *Giants Magazine*, (no. 2: 1987), p. 37.

112. *Ahead in the Count: 130 Years of Women & Baseball: 1995 Colorado Silver Bullets Souvenir Program; Michael* Learmouth, *San Jose Metro*, August 21, 1997.

113. *San Jose Mercury*, March 8, 1924; March 27, 1924; February 10, 1930; February 11, 1930; *Nikkei Heritage, Diamonds in the Rough: Japanese Americans in Baseball*, (Spring, 1997), 8; *Chinese Digest*, March, 1938..

114. *Los Angeles Times*, March 22, 1908; March 14, 1915; March 7, 1925; February 18, 1931; *Daily Palo Alto*, April 20, 1911; *Pacific Commercial Advertiser*, December 23, 1911; March 12, 1913; March 12, 1914; *Appleton Post-Crescent*, June 10, 1931; *San Francisco Examiner*, May 3, 1936; *San Jose Mercury*, May 2, 1942; Yee, "Chinese," pp. 2, 3.

115. *Marion Star*, April 9, 1940; *Pacific Citizen*, July 12, 1947; Arizona State On-line, accessed March 7, 2001.

116. www.liu.edu., accessed February 8, 2003; *New York Times,* April 16, 1941; *Berkshire Evening Telegram,* August 2, 1952; William T. "Buck" Lai, *Championship Baseball From Little League to Big League,* (New York Prentice Hall, 1954.)

117. Nakagawa, *Through a Diamond,* 92-93; Okihiro, *Cane Fires,* 94-95.

118. *Los Angeles Times,* May 30, 1947; *San Jose Mercury* May 3, 1946; August 1, 1947; August 15, 1947.

119. Harris, "An Outfielder," p. 58; *Pacific Citizen,* March 11, 1950; *Nichi Bei Times,* January 1, 1973.

120. *Pacific Citizen,* April 15, 1943; March 11, 1950; June 8, 1973; *Sacramento Bee,* June 15, 1935; *San Francisco Examiner,* March 12, 1950; May 24, 1951; May 20, 1956; *San Jose Mercury,* March 1, 1964; March 4, 1964; March 8, 1964; *Honolulu Star-Bulletin,* June 8, 1951; *New York Times,* May 11, 1958; *East/West,* April 3, 1968; *Nichi Bei Times,* March 25, 1972; January 1, 1973; September 1, 1973; *Rafu Shimpo,* March 18, 1972; Cisco, 27;

121. *San Jose Mercury,* August 4, 1908; *Pacific Commercial Advertiser,* July 6, 1912; March 25, 1914; January 2, 1915.

122. John Holway, *Voices from the Great Negro Baseball Leagues,* (New York: Dodd, Mead, & Company, 1975), 102.

123. Ethnic Studies Oral History Project, Remembering *Kakaako,* v. 3, (Honolulu, HI: University of Hawaii, Manoa, 1978), 525-526.

124. *Seattle Post-Intelligencer,* January 22, 1941; Beth Bailey and David Farber, *First Strange Place: The Alchemy of Race and Sex in World War II Hawaii,* (New York: The Free Press, 1992), 166; *Honolulu Advertiser,* July 16, 1947; *Honolulu Star-Bulletin,* August 28, 1948; September 4, 1948; July 27, 2000; Suehiro, *Honolulu Stadium,* 56-57.

125. *Official Baseball Annual 1956, Rules, Teams, Photos,* (Wichita, KA: National Baseball Congress, 1956), 14-19.

126. www.hawaii.edu, accessed February 19, 1998; Cisco, *Hawai'i, Sports,* 12, 16-17; *Honolulu Advertiser,* March 31, 1935; *Honolulu Star-Bulletin,* April 5, 1950; January 27, 1951; April 23, 1999.

127. Cisco, *Hawai'i Sports,* 21-24.

128. Ron Kroichik, "USF's Title Hopes Are on the Horizon," *San Francisco Chronicle,* April 3, 1998; "Unblemished," *Asian Week,,* June 29 2001-July 5, 2001.

129. *Honolulu Star-Bulletin,* August 21, 2001; www.gostanford.com, accessed April 3, 2005.

130. www.huskerwebcast.com, September 12, 1999; Eithen Leiser, "Komine Shucks Hitters in the Cornhusker State," www.asianweek.com, July 25, 2002.

131. Stanford vs. California State University, Fullerton, Baseball Program, Stanford University, February 2, 2002; www.bigwest.org., accessed December 5, 2004.

132. www.majorleaguebaseball.com, accessed July 13, 1997; *Helena Independent,* July 6, 1940; *Pacific Citizen,* January 21, 1950; *Chinese Press,* July 21, 1950; *Hawaii Herald,* February 21, 1950; *New York Times,* August 16, 1953; *Santa Ana Register,* April 2, 1960; "Diamonds in the Rough, *Nikkei Heritage,* 15 (Spring, 1997), p. 11; *East/West,* August 15, 1984; Bert Elijea, "Silver and Gold for Amy Chow," www.asianweek.com, June 17, 1999; *Honolulu Star-Bulletin,* April 22, 1940; June 15, 1951; May 30, 1998; www.gobears.com, February 6, 2001; Ethen Leiser, "UCLA's Sua Stays Cool Under

Fire," www.asianweek.com.,June 15, 2001-June 21, 2001; www.usasoftball.com/ Women/ Olympics/2004Olympic games, accessed March 18, 2005., accessed March 18, 2005.

132 http://epicanthus.net/2007/06/24/asian-american-trio-heart-and-soul-of-college-world-series-baseball-champ-oregon-state-beavers/

133. Seymour, *The People's Game*, 566.

134. *Sporting Life*, January 30, 1915; *Honolulu Star-Bulletin*, November 4, 1949; April 16, 1961; Suehiro, *Honolulu Stadium*, 27.

135. *Honolulu Star-Bulletin*, November 29, 1999.

136. Asian *Week*, April 8, 1998; "Dodgers' Ng Subject of Racial Remarks," November 21, 2003.

137. *San Jose Mercury*, January 18, 1965; Martinez, "League," March 29, 2000; *Pacific Citizen*, March 31, 1951; Michael Lewis, *Moneyball: The Art of Winning An Unfair Game*, (New York: W.W. Norton, 2003.)

138. *San Francisco Examiner*, May 23, 1956.

139. Yoshimi Ishikawa, *Strawberry Road: A Japanese Immigrant Discovers America*, Eve Zimmerman (trans.) (Tokyo, New York and London: Kondansha International, 1991), 130-131.

140. Clark Walker, *Asian Week*, August 29, 1997; Jeff Weinstock, "Park's Place," *Sport*, August, 1998; *Los Angeles Times*, September 14, 1997.

141. *San Francisco Chronicle*, August 18, 1947.

142. Ishikawa, *Strawberry Road*, 130-131.

143. Harold Peterson, *The Man Who Invented Baseball*, (New York: Charles Scribner's and Sons, 1973). 162.

144. *East/West*, July 20, 1983; Carolyn Jung, "Assimilation," *San Jose Mercury*, July 17, 1996.

145. Ethen Leiser, "On Threshold of Greatness," *Asian Week*, July 13-July 19, 2001; Richard Lapchick, "Asian. American Athletes: The Past, Current, and Future,"www.sportsinsociety.org., accessed March 24, 2003.

146. *East/West*, June 3, 1981; Associated Press Online, "Philly Chinese Leaders Rip Ballpark," June 7, 2000.

147. Ethen Leiser, "Out After a Song," *Asian Week*, August 24-August 30, 2000. "

148. L. John Wertheim, "When A Bowl Game Isn't Football," *Sports Illustrated*, (May 15, 2000), p. 50.

149. Melwani Lavina, Little India, May 31, 1995, Rob Nixon, As American As Cricket, *The Atlantic Monthly*, July, 2000.

151. *Rafu Shimpo*, September 3, 1974; *Asian Week*, August 29, 1997; *Honolulu Star-Bulletin*, September 12, 1999.

152. Emil Guillermo, "Our Benny," Asian Weekly, April 6-April 12, 2000; www.athletesdirect.com, accessed January 12, 2001; *Cincinnati Post*, May 18, 2000; "High School Retires SF Giants' Uniform, www.asianweek.com, January 16, 2004;, http://www.singaporesoxfan.com/2004/10/dave-roberts-japanese-base-stealing.html; Yong-Yi Zhu, Holy Johnny Damon And Fenway Disciples, www.tech-mit.edu, April 23, 2004.

Chapter Four: Touchdowns and Goals

American football is not typically the first thing we associate with the Hawaiian Islands. Texas might come in mind. In Texas, folks do not just go wild over the Dallas Cowboys; they even take their high school football seriously. They even take cheerleading at football games seriously. Ohio, Nebraska, and Alabama, to be sure, might also well challenge the Lone Star State for the perhaps dubious title of the most football-obsessed chunk of the United States.

The nastier among us might say that, of course, Texas and those other states live and die for football. In what else can their residents express much pride? Certainly, Hawaiians with their beaches, surfboards, volcanoes, and endless waves of tourists to distract them have better things to do with their lives than worry about whether some seventeen-year-old can catch the ball over the middle or cover the corners. Still, Hawaiians, like Texans, are a bit more complicated than the regional stereotypes make them out to be. Indeed, sports have constituted an interesting part of Hawaiian cultural history. And American-style, as opposed to association or rugby, football has attracted the participation and patronage of countless Hawaiians of racially and ethnically diverse backgrounds.

For years, one of the most popular sports attractions in Hawai'i was "barefoot" football. Barefoot football leagues engaged the athletic ability of diverse young and mature males of working class backgrounds. Size in the barefoot leagues erected few obstacles to smaller Hawaiian athletes. One scholarly observer of Hawaiian culture in the 1930s pointed out in regarding Chinese Hawaiian athletes: "In football, their average light weight puts Chinese at a disadvantage against haoles and <Native> Hawaiians. Yet they hold their own in the celebrated 'barefoot leagues.'" [1]

Barefoot teams might, moreover, represent various plantation work forces. Since in barefoot football, one did not need size to excel, the game relied upon quickness, stealth, teamwork, and the ability to kick the ball barefooted with strength and accuracy. Chin Do Kim became known as the "world champion barefoot place kicker." He reportedly once barefooted a phenomenal 78 yard field goal for the University of Hawai'i eleven, for whom he also played guard and served as co-captain. Probably the first Asian Pacific American to play professional football on the mainland was Walter Achiu, a running back and barefoot kicker of mixed Chinese and Native Hawaiian ancestry. Achiu competed for the Dayton Triangles in the 1920s after a football career at the University of Dayton. Unfortunately, at least initially he apparently denied possessing Chinese ancestry in order to avoid the anti-Chinese sentiments of many white mainland-ers. [2]

The football played in cleats was also admired on the islands. High school football made headlines in Honolulu in the 1930s and 1940s. Meanwhile, Honolulu high schools recruited talent from Maui and other islands. For example, the great Wally Yonamine led his Maui eleven to a league championship and then Farrington High School in Honolulu secured him for his senior year. Indeed, Hawaiian high schools in the 1940s earned the reputation as nurturers of swift, elusive, and versatile running backs such as Yonamine and Herman Wedemeyer, who played for St. Louis Preparatory School in Honolulu before gaining fame with an eleven representing little St. Mary's of Moraga, California.

When a football team known as the Hawaii All Stars toured the mainland after World War II, mainlanders were impressed. This team, coached by Chin Do Kim, consisted of some of the finest amateur and semi-professional gridders around. The names of the players expressed the multi-ethnic character of Hawaiian sporting practices. Yonamine was one of the stars. But he shared the field with likes of Young Suk Ko, Bill Apau, Isso Ito, Henry Hosea, John Kapuna, and Richard Asato. After seeing the Hawaii All Stars tie his San Jose State team, player Chuck Mallory insisted that Yonamine was as good as Wedemeyer, who at that time was an All American. Mallory told the press, "Good players must be a dime a dozen in the islands."[3]

Few confused the University of Hawai'i eleven with the football power-houses that emanated from Notre Dame or the University of Southern California, but it often held its own against respectable mainland opponents in the 1920s, 1930s, 1940s, and 1950s. Annually, Honolulu football fans were treated to the sight of at least one "big time" mainland eleven team crossing the Pacific to play the "Rainbow Warriors." More often than not the University of Hawai'i lost and sometimes by large margins. However, they won some games and opponents did well not to take the largely non-white Rainbow Warriors for granted. In 1925, Asian Pacific Islander standout Willie Wise helped lead the UH eleven to a decisive 41-0 victory over the visiting Colorado Agricultural College, later known as Colorado State. In 1954, the University of Nebraska traveled to Hawai'i and humiliated the Rainbow Warriors, 50-0. The next year, the University of Hawai'i stunned the Cornhuskers, 6-0, in Lincoln, Nebraska.[4]

During the 1930s, five foot five inch and 140 pound Tommy Kaulukukui starred as a running back for the University of Hawai'i. Like Wedemeyer and Yonamine, Kaulukukui was a splendid all-around athlete who excelled in baseball and basketball as well as football. In a game against UCLA in 1935, Kaulukukui burned his big time opponents with a long kick off return of 103 yards for a touchdown. In probably not one of his grander moments, the great American sportswriter, Grantland Rice, called Kaulukukui "Grass Shack" in reference to a popular, but patronizing song about Hawai'i. The *Los Angeles Times*' Jack

Sanger called Kaulukukui "cookie" because "he looked mighty sweet and wrote that the Hawaiian "learned to shake his hip from the native Hawaiian hula-hula dancers." Kaulukukui did more than just return a long kick off against the Bruins. "The tiny Hawaiian-Chinese was a constant threat," turning in one run from scrimmage of forty-five yards, two of twenty yards, and passing and catching the ball impressively. When UH edged the University of Utah, Kaulukukui tossed the winning touchdown pass. The press reported, "<T>.he tiny Hawaiian ran back, with towering Ute linemen swarming after him ... calmly flipped the ball over the enemy secondary to Ernest Moses who fell over the goal." Kaulukukui also earned small college All-American honors, went on to coach his alma mater's eleven, and became a member of the National Football Hall of Fame.[5]

Tommy was not the only Kaulukukui to star for UH. In the late 1930s, UH upset San Jose State College, which had been enjoying an eleven game winning streak. This time, Tommy's brother Joe was the big star as his team edged the Californians, 13-12. Eight years later, another brother, Sal, quarterbacked UH to an upset victory over the heavily favored Fresno State, 7-2. Unkei Uchima and Wallace Lam Ho helped as well.[6]

Mainlanders have long been struck by the multi-racial, multi-ethnic character of the University of Hawai'i football teams. At the same time, UH listed its players ancestry in its programs. The *Pacific Citizen* declared it was the only college football program to do so. In the fall of 1938, the University of Hawai'i squad arrived in Los Angeles en route to a game in Denver against the University of Denver. The *Los Angeles Times* noted the twenty-four players on the traveling squad "representing fifteen distinct racial groups—including Koreans and Scandinavians." A player named Kaye Chung captained the University of Hawai'i squad. Ten years later, some of the standout performers on the University of Hawai'i squad were backs Sal Kaulukukui, Wally Lam Ho, Johnny Dang,, Jyun Hirota, as well as end Harry Kahuanui, who became the first UH gridder named to the prestigious East/West Shrine All-Star game. The *Pacific Citizen* observed that several of UH"s football players were Nikkei—players such as Hirota, Richard Mamiya, Jimmy Asato, Herbert Doi, Unkei Uchima, Sadao Watasaki, James Satao, Saburu Takesaeu. In 1950, Herbert's brother, Mansfield, was unanimously selected as team captain. Moreover, Harold Kometani served as an assistant coach. In more recent years, the University of Hawai'i gridders continued to represent the islands' diversity. For example, pro standouts Mark Tuinei, Merv Lopes, Ma'a Tanuvasa, Al Noga and Jesse Sapolu have played for the University of Hawai'i. Playing on the 1995 squad were Tad Yamashita, defensive back, Joe Wong, a 295-pound guard, Bobby Singh, a 300 pounder from British Columbia, and Randall Okimoto, a slotback of Japanese, Portuguese and Guamian ancestry. In the early 2000s, Timmy Chang was a record-breaking quarterback for June Jones' wide open offense. An all-WAC freshman of the year in 2000, Chang's passing was not the only reason why UH got into some post-season bowl games. For one thing, Vince Manuwai was a standout defender who became the first UH gridder to be nominated for the prestigious Vince Lombardi Award.[7]

Reinforcing the multi-ethnic character of the University of Hawai'i football tradition is that two former head coaches—Kaulukukui and Jim Asato were Asian Pacific. Today, the team's coaching staff wears Palaka shirts on the sidelines. This is done to honor Hawaiian multi-ethnic, multi-racial plantation workers, who also wore Palaka shirts. [8]

Semi-professional elevens thrived on the islands for years. In the early 1920s, the Associated Press affirmed the prowess of Frank Kanae, a forty year old Hawaiian who had been playing football on the islands for twenty-five years. A father of sixteen children, Kanae was known as "cannon ball" because of the hard charging way he battered the line. Kanae was born on Molokai but schooled on Oahu at St. Louis College and Kamehameha. He had played on several Honolulu elevens over the years but most recently for a team representing the city's Palama district. In 1923, a Honolulu Town team consisted of Asian Pacific Islander athletes such as William Wise, F.H. Tong, and Nick Hoopii. The Thundering Herd team included athletes such as Frank Anahu and Jiro Sato. In 1934, the University of California football team came to the Islands where it lost to the Honolulu Town Team, 26-15, on Christmas Day. In 1936, an all-star team of college greats traveled to the islands. There they took on and beat the Honolulu Town squad. Nevertheless, the mainlanders were impressed with Hiram Kaaqua's skills and skin color as he was dubbed the "Black Grange" in reference to one of America's great gridders, Red Grange. In 1941, according to scholar Frank Ardolino, Jackie Robinson could not find integrated professional teams on which to play on the mainland after leaving UCLA. Robinson, a great all-around athlete, wound up crossing the Pacific to compete for the Honolulu Bears of the Hawai'i Senior Football League. Opposing the University of Hawai'i eleven, as well as the Nua Alis and Healanis squads, the Bears gave players unique contracts. Robinson, for example, was paid $100 a game and a bonus if the Bears won the league championship. In addition, Robinson received a draft-deferred construction job near Pearl Harbor. In 1946, one potent semi-professional squad called the Leialums toured the mainland after World War II as the aforementioned Hawaii All-Stars. During one game against the University of Portland, Yonamine scored six touchdowns and kicked ten extra points. The next year, the All-Stars defeated the University of Portland again. Yonamine was no longer with the squad. But Jim and Dick Asato each scored touchdowns. After World War II, as well, a professional team called the Hawaiian Warriors competed in the minor league Pacific Coast Football League. Like the better known Green Bay Packers, this eleven was community owned. Thousands of fans reportedly bought shares in the Hawaiian Warriors—shares worth ten dollars each. The Hawaiian Warriors were multi-racial and multi-ethnic. In 1946, the Warriors fielded athletes such as all-league quarterback Joe Kaulukukui and end Joe Chong. The 1948 squad started the season with all but two of its players hailing from the islands. For instance, the *Honolulu Star-Bulletin* depicted team member William Apau as an Hawaiian Chinese and a "big, smart—slashing tackle." The starting backfield for the 1948 squad's opening game consisted of Yonamine at one halfback and Joe Corn, a player possessing English, Portuguese, and Native Hawaiian ancestry, at the other. At quarterback was Al Chang, while Wally Lam started at fullback. The Hawaiian Warriors were considered the best drawing team in the Pacific Coast League. However, in 1949, a waterfront strike in Honolulu made it impossible for the squad to travel to the mainland. According to one San Francisco *Examiner* sportswriter, the Pacific Coast League could not stand to lose the Warriors and folded.[9]

Mainland football coaches have long known that Hawai'i cultivated some fine football talent. St. Mary's College attracted a number of Hawaiian players, the most notable of whom was, of course, Herman Wedemeyer. An elusive ball carrier and dependable defender of mixed European, Native Hawaiian, and Chinese ancestry, Wedemeyer dazzled Bay Area college football fans during the mid-1940s. In the early 1950s, Southern California junior colleges such as Compton and Pasadena lured Hawaiians eastward so adeptly that some observers feared for the future of the University of Hawai'i's grid fortunes. Oregon State also developed a link between Corvallis, Oregon and the islands. "Honolulu" Harold Hughes played for Oregon State before joining the professional Boston Braves in the 1930s. In the 1950s, this trans-Pacific link brought to Beaver football a sturdy lineman in Herman Clark and a versatile tailback in Joe Francis. In the last fifty years Hawaiian football players frequently found their way into Michigan State University, University of Southern California, University of Utah and Brigham Young University uniforms.[10]

Professional football coaches have used Hawaiian players. Wedemeyer rarely shined in the pros as he did in college. Even before he left St. Mary's, the San Francisco 49ers, then competing in the All-American Football Conference (AAFC), expressed interest in him. The National Football League's Los Angeles Rams drafted Wedemeyer, but the Los Angeles Dons of the AAFC, however, signed him for a two-year, $47,500 contract. After playing with the Dons in 1948, Wedemeyer was let go and wound up on the Baltimore Colts, then also a member of the AAFC. The Colts released him and Wedemeyer tried to catch on with the 49ers, but while he remained a Bay Area favorite, the San Francisco team cut him. Subsequently, Wedemeyer went into island politics, but became most famous as a supporting actor on the *Hawaii 5-0* series. Wedemeyer died in 2000. St. Mary's, consequently, honored the memory of the great running back by establishing a Herman Wedemeyer Endowed Scholarship Fund. Yonamine signed by the San Francisco 49ers for the 1947 season, but played just one year for the fledgling franchise. Linemen Herman Clark and Charlie Ane, nevertheless, starred in the National Football League in the 1950s. And Mel Tom, Rockne Freitas, and Jesse Sapolu shined as well in the NFL in more recent years.[11]

Football and Community

It has been relatively hard for ethnic communities to organize American football squads. Baseball has not needed the expensive equipment often required in American football. Basketball has not needed eleven players on each side. Nevertheless, since early in the twentieth century, football squads, American and soccer-style, were organized to represent Asian Pacific community strivings.

Soccer-style and rugby football attracted the participation of Asian and Asian Pacific American students at American universities on the East Coast in the 1910s. In 1917, Chinese student soccer teams were formed in Boston and New York City. The next year, those teams merged into the New York Chinese Students' soccer team and competed against other clubs. On the West Coast, Chinese Americans at Stanford and the University of California established soccer teams. In the fall of 1920, the *San Jose Mercury* reported on a soccer association formed in the San Francisco Bay Area. Among the participants were teams representing Stanford University, the University of California, the Italian Club of San Francisco, and the Chinese YMCA of San Francisco. In 1917, Japanese students at Stanford assembled a rugby squad and reportedly challenged Chinese students at the University of California for a match. [12]

In terms of American football, an Associated Press account published in the *Los Angeles Times* told of a "slit-eye game" in 1909 between Japanese and Chinese athletes in San Francisco. The "Chino-Jap footballists" ended the highly attended game on a sour note. The "Mikado Men" won the game but the "Chinks <s>wipe<d> the ball." Things turned violent on the gridiron where three members of the Japanese Fuji Club eleven were hurt. And a melee in which spectators and players participated ensued after the game. The fracas broke out because while the Fuji Club came out on top of a 10-0 victory, the losers took the ball, which the winners claimed rightly belonged to them. The Fuji Club's captain swore that his team would never play the Chinese squad again. And both teams said they would switch over to rugby as Stanford and Cal had in the wake of increasing controversy over American football in various colleges across the country. [13]

A Chinese American squad was organized in the San Francisco Bay Area during the late 1910s. Called the Kai Kee team, it was coached by a former University of California player named Son Kai Kee. The squad apparently had trouble finding opponents. The *San Francisco Chronicle* explained that part of the problem was that its members worked during the week. Yet the Kai Kee team optimistically challenged any eleven averaging 145 pounds per player or less. Among the opponents the Kai Kee team expected to play were an eleven representing the "Deaf and Dumb" school in Berkeley and a team of Japanese students at the University of California. In the early 1920s, Son Kai Kee organized and coached the Wa Ku football team, which held practices at Davies

Field in downtown Oakland and played games at San Francisco's legendary Kezar Stadium.[14]

Meanwhile, Kamehameha's football teams represented indigenous Hawaiians on Oahu. Playing on the 1915 squad were athletes such as Richman-Dower, H. Bertelmann, Pereko, C. Bertelmann, Kamuka, and. L. Bertelmann. In the early 1930s, Kamehameha traveled to the mainland and beat a Chaffey Junior College eleven, 12-0. A player surnamed Aikue scored one of the touchdowns.[15]

During the 1920s, the Yoke Choy Club was founded in San Francisco's Chinatown. According to pioneering Chinese American historian, Thomas Chinn, Yoke Choy means " disseminate knowledge." The Yoke Choy Club was intended to promote Christianity, love of music, and athletics among members. Its football team played against other Chinese American elevens, as well as Japanese American squads. In 1932, the Yoke Choy eleven opposed a squad representing the Chinese Poly Club in a game that was staged as a benefit for Shanghai refugees. It also played against non-Asian Pacific American teams. In 1931, the Yoke Choy squad took on white teams in the McNamara Grid League, which held its games at Golden Gate Park. [16]

In the meantime, Chinese Americans in Oakland and Fresno organized football teams. In 1925, the *Los Angeles Times* reported on a game between "Chinese gridiron teams" from the two California cities for the "Chinese Championship of Northern California." Joe Yuen captained the Fresno eleven while his Oakland counterpart was Al Chin. The game ended in a scoreless tie, mainly because of inclement weather. The rain and mud, according to the *Times'* account, excluded the use of "wily Oriental strategy." Oakland's Larry Wong proved the best ball carrier, while Fresno's Bill Dott did a good job of punting in the slop.[17]

In the 1930s, Chinese American community football teams were quite active. In 1935, a team of youngsters called the Chinese Crusaders represented Oakland's Chinese American community. For several years during the 1930s, a Los Angeles squad of Chinese Americans players met a rival eleven from San Francisco in a game dubbed the Rice Bowl. In 1936, the *Los Angeles Times* declared, "Pasadena has its rose bowl--other cities have sun bowls, cotton bowls, but thanks to football minded Chinese San Francisco has its Rice Bowl--for the Pacific Coast Chinese football championship." Cotton Warburton, a great USC All-American, was recruited to coach the Los Angeles squad, while St. Mary's Bill Foster coached the San Franciscans. In January, 1937, for example, the San Francisco team beat their Los Angeles rivals, 6-0, at the University of San Francisco. Although the game was held in the rain an apparently nice crowd of spectators appeared and contributed funds to the Chinese war effort against Japan. The half time show consisted of a Lion Dance engaged in by a Chinatown Boy Scouts troop, as well as a performance put on by San Francisco's Chinese Catholic Mission's Drum and Bugle corps. The Rice Bowl was also staged in Los

Angeles, where, according to the San Francisco coach, Bill Fisher, it also proved a hit with the local Chinese American community.[18]

The Rice Bowl asserted Chinese American cultural citizenship—an assertion of distinctiveness and similarity to other Americans in the 1930s. The white press sometimes dimly perceived this assertion. Writing on the scheduled Rice Bowl in February, 1938, the *San Francisco Chronicle*'s Bob Stevens declared: "Those little Orientals who ignore the seasons and poo-poo the numbers on the grocers calendar will haul their honorable selves out to Ewing Field this Saturday afternoon to engage in the most unique football game on the books—The Rice Bowl Business." Nevertheless, Stevens admitted, the San Francisco eleven, which he called the "local pigtails," included some fine former high school players.[19]

A Northern California Chinese Football League was organized in the fall of 1940. Among the elevens involved were St. Mary's Unknown Packers, the Black Panthers from Sacramento and the Young Chinese from Oakland. Games took place at an old stadium in San Francisco's Golden Gate Park.[20]

The St. Mary's football team acquitted itself well against other Chinese American squads. Yet its gridders represented the entire Bay Area Chinese American community against non-Chinese Americans. In the fall of 1938, the Unknown Packers defeated a team of Japanese Americans, 12-0. Unfortunately moved by the bitter war then waged across the Pacific the *Chinese Digest* exulted, "Packers 12, Japs 0."[21]

Four years earlier, Asian Pacific tensions spilled over into a *Chinese Digest* account of a game between Pasadena's Crown City Japanese and the Los Angeles Chinese. The game ended in a 6-6 tie. However, according to the *Chinese Digest*, the Crown City coach officiated the game held at Pasadena Junior College and called many unfair penalties on the Chinese American players.[22]

San Francisco's Chinese American displayed support for local college football programs. In November, 1940, the *California Chinese Press* furnished readers with substantial coverage of the upcoming "Big Game" between the Rose Bowl bound Stanford eleven and its East Bay rival from the University of California, Berkeley. It published, moreover, an advertisement for the Club Shanghai's "Big Game" rally.[23]

Japanese Americans also used football as a way of sustaining a sense of community. In 1928, the *San Francisco Chronicle* reported on a game between the Japanese American Showa Club and the Chinese Tung team. The Showas won the game at Ewing Field in San Francisco, prompting the *Chronicle* to declare that the Japanese American gridders were too speedy "for the bigger boys from Grant Avenue." The *Chronicle* also announced it heard rooters mix "Hold that line" with "strange sounding exhortations."[24]

According to the *Pacific Citizen,* the original Rice Bowl pitted two San Francisco-based teams--one Japanese American and the other Chinese American. It claimed that the games were well played and well attended. However, the

"Japanese aggression in Manchuria and China" put an end to the rivalry. The *Pacific Citizen* reported that Chinese American elders even locked up their sons to keep them from playing Japanese Americans.[25]

These early Rice Bowl games were well publicized and highly competitive. In 1931, the war clouds hanging over Manchuria forced a postponement. In 1934, the *Nevada State Journal* showed a photograph of Japanese American football players ready to take on the "Chinese All-Stars" at San Francisco's Kezar Stadium. Coached by a former Stanford player named Tommy Glover, the team practiced daily at Golden Gate Park. At least one European American coach internalized the emotions provoked by the early Rice Bowl games. Benny Lom, an All-American player at Cal, coached the Chinese American squad until it was defeated. Then, Lom resigned.[26]

The program for the 1934 "Big Game" between Stanford and Cal informs us that the preliminary "kids game" pitted the McKevvits Lions against the Lumpe Lions. Both teams were sponsored by the Lions Club in the San Francisco East Bay and all of the players save one, were Japanese American. Indeed, according to the *Pacific Citizen,* Japanese Americans in California organized several talented Nisei elevens. The best were the Berkeley Niseis, Alameda Taikus, Los Angeles Olivers, and Los Angeles Spartans. These teams were light and fast and were constituted by athletes with high school football experience and a few college veterans, although most of the players were considered "too small" for college football. [27]

In the concentration camps, Japanese Americans expressed enthusiasm for football. At Manzanar, male internees played the game. Internees also poignantly tried to retain their connections to the outside world by way of football. In 1942, the *Los Angeles Times* reported that at the Gila camp in Arizona internees who had attended the University of Southern California (USC) and Cal staged separate rallies before a big game between the USC and Cal football teams.[28]

After World War II, community teams continued to emerge. In 1949, Chinese San Franciscans were represented by an eleven called the San Francisco Eagles. The Sacramento Panthers, meanwhile, represented Sacramento's Chinese community. At the same time, the *Pacific Citizen* observed a decline in Japanese American community teams after World War II. It explained that the Nisei had gotten too old, while the Sansei were too young.[29]

In Hawai'i, community often connected to class, as well as ethnic and racial boundaries. Barefoot football teams in the 1920s and 1930s represented the working class, Honolulu neighborhoods of Kalihi, Waipahu, Punchbowl, Kakaako, and Palama. Albert Adams, a Portuguese Hawaiian, told oral historians in the 1980s that some of these teams included players of Japanese, Native Hawaiian, and occasionally Chinese ancestries. [30]

Barefoot football leagues continued to exist after World War II, although their peak years had faded. In December, 1949, the Primo Athletic Club from Honolulu's Kakaako district team defeated Palama before 2500 fans at Honolulu

Stadium. Masa Morita was the big star for the victors. Helping Morita was Harry Kikuyama. Palama was led by Ray Apaa, Charley Choo, and Ted Hasegawa.[31]

Ethnic-based football teams were formed on the Islands. After World War II, Japanese Hawaiians organized a "Go For Broke" to represent Hawaiian veterans of the 442nd. Among the team's leading players were Sadao Watasaki and Unkei Uchima.[32]

Before and after World War II, therefore, Asian Pacific American communities expressed substantial affection for American football. Ethnic newspapers consistently pointed with pride to players who represented their communities well on the gridiron. In the fall of 1949, for example, the *Chinese Press* noted that a Chinese American named Chuck Toy starred on the Fresno State eleven. Since Toy served frequently as a Chinese American surname, the *Chinese Press's* allusion to the Fresno State standout is understandable. A Fresno State publicist, however, wrote to the *Press*, complaining that "Toy is not Chinese boy—Just plain white American."[33]

Meanwhile, the youthful San Francisco 49ers, attempting to establish a permanent presence in a city and region in which college football and PCL baseball had long reigned, built and solidified bridges to San Francisco's Chinese American community. The 49ers biggest star at the time was former Stanford great, Frankie Albert, who showed up at least occasionally at San Francisco Chinatown functions. In the spring of 1950, for instance, Albert acted as the major celebrity at a Chinatown banquet honoring young male Chinese American athletes.[34]

Pacific Islander and Mainlander Stars

In the late 1910s, St. Mary's College of California began a minor tradition of recruiting Hawaiians for its football teams. St. Mary's was not the first mainland college or university to do so. For example, an Hawaiian named Atherton Gilman not only played tackle for Harvard University in 1915, but became an All American. Interestingly, another Ivy League school, the University of Pennsylvania, considered suiting up an Asian Pacific football player. In 1906, according to a *San Francisco Chronicle* report, "Takaki, the Jap" almost made the football team but failed because of a weak heart. In 1915, the *Chicago Tribune* declared that Wah Kai Chang was "the first Chinese to receive recognition for football work in an American college" when the Hawaiian competed for the University of Chicago as a freshman.[35]

Readers of the *Fort Wayne News* in 1916 learned about a "<s>crappy <c>hink" named Pao Shun-Kwan who played quarterback for Rensalear Polytechnic. "Formerly of Shanghai," the young athlete competed for the freshman and reportedly did well enough to make it to the varsity. The sportswriter declared, "The young Chinaman is fast on his feet, uses good judgment in running the team, and his 'celestial smile' always looms up somewhere in the thick of the scrap." The next year, the *Washington Post* named Kwan as quarterback on an "All-American" team of players with foreign sounding names. The *Post* maintained, "They're all playing formal football and mighty good football, and they're all Americans, too."[36]

The St. Mary's 1918 football squad featured three Hawaiians as backfield members. Ed Hughes of the *San Francisco Chronicle* described Correa, Kauhane, and Naiphaa as "boys <who> are well groomed in football…They are fast, tricky runners and know how to protect themselves in the open field." Prior to coming to the mainland Noble Kauhane and Bill Nahipaa had competed for Punahou Preparatory School. St. Mary's also fielded a center named Heirero, who came to the California college from Guam.[37]

Nearby, the University of California, Berkeley squad called on the services of Chinese American, Son Kai Kee. Ed Hughes wrote, "Ki-Kee <sic>, a Chinese, is trying for an end position. He is rather light, but he is fast and will be given every chance to show what he can do." The *Oakland Tribune*'s Herbert Hawes claimed that "little Kai Kee—the slippery Chinese boy" had played quarterback on the freshman squad and was actually playing fullback for the Cal varsity. Hawes maintained that "he is fast as lightening and not very easy to tackle," although somewhat small for a fullback.[38]

In the 1920s, Arthur Matsu surfaced as one of the finest college quarterbacks on the East Coast. At that time, the single wing offense dominated in American football. In the single wing, the quarterback called signals, handled the ball, and did a great deal of blocking. However, the single wing quarterback did relatively little running or passing. Formerly starring at quarterback at Cleveland High School in front of the great Benny Friedmann, Matsu garnered a great deal of praise while with the William and Mary University eleven. The *Washington Post* declared that "fans say <Matsu>has displayed genius in his field marshaling." The *Post* maintained that "Matsu, an American-born Japanese, played a star game for the visitors" against Syracuse. When William and Mary easily downed Kings College, 37-0, Matsu, who was actually a Canadian-born "hapa" reportedly "outgeneraled" the opposition. After his college playing career ended, Matsu competed for a year professionally with the Dayton Triangles and then served Rutgers as an assistant football coach and sports publicity director.[39]

The 1930s witnessed several players of Asian Pacific ancestry competing on mainland teams. In the mid-1930s, Ed Yee, a Chinese American played end for San Francisco State College, while Irwin Chan suited up for Fresno State College. Around the same time, Tin Yan Jim On started at center for North Dakota State. In 1938, the *Los Angeles Times* reported on the "All Nations" backfield at San Diego State College. In addition to halfbacks Art Metzger and Frank Galindo, described as German and Mexican American respectively, Hideo Higashi started at fullback along with "Indian" quarterback Allen Louie. In the fall of

1938, the *Times* called Cal Poly Pomona's Kazuma Hisanaga "one of the best blockers in the loop." Meanwhile, the Wai brothers from Hawai'i, Francis and Conkling suited up in UCLA uniforms and got plenty of playing time on Bruin teams which featured great football players such as Kenny Washington and Jackie Robinson. Possessing Chinese and indigenous Hawaiian ancestry, Francis earned a posthumous Congressional Medal of Honor for the heroism he displayed while serving in the Philippines. Hawaiian Bill Anahu became an outstanding end for Santa Clara College in the late 1930s, playing "vicious football" for the Broncos at the 1938 Sugar Bowl. During World War II, Anahu was killed in action. Meanwhile William Kanakanui, Jr., stood out as a tackle for the Naval Academy, while competing as well for the school's swimming team.[40]

The versatile Bill Kajikawa became an all-conference fullback for Arizona State in the 1930s after competing as a multi-sport athlete at Phoenix Union High School, where he was all-state in football for two years. According to the *Pacific Citizen,* Kajikawa was a fine passer, who earned small college All-American honors. After graduating, Kajikawa coached freshman football at his college alma mater. Apparently, Kajikawa's ancestry rendered him not the most popular choice for the post. In 1959, Frank Kush, then head football coach of Arizona State, named Kajikawa freshman coach. Kush remembered that Kajikawa "was great around young people because he really cared." Kajikawa also assumed recruiting duties for Arizona State in Hawai'i, bringing some talented Hawaiian players over to Tempe. [41]

During World War II, Herman Wedemeyer glittered as the greatest Hawaiian player of his time. Typically during the first half of the twentieth century, freshmen were not eligible to play in varsity sports. World War II, however, inspired a change in the freshman eligibility rules and Wedemeyer made an immediate impact on the Bay Area and national football scene. At five feet ten and 164 pounds, Wedemeyer appeared hardly as an imposing physical presence. Still he played football with a carefree, infectious, and unselfish style rooted in his Hawaiian childhood. Wedemeyer recalled to *Sports Illustrated* writer Ron Fimrite:

> I was born on the Big Island (Hawaii) in an area so remote that we had no paved roads. We used cornstalks for goalposts, and we played a type of touch football with as many as 30 on a side. Let me tell you, you learned to dodge with that many people trying to catch you. And we threw the ball around all the time. According to our rules, you could pass the ball forward or backward whenever you pleased. It was chaotic. But I took that style of play with me to St. Mary's. [42]

Wedemeyer, consequently, earned recognition not only for dazzling long runs with the ball, but for lateraling the pigskin off to teammates enroute to a touchdown himself—perhaps an informative example of the Hawaiian aloha spirit in action. Yet, mainland observers were struck by the fact Wedemeyer was not just a very talented football player, but that he was a talented football player from Hawai'i. Indeed, Wedemeyer's feats often encouraged comments that suggested Hawaiians, regardless of racial and ethnic ancestry, comprised a distinct and exotic ethnic group.[43]

Historian James N. Gregory in *American Exodus* insightfully asks readers to consider the people who migrated to California from Oklahoma and Arkansas during the 1930s as belonging to a discrete ethnic group. One problem, he admits, in doing so is that the Dust Bowl migrants too rarely identified themselves as belonging to an "Okie" culture. Such identification, for good or bad, was thrust upon them by public officials, civil authorities, educators, and the popular media. Likewise, the sporting press and others seemed determined to confer a unique, exotic Hawaiian ethnic identity on athletes such as Wedemeyer.[44]

Clearly, the Bay Area fell in love with the Hawaiian halfback. His coach Jimmy Phelan enthused, "It took me less than two minutes to see that I had the football player every coach dreams about, but seldom gets…Here was a kid who had everything—speed of foot and body and hands, speed of brain, perfect coordination, amazing flexibility, and the ability to be at his best when you needed him the most." In 1943, the *San Francisco Examiner*'s Prescott Sullivan wondered why Wedemeyer did not achieve All-American mention. Sullivan quoted the respected Bay Area football coach Buck Shaw, who maintained that Wedemeyer was "so good that it's hard to believe he's playing his first season of college ball." In 1945, the *San Francisco Chronicle*'s Bill Leiser celebrated the fact that the "21 year old Hawaiian-Chinese boy" would return to St. Mary's after a year in the merchant marines and wrote a year later, "Hawaiian-born Herman, so small it's impossible to believe when you see him off the field he can do what he does on it, takes his place as the greatest Coast-developed player of all time, a distinction previously owned by the big U.C.LA. back, Kenny Washington." During Wedemeyer's senior year, the *San Francisco Chronicle*'s Will Connolly called "the mild mannered Hawaiian the most exciting player we ever laid eyes on—anywhere, anytime, on any team." Connolly predicted that Wedemeyer was "destined to become a legend in these parts." In the late 1960s, Ron Fimrite wrote in the *San Francisco Chronicle,* "the combination of <Wedemeyer's> Hawaiian ancestry and truly remarkable versatility captured the fans of an entire nation of football freaks."[45]

One might expect Bay Area sportswriters to laud Wedemeyer, but Easterner Grantland Rice claimed the "Hawaiian centipede" was one of the most versatile backs he had ever seen" and the greatest all around athlete in America. When Wedemeyer starred in the Sugar Bowl game, Rice noticed:

> Wedemeyer looked smaller than he was. But I noticed that in addition to good legs and a halfbarrel chest, he had a pair of great-looking hands, developed from pushing hand

trucks loaded with cases of pineapples, a job that called for
both strength and dexterity. This work undoubtedly helped
him to get that firm grip on a football, so that he seems almost
to palm it as he roves around looking for a pass opening.

And the All-American Review Board said of Wedemeyer in 1945, "statistics and
technical skill cannot be discounted but it's the utter nonchalance and wizardry
of Wedemeyer that keeps customers jumping up and down."[46]

Furnished with an exoticized Hawaiian ethnic identity, Wedemeyer, according to much of the press, shined as not just an elusive ball carrier. He was,
according to the *San Francisco News*'s Jack Rosenbaum, "hula hipped." Much
was made of Wedemeyer's supposedly easy going, Hawaiian personality and
physical characteristics. Will Connolly described "<t>he dark complexioned"
Wedemeyer as "rugged and elusive." Yet, as well, Wedemeyer "laughs
throughout practice." The *San Francisco Chronicle* quoted his coach, Jimmy
Phelan, declaring: "I like to coach the Hawaiian boys...they have a good sense
of humor, have played the game since they crawled out of the cradle---and are
they durable." Writing for *Collier's* magazine, Emmons Byrne asserted, "Despite his name. Wedemeyer is a true Hawaiian with a statuesque frame and
swarthy complexion.[47]

Another elusive, versatile Hawaiian gridder was provided with an Hawaiian ethnic identity even though he possessed Japanese-Okinawan ancestry.
Wally Yonamine, while trying out for the San Francisco 49ers in 1947, "hula-
hipped his way for another ten additional yards," according to *San Francisco
News* reporter Don Selby. And even the *Pacific Citizen* hailed Yonamine as a
"hula hipping Nisei halfback from Hawaii." [48]

Press attention was heaped upon Yonamine's Hawaiian origins when he
and another Japanese Hawaiian, center Henry Hosea, arrived at the 49ers training camp. The *San Francisco Chronicle* and *Examiner* represented Yonamine as
a lovable, Pidgin English speaking character. In reporting on an ostensible conversation between 49er coach Buck Shaw and the "Hawaiian HB," the *San
Francisco Chronicle* quoted Yonamine as complaining, " I don't eat. I lose 12
pounds." When Shaw asked if Yonamine got enough food Yonamine supposedly replied, "No. No. That's not it. But coach, why we get no rice?" Since Yonamine became a hot prospect, the *Chronicle* maintained, Yonamine procured
all the rice he wanted.[49]

In a similar vein, Curly Grieve, a sportswriter for the *San Francisco Examiner* described Yonamine as the "happy Hawaiian." Under the headline,
"Wally Eats Rice. Can He Run?," Grieve's article pointed out that star 49er
quarterback Frankie Albert admired Yonamine's toughness. It also claimed that
after Yonamine evaded tacklers for a twenty yard run, "the dark skinned Hawaiian" turned to the sidelines and quipped, "You think too much hula." The
players on the sidelines laughed at the rookie, who reportedly enjoyed, as any

native boy might, walking around barefooted. According to the *Examiner*, Yonamine confidently expected to make the 49ers. He was quoted as saying, "I not worried...All my pals in Honolulu send me letters saying I getting lots of newspaper stuff."[50]

The *Pacific Citizen*, meanwhile, celebrated Yonamine's emergence as a potential Japanese American star. After Yonamine stood out in a 49er intersquad game in Salinas, the Japanese American Citizens' League publication declared, "<T>he Hawaiian Nisei who is the most highly touted rookie in the All-American Football Conference proved himself to be a press agent's dream" Of the 3500 attending the game which featured 49er greats such as Frankie Albert and Norm Standlee, 400 Nisei showed up, according to the *Pacific Citizen.* And half of the Nisei in attendance were Japanese American GIs studying at Monterey's Military Intelligence School. The weekly recognized that the Maui native was signed because of his ability but since Japanese Americans arrived to watch Yonamine perform in intersquad games held in Salinas and San Jose, the *Pacific Citizen* speculated that the 49ers were hoping that Yonamine might also draw paying customers into Kezar Stadium from the Bay Area's Nikkei population. It mentioned the Sacramento Solons' attempt to do the same thing by recruiting Nushida and Horio but added, "<N>either Nushida or Horio was the standout star which Yonamine promises to be."[51]

Hal Wood, a West Coast UPI reporter, tried to provide a multi-dimensional approach to Wally Yonamine's advent as a professional football halfback, despite a headline to his article reading, "Jap Gridder Fears No Pro Behemoths." Wood wrote, "This year the San Francisco Forty-niners will introduce to the fans across the nation one Wally Yonamine (pronounced Yon-a-mean-e), a full blooded Japanese who never set foot on the U.S. mainland until 1946, as one of its backfield stars." Despite "his ancestors," Wood maintained, Yonamine "absorbed the game of football just as the average U.S. mainland boy does in his school days." Wood reported that Buck Shaw was enthusiastic about Yonamine's potential. He would give the 49ers needed speed and, in the process, become "one of the sensations of the" All-American Football Conference. He could do it all, Shaw declared—run, pass, and kick, as well play defense. Admittedly. Yonamine was small for a pro football player. At 170 pounds, he was big for a "Japanese," Wood insisted. Moreover, he had the power of a 200 pounder and was not afraid to take on "any man on the gridiron." Yonamine told Wood, "I don't care how big or small they are. I feel that I can handle myself in any competition."[52]

Yonamine, however, proved not to be such a "happy Hawaiian" as he, but not Hosea, made the team. When the 49ers defeated the Brooklyn Dodgers in the opening game of the 1947 season, the *Chronicle* reported that the "Japanese American halfback from Hawaii" did not play much. Coach Shaw confessed that Yonamine expressed concern about gaining acceptance. Hal Wood reported Shaw admitting that "the kid is tied up a bit, just as you or I would be if we were

playing as the only white man on an all Japanese team." Shaw was quoted as
saying that Yonamine "is extremely conscious of being a Japanese. I try to tell
him everything is okeh, but he worries anyhow."[53]

Despite Shaw's assurances, Yonamine generally languished on the 49er
sidelines throughout the 1947 season. The *Chronicle* commented:

> Wallace Yonamine, Hawaii-born Japanese, gets all tied
> up on the San Francisco 49er bench and can't do his best work
> when sent in at halfback....Yonamine is afraid the big crowds
> at Kezar--biggest he's ever seen in his life--won't accept him
> as a U.S. citizen, because of his ancestry. In Honolulu, yes; on
> the mainland, no. That's what he thinks, though he's an ex-GI."

The San Francisco daily, in the meantime talked to San Jose State's Babe
Nomura about whether he had experienced any bigotry while competing for the
Spartans. Nomura responded that he had encountered no problems: "I don't
know what you're talking about. Everybody treated me fine. At home and on the
road." His coach, Bill Hubbard, maintained that Nomura was popular with his
teammates and cheered at both home and away games.[54]

Yonamine's career in professional football was not quite over. He tried to
compete with the 49ers in 1948 season, but a hand injury incurred while playing
baseball on the islands helped keep Yonamine off the 49er roster. He, then,
joined and starred for the Pacific Coast Football League Hawaiian Warriors. In
one game against the San Francisco Clippers, Yonamine took part in each of the
touchdowns the Warriors scored in a 19-6 victory. He passed for one, twenty-
four yard, touchdown, ran back an interception sixty-three yards for another
touchdown, and carried the ball thirty-four yards from scrimmage for a third
touchdown. In 1949, Yonamine tried to make the 49ers final roster, but was
cut.[54]

Yonamine and Wedemeyer were not the only island football players for
whom an Hawaiian ethnic identify was constructed. The University of Southern
California suited up a "Honolulu Halfback" after World War II. According to a
San Francisco Examiner report, John Naumu caught his coach's eye "like a hula
girl." The *Pacific Citizen* pointed out Naumu also possessed Japanese ancestry.
Indeed, Naumu's emergence as "a new Hawaiian rage" apparently caught the
Southern California press by surprise. But, according to one UPI report, "this
astonishment at 'finding' the dark-skinned wiry touchdown-running Mr. Naumu
is bringing a lot of laughs from the barefoot leagues of Honolulu." Well in his
twenties by the time he headed to USC, Naumu had been well known as a luminary in Honolulu football circles before the great Wedemeyer. [55]

In 1950s, several Hawaiians attracted the ethnicization process. University
of Dayton back Leroy Ka-ne was named to the East-West Shrine All-Star game
annually held in San Francisco. Ka-ne, the *San Jose Mercury* declared, was a

"hard running Hawaiian back" and the first Hawaiian to ever play on the East All-Star team. His real name, the *Mercury* advised, was Peter Patrick Wialaahea Ka-ne, but his teammates gave him nicknames such as "the Savage," as well as "Coconut," Pineapple," and "Hyphen." A year later, the program for the East-West Shrine football game in 1951 informed readers that Oregon State lineman Herman Clark hailed from Honolulu. The 295-pound Clark was reportedly the largest lineman competing on the Pacific Coast. A varsity swimmer, as well, Clark's hobby was apparently playing a ukulele and "singing Hawaiian style." In the mid-1950s, the *Sports Review Football Annual* described Oregon State's Joe Francis as a "hula hipped Hawaiian tailback." Writer John Eggers asserted that "Honolulu Joe...like all Hawaiians...loves his native music and in moments of relaxation packs a mean baritone imparting island tunes."[56]

The example of the University of Hawai'i team's efforts on the part of Hawaiian statehood and tourism also represents the ethnicization process. In 1948, the University of Hawai'i players traveled to East Lansing, Michigan to oppose a fine Michigan State squad. Before the game a group of players, as well as the university's athletic director, Iwao Miyake, staged a presentation at an East Lansing hotel. In order to expand tourism to the islands and make the case for Hawaiian statehood, the players entertained the audience with ukuleles and Hawaiian songs. Hawaiian Olympic swimmer and Michigan State student, Thelma Kalama, showed up to do some hula dancing. Meanwhile, Miyake lectured the audience on Hawaiian history and translated the songs and dances for the mainlanders.[57]

Several other Asian Pacific American gridders attracted attention in the 1940s. Frank Miyaki, a "triple threat Nisei" suited up for Washington State in the early 1940s after starring on Spokane's Central High School eleven. Jack Yoshihara helped Oregon State get into the 1942 Rose Bowl, while a few years later another Nisei, Joe Nagata, quarterbacked for Louisiana State when it appeared in the 1944 Orange Bowl. Southern California's Redlands College was led by the accurate passing of future Hawaiian Warrior Al Chang in the early 1940s. Toward the end of the decade, Leonard Wong starred at fullback for Redlands. During World War II, the University of San Francisco suited up Sam Kim, a Korean American from Southern California. Ted Kahananui started at center for Colorado State in 1944 and 1945. Huron College in South Dakota suited up Hawaiians Roy Hatate and Hen Lum during World War II, while Albert Nakazawa played for Valpariso and Bright Onoto competed for Hillsdale College. Honolulan Charley Liu was described "as a magician among T-Formation quarterbacks" while with the University of Portland in 1945. And Herbert Innaka, an Hawaiian Nisei, starred in the College of Idaho's backfield in the late 1940s.[58]

After World War II, George Fong developed into a stalwart backfield player for a fine University of California eleven. When the 1946 college football season ended, Fong was voted "the most courageous and inspirational member of the...squad." Referring to Fong's high school and San Francisco Chinatown's main thoroughfare, sportswriter Will Connolly wrote, "Poly High and Grant Avenue should be proud of Fong." Before Cal played the Navy Academy, head coach Pappy Waldorf named Fong team captain for the game. Given the troubling history of Chinese Americans in San Francisco, Connolly responded with a curious remark that the recognition accorded Fong "could only happen in this cosmopolitan community." Connolly declared, "The rest of the country considers a Chinese an exotic creature, but in this town and environs US citizens of Chinese ancestry are accepted as one of the boys." Connolly's colleague Bill Leiser expressed similar pride in Bay Area racial liberalism and pointed out that "it's a given that this is the first time Midshipmen have ever played against a team captained by a real Chinese." For some reason, however, a football expert named Dr. Lucien Stark, named Fong to his eighteenth annual "All-America jawbreaker" team. [59]

Japanese American Babe Nomura joined San Jose State College's backfield after the war. Before evacuation, Nomura had starred at halfback for Hollywood High School. In 1945, Nomura tied the Los Angeles Junior College record for touchdown passes with fifteen, while honored on the All Southern California Junior College Team. In one game against Pasadena Junior College, Nomura tossed three touchdown passes and returned a punt forty-five yards to help his team win. Playing with Nomura was a quarterback surnamed Wong. Bill Leiser expected Nomura would help the Spartans immensely in 1946. He predicted, "Babe Nomura whose passes clicked for 15 touchdowns last fall, will pass some more." The *San Francisco Chronicle* referred to Nomura as "a very fast and shifty runner, and a good passer," while the *San Francisco Examiner* called Nomura an "elusive Japanese pass throwing left half." Nomura's ability as a broken field runner was apparently more in evidence for the Spartans than his passing. Playing with Nomura on the San Jose State eleven was an another Nisei, lineman Jake Kikuchi.[60]

Chinese Hawaiian quarterbacks suited up for Santa Clara College and the University of Oregon after World War II. At Santa Clara, Abe Dung played quarterback and defensive back. In fact, Dung scored on a 93-yard touchdown against rival St. Mary's. Dung also starred in Santa Clara's upset victory over the Bear Bryant coached University of Kentucky team in the 1950 Orange Bowl. The *Chinese Press* maintained he was one of the best punters in Santa Clara's history. The *Chinese Press* also acclaimed Dung as "175 lbs of dynamite" in 1950. Joe Tom played quarterback for the University of Oregon behind future pro great Norm Van Brocklin. The *San Francisco Chronicle's* Will Connolly mistakenly called Tom a "Japanese boy," but described him as a good ball handler and tricky faker whose 5 ft. 8 inch frame hurt him in big time college football. Both Dung and Tom were vaunted high school athletes in Hawai'i. [61]

During and after World War II, St. Mary's recruited more gridders than Wedemeyer from the Hawaiian Islands. Born on a South Pacific island called

Pupi, Packard Harrington was a contemporary of Wedemeyer's. Harrington became a stellar backfield player of Irish-Samoan ancestry. His family moved to the Hawaiian Islands, where he starred in football for Iolani High School before fighting in Europe during World War II. Harrington shined especially on defense for the St. Mary's Gaels, earning all-West Coast honors in 1948. In 1950, the Cleveland Browns drafted Harrington in 1950 but the Hawaiian could not make it in the pros. [62]

Aside from Wedemeyer and Yonamine, a few other players of Asian Pacific ancestry played professionally for U.S. mainland and Canadian teams before 1950. Al Lolotai, described by the *Los Angeles Times*, as a "big Samoan" suited up for the Washington Redskins and the Los Angeles Dons. Part-Indigenous Hawaiian Joe Corn joined the Los Angeles Rams in 1948. John Kaleimamo played center for the Sacramento Nuggets of the Pacific Coast Football League with Paul Kuwabara, who had previously competed for Sacramento High School and Sacramento Junior College.[63]

During the 1950s, Stanford and other universities launched searches for Hawaiian talent. One of the players Stanford landed was Packard's brother, Tausau (Al) Harrington. Another was Al Napoleon. Both were wily running backs from Honolulu. According to sportswriter Will Connolly, Harrington had upset the Stanford coaching staff when he nicked himself doing a Samoan ceremonial dance. The "handsome Polynesian," Connolly maintained, would be a big draw because "of his exotic background." Interestingly, Al Harrington joined Herman Wedemeyer on the *Hawaii 5-0* cast. Harrington, indeed, became a featured actor on the popular series. The University of Southern California, meanwhile, recruited Charlie Ane, Harold Han, and Sal Naumu from the Hawaiian Islands. Ane was a large and versatile lineman, while Han was good enough lineman to compete in the Shrine East-West football game in San Francisco in 1953. Ane, however, was special. In 1952, the *Sporting News* ran an account on Ane by the respected Los Angeles sportswriter Rube Samuelson. Headlined "Hawaiian Ane One Hula-va Tackler," Samuelson claimed that the "happy go lucky" Ane possessed "Chinese, Samoan, and English" ancestors and had become the most famous Hawaiian gridder since Wedemeyer. Ane would subsequently star for the Detroit Lions. Oregon State recruited Joe Francis, as well as Herman Clark. And while the talented Francis never made it beyond being a backup quarterback for the Green Bay Packers, Clark was a solid lineman for the Chicago Bears. At the same time, smaller college programs also picked up Hawaiian talent. In 1950, Williamette suited up Al Minn, Bill Kukashika, Newt Kehahio, Bill Ewalika, Charles Nee, and Jimmy Noa.[64]

Also in the 1950s, San Jose State and Fresno State suited up several players of Asian Pacific ancestry. Japanese Americans such as Hash Takata, guard, Jim Kajoka, tackle, and Tom Yagi, center, played on the 1952 squad. What is more Larry Shishido served as student manager, while Lincoln Kimura was in the midst of a long time career as a trainer for not only San Jose State, but also eventually the San Francisco 49ers. Two years later, Hawaiian Melvin Soong played halfback for the Spartans, along with linemen Tom Yagi and James Hakagawa. In 1956, halfback Ken Matsuda wore a San Jose State uniform, as well as Hawaiian guard Charlie Kaaihue. Fibber Hirayama was a backfield star for Fresno State in the early 1950s. Ten years later, Larry Iwagaki was an all-league halfback for the Central California school. A graduate of Reedley High School, Iwagaki later coached and taught at his high school alma mater. In 1958, Hawaiian John Kapele was an all-conference tackle for BYU.[65]

Japanese American Pete Domoto was an outstanding lineman for Cal in the late 1950s after coach Pete Elliot shifted him from fullback. Playing guard for the eleven which achieved a conference title and a berth in the Rose Bowl, Domoto was named team co-captain for the 1959 season.[66]

Since the 1950s, a number of Asian Pacific gridders have not only competed on the college and professional levels, but have excelled. Many of these players have possessed Pacific Islander ancestry. In fact, during the last twenty years or so, some very fine athletes of Samoan ancestry have appeared in big time college football ranks, as well as the pros. In the late 1950s and early 1960s, Kenji Sasaki competed for the University of California. In 1960, Herb Yamasaki gleamed as one of the top linemen on the San Jose State Spartans' squad before playing semi-professionally with the San Jose Apaches. [67]

Several Hawaiians made their way to East Lansing, Michigan, and the Michigan State squad. Tommy Kaulukukui developed a friendship with Biggie Munn, a one-time Michigan State coach and athletic director. Kaulukukui, subsequently, did graduate work at Michigan State and became a big booster of the school to Hawaiian athletes, one of whom was his nephew Bill Kenney, a barefoot place kicker of some skill. Bob Apisa was a solid performer for Michigan State in the mid-1960s. The press hailed the fullback as a "215 pound, linecracking Hawaiian." Herman Wedemeyer's younger brother Charlie became a fine defensive back for Michigan State University in the late 1960s. Previously, Charlie had played for Punahou, where his quarterbacking skills garnered mention in *Sports Illustrated*'s "Faces in the Crowd" section in 1965. After graduating Michigan State, Charlie Wedemeyer remained on the mainland to do high school coaching. In California, Wedemeyer became a popular and successful coach at Los Gatos High School. Sadly, he contracted Lou Gehrig's Disease. Happily, he has put up a long and courageous battle against ALS.[68]

Roman Gabriel ranks clearly as one of the most famous football players of Filipino ancestry. While his mother was white, his Filipino father, Roman Ildefonso Gabriel Sr., worked as a cook for a railroad company after a stint in an Alaska cannery. Born in Wilmington, North Carolina, Gabriel starred as a quarterback for North Carolina State University in the late 1950s and early 1960s. The Los Angeles Rams then drafted him in the first round. Well over six feet tall, Gabriel quarterbacked the Los Angeles Rams for twelve years, during which time he was acknowledged as one of the better professional quarterbacks around. After finishing with the Rams, Gabriel put in four more years with the Philadelphia Eagles. Admittedly, football historians do not confuse Gabriel's accomplishments with those of Johnny Unitas or Joe Montana. Playing sixteen years as a quarterback in the NFL, nevertheless, was and remains impressive. After Gabriel's playing career ended, he became head football coach for Cal Poly of Pomona and then an assistant for the Boston Breakers of the United States Football League.[69]

Sei Miyama was a Gabriel contemporary. The Japanese American quarterbacked for Richard Nixon's alma mater, Whittier College in Southern California. At five-feet-seven, Miyama stood as unlikely pro material. The *Los Angeles Times*, however, considered Miyama an excellent small college quarterback. Indeed, he ranked eleventh among passers in the NAIA.[70]

Jackie Thompson was a more famous college football quarterback. Called the "Throwin' Samoan," Thompson starred for Washington State University in the 1970s. Like Gabriel, Thompson was drafted to play in the NFL. Compared to Gabriel's, Thompson's professional career was relatively brief. And outside of one year with the Tampa Bay Buccaneers, Thompson generally rode the bench. Nevertheless, in 2000 *Sports Illustrated* honored Thompson as the thirty-third best athlete in Washington's history. A few years after Thompson left Washington State, the Pullman school started another fine Samoan quarterback named Samoa Samoa.[71]

In the meantime, one standout Samoan gridder met a tragic end outside of an Amarillo, Texas, bar. Born in American Samoa but a resident of Honolulu, Ramse (Ram) Faleafine had left the islands to become the second leading ground gainer for West Texas State. However, the twenty-two-year-old was shot to death in 1971 following an argument.[72]

Hawaiians Mel Tom and Rockne Freitas were solid NFL performers in the 1960s and 1970s. A San Jose State star, Mel Tom, performed for several years as a fine defensive lineman for the Philadelphia Eagles and Chicago Bears in the 1960s and 1970s. Tom's daughter, Logan, became an All-American volleyball for Stanford in the early 2000s. A graduate of Kamehameha, Rockne Freitas played for Oregon State before joining the Detroit Lions.

In the 1970s, Arnold Mogado was just one of many fine athletes of Asian Pacific American ancestry to play football. A Hawaiian of part-Japanese ancestry Mogado starred for Michigan State before joining the Kansas City Chiefs. Japanese American Chuck Hirota quarterbacked and served as tri-captain for the University of Redlands squad. Nisei Don Chikami played halfback for Whittier College. Frank Manamaluena starred as a linebacker for San Jose State in the late 1970s. And Milt Holt was a "Japanese looking" quarterback for Harvard University. A Hawaiian of mixed racial and ethnic ancestry, Holt played previously for Kamehameha High School in Honolulu.[73]

In 1983, the San Francisco 49ers signed Daryl Wong as a free agent quarterback from Dartmouth. Wong's chances of making the team were limited and his chances of starring while Joe Montana reigned were infinitesimal. His story, nevertheless, is interesting. A native of San Francisco, Wong had stood out at Lowell High School in football, baseball, and tennis. Future 49er coach, George Seifert, had tried to recruit Wong for Stanford, but the San Franciscan chose Dartmouth instead. Wong told *East/West* reporter Mark Jue that he thought racial bias kept him from the starting line-up until late his Dartmouth career. But he was good enough to attract the 49ers' curiosity after graduation. When asked by Jue, why more Asian Americans did not play football, Wong responded, "I think it's the stereotype of football being brute force and the fear of injury that dissuades Asians from playing. Nobody likes to get hurt. In reality…football requires quickness and thinking. I wish more Asians would play."[74]

Wong, subsequently, tried out for the San Diego Chargers after the 49ers famed coach recommended him to the Southern California team. At the time, Wong told *East/West* that the "Asian community" was behind him when he sought a 49er roster place. He added, "Professionally, Asians have been successful in all aspects of life, but we haven't made a dent in athletics yet."[75]

Meanwhile, college and professional football coaches were discovering plenty of talented players with Pacific Islander ancestry. Jack Thompson's alma mater Washington State suited up several Pacific Islander players on its 1984 squad. Coach Jim Walden could call upon the services of defensive tackle Tokoumu Palilei, as well as linebackers Malo Taupoa, and Junior Tupola. Walden valued Tupola, in particular. The coach said, "He can be the most dominating player on the field."[76]

By this time, college and professional coaches such as Walden looked fondly upon the muscular and often very large bodies belonging to gridders of Samoan ancestry. Manu Tuiasosopo starred as a defensive lineman for UCLA from "far off-Samoa," according to *Sports Illustrated* and then went on to distinguish himself with the Super Bowl winning San Francisco 49ers. Jesse Sapolu starred as a versatile lineman for the 49ers, while Mark Tuinei blasted holes for the Dallas Cowboys' Emmet Smith. Tuinei tragically died of a drug overdose in 1999. UCLA's rival the University of Southern California recruited Junior Seau out of Oceanside, California. Seau, who could not speak English until he was seven, became one of the most feared linebackers in professional football for the San Diego Chargers during the 1990s after an All-American career at USC. Sportswriter Michael Silver called Seau in the 1990s the most intense player in the NFL since Ronnie Lott. As of this writing, the veteran Seau suits up for the New England Patriots.[77]

Other players of Pacific Islander and Asian backgrounds have competed in big time college and professional football in the last decades of the twentieth century. Hawaiian Wilson Faumina starred as a linebacker for San Jose State University in the 1970s before going on to a solid career with the NFL's Atlanta Falcons. Kaulana Park, recruited out of Kalua, Hawai'i, became a standout fullback for Stanford in the 1980s. Park played on a college team which also suited up Hawaiians Mark Hashimoto and Bill Pimental, as well as mainlanders Andy Hsu, Don Ting, and later in the decade, a fine defensive back named Tuan Van Le. Meanwhile, Vietnamese American Mike Nguyen played end for UCLA, while Korean immigrant John Kim placekicked for the Bruins. Tongan brothers Peter and Tom Tuipuloto became two of the many Pacific Islanders to compete for Brigham Young University. Peter, subsequently, played professionally in Canada. Suiting up the University of Pacific in the late 1980s was Hawaiian defensive end Chad Kurashige. Possessing Asian Indian ancestry, Sanjay Beach played offensive end for Colorado State University in the late 1980s and then had a brief career in the NFL. In 1990, offensive lineman and Korean American Eugene Chung became the first Asian American drafted in the first round by a National Football League team. Chung, however, proved a disappointment to the Atlantic Falcons and he never really became a better than competent NFL lineman. In the early 1990s, George Malauulu played quarterback for the University of Arizona, which also suited up Mu Tagoai and Pulu Poumele. Michah Matuzaki caught four touchdown passes in one game for BYU. Hapa Mike Koslowski stood out as an end for BYU and then played for the Chicago Bears. Joey Getherall, who possesses Japanese ancestry, played end for Notre Dame. Wearing University of Utah uniforms in the late 1990s were place kicker Ryan Kaneshiro, a multi-team athlete at Iolani High School in Honolulu, and dominating lineman Ma'ake Keamoeatu. At around 300 pounds, Neo Aoga was an unusual quarterback when he took snaps at Azusa Pacific in Southern California. In 2002, Emil Aguinaldo wrote about Harvard lineman Jamil Soriano, a three hundred pounder with a Pakastini American mother and a Filipino American father.[78]

Late in the 1990s, there were fewer better college defensive players than Kailee Wong, a Stanford performer possessing a combination of Native Hawaiian, European, and African ancestry. While his surname suggests he has Chinese roots, Wong's mother, according to *San Jose Mercury* sportswriter, John Akers, declared he has merely "traces of Asian blood." Apparently, Wong's father adopted the surname to honor the man who raised him. Interestingly, when the Stanford squad visited Northwestern University a number of Asian students showed up to hail Wong as a football hero of Chinese ancestry. Wong subsequently played in the National Football League. Hawaiian Tafitti Uso was one of Wong's teammates at Stanford. A talented pass receiver Uso later transferred to the University of Hawai'i, where he played his last varsity season in front of his hometown fans.[79]

At Georgia University, Hines Ward glittered as a wide receiver. Part Korean and African American, Ward became a Pittsburgh Steeler in 1998 and one of the better pass receivers in the NFL. Another rookie on the Steeler 1998 squad was Hawaiian Chris Fuamatu-Ma'afala, a giant, 275 pound running back who starred for the University of Utah.[80]

Johnny Morton, possessing Japanese/African American ancestry, starred as a receiver for USC. He, subsequently, developed into a big-time pass catcher for the Detroit Lions before moving on to the 49ers. Morton's brother Chad also played for USC and then the NFL.

In climate and social composition, there are few places in the United States more different than Hawai'i than Utah. Nevertheless, football programs at the University of Utah and Brigham Young University have consistently recruited talented Hawaiian football players in the late 1900s and into the early 2000s. Even stranger, it would seem, was the case of Brian Ah Yat, who starred at quarterback for Montana University in the late 1990s. Indeed, according to a *Sports Illustrated* article, six. Hawaiians played on the Montana University squad in the fall of 1997, although writer Ivan Maisal claimed that "Ah Yat may be the best player to come though a pipeline that, on and off for four decades, has sent football players from the islands to the Big Sky country." A key to Montana's success in recruiting Hawaiian players in the 1980s and 1990s was Hawaiian Tommy Lee. A Montana University's assistant coach in the 1980s, Lee became an assistant at the University of Utah, "which," Maisel wrote, "by no coincidence has 12 Hawaiian players <in 1997>." Maisel quoted Lee remarking that "<y>ou sign one or two <Hawaiians>, they enjoy it, and by word of mouth, more kids get interested." After leaving Montana, Ah Yat, quarterbacked the Honolulu Hammerheads of the Indoor Professional Football League before joining the Canadian Football League.[81]

The presence of Asian Pacific Islanders on American professional football team became more noticeable by the early 2000s. Hawaiian Joe Wong transferred from the University of Hawai'i to Brigham Young University (BYU), where he became a stand out lineman. Spencer Folau graduated from Sequoia High School in the San Francisco Bay Area. From there, he headed to the University of Idaho, where he starred as an offensive lineman. A native of Tonga, Folau began his pro career with the Rhein Fire of the World Football League. He, subsequently, made it with the Baltimore Ravens. Edwin Mulitalo played with Folau on the Ravens. From Daily City, California, Mulitalo competed for the University of Arizona before heading to the NFL. Ma'a Tanuvasa became a solid NFL defensive lineman after a career at the University of Hawai'i. Hawaiian and former University of Colorado lineman, Chris Naeole became a fine NFL guard. Tight end Itula Mili left Hawai'i for BYU and eventually developed into a veteran NFL tight end. Lonnie Palelei went to high school in Missouri before journeying west to suit up for the University of Nevada, Las Vegas. Palelei then became an offensive guard in the NFL. [82]

In size, Marques Tuiasosopo looks more the part of a quarterback than Neo Aoga. Manu's son and reportedly a grandson of a chief of a small village on American Samoa, Marques Tuiasosopo's tremendous athletic ability encouraged his coaches at the University of Washington to switch him from quarterback to defensive back. However, he returned to quarterback and a record setting one at that—as he became the first player in college football to run for 200 yards and pass for 300 more in a game. Tuiasosopo was later drafted by and played for the Oakland Raiders. His brother Zach also played for the University of Washington.[83]

At BYU, Norm Chow fashioned an impressive reputation as a keen molder of quarterbacks and creative offensives. A graduate of Punahou in Honolulu, Chow became a stand out guard for the University of Utah in the late 1960s. He performed briefly as a professional in Canada before a knee injury ended his playing career. Chow coached high school football in Hawai'i before pursuing a college career on the American mainland. A Ph.D. in Educational Psychology, Chow served as offensive coordinator for many years at BYU, mentoring talented Cougar quarterbacks such as Jim McMahon and Steve Young. Passed over when he wanted to take on the Cougars' head coaching job, Chow left BYU in 2000 to coordinate the offensive at North Carolina State and then was hired by the University of Southern California, where he was the highest paid assistant coach in the United States. After Stanford apparently seriously considered hiring Chow as head coach, he moved on to the NFL's Tennessee Titans who paid the Hawaiian a million dollars to coordinate their offense.[84]

The fact that Chow has been passed over for Division I head coaching jobs has caused consternation among Asian Pacific Islander American football followers and some non-Asian Pacific Islander Americans as well. While doing commentary for USC game on ABC, Dan Fouts, a former quarterback great at Oregon and in the NFL, expressed surprise that Chow had not gotten a head football coaching job. Chow has told the press that he would welcome the opportunity to become the first Asian Pacific Islander American to coach a Division I team:

> That's very important to me...People can say what they want, but I would like that opportunity to do that....Because you're the first! There are not that many of us that are in this profession. I have seen the good things. I have seen the bad things. I have seen the prejudices. All you can do is work as hard as you can. If you get caught up in that, you're in big trouble. I was taught a long time ago, just to do the best that you can and whatever happens will happen.[85]

Chow, according to the *Asian Week's* Sam Chu Lin, has had to put up with overt racial stereotyping. He recalled s meeting he attended at BYU. A school administrator, in discussing the construction of a new building: said, "We have all of the Chinamen lined up ready to work on it." Recalling the statement, Chow added, "As far as I was concerned, this was the 20th Century. That comment didn't have to be made. I saw very little remorse after that. There was a form letter that came out apologizing to everybody. I just happen to be the only

'Chinaman.'" This incident helped convince Chow that it was time to leave the BYU campus.[86]

Other Hawaiians served as college coaches on the American mainland. Tommy Lee was as an assistant coach for many years at the University of Utah. A small college All-American at Williamette College in Oregon, Lee coached on the Hawaiian Islands and the American mainland after playing a year in the Canadian Football League. Among the many stops Lee's career took were in Toronto for the CFL Rough Riders and San Antonio for the World Football League. A former quarterback backup to Warren Moon at the University of Washington, Duane Akina was associate head coach of the University of Arizona in the early 1990s and mentored the Wildcats' quarterbacks.[87]

Dat Nguyen deserves special notice. In the late 1990s Dat Nguyen led Texas A&M in tackles and astounded observers when he made twenty tackles against UCLA in a Cotton Bowl game. According to a nice article by the *Los Angeles Times'* Jim Hodges, Dat Nguyen was born in a refugee camp near Little Rock Arkansas. Then his family settled in Rockport, Texas. His father was a shrimper by trade. In Rockport, Texas, however, Vietnamese shrimpers encountered protests from resentful white Texan shrimpers. Dat's parents then operated a Chinese-Vietnamese Restaurant. Dat did not play football until eighth grade, at which time the gridiron lured him away from street life. He then went on to play high school football with his brother Hung. His relative lack of size posed an obstacle to Dat's desire to extend his football career beyond high school. Nevertheless, Jim Hodges claimed, "American food, eaten at the house of a friend helped...So did time in the weight room. As his body and his legend grew in South Texas, recruiters began to call."[89]

UCLA ranked high among the schools trying to lure Dat into their university. In the early 1990s, Mike Nguyen lettered as a pass receiver for the Bruin squad. Later in decade, he tried to recruit the Texan to Westwood. Mike Nguyen was persuasive, Dat confessed: "He was talking about how Jackie Robinson started the black thing, the African-American thing out there at UCLA....He wanted me to help him start an Asian thing there. It was a neat deal." It was not, however, neat enough as Dat accepted a scholarship to play football at Texas A&M, where he led the team in tackles three years in a row and headed to All-American distinction in 1998. And while reporters asked his A&M teammates if he spoke English, Nguyen earned not only All-American credentials, but also the prestigious Lombardi and Bednarik Awards given to the best college defensive player and best college linebacker in the country respectively.[90]

By the spring of 1999, Nguyen faced the prospects of going professional. The Dallas Cowboys drafted him; thus making Nguyen the first Vietnamese American drafted into the NFL. While excited and grateful, Nguyen also expressed a certain amount of trepidation. Journalist Mike Freeman quoted Nguyen: "I wonder if I will go through the kind of racism that African-American players went through when they first came into the league." At the same time, Nguyen hoped he could emerge as a role model for other Asian Pacific American athletes. After 2005 and several fine years with the Cowboys, Nguyen retired from the NFL.[91]

More players of Southeast Asian backgrounds have appeared on big time college teams. Hailing from Rockport, Texas, as well, Tren Van Nguyen played defensive back for the University of Texas in the early 2000s. Born in Malaysia, Minh Nguyen was a lesser known but still formidable gridder. Nguyen played high school football in Anaheim and was named his league's defensive player of the year. Nguyen moved on to Cal, where he played solidly as a linebacker in the early 2000s.[92]

In 1999, Joe Salave'a, then with the Tennessee Titan, pointed out that Asian Pacific Islanders experienced discrimination in the NFL. He told *Asian Week,* "There was discrimination, but I let it all slide by. I really didn't let it get to me and I didn't get caught up in it. I don't know, maybe you can call it ignorance, but I didn't care for it."[93]

Another Asian Pacific Islander American gridder confronted a different kind of discrimination. In 2002, Esera Tualo, a star at Oregon State before embarking on a nine year NFL career, announced he was gay. Tualo declared that he was tiring of living a double life—of pretending to be heterosexual for less than open minded teammates, coaches, and fans. "They didn't know who Esera Tuaolo is," he said. "What they saw was an actor."[94]

Still, college and pro teams, as the new century dawned., caught on more than ever to the possibility that Asian Pacific Islanders could help them win. *Asian Weekly* sportswriter, Brian Liou, wrote in 1999 that "Asian Americans grind it out each Saturday" in the Pacific 10 conference. Tom Holmoe, then Cal's coach, declared, "It's the simple fact that Hawaii and other Polynesian Islands has some really good football. A lot of players from the islands are fantastic players...there's no reason why they shouldn't succeed." [95]

Samoans, in particular, have contributed to college and pro football teams in the United States. In 2003, journalist David K. Choo declared that over 200 athletes of Samoan descent competed in Division I college football, while the NFL employed twenty-eight. Choo added that sixty percent of UH's football team was comprised of Samoans and part-Samoans such as Isaak Sapoaga, a 310-pound lineman, who had suited up for California's College of the Canyons before heading to Oahu.[96]

The issue of Asian Pacific Americans in the head coaching ranks still rankles. Writing in *Asian Week,* Jon Chang noted that many sportswriters expressed understandable concern about the insufficient number of African American head coaches. However, he wrote that these sportswriters seemed unconcerned that no Asian Pacific American served as a college head football or, for that matter, basketball coach: "Did any of these sportswriters or activists mention that? Did any of them mention the lack of Latino and APA coaches in American sports at all? No! So, all of their laments and handwringing about "diversity' ring a little hollow?" Why would an Asian Pacific American head coach such as Norm Chow make a difference? Chang responded, "First, a football coach is leader, educator and role model for the university and the community at large. An APA football coach adds yet another facet to the diamond called America. Finally, with all the clamoring for diversity, the opportunity is here. The response dead silence. Where are the activists and sportswriters now.?"[97]

In 2007, however, the U.S. Naval Academy became the first Division I school to choose an Asian Pacific Islander as a head football coach. Raised in Hawai'i, the Samaon-born Ken Niumatolo starred as a quarterback for Honolulu's Radford High School. After graduation from Radford, Niumatolo remained on Oahu to play for the University of Hawai'i. At Navy, he served as an assistant coach for ten years before moving into the head coaching job.[98]

Crossing Borders, Crossing Goal Lines

Asian Pacific Americans have competed with and against non-Asian Pacific Americans in football below the four-year college level. This was, of course, common on the Hawaiian Islands even before the twentieth century. In the 1890s, D. Kupihea and E. Hapai competed for a Honolulu team called the Defenders. A. Wang played for the College of Hawaii in 1915. Lam Nan, Kam Moon, and Ten You suited up for Mills School. Punahou's squad in 1912 included an athlete named E. Liu. And McKinley High School fielded a culturally diverse assortment of gridders in the early twentieth century such as baseball great Lai Tin, in addition to Jiro Morita, En Choi, Foo Kau, Sam Kahalewai, and C. Chang.[99]

Before embarking on a professional baseball career on East Coast, Andy Yamashiro attended Temple Preparatory School in Philadelphia. There, he performed for the school's football team, causing a bit of curiosity on the part of the national press. Yamashiro played right guard for the Temple eleven and had done a good job when his team took on La Salle. A wire report claimed that Yamashiro was called 'Yim" by his teammates but preferred "a less familiar name." The Hawaiian told the press, "I like football very much...Baseball , though, I think is better. You can use your hands in baseball but not in football. I don't quite get the idea." The five-foot-five inch, 135 pound Yamashiro was studying dentistry at the time.[100]

In 1920, the *Los Angeles Times* reported on "<a>...Japanese end," named Sakamoto, who played on Poly High's varsity eleven in Los Angeles. Some weeks later, the same daily published a discussion of Tojo, a guard for Santa Monica High. According to the *Times*, "<h>e is aggressive and can hold his own in the best of company." Toward the end of the 1920s, Frank Ichishita played fullback for San Jose High School. In one game against Mountain View High School, Ichishita stood out by scoring both of his team's touchdowns as San Jose won, 12-7.[101]

During the 1930s, Chinese and Japanese Americans played plenty of high school and junior college football despite the general assumption they were too small to compete in such a tough game. In 1932, Howard Ah Tye, quarterback, and Donald Kitazuma, guard, suited up for the Sacramento Junior College squad. On nearby high school elevens, Frank Yamada, George Noda, and Shigeo Ishi performed for Elk Grove. Meanwhile, Johnny Takahashi served as a 127-pound quarterback and the fastest man on the Long Beach High School team. And, according to the *Chinese Digest*, George (Tiny) Leong emerged as "one of the best football linemen Commerce High <in San Francisco> ever turned out." The *Chinese Digest* also reported that Frank Chin played for Union High in Salinas, California, in 1935 and complained that it was too bad that Union High had such a good team, because Chin would have starred on most high school elevens. In San Francisco, Marshall Leong became an all-star tackle for Mission High School, while Moriumu Yasuda quarterbacked for Galileo High School. In Hayward, Ernest Lee made all-Alameda County as a tackle. In Southern California, Hideo Higashi quarterbacked the Santa Ana Junior College team and Chaffy's Kobei Shogi led the Orange Empire Junior College League in scoring. Near San Diego, Minora Hatado and Moruki Koba stood out for the Coronado High School team. Starring on Torrance High's eleven in 1939 was fullback Akigee Shimatsu, described by the *Los Angeles Times* as "a hard hitting 150 pound Japanese lad." Los Angeles's Lincoln High, according to the *Times*, was led by "Chinese gridder" Allen Dong, a guard who was "squat, chunky...looks like a walking watermelon."[102]

During the early 1940s, Tarro Inoyue lettered at Los Angeles City College and such young men as Jimmy Chinn and Bill Dong played high school football for Watsonville High School in California. Wally Wong competed for Watsonville High School later in the 1940s. He, subsequently, quarterbacked the Hartnell Junior College eleven in nearby Salinas. In 1942, Bobby Balcena earned 2nd team all-league honors while playing end for San Pedro High School. In 1943, Willie Wong became an all-league guard while suiting up for San Fernando High School. That same year, "Charlie Chan, a robust Chinaman" suited up for San Francisco's Sacred Heart eleven, while Willie Kong competed for Oakland High School along with the great Jackie Jensen. According to the *Korean Independence*, Korean American Luther Hahn starred on and captained the Delano High School team in California during the fall of 1944. In the fall of 1946, the *Los Angeles Times* reported that Kyoshi Tomikawa and Seiji Saito played on the University High squad in Los Angeles. Shoji Shimimoto competed at left guard on San Francisco's Mission High eleven in 1947, while Yosh Kiyokawa quarterbacked the Hood River High team in Oregon. Meanwhile, the *Philippines Star Press* pointed out that Sammy Garcia was a fullback for Hartnell Junor College. In 1949, Fred Yamashito captained the Hyde Park High School eleven in Chicago, while Ted Matsunaga captained the Garden Grove varsity squad in Southern California. A 135 pound halfback Ralph Kubota starred on Los Angeles's Compton High team. And while they did not make the Cal varsity, My Nin Wong, Jimmy Jiu, and Richard Ng competed on the junior varsity squad. Gordon Chen, at the same time, was a halfback on the Stanford JV team.[103]

Asian Pacific Americans played plenty of high school football during the second half of the nineteenth century. In 1950, Stan Ozaki of Poly High School was named to the second team all-San Francisco backfield. Meanwhile, halfback Chang Tsang of Oakland Technical High School was honored as a member of the all-Oakland Athletic League team and Ah Nin played guard for Washington High School in San Francisco. In 1953, Yosh Katsura earned a letter playing for Cal's junior varsity team. In 1954, Kent Ikeda won all league backfield honors for San Mateo High School. In 1967, Dick Sakai played halfback for Gardena High School in Southern California. Wes Okamura stood out at cornerback for Andrew Hill High School in San Jose in 1976. The same year Allen Tagami starred as an end for Watsonville High School. In the mid-1990s, Albert Tuipulotu, the nephew of the aforementioned Peter and Tom, developed into a star running back for San Mateo High School. In the late 1990s, Herman Ho-Ching ranked as one of the best prep running backs in the country while at Long Beach's Poly High School. [104]

Asian Pacific American high school coaches can more easily be found in Hawai'i than on the American mainland. Native Hawaiian William Wise coached Kamehameha when its eleven invaded California to play Chaffey Junior College in 1932. Henry Kusnoki coached Wally Yonamine and several fine high school teams for Farrington during the 1940s. In 1949, the great Keo Nakama coached football at Leilehua High School.[105]

In the late 1990s, efforts to promote women's professional American football were underway in places like the Hawaiian Islands. While not financially successful, they provided opportunities for women such as Debbie Nojima, a pediatrician who happened to compete for a team called the Hawaiian Wave. A starting fullback at five feet and 130 pounds, Nojima had previously played rugby at the University of Colorado and had long loved American football and idolized the great running back, John Riggins. She told the press, "I didn't do it to make a statement....If it does, maybe that's a happy side benefit. I think it's neat to get dirty and mix it up, and then be able to put on a dress and go to a meeting. Being female is just being a person."[106]

Soccer and Rugby

Other forms of football such as soccer and rugby may not attract as much support as American football, of course, does in the United States and, to some extent, Canada. Nevertheless, they have attracted the skills of Asian Pacific Americans. Hawaiian school soccer teams regularly featured the athletic talents of Asian Pacific Islanders in the early 1900s.

For example, Lai Sin, Joseph Kong, Charles Kapukui, Henry Paoa, the cousin of the great Duke Kahanamoku, and two Hawaiian Travelers baseball players, Foster Robinson and Chinito Moriyama competed for St. Louis College in the 1910s. Haka Y. Lee competed in soccer and American football at St. Louis before trying to make the De Pauw football team in 1915. Lee wrote home, guessing that he was "the first Oriental to join an Indiana football camp." Kamehameha fielded a soccer team in 1912 that included athletes surnamed Akana, Kauihani, Morse, Kalai, and Desha, while Wai On, Hu Siong, Robert Kapunai, B. Ka-ne. John Kalu, and Charlie Pang played for Iolani and George Desha and Ah Fook competed for Hilo. We have already noted that Chinese and Japanese students at American colleges participated regularly in soccer matches in the late 1910s and 1920s. We did not mention that "Lung, a full-blooded Chinaman at inside left on the Columbia University soccer football team is one of the squad's most expert players," according to a press account published in the *Bismarck Daily Tribune* in 1916. In the 1920s, scholar Russell Means observed that in 1923 Fresno High School had a soccer team on which one Chinese American and three Japanese Americans competed. Means added that one of the Japanese American players was elected team captain. Chung Chan was born in San Francisco, but lived in Hong Kong before going to Hamilton College. Chan joined the college's soccer team and, in 1928, was also chosen as team captain. In 1935, Korean Hawaiians supported a soccer team in Honolulu—a team coached by Chang Sun Inn. And UH's Ismei Hapai and Bill Ahuna were two of the best players on the islands. During World War II, Los Angeles was home to several active, multicultural soccer teams. The *Los Angeles Times* claimed in January, 1943, that the "most colorful" soccer team around was the Hollywood Hispanos. "Little Robert Cheng" became the team's "sensational Chinese star." In 1947, a young man with the Sikh surname of Singh competed for the University of California's soccer team. Peter Wong was named Most Valuable Player on Stanford's soccer team in 1956. In the 1970s, Filipino American John Anton played soccer for the University of San Francisco. Twenty years later, Vijay Agarwal was a Texan born athlete who competed for UCLA.[107]

In recent years, Canadian born Mark Chung has emerged as one of the better midfielders in North American professional soccer circles. Now a U.S. citizen and resident of Florida, Chung starred for the University of South Florida soccer team before going professional with the Continental Indoor Soccer League. Subsequently, Chung performed for Major League Soccer's (MLS) New York-New Jersey MetroStars, as well as other team's such as the San Jose Earthquakes. Possessing Chinese and Jamaican ancestry, Chung won the MSL's Fair Play Award twice and earned a reputation for bearing an "unflappable demeanor." When Chung joined the MLS's San Jose Earthquakes, he teamed up with the talented Hawaiian, Brian Ching.[108]

As soccer has grown in popularity among young women in America in the late 1900s, a number of fine Asian Pacific female players competed on high school and college squads, as well as national teams participating in the Olympics and World Cup. In the early 2000s, Allison Hamada and Natasha Kai starred on Oregon State's and UH's soccer teams respectively. One of the best young female players in the country in the late 1990s was Tiffany Roberts. A midfielder, Roberts played for the powerful University of North Carolina female soccer team and, better yet, was the youngest player on the gold medal winning U.S. women's Olympic team in 1996. In 1999, she suited up for the World Cup winning U.S. team. Known as the "little animal" because of her determined defensive prowess, Roberts, moreover, can claim Filipino ancestry. One of Roberts' teammates at the University of North Carolina was Lorrie Fair. An All-American defender, Fair joined the U.S. women's World Cup team in 1999. Possessing a Chinese mother, Fair also has a twin sister, Ronnie, who ranked as one of the stars of Stanford's female soccer team in the early 2000s. [109]

In rugby, Hawaiian Sing Chong Pung starred for Stanford in 1911, a time when the school had banned American football and rugby was its big time sport. Japanese students at Stanford formed a rugby team in 1917 to challenge Chinese students at the University of California. At least two players of Japanese ancestry started for Southern California teams in the late 1930s. Santa Ana Junior College suited up a player named Kobayashi, while a Yoneda started for the Santa Barbara Athletic Club. Several years later, Tongan Vaea Anitoni migrated to California, where he established himself as one of the top rugby players in the United States while competing for the Pomona Rugby Club and the San Francisco Olympic Club.[110]

Conclusion

Often described as small compared to people of European or African ancestry, Asian Pacific people have not only played American football—a sport where size and strength often seems paramount--but they have excelled in the sport. For much of the twentieth century, nevertheless, an American football player of Chinese, Japanese, or Korean ancestry struck many followers of the sport as exotic. A telling incident took place during the 1941 football season. A group of Wall Street stockbrokers decided to act upon their amusement over the great many small college football teams whose gridiron exploits gained access to the sporting pages. They had not heard of any of these schools and doubted many football fans had either. They decided to invent a small college and its football team. They came up with Plainsfield Teachers College and a college publicity director with the name of Jerry Croyden. Late every Saturday afternoon during the football season, someone identifying himself as Jerry Croyden would call the New York City newspapers and the wire services based in New York City with the results of Plainsfield's latest game. Plainsfield, it seemed, mounted one impressive victory after another against invented foes such as Scott College. Leading Plainsfield in its victory parade was none other than "its stellar

Chinese back," John Chung. If the hoax had not been uncovered, it is possible that John Chung would have received little All-American honors.[110]

What are we to make of these stockbrokers' need to invent a Chinese American back? We might say that John Chung expressed a belief that Chinese Americans could play "stellar" football. On the other hand, we might consider John Chung as representative of an effort, intentional or not, to demean Chinese American males as unmanly, as well as un-American—that in reality they were incapable of playing the great American college football game and to think otherwise deserved derision.

The presence of Asian Pacific Islander athletes on American gridirons can no longer so easily be derided. Upon getting drafted by the Cowboys, Dat Nguyen maintained, "Asians are still rare in the field...But hopefully there will be others behind me because football is definitely catching on with this generation of Asians." Eugene Chung told journalist Brian Liou that he was not surprised by the growing interest in American football among people of Asian Pacific Islander ancestry, "I think as this generation gets older, the baby boomers and the first generations who first migrated here have let their children play more sports...We are so exposed to sports by the media. There's a lot more exposure than, say, when I was growing up." Kailee Wong maintained that not all Asian Pacific Islanders were short and scrawny. Samoans, Tongans, and Hawaiians were built for football, the linebacker declared. Moreover, "we do have football organizations in the Polynesian Islands with good coaches, and that's why you are starting to see more APIs in the NFL now." For example, in the 2006 Super Bowl, the victorious Pittsburgh Steelers fielded an amazing defensive back from USC, Samoan American Troy Polamalu. On the losing side, the Seattle Seahawks featured a prodigiously talented rookie linebacker, Lofa Tatupu, another USC standout but also son of Samoan American standout Mosi Tatupu, who starred for USC before playing several years in the NFL. And while he has yet to compete in the Super Bowl, Brandon Chillar, a linebacker of Asian Indian and Jamaican ancestry, departed from UCLA to become an outstanding competitor for the St. Louis Rams.[112]

Still, the ability to play American football may not strike many of us as worthy of praise. Like boxing, American football has nearly always been considered and eulogized as integral part of the male domain. Thus, perhaps to the extent that Asian Pacific American communities and individuals have backed American football, they have frequently done so at the expense of Asian Pacific American females. Since size and strength has never really been as important in soccer, young Asian Pacific American females are presently in the process of demonstrating that their athletic passions and abilities neither begin nor end with gymnastics and figure skating. Competing in highly physical games such as American football and soccer, Asian Pacific American athletes have, regardless of gender, defied stereotypes that depict Asian Pacific people as physically passive.

Tiffany Roberts and Lorrie Fair have helped to shatter some of the cultural restraints imposed upon Asian Pacific women. Yet through their contributions to American soccer, Roberts and Fair have also asserted their cultural citizenship across racial and gender borders.

Notes

1. Burrows, *Hawaiian*, 83.

2. *San Jose Mercury*, October 9, 1946; 1990; Total Football, Bill Kwon, "Two Men Who Won't Soon Be Forgotten," *Honolulu Star-Bulletin*, June 26, 1997; www.alohafame.com.

3. *San Jose Mercury*, October 10, 1946;.October 11, 1946; October 15, 1946.

4. *Helena Independent*, December 13, 1925; Lyle E. Nelson, "A Real Upset," *College Football Historical Society*, (May, 1996), p. 11.

5. www.alohafame.com, accessed March 21, 1999; *Los Angeles Times*, November 6, 1935; December 5, 1935; *Helena Independent*, December 15, 1935.

6. *Los Angeles Times*, December 4, 1938; *New York Times*, November 12, 1946.

7. www. hawaii.edu, accessed March 21, 1999; *Pacific Citizen*, October 11, 1947; March 11, 1950; *Honolulu Star-Bulletin*, December 6, 1949; Jaymes Song, "Ready, Set, Hike" *Asian Week*, September 7-September 13, 2001.

8. www.hawaii.edu, accessed March 21, 1999..

9. *Los Angeles Times*, January 19, 1936; November 3, 1938; *San Francisco Chronicle*, September 27, 1947; *San Francisco Examiner*, December 7, 1949; December 12, 1949; *Honolulu Star-Bulletin*, January 4, 1923;; August 19, 1948; September 11, 1948; September 18, 1948; ;October 1, 1948; October 7, 1948; Bill Kwon, "Two Men," June 26, 1997; *Charleston Daily Mail*, January 5, 1923; *Reno Evening Gazette*, December 26, 1934; *Pacific Citizen*, October 11, 1947; *San Francisco News*, November 8, 1947 www. hawaii.edu, accessed August 6, 1999; Gill, 227; Frank Ardolino, "Jackie Robinson and the Honolulu Bears," *The National Pastime*, (no. 15, 1995). 68; Ethnic Studies Oral History Project, *Kalihi, Place of Transition*, v. 3, (Social Science Research Institute, University of Hawai'i, Manoa, 1984), 837-838.

10. *Sport*, December, 1951; East-West Shrine Football Program, Kezar Stadium, San Francisco, December 19, 1951.

11. *Los Angeles Times*, December 29, 1946; October 27, 1948; *Honolulu Star-Bulletin*, July 27, 2000.

12. *Chinese Students*, December 1, 1918; *San Jose Mercury*, October 1, 1920; *Mind and Body*, December, 1916; *Daily Palo Alto*, February 2, 1923.

13. *Los Angeles Times*, December 27, 1909.

14. *San Francisco Chronicle*, November 14, 1919; Ma, *Oakland*, 54.

15. *Honolulu Star-Bulletin*, November 11, 1915; *Nevada State Journal*, December 27, 1932.

16. Thomas Chinn, *Bridging*, 125-128; *San Francisco Chronicle*, December 13, 1931; *San Francisco Examiner*, February 8, 1932.

17. *Los Angeles Times*, January 26, 1925.

18. *Los Angeles Times*, December 20, 1936; *Chinese Digest*, November 22, 1935; January 1937; *San Francisco Examiner*, December 21, 1937.

19. *San Francisco Chronicle*, February 8, 1938.

20. *Chinese News*, November 1, 1940.

21. *Chinese Digest*, December, 1938.

22. *Ibid.*, October 30, 1936.

23. *California Chinese Press*, November 29, 1940.

24. *San Francisco Chronicle*, January 21, 1928.

25. *Pacific Citizen*, October 4, 1947.

26. *Washington Post*, December 22, 1931; *Nevada State Journal*, December 6, 1934; *Los Angeles Times,* August 15, 1936.

27. Stanford vs. California, Program, November 24, 1934, Memorial Stadium, Berkeley, California; *Pacific Citizen,* October 4, 1947.

28. *Manzanar Free Press*, September 2, 1944; *Los Angeles Times*, November 6, 1942.

29. *Chinese Press*, November 11, 1949; *Pacific Citizen*, October 4, 1947.

30. Ethnic Studies Oral History Project, *Kalihi*, v. 1, 167; Suehiro, *Honolulu Stadium*, 72-73.

31. *Honolulu Star-Bulletin*, December 5, 1949.

32. *Pacific Citizen*, October 11, 1947.

33. *Chinese Press*, December 16, 1949.

34. *Ibid.*, June 2, 1950.

35. *San Francisco Chronicle*, September 22, 1947; March 21, 1907; *Chicago Tribune*, January 15, 1915.

36. *Fort Wayne News*, December 9, 1916; *Washington Post*, December 2, 1917.

37. *San Francisco Chronicle,*, October 19, 1918; October 28, 1918; *Honolulu Star-Bulletin*, October 15, 1915.

38. *San Francisco Chronicle,*, October 3, 1918; *Oakland Tribune* November 1, 1918.

39. *Washington Post*, October 12, 1924; November 2, 1924; November 6, 1924 ; *New York Times*, November 8, 1940; *Pacific Citizen*, September 13, 1947.

40. *Honolulu Star-Bulletin*, November 2, 1948; *Chinese Digest*, November, 1935; April, 1937; *San Jose Mercury*, October 22, 1937; November 6, 1937; *Los Angeles Times*, August 16, 1936; November 3, 1938, November 11, 1938; *San Francisco Examiner,* January 6, 1938; Ethen Leiser, "A War Hero Remembered" *Asian Week*, July 27-August 2002; US Census, Manuscripts, City and County of Honolulu, 1930.

41. www.asuonline, accessed May 23, 2002; "Tempe Oral History Project," Mary Pry Interviewer, Bill Kajikawa, www.tempe.gov; May 25, 1995; Pacific Citizen, September 13, 1947.

42. Ron Fimrite, "Little St. Mary's Big Star," *Sports Illustrated*, October 26, 1996.

43. *San Francisco Chronicle*, October 9, 1944; October 28, 1947.

44. James N. Gregory, *American Exodus: The Dust Bowl Migrations and Okie Culture in California*, (New York and London: Oxford University Press, 1989), 140-141.

45. *San Francisco Examiner*, December 3, 1943; *San Francisco Chronicle*, September 9, 1945; October 21, 1947; October 17, 1968; Fimrite, "St. Mary's"; Rice, "Who is Our Top Athlete?" *Sport*, October 1946. Bill Leiser, "The Coast," *1946 Illustrated Football Annual*, p. 46; Bernie McCarthy, ""Squirmin Herman and the Whiz Kids," *College Football Historical Society*, vol. 22, 1987, p 4.

46. Rice, "Top Athlete," McCarthy, "Squirmmin," p. 4.

47. *San Francisco News*, August 11, 1947; *San Francisco Chronicle*, September 2, 1943; September 10, 1943; Emmons Byrne, "The California Whiz Kids," *Colliers*, January 5, 1946.

48. *San Francisco News*, August 2, 1947; *Pacific Citizen,* July 12, 1947.

49. *San Francisco Chronicle*, August 1, 1947.

50. *San Francisco Examiner*, August 5, 1947; August 10, 1947.

51. *Pacific Citizen*, August 16, 1947; August 23, 1947.

52. *Oxnard Press-Courier,* August 6, 1947

53. *Oxnard Press-Courier,* August 6, 1947; *San Francisco Chronicle*, September 27, 1947.

54. *Pacific Citizen,* September 13, 1947.

55. *Honolulu-Star Bulletin*, August 17, 1948; *Los Angeles Times,* November 29, 1948; San *Francisco Chronicle,* July 16, 1949.

56. *Oxnard Press Courier*, November 2, 1946; *San Francisco Examiner*, September 8, 1947; *Pacific Citizen*, November 29, 1947.

57. *San Jose* Mercury, December 10, 1950; East West Shrine Football Game, Kezar Stadium, San Francisco, California, December 19, 1951; *Sports Review Football Annual*, 1957.

58. *Honolulu Star- Bulletin*, October 1, 1948.

59. *Ibid*., November 9, 1949; November 12, 1949; October 3, 1953; Leiser, "Coast;" *San Francisco Chronicle*, September 5, 1943; *Pacific Citizen,* September 13, 1947; September 20, 1947; February 18, 1950; Gary Y. Okihiro, *Storied Lives: Japanese American Students and World War II*, (Seattle : University of Washington Press, 1999), 90, 92.

60. *San Francisco Chronicle,* September 27, 1947; September 29, 1947; *Waterloo Daily Courier,* November 30, 1947.

61. *Los Angeles Times,* October 4, 1941; November 10, 1945; *San Francisco Chronicle*, April 6, 1946; September 18, 1947; *San Francisco Examiner*, September 6, 1947; Leiser, "Coast,", p. 54.

62. *Chinese Press*, November 10, 1950; January 9, 1949; *San Francisco Chronicle,* August 7, 1949; *Los Angeles Times,* January 3, 1950.

63. *San Francisco Chronicle*, September 7, 1947; *San Francisco Examiner*, September 8, 1946; Byrne, "California Whiz Kids." *Coschocton Tribune*, July 2, 1950.

64. *Los Angeles Times*, December 4, 1936, September 11, 1948; *Honolulu Star-Bulletin*, October 7, 1948; *Chinese Press*, January 13, 1949; Gill, 237; US Census, MS, 1930; *Pacific Citizen,* November 15, 1947; David K. Choo, "The Polynesian Powerhouse: University of Hawaii Football Counts On Its Samoan Connection, *Pacific Magazine and Islands Business,* www.pacificislands.com,, July 2003.

65. Rube Samuelson, "Hawaiian Ane One Hula-Va Tackler USC Foes Learn, *Sporting News,* December 3, 1952; San Jose State College v. Stanford University, Football Program, Stanford Stadium, October 13, 1956. University of Southern California v. California, Football Program, Memorial Stadium, Berkeley, California, October 20, 1951; *San Francisco Examiner,* December 23, 1953; *Honolulu Star-Bulletin*, April 6, 1950; Irv Goodman, "Pro Football Preview," *Sport,* September, 1956, p.77.

66. San Jose State College vs. Stanford University, Football Program, Stanford Stadium, November 1, 1952; November 13, 1954; October 13, 1956; *La Torre*, San Jose State College Yearbook, 1957; *San Francisco Chronicle,* September 4, 1955; *Sports Illustrated,* September 22, 1958, p. 106; *Nichi Bei Times*, January 1, 1973.

67. *Sports Illustrated*, September 22, 1958; *San Francisco Examiner*, November 29, 1959.

68. *San Jose Mercury*, April 24, 1960; August 30, 1964; San Francisco Examiner, November 27, 1961.

69. Will Grimsley's, "Kenney's Toenails Need Special Care," *St. Joseph Herald Press*, October 15, 1965; November 18, 1965; *Sporting News,* September 25, 1965; *Sports Illustrated*, January 4, 1965; *Honolulu Star-Bulletin*, January 15, 1999; Mark Purdy, "Wedemeyer Retains Vitality," *San Jose Mercury*, July 22, 1998.

70. *Filipinas*, January 2000, p. 41; *Frederick Post*, February 7, 1983.

71. *Los Angeles Times*, October 18, 1961; December 7, 1961.

72. *Sports Illustrated*, September 25, 1978, p. 57; December 27, 1999-January 3, 2000; *Sporting News*, November 1, 1980.

73. *Sporting News*, August 2, 1971.

74. *Pacific Citizen*, October 25, 1974; December 6, 1974; December 20, 1974; *Sports Illustrated*, September 11, 1978, p. 76.

75. *East/West*, June 15, 1983.

76. *Ibid.*, May 23, 1984.

77. Washington State University vs. Stanford University, Football Program, Stanford Stadium, October 20, 1984.

78. www.juniorseau.org.com, accessed May 7, 1998 ; Sports Illustrated September 11, 1978; Michael Silver, "The Last Best Word," January 23, 1995, p. 32; AP Online, May 7, 1999.

79. *San Jose Mercury*, December 12, 1976; November 7, 1996; San Jose State University v. Stanford University, Football Program, Stanford Stadium, September 27, 1983, San Jose State University vs. University of Pacific, Spartan Stadium, November 7, 1987; San Jose State University vs. Stanford University, Football Program, September 30, 1989, Stanford Stadium; Mike Freeman, "A Win-Nguyen Situation for NFL," *San Jose Mercury*, April 13, 1999; Burt Takuchi, "Asian Pacific Americans On The Gridiron," www.nichibeitimes.com., November; www.sdsu.edu, accessed September 17, 2001; www.utah.edu; accessed September 16, 2001; San Francisco Forty Niners 1986 Yearbook; Emil Guillermo, "Good and Plenty" *Asian Week*, , November 29-December 2, 2002.

80. John Akers, "Fanfare for Wong Spreads," *San Jose Mercury*, August 31, 1997; Stanford v. Oregon Football Program, Stanford Stadium, September 27, 1999; Stephen Tsai, "Former Punahou Leaves Stanford for UH," *Honolulu Advertiser*, June 9, 2000.

81. Bill Wong, "Leveling the Playing Field, *Asian Week*, July 16-July 13, 1998; *Sport*, September, 1997;

82. Ivan Maisel, "Beach Ball," *Sports Illustrated*, August 25, 1997.

83. www.utah.edu, accessed November 12, 1999; Brian Liou, "The API Line-up," www.asianweek.com., October 14, 1999.

84. Gail Wood, "Tuiasosopo not pretty, but he just wins," Gannet News Services, December 29, 2000.

85. www.byu.edu, November 12, 1999; Ivan Maisel, "Signing Daze," *Sports Illustrated*, February 24, 2000; www.HonoluluAdvertiser.com, January 11, 2001; www.asianweek,com, February 11, 2005.

86. Sam Chu Lin, "Norm Chow Leads USC's National Football Title," www.asianweek.com, January 10, 2004.

87. *Ibid.*

88. www.utah.edu, accessed November 12, 1999; *Sports Illustrated*, September 11, 1978, p. 63; Stanford vs. Arizona University Football Program, Stanford University, October 17, 1992.

89. *San Jose Mercury*, December 31, 1997.

90. *Ibid;* Richard Lee, "A Scoring Drive," *Asian Week*, December 24, 1998-December 31, 1998; Lydia Lum, "Breaking Football's Color Barrier," *Black Issues in Higher Education*, April 15, 1999, p. 50.

91. Mike Freeman, "A Win-Nguyen Situation," *San Jose Mercury*, April 13, 1999; Lum, "Breaking," 50

92. www.macbrown-Texas-football.com, accessed January 20, 2004; www.gobears.com, accessed February 10, 2003.

93. Liou, "API."

94. Brian Kluepfel, "Tuaolo Emerges from the NFL Closet," *Asian Week*, November 1, 2002-November 7, 2002.

95. Liou, "API."

96. Choo, "Polynesian Powerhouse."

97. Jon Chang, "Where Are the APA Football Coaches," *Asian Week*, December 13-December. 19, 2002.

98. Jill Lieber Steeg, "New Navy Coach Niumatolo is Big Fan of Old One," www.usatoday.com, December 19, 2007.

99. *Hawaiian Gazette*, November 29, 1895; *Pacific Commercial Advertiser*, November 4, 1911; October 26, 1912; November 4, 1914; *Honolulu Star-Bulletin*, October 9, 1915; October 11, 1915.

100. *Honolulu Star-Bulletin*, November 21, 1916.

101. *Los Angeles Times*, December 1, 1920; December 11, 1920; *San Jose Mercury*, October 17, 1929.

102. *Sacramento Bee*, September 17, 1931; September 23, 1932; *Los Angeles Times*, September 18, 1932; November 8, 1935; November 11, 1938; November 16, 1938; October 9, 1939; October 14, 1939; *Chinese Digest*, November 15, 1935; November 13, 1936; *San Francisco Examiner*, October 17, 1936; *San Jose Mercury*, October 22, 1937; *San Francisco Chronicle*, February 8, 1938.

103. *California Chinese Press*, January 13, 1941; *San Francisco Chronicle*, October 2, 1943; October 9, 1943; *Chinese Press*, January 7, 1949; February 4, 1949; *Korean Independence*, January 11, 1945; *Los Angeles Times*, January 22, 1942; December 16, 1942; December 17, 1943; October 17, 1946; *San Francisco Examiner*, September 10, 1947; *Philippines Star Press*, December 8, 1947; *Pacific Citizen*, November 15, 1947; January 7, 1950.

104. *San Francisco Examiner*, November 29, 1950; December 3, 1950; *San Francisco Chronicle*, September 7, 1950; December 7, 1953; December 10, 1954; San *Jose Mercury*, December 11, 1976; December 12, 1976; November 7, 1996; Lee, "A Scoring Drive."; *Los Angeles Times*, October 7, 1967.

105. *Williamsport Grit*, January 3, 1932; *Honolulu Star-Bulletin*, December 6, 1949; *Pacific Citizen*, January 14, 1950.

106. Dave Reardon, "Pigskin Pediatrician," www.islandscene.com, January 5, 2000.

107. *Pacific Commercial Advertiser*, November 11, 1911; January 2, 1912; January 3, 1912; March 3, 1912; March 2, 1914; January 23, 1915; October 16, 1915; *Honolulu Advertiser*, March 3, 1935; March 25, 1935; *Bismarck Daily Tribune*, January 8, 1916;

Mears, *Resident*, 366; *San Jose Mercury*, July 13, 1928; *Los Angeles Times*, January 17, 1948; *San Francisco Examiner*, November 27, 1947; *Stanford Daily*, May 29, 1956; *Philippine News*, January 24-Janurry 30, 1974; www.indianfootball.com, accessed May 11, 2000.

108. Brian Kluepfel, "Mark Chung: American Soccer's Coolest Man" *Asian Week*, November 22, 2002; November 28, 2002.

109. www.conthewww.com, accessed January 20, 2000; Emil Guillermo, "Asian vs. APA," www.asianweek.com, July 8, 1999; www.hawaii.edu, accessed February 10, 2003; www.osubeavers.com, accessed February 11, 2001.

110. *Pacific Commercial Advertiser,* November 28, 1911; *Daily Palo Alto,* February 2, 1923; *Los Angeles* Times, January 17, 1938; February 19, 1938; "Kurt Oeler, Vaea Anitoni, *Encyclopedia of Ethnicity and Sports in the United States,* edited by George B. Kirsch, Othello Harris, and Claire E. Nolte, (Westport, Connecticut: Greenwood Press, 2000), 29-30.

111. Biff Bennett, "SPORTalk," *SPORT*, December, 1951.

112. Lum, "Breaking," p. 50; Liou, "API."

Chapter Five: Courts and Communities

Great Depression San Francisco embraced two urban hotbeds of ethnic basketball. One of these hotbeds consisted of the adjacent Italian American neighborhoods of North Beach and Russian Hill--neighborhoods from which the great baseball player Joe Dimaggio was launched. Just as important in his sport was a Russian Hill, Italian San Franciscan named Angelo "Hank" Luisetti, who at Stanford University became the Michael Jordan of the late 1930s. North Beach and Russian Hill playgrounds, old-timers recall, were filled with youngsters playing either Dimaggio's or Luisetti's sport.

Bordering on North Beach and Russian Hill was the other center of city basketball in San Francisco—Chinatown. To be sure, no one as notable as Luisetti emerged from the crowded Chinese American ethnic enclave, which had only one decent playground during the depression years. Chinese American youngsters of both sexes, nevertheless, played basketball with skill and verve. A few even became local legends given ethnic-based and often tiresome nicknames by the press. There was Robert "Egg Foo" Lum, the scourge of lightweight basketball in San Francisco during the late 1930s. A decade later, Willie "Woo Woo" Wong illuminated high school and community basketball. His sister, Helen, was probably as good a female basketball player as there was in San Francisco during the late 1940s. Nowadays, few of us associate Chinese Americans with fervent and skilled basketball playing. Nowadays, however, too many of us still see the world through stereotypes, although perhaps Yao Ming is changing the way many of us look at the basketball skills honed by people of Chinese descent.

The popularity of community basketball in San Francisco's Chinatown, nevertheless, should not surprise us. For San Francisco's Chinatown, basketball seems to have occupied the same role as in other urban ethnic communities. Historian Peter Levine writes in regards to Jewish American city basketball: "Not surprisingly, in urban, ethnic working-class neighborhoods, a game open to improvisation and requiring little space or equipment proved attractive to children." At the same time, unlike other team sports, basketball did not require nine, ten, or eleven on a side nor expensive equipment and uniforms. Urban ethnic community teams were, therefore, easier to organize than baseball and especially football teams.[1]

Chinese Digest sportswriter, Frank Hee, reported in 1939 that "the Chinese in America have been growing in leaps and bounds toward the betterment of sports and this is especially so in basketball." He added, however, that San Francisco Chinese Americans had been playing basketball since 1919 when a team representing Chinatown's Boys Scouts of Troop E was formed. In 1940, a writer for the *California Chinese Press* boasted that "Chinatown is one of the bright spots of basketball in San Francisco." This writer pointed out that three hundred Chinese Americans children passed up Chinese school to make it to the Cow Palace, a ten thousand seat arena just south of San Francisco, sufficiently early to see Hank Luisetti play for the Olympic Club five against his alma mater's squad.[2]

Community Basketball

Basketball helped maintain a sense of community among early twentieth century Asian Pacific American mainland college students. According to *Mind and Body*, Chinese American students at Cal and Stanford formed basketball teams in 1916. In 1922, a Japanese Stanford team pounded an ethnically similar squad from USC, 43-3. Fred Koba, who played varsity basketball for Stanford, led the way with twenty points. During the early 1920s, Stanford's Japanese Club participated in the university's male intramural league. After the Nikkei squad beat Encina Hall's first floor five, the *Daily Palo Alto* maintained, "The large Encina men seemed to have the edge in guarding but the Japanese players were much faster and more clever with their passes and shooting."[3]

In 1929, Oakland's Waku Auxiliary organized a female Chinese American basketball team. The squad toured Northern California, playing Chinese American girls in San Francisco and Locke. The youthful Oakland athletes also competed in volleyball, softball, and track and field.[4]

In Great Depression Los Angeles, Chinese Americans of both sexes in Los Angeles played and supported basketball. For example, during the spring of 1938, the Federation of Chinese Clubs in Los Angeles organized a basketball tournament to which Chinese American and non-Chinese American teams were invited. On the male side, the Korean All Stars beat the Wah Kue team, 29-24. The Chinese American Lowa five won its game against the Twin Dragons from San Francisco, 23-20. On the female side, a Chinese American squad representing the Mei Wah and Lowa Girls defeated the Independent Colored Girls, 14-11.[5]

In 1931, the Mei Wah Club formed as an organization of young women devoted to basketball and athletics. Members proclaimed that Chinese Americans strove to "do our utmost to uphold the traditions of sportsmanship" and make friends "through our athletic, social, and philanthropy activities." Several of the Mei Wah Club members were related to one another. The Lowa Auxiliary Girls' Club was founded in the mid-1930s for young women who wanted their own basketball team. They started without formal sponsorship and received coaching from a woman named Eloise Wong. They held practices at the 21st. Street Playground and Poly High School's gym. The Lowa female basketball team continued playing until World War II, during which time the players became more involved in bowling and tennis. The Lowa male team, meanwhile, played more than just Los Angeles teams. The squad traveled to Tijuana, Mexico City, Santa Barbara, Bakersfield, and San Francisco to oppose local fives. [6]

The Lowa male contingent was apparently one of the best amateur teams in Southern California outside of the college game. In 1937, the Lowa five took on a team representing Whittier's Chamber of Commerce in the championship game of Southern California's Open Tournament. The *Los Angeles Times* described the Lowa team as consisting of "Orientals" over six feet tall and sufficiently skilled to beat formidable opponents with college performers. George Tong was a team leader. Called a "scintillating center," the *Times* could not understand why he thought he was not good enough to try out for the USC basketball team when he was an undergraduate there. [7]

Chinese Americans in Oregon organized basketball teams in the 1930s. In the mid-1930s, the Wah Kiang Club basketball team became the house league champion of Portland's YMCA. The Chung Wah female team represented Portland Chinese community in the late 1930s. This team was led by a standout player named Lalun Chun. Several years earlier, Chun had captained the local Beaverton High School female basketball team. [8]

In Northern and Central California, Chinese communities were represented by plenty of basketball squads during the 1930s. As early as 1923, Sacramento's Chinese Athletic Club supported a basketball team of males nineteen and over in the city's Playground Basketball League. In 1928, a San Francisco Chinatown team won the eighty-eight pound division in a citywide tournament. According to the *San Francisco Chronicle*, this marked the first time that Chinese American boys had entered the tournament. In 1930, the *San Francisco Chronicle* reported that youthful Chinese Americans played basketball in San Francisco in the eighty-five, 110, and 130 pound divisions. The next year, the *Chronicle* announced that the "Namwah Chinese cagers" and the "Tahmies Chi-Fornia" were practicing for a big game. Apparently, the "Namwah" team "claim<ed>... the distinction of the best Chinese lightweight cage squad west of the Rocky Mountains." The True Sunshine team, comprised entirely of Chinese surnamed players, competed in San Francisco's Episcopal Basketball League during the 1930-

1931 season. In 1934, Chinese American girls attending St. Mary's Catholic Church were represented by a team in San Francisco's Catholic Girls Basketball League. San Francisco's Chinese Girls Scouts Troop #13 had a basketball team in the mid 1930s, while a male five represented San Jose's Chinese Students Club. In 1935, the Nam Wahs beat a team from the Japanese Reform Church in San Francisco's Pacific Amateur Athletic Association tournament for 120 pounders. In San Jose, the San Jose Chinese, led by H. Lee's seventeen points, defeated the Stanford Chinese 27-23 in February, 1936. In Salinas, California, Chinese Americans had organized a basketball team in 1936. Chinese Americans in Bakersfield, California supported a Cathay Basketball five in 1936. Around the same time, three basketball teams represented the noted Chinese American community of Locke, California. Yet since many of these community teams played fives associated with other racial and ethnic groups, at least a few ugly incidents were impossible to avoid. For example, in 1937 a *Chinese Digest* reporter bitterly condemned the *Willits News* in Northern California. Apparently in describing a game between the Willits Lions and a Chinese YMCA five, the Willits News called the Chinese players "Chinks." The *Chinese Digest* reporter said that upon reading this article: "We just blew up (and so would you protest vigorously if you had read it.)" [9]

Ethnic-based basketball teams emerged on the Hawaiian Islands before the twentieth century. In 1899, Kamehameha girls' basketball squad included Elizabeth Robinson, Angelina Wohler, Rose Alaron, Hawley Stone and Emily Alexander. In 1903, the *Pacific Commercial Advertiser* in Honolulu reported on a game between the YWCA second team and the Kamehameha School Girls Team. A few of the girls competing on the victorious Kanehameha squad were Kai Walau, Lori Wonghong, and Acho Achu. In 1911, the squad was captained by Flora Kaai and included Emma Ukauka, Julia Pahia, and Emma Malakaua. [10]

In Hawai'i, Loui Leong Hop reported, basketball was popular with "Chinese boys." The sportswriter declared, "While small in most cases, they utilize superior speed and teamwork to attain victories and championships." An organization called the Association of Chinese Athletics, "always enter title contending quintets in local senior leagues." Suiting up for the ACA in 1935 were George Ching,, S. Lee, B. Wong, W. Mau, R. Tom, H. Lau, W. Lee, and A. Fong. The James Chong Clothiers' five was a top Chinese Hawaiian squad in the 1930s. Richard Tom and Walter Wong were two of the team's better players. [11]

Korean and Filipino ethnic teams competed in on the islands in the 1930s. An Oahu All-Star Filipino five included Marcus Sibalon, Jesus Caballero, Teadro Ballasteros, and Vicente Rausa. J. Lee, S.A. Kim, H. Lee, P.S. Lee, P. Kim, and C. Park played for a Korean Hawaiian team called the Delta Frats. [12]

Japanese Americans enthusiastically embraced community basketball before World War II. As early as 1916, a team of 110 pounders played in San Franisco's Pacific Athletic Association Basketball League. A few years later, Japanese Americans could go to their own YMCA branch which was set up in an old mansion, the attic of which was turned into a gymnasium. Called the Spartans, this squad consisted entirely of Japanese American players. Playing under a ten foot ceiling that slopped to five feet near the sidelines, Japanese American basketball participants learned how to put up flat shots that caromed into the basket off the backboards. Apparently, Japanese American YMCA athletes learned their basketball very well. In 1930, the *San Francisco Chronicle* reported on a game in which a Japanese American YMCA team trounced a squad representing the Boys' Club, 58-1. [13]

In the decade before World War II, Japanese American basketball leagues pervaded Northern and Southern California. The *San Francisco Examiner*, in 1934, described a contest between 120-pound division teams representing the Japanese American Reform Church and the Chinese American South Athletic Club. The same year, according to the *San Francisco Chronicle*, a five sponsored by the San Francisco Japanese YMCA was scheduled to play a team of University of California Japanese American players coached by former Cal player, Ted Obashi. A year later, construction on a new "Japanese Y" was underway in San Francisco. Built on the city's Buchanan Street, it hosted several recreational leagues. One of the teams involved was called the Greyhounds because the players were so quick. In Alameda, the Japanese American Young Men's Buddhist Association (YMBA) had developed a winning basketball team. Also in Northern California, the Mount Eden Japanese American Citizens League (JACL) and the Santa Clara JACL sponsored basketball teams. In Southern California, a Japanese American Union tournament took place at Chapman College in Orange County early in 1939. Among the teams participating were the Utes, Wanjis, Bruins, Boyle Heights Cougars, Long Beach Asahis, the Golden Bears and Crown City. A few months later, Chapman College hosted a game between the San Francisco Mikados, the Northern California Japanese American champion, and the Utes. The visitors won, 37-27 and then beat the Southern California champion Cardinals, 51-35. [14]

In the early 1930s, a team called the San Jose Zebras was formed with players of Japanese descent. Many of these young men were high school graduates apparently too short to play college basketball. The Zebras, sponsored by San Jose's Buddhist Church and coached by a European American, opposed Japanese American teams all over the state. However, they also competed against non-Japanese American squads. In 1934, for instance, the *San Jose Mer-*

cury reported that "a high powered Japanese basketball team under the banner of the Young Men's Buddhist Association" beat Santa Clara High School, 32-28. This YMBA five, the *Mercury* declared, was one of the best amateur contingents in the area. What had made the Zebras effective, according to the *Mercury*, was an unsurpassed unity among the players—a unity that translated into game winning teamwork on the court. Unwilling to neglect the usual references to the size of Asian Pacific American athletes, the *Mercury* declared that the Zebras were "mighty mites, lightweight in proportion, but experts in ability." [15]

In Stockton, California, the Young Women's Buddhist Association's "Busy Bees" built a winning tradition. Organized in 1923 by the Stockton Buddhist Church, the Busy Bees reportedly played 236 games from 1928 to 1940 and lost only four of those games. During the 1939-1940 basketball season, the Busy Bees made a 2500-mile tour of the U.S. southwest. Their coach, George "Pop" Suzuki became something of a Japanese American community legend. [16]

Scholar Harry Kitano maintained that second generation Japanese Americans acquired a great deal of satisfaction out of the basketball leagues and tournaments in which they participated in the 1930s. They could achieve a sense of independence, see a piece of the world outside of their particular communities, interact with other Nisei, and all in all develop more self esteem. They could, Kitano claimed, become big fish in little ponds. Kitano quoted one former player: "I used to wait for the all-hi tournament. It was the time when all the Nisei going to different high schools in San Francisco would get together and compete. We'd have rooting sections and trophies. And then a big victory dance." Kitano went on to argue that for the Nisei, basketball teams became primary reference groups and playing basketball became a vehicle of acculturation. Japanese American basketball players and supporters, moreover, seemingly resisted efforts at using basketball to totally erase racial and ethnic lines. Kitano wrote that during the 1930s, the Mikado basketball team of San Francisco left the local Japanese American basketball league to participate in an interethnic league. He pointed out that many upset Nisei in San Francisco pressured the Mikados to return to the fold the next season. [17]

During the 1940s, Chinese Americans remained very active in basketball. In 1941, a *California Chinese Press* sportswriter expressed confidence that San Francisco's Chinatown shined as a citadel of city basketball. The occasion was the victory of a team of male cagers sponsored by Chinatown's St. Mary's Church. Led by Willie Wong, the Chinese American squad beat a five representing the Mission Delores for the lightweight Catholic Youth Organization (CYO) championship. The *California Chinese Press* also noted in 1941 the existence of the Chi-Nettes, a female team representing Sacramento's Chinese Americans. The Lowa men's team endured. The *California Chinese Press* called it "the tallest and biggest quintet in Chinese basketball." Captain and center

George Dong was the tallest player at 6 ft 2 inches and Frank Dong was the smallest at 5 ft. 11 inches. Also in Los Angeles, the Cathayette Girls' Club formed a basketball squad. Generally comprised of high school students interested in playing tennis and bowling, as well as basketball, the Cathayette Girls' Club claimed no formal sponsor until the mid-1940s, but existed until the early 1950s. Elsie Wong, who also was involved with the Lowa Auxiliary team, helped the Cathayette athletes as well. [18]

In New York City, the Chinese Athletic Club supported a basketball team as did the Japanese Christian Federation. In April 1943, the two squads hooked up for a game to decide "Oriental American basketball supremacy." The Chinese Athletic Club won the game, the proceeds from which was to benefit the Church of All Nations in addition to other charities.[19]

These community basketball teams often seemed to harbor an empowering influence on participants and supporters. In 1943, a group of young Korean American women in Los Angeles expressed pride in the basketball team they formed as members of the Korean Christian Association (KCA). One of these young women, Virginia Chung, reported in the *Korean Independence* that the KCA female basketball team had just defeated a "colored girls team combined from Poly and Manual Arts High Schools." Playing at a gym on Whittier Boulevard, the KCA squad barely won 15-12 and the losers challenged the "Little Foxes for a rematch." Chung, then, urged readers in Los Angeles's Korean American community to "<c>ome and see the only Korean girls basketball team ever to be organized."[20]

In San Francisco, a group of Filipino young men assembled the Mango Athletic Club in 1940. Most of the original members lived in the city's Western Addition and sought some recourse for the lack of recreational outlets available to them. They organized competitive teams in baseball, volleyball, and sandlot football, but their basketball team gained the most attention. Initially, they had hoped older and better off Filipinos would sponsor their teams, but the Filipino American elders wanted to see how they competed before committing themselves and their hard-earned money. After they started winning games, the Mango Athletic Club members received sponsorship offers from the elders. By then, however, the Mangos were not interested. They enjoyed competing on their own. Practicing at a YMCA facility in the Western Addition, the Mango Athletic Club five became the preeminent Filipino American basketball team in Northern California and one of the best Asian Pacific American aggregations in the nation.[21]

In the Japanese American concentration camps, young internees engaged in basketball. Basketball teams represented the various camps such as the one at Topaz. The Topaz five, for instance, beat a local high quintet on January 1, 1943. Later in the month, a team from the Postan, Arizona camp opposed an American Indian five from Parker, Arizona. Led by "Sunshine Willie" Fisher's twenty-eight points, the Parker squad easily won, 71-35. During the winter of 1943-1944, the Heart Mountain All Stars, consisting of fine all around athletes such as Babe Nomura, played competitively against some of the better independent amateur teams in the region. When the San Jose Zebras were relocated they took their uniforms with them. Eventually, they wound up at Heart Mountain, where their dominance sometimes stirred controversy. Jack Kumotomi, who reported on sports for the *Heart Mountain Sentinel*, lamented that the Zebras were running up scores against less talented opponents. He wrote, "This seems to reflect poor judgment on the part of the coach and also of the Zebra partisans, who clamored and agitated for such an incident." However, because there were no indoor facilities for basketball at Heart Mountain, where winters could get a little colder than freezing, basketball games were often cancelled. Outside of the camps, the Salt Lake City JACL was represented by a junior male team, while the JACL also sponsored squads in Pocatello and Idaho Falls, Idaho. In Denver, meanwhile, a formidable five sponsored by Cary's Malt Shop competed in the City League. According to the *Pacific Citizen*, this squad consisted of Nisei males from San Francisco, Los Angeles, and San Jose. Obviously, they were in Denver to escape the concentration camps that trapped Pacific Coast Japanese Americans. The *Pacific Citizen* maintained that "<d>ue to their aggressiveness and speed, they've been able to win their share of games against much taller competition."[22]

After World War II, plenty of basketball was played whenever significant Asian Pacific American communities existed. The San Francisco Bay Area prevailed as a stronghold of Asian Pacific American community basketball. In March, 1949, for example, the Catholic Bishops Relief Fund games were held in San Francisco. In one match up, a team of Japanese American War Veterans beat the San Francisco Chinese, despite the efforts of Willie "Woo Woo" Wong. In another game, a Nisei female team defeated the St. Mary's Saints, even though sixteen-year-old Helen Wong scored a game high 24 points.[23]

Also in San Francisco, annual Chinatown basketball festivals had been staged since before the war. Sponsored by Chinatown's St. Mary's Church, the festival was held at Kezar Pavilion situated in San Francisco's Golden Gate Park. In 1949, the festival consisted of three games. Males participated in two of the games, while females played in one. The last game of the evening pitted the male San Francisco Chinese Saints, the reigning "Oriental American Champs" out of St. Mary's Church, against the Filipino All Stars from Manila. Typically playing in this festival was the female counterpart to the San Francisco Chinese team--the Helen Wong-led squad representing St. Mary's. In 1947, the team won San Francisco's CYO championship. The next year St. Mary's came in second. Besides Helen Wong, the St. Mary's team included Susan Ng, Louise Wong, Monica Chang, and Francine Ong.[24]

The annual Pacific Athletic Association (PAA) Tournament was the major event in San Francisco Bay Area basketball circles, outside of the college game. Chinese Americans had typically competed in lighter weight divisions before the end of World War II and done well. However, the PAA attracted the skills of some of the finest male basketball players in the San Francisco Bay Area, including future and former all time greats such as Luisetti, Fred Scolari, and Don Barksdale. Until 1946, however, no team of Chinese Americans had entered the tournament against such formidable foes. That would change with the appearance of an all Chinese American team representing the Mierson Product Company. According to the *San Francisco Examiner,* George Wong managed the team, which included Benton Wong, Earl Gee, Steven Won, Horace Huey, Chung Wong, Ulysses Moy, Bill Louie, Henry Chin, as well as George Wong. The tallest player was five feet nine inches, while Steven Won was reportedly the shortest at five feet six inches. The Mierson aggregation was not expected to beat the Auten five from Palo Alto in the tournament's first round. However, the not very respectful headline "Wongs Tong Score 47-43 Victory," drew attention to what the *San Francisco Examiner's* Harry Borna wrote: "Eight little Chinese boys got the thirty-eighth annual *San Francisco Examiner* Pacific Association cage tournament to a sensational start in Kezar Pavilion" in defeating the bigger Auten five. Even though the Auten squad tried to rough up the Mierson players, "the little men from Chinatown" won because of their effective dribbling and passing. Borna, consequently, predicted the Mierson five would become crowd pleasers in San Francisco basketball circles. Unfortunately, they would not move beyond the second round, but they had started a chapter in Chinese American basketball history that the San Francisco Chinese Saints team gladly took up after it was formed in 1947.[25]

In 1949, the *San Francisco Examiner* mixed stereotypes in with admiration as it reported on the aforementioned "Chinese basketball festival" staged at Kezar Pavilion: "There won't be a lanterns hung at Kezar Pavilion this afternoon, but the annual Chinatown Basketball Festival won't lack color." The next year the San Francisco Chinese "Saints" hosted and defeated a "Nisei All Star" squad from Hawai'i, 50-40 at the festival. The undefeated St. Mary's Chinese Girls Saints beat the Oakland Sacred Heart Girls, 43-28.[26]

The San Francisco Chinese Saints earned a great deal of notice from European American observers. In 1950, *San Francisco Examiner* sportswriter Bob Brachman described the San Francisco Chinese players as "always colorful." The "clever little Chinese" staged an "artistic display of short, jolting passes and stop and go dribbling." Brachman claimed that the "daring little Chinese...because of their nimbleness have been accused of coming up out of the holes in the floor." The *San Francisco Chronicle* agreed that the San Francisco Chinese five was "one of the Bay Area's most colorful basketball teams" and that "despite a lack of height has consistently been one of the better club quintets on the local courts." [27]

The sustained enthusiasm for basketball in San Francisco's Chinatown after World War II was no doubt fueled by community leaders such as Lillian Yuen, who served as director of the Chinatown playground on Sacramento Street. For Yuen, basketball offered the kind of recreation that diverted Chinatown youths from vice and crime. She maintained that "when the pool-halls are empty the basketball league at the playground must be underway." Without basketball and other wholesome forms of recreation, she argued, too many Chinatown youths engaged in 'puncturing tires, breaking windows, and jamming parking meters.'"[28]

Other Asian Pacific American communities outside of San Francisco's Chinatown nurtured basketball teams after World War II. In 1947, the first Nisei basketball team to enter competition in New England came from Boston. Many of the Boston Nisei Club's players originated from California and Hawai'i, and accumulated plenty of competitive experience before heading to New England. The Salt Lake City Seagulls represented that city's Japanese American community. Meanwhile, the San Jose Zebras remained active World War II. In 1947, the *San Jose Mercury* insisted that "local basketball fans will have a real treat" watching eight Nisei teams vie in a tournament to settle the Japanese American basketball championship of Northern and Central California. The Zebras, who had just won the first half championship of San Jose's City League, would host teams such ass the Sacramento Maroons, Berkeley Nisei, co-champion of the Northern California Nisei Athletic Union, Presidio All-Stars, Reedley YBA, Central California champs, San Francisco Drakes, Oakland Paramounts, and San Mateo AC. A girls game between Sacramento and Mountain View teams was also featured. Starring for the Zebras in those years was Babe Nomura and T-Bone Akizuki. .In 1950, the Zebras competed in San Jose's City Adult League and won the championship of the Western Young Buddhist League by beating the Sacramento Maroons, 66-51, at San Jose High School. In 1955, the Zebras competed with players surnamed Sakamoto, Inouye, Nakatami, Fujimoto, Moon, and Alexandro. In other parts of California, Stockton's YMBA and YWBA merged into the Young Buddhist Association, which, in turn, sponsored the Busy Bees continued success. Boys' teams, by the way, were also sponsored. Sacramento's Japanese Americans were represented by the Stags as well as the Maroons, while the Los Angeles Trading Lords and the San Francisco Associates were also powerful Japanese American male fives.[29]

Filipino American basketball did not subside after the war. A quintet representing the Filipino Mango Athletic Club continued to play in the San Francisco Bay Area.. During the late 1940s and early 1950s, the Mango team competed in three National All Oriental tournaments held in Seattle and San Jose. The Saga basketball squad, moreover, represented Stockton's Filipino

American community. Its players were generally discharged veterans. In 1948, Stockton High School was the site of a tournament sponsored by the Filipino Catholic Youth Society. Led by high school star Eddie Chavez, Vallejo's Filipino Youth's Recreation Program won the tournament. In Hawai'i, the Hawaii Fil-Vets Club sponsored in 1948 a basketball team consisting of many veterans of the Filipino Infantry Regiment which fought in World War II. In Honolulu at the same time, Filipino Americans formed a basketball league. Among some of the other island Filipino teams were the Waialu Fils, Hil-Fil All-Stars, the Lanai Filipino Youth Organization, and the Waipahu Fil Americans. In December, 1948, the Filipino Catholic Youth cagers won the seventeen year old division championship in Seattle's Park Department's Queen Anne Lions Marine Reserves Tournament. San Jose in 1950 served as the site of a Filipino American basketball tournament drawing male teams from Oakland, San Francisco, Livingston, Stockton, Livermore, and San Jose.[30]

In 1946, the *Korea Independence* published a notice written by Mary Lyou, who reported on the Kon Wha Girls, "a sport loving group whose desire it is to have a victorious basketball team this season." In Honolulu, Korean Americans forged a basketball league with teams representing the Moiliili Realty Company, Makiki Nursery, the Delta Frats, coached by Harry Chung, and Radio Appliance, headed by Art Kim who was something of a legend in Honolulu basketball circles.[31]

In the late 1940s, Japanese Hawaiians supported a team called the AJA (Americans of Japanese Ancestry) or Nisei All-Stars. On the islands, the AJA squad opposed in the late 1940s such teams as the University of Hawai'i five and the visiting Oakland Bittners, a powerful amateur Bay Area five led by Don Barksdale. In one game against the University of Hawai'i early in the 1948 season, the AJA squad lost 56-39, as Rainbow captain Bobby Wong scored fourteen points for the winners. A few nights later, the Bittner's trounced the Nisei cagers, 93-44. However, the *Honolulu Star-Bulletin* declared that "although dwarfed and outclassed by the Bittners...the local cagers put up a spirited battle all the way." Dick Shimomura, the "five foot forward," scored fifteen points for the Nisei five. The Nisei All Stars entered the All-Oriental Basketball tournament held at San Jose State College in December, 1949. There, according to the *San Francisco Examiner*, 2500 packed into the small college gym to watch the All Stars defeat the San Francisco Chinese, 42-39; thus ending the San Franciscans two year championship reign. In the consolation game, the San Jose Zebras defeated a Japanese American squad from Chicago known as the Huskies—a team that would appear at Chicago Stadium to play in a preliminary game before a contest matching the Chicago Stags and the Rochester Royals. The Japanese Hawaiians barnstormed the mainland during the spring of 1950, defeating a five of San Francisco Japanese Americans in the process, 48-41 and losing the aforementioned game with the San Francisco Chinese. They, then, moved on to the Fifteenth Annual Nisei Basketball tournament held in Salt Lake City. There, they lost in the championship round to the San Jose Zebras, who were making their first appearance in the tournament.[32]

The Honolulu AJA's actually sponsored two all-stars teams in the spring of 1950—the one that headed to the American mainland and another that toured Japan. The latter team ran into problems with the AAU, which initially sought to ban its trek to the west. The AAU claimed that the AJA was not good enough to represent the United States abroad and that Japan had not yet been readmitted to the World Basketball Federation in the wake of World War II. Hawaii's AAU was not too happy either. It argued that the AJA's trek to Japan would mean that several of the islands' best basketball players would leave the Honolulu's AAU league less competitive. Eventually, the AAU relented and sanctioned the AJA team's trip to Japan. Once there, the AJA five defeated a team of Japanese college all-stars, 68-48, before 10,000 spectators at Tokyo's Sports Center. According to the *Hawaii Herald*, many Nisei GI's showed up to root for the AJA five.[33]

The AJA also operated a league with teams representing rural Oahu communities—communities such as Aiea, Wahiawa, Ewa, Pearl City, Waipahu, and Waialua.. AJA basketball was a source of pride for post-World War Hawaiian Nikkei and a training ground for Japanese American basketball players. An AJA spokesperson, Eddie Tanaka, admitted that "as Japanese are a small race, the going was tough and only a handful were able to compete in the top-notch division." However, he proclaimed, "AJA basketball players need no longer take a back seat to other nationalities any more. Gone is the day when their number were limited in the senior league." Moreover, in the mid-1950s, Japanese Americans in Honolulu also supported a Nisei Basketball League with teams such as Nippon Theater, Ebisu Caterers, and Aiea Japanese American Club.[34]

During the 1950s and after, basketball maintained its hold on San Francisco's Chinatown. The San Francisco Chinese continued to compete effectively during the decade. In 1950, the Chinese American five joined t an amateur organization called the Central California Basketball League, consisting of teams such as those sponsored by the YMI, the South City Windbreakers, and the Marin Town and Country Club. In 1951, player-coach Willie Wong scored seventeen points in leading his five over the University of San Francisco Freshman squad, 56-43 in a PAA tournament game. In 1953, the San Francisco Chinese entered a PAA tournament ultimately won by the Bill Russell led University of San Francisco Freshman team. In 1955, the San Francisco Chinese played and lost to a fine USF frosh team, 82-60.[35]

In subsequent years, the San Francisco Chinese took on teams from Taiwan and the Chinese mainland. In 1969, the five beat a team from the Republic of China, 64-61, at the USF gym. Twelve years later, *East/West* reported that the San Francisco Chinese squad would embark upon a tour of mainland China organized by Perry Chu, the director of San Francisco's Chinese Recreation Center.ter. According to player Keith Lee, the team consisted of veterans of high school and community college basketball who had previously toured Taiwan but would make their first venture onto the mainland. Lee explained, moreover, his attraction to basketball in a way that echoed the sentiments earlier uttered by Lillian Yuen. "To me, basketball...is a good thing. It's always been a constructive form of burning off energy." He bemoaned, however, the lack of a Chinatown league for young people in the 1980s. "I think if the community had a league, it would give the kids more incentive to get involved."[36]

Nevertheless, San Francisco's Chinatown persevered as a incubator of Asian Pacific American community basketball. In 1970, the Chinese Recreation Center hosted the Old Timer's Cage Classic, with adult teams representing Larry Mar's Bowling, Won Chong's Bean Sprouts, and Tony Auto Parts. It continued to sponsor an annual Chinese New Year Basketball Classic. In 1982, for instance, twelve teams participated in the event held at the Chinese Recreation Center. The Chinatown YMCA organized a basketball association for boys and girls ranging in age from eight to twelve years old. Games were held Saturday mornings and each player, regardless of skill level, competed for at least one half.[37]

Meanwhile, the San Jose Zebras remained a source of Japanese American community pride. In 1964, San Jose's Japanese American community honored the Zebras with a dinner-dance reunion. Among the guests invited was Everett Roseveaux, the European American who coached the Zebras in the 1930s. And forty years later, Zebra basketball still inspired the participation of Japanese American youths in the San Jose area. [38]

In Southern California during the 1970s, Japanese American community basketball thrived. In 1972, the Japanese American Optimists Club sponsored a girls basketball jamboree in Los Angeles. Teams from West Los Angeles, Gardena, and Hollywood participated. The Gardena F.O.R. tournament developed into a cherished event in Japanese American basketball circles. One of the oldest Japanese American tournaments in the United States, it replaced the aforementioned Salt Lake City Nisei tournament in 1960. The F.O.R. stands for Friends of Richard—Richard Nishimoto who played basketball for Gardena High School but died in 1959 at seventeen. Since its inception the Gardena F.O.R. tournament has not only attracted fine Japanese American teams, but also the likes of the San Francisco Chinese Saints. Also in the 1970s, Sacramento played host to a Japanese American invitational tournament for boys and girls squads. In 1977, the San Francisco Ardenettes led by Lorraine Hirano won the girls' division. [39]

In Southern California, as well as other regions, teams and leagues were organized for both girls and boys. However, as in many youth programs, regard less of ethnic base and decade, some of those involved craved victory a llittle too fanatically. Ed Takahashi, a primary architect of Japanese American girls' basketball in Southern California, complained in *Rafu Shimpo* that some of the coaches recruited players unscrupulously. Indeed, the problem of recruiting across racial and ethnic lines has cropped up enough to arouse Japanese American league administrators to mandate that teams possess a certain number of Nikkei and that all players possess some kind of Asian Pacific ancestry.[40]

In San Jose, Filipino/a American community leaders sought to establish the Filipino Service Center in the 1970s as a means of providing recreational and health services to the areas developing Filipino/a population. One of its more successful initial endeavors was a basketball tournament. Youth from nearby Mountain View, Gilroy, Morgan Hill, Santa Clara, Milpitas, and Palo Alto, as well as San Jose participated in this tournament.[41]

In Los Angeles in 1980, Asian Pacific American community activists used sports such as basketball to steer youth away from drug abuse and crime. The Asian American Drug Abuse Program sponsored a basketball team, as did the Korean Youth Center. High School gyms were utilized for practice sessions and games and the level of participation was reportedly high.[42]

The Korean Youth Center, indeed, had a challenge on its hands in servicing the growing Koreatown in Los Angeles. The KYC believed that a basketball program for Koreatown youth was vital. According to *Rice Paper*, a publication of the Asian American Drug Abuse Program:

> Too often access to facilities is limited, youth themselves often don't feel comfortable competing in non-Korean settings, because of language, cultural, and physical differences, in addition there are few organized sport or recreation associations that would help to foster the social and physical interaction with others that take place in a supervised activity such as the basketball program.[43]

In the 1990s, we could have found evidence of pan-Asian Pacific American community building and maintenance in a group of street basketball players in Flushing, Queens, New York known as the Asian Basketball Clique. According to its poetic website author, the Asian Basketball Clique "are all asian/ only by coincidence/ I imagine one day/we will grow to be/ the International Basketball Clique." A.B.C. was started in 1994 by students attending Townsend Harris High School. A.B.C.'s "founding fathers...are (in alphabetical order) Jack Chen, Cannon Chu, Michael Liou, Joseph Meng, and Vincent Yu." The website assured readers that "Our minds are set to pursue the never-ending quest for a good basketball game" and that A.B.C.'s "summer-only season unofficially begins with the first available game in the month of

May. Our home court is located at Memorial Park (149 St. & Willets Point Blvd.) in Flushing, Queens, N.Y."[44]

Other websites announced that Asian Pacific American community basketball flourished at the end of the twentieth century. One proclaimed that on Memorial Day weekend of 1999 the nineteenth annual North American Chinese Asian National Basketball tournament would he held at Seton Hall University in New Jersey. Among the teams invited were the defending "Men's Elite Open Champion" the durable San Francisco Saints along with male squads from all over the United States and Canada. For the first time, a "Women's/Girls Elite Open" would be staged. In Seattle, the Asian Sports Club offered a year-round basketball program for young people of both genders. On its website, the Asian Sports Club proclaimed: "Our goal is to encourage our youths' contribution beyond their participation as players.[45]

In places like Los Angeles and the San Francisco Bay Area, Asian Pacific American basketball teams and leagues prospered into the 2000s. In San Francisco, the Enchantees have been one of the best girls' teams in the region. The San Jose Community Youth Service basketball program is part of the legacy of Zebra basketball. The organization has shown a commitment to the Positive Coaching Alliance which seeks to "Honor the Game" by "creat<ing> a positive environment with effort and improvement, not winning and losing, being our main focus."[46]

Diverse Asian Pacific American communities have shown their support for Asian Pacific players and teams competing in the United States. In 1998, 500 Filipino Americans bought tickets to watch the Philippines National team play the University of Minnesota. A few years later, Chinese Americans and other Asian Pacific Americans began to get excited about the prospect of Chinese nationals such as Wang Zhizhi and Yao Ming entering the NBA. When Wang Zhizhi joined the Dallas Mavericks in the early 2000s, journalist Sam Lee noted the growing Chinese American fan base for NBA basketball in Texas. Moreover, Asian Pacific American parents in and around Dallas were sending their children to the Mavericks' summer basketball camp. Chinese officials hoped, in the meantime, that Yao Ming would join a good organization in a city possessing a large Chinese American population. [47]

In the summer of 2002, "Yao-Mania" swept Houston's Chinese American community as the Houston Rockets prepared to draft Yao Ming. The *Houston Chronicle's* Rachel Graves quoted Houston's city council member Gordon Quon, " <Yao Ming> helps break stereotypes…That has to make you feel proud as a Chinese-American, that black kids or Hispanic kids or white kids would also want to be Yao." Leaders of Houston's Chinese American community urged the tall center to come to Texas, promising that the community had hundreds of restaurants to fatten Yao Ming and offering their services to Yao of a Mandarin translator.[48]

The Stars

Basketball players of Asian Pacific ancestry have long competed on a college and even professional level. Given the stereotypes many of us harbor of Asian Pacific people this might seem surprising. However, considering the historical popularity of basketball in Asian Pacific American communities perhaps we should not express too much amazement as we discover top-notch male and female basketball players of Asian Pacific ancestry.

In the 1920s and 1930s, a few Japanese Americans competed for mainland college fives. During the early 1920s, "Fred Koba, the diminutive forward" suited up for the Stanford varsity five, while Arthur Matsu played basketball as well as football for William and Mary. In the early 1930s, the *San Francisco Chronicle* praised the play of Ted Obashi, a six foot guard on the University of California squad. Obashi, the *Chronicle* assured its readers, was man enough to take on big time basketball. He can, the *Chronicle* explained, "hold his own with the tallest when the play gets rough." In later years, Koba coached top Japanese American youth teams such as the Greyhounds and Mikados.[49]

A Nisei from Utah, Wataru Misaka starred on the University of Utah team during and after World War II. A son of a barber, he had grown up in the working class neighborhoods of Ogden, Utah before going on to Weber Junior College and the University of Utah. The University of Utah team glittered as one of the best college teams in the country and Misaka participated in both the NCAA tournament and at one time the equally prestigious National Invitational Tournament held in New York City's Madison Square Garden. The five foot eight inch Misaka shined as a defensive wizard, but he also scored three crucial baskets against Dartmouth to help Utah get into the 1944 NCAA finals. Getting Misaka's nativity wrong, sportswriter Hugh Fullerton Jr., enthused in 1944, "wonder if there's any place but America where you'd see the kind of sportsmanship the Garden fans displayed when they gave a big hand to Utah's Wat Misaka, Hawaiian-born Japanese? The kid deserved it, too." And the famed Bob Considine told readers, "One of the biggest cheers of the basketball season went to Wat Misaka, University of Utah's American-born Jap, when he left the floor after his fourth personal foul in the Western NCAA finals at Kansas City." In 1947, Misaka limited Kentucky's great Ralph Beard to only two points in the NIT championship. A UPI account of the game was headlined, "Jap Runt Stars in Ute Victory," and declared that basketball fans "had to stoop down to pat the brunette thatch of little Wat Misaka, the Japanese kid who has improved on the invention of the dynamo." [50]

Misaka recalled getting positive treatment at the University of Utah, while competing in New York City. However, his college career was not free of racial incidences. For example, Misaka remembered that when playing on the road against Utah State, white fans yelled "Get the dirty Jap."[51]

The New York Knicks signed Misaka to a 4,000 dollar contract. A press account said that the "flashy little Japanese-American" had a chance to contribute to the Knicks because coach Joe Lapchick liked small players. The *Pacific Citizen* proudly reported on Misaka's achievement, informing readers of Misaka's first appearance in a Knick uniform against the Washington Capitols. The JACL"s weekly reproduced a wire report on the game in which "little Wat Misaka of Ogden" appeared. However, after getting into five games, the Knicks cut Misaka. Misaka claimed he was treated unfairly by Lapchick. For example, Lapchick put him at forward where taller players could post up on him. Lapchick cut Misaka shortly before Christmas of 1947. Misaka maintained, "I think I was cut possibly because I was Japanese American. Though I have no real evidence of this, I know that Japanese Americans were not appreciated as fans back then." The *Pacific Citizen* asserted that Misaka might have been the victim of bad timing. A rival professional league had just folded and the Knicks hoped to sign some of that league's former players such as the great George Mikan. Thus, the New York team felt it had to cut Misaka and another player to make room for the prospective signees. Misaka later told a *Los Angles Times* reporter that while he did not face overt discrimination as a Knick no player except for star guard Carl Braun was particularly friendly toward him. Abe Saperstein, who ran the Harlem Globetrotters, apparently offered Misaka a chance to play with his famed touring team. Misaka decided instead to stay in Utah, work as engineer and coach Japanese American basketball teams.[52]

Aside from Misaka other Japanese Americans played college basketball during World War II even though in 1950 the *Pacific Citizen* lamented, "because of the fact that few Nisei meet the height requirements of modern-day basketball only a handful have played on college varsities in recent years." Nevertheless, it pointed out that in addition to Misaka, Shig Maruo competed for Springfield College, while Johnny Oshida played for the University of Illinois Navy Pier. Moreover, Bright Onodo played basketball for Hillsdale College in 1944, while Kazuo Tada left a concentration camp to suit up for Nebraska Wesleyan and Sei Adachi joined Huron College's squad. In Michigan, Tom Sugihara and Paul Hiyama suited up for Kalamazoo College. The fact that both Sugihara and Hiyama stood about 5 ft. 4 garnered national publicity for Kalamazoo as "the shortest basketball team in the nation."[53]

During the late 1940s, there was no better amateur basketball player in San Francisco than Willie "Woo Woo" Wong. It may not have been much of an honor, but in 1950 Roger Williams of the *San Francisco News* picked Wong as a member of the 2nd all short team of San Francisco basketball players active since 1925.[54]

In 1948, Wong joined the University of San Francisco Dons squad. His freshman year at USF must have seemed promising. USF varsity coach, Pete Newell, praised Wong's shooting and passing ability and expressed the hope that the San Franciscan would "become the first great Chinese basketball player the United States has ever known." In November, 1949, a USF football program displayed an advertisement for the upcoming Dons' basketball season. The advertisement touted Wong as a leading newcomer. Wong, indeed, made the USF varsity, which was the defending NIT champion. The *Chinese Press* perhaps exaggerated Wong's importance to Coach Pete Newell. It described him as the "sharp shooting sophomore star of the University of San Francisco basketball team." It also informed readers that Wong was probably the first Chinese American varsity player to appear in New York's famed Madison Square Garden and that hundreds of New York Chinese Americans showed up at the game to welcome the San Franciscan. To publicize USF's appearance at Madison Square Garden, newspapers such as the *New York Times* and *San Francisco Examiner* printed photos of the five-foot-four inch Wong with six-foot-six inch teammate, Don Lofgren. In one photo, which once again stressed the so-called diminutive nature of Asian Pacific Americans, Lofgren held Wong aloft on his shoulders, allowing the Chinese American to dunk the ball. The *New York Times* also predicted that the "Chinese sophomore…may electrify the Garden spectators with his speed." Wong rode the bench for most of the season, however, and subsequently dropped out of the USF basketball program. He then returned to the San Francisco Chinese Saints as a player-coach. As far as the *Chinese Press* was concerned, Wong remained "Mr. Basketball of Chinatown."[55]

Several other players of Asian Pacific ancestry have gotten more playing time in major and not so major college basketball programs and even in the National Basketball Association (NBA).The aforementioned football star, Al Chang, played guard for Redlands in the early 1940s, while John Nishiyama started for Occidental on the eve of Japanese American internment in 1942. Jimmy Wong captained and starred on the San Francisco State College five during the 1949-1950 season.[56]

The University of Hawai'i often was represented by fine basketball players who could effectively compete against mainlanders. Early in 1947, UH dispatched its basketball team to the American mainland where it played in the famed Madison Square Garden. Because of its unique ethnic composition, the team garnered a semblance of publicity from the *New York Times,* which published a photo of coach Bert Chan Wa conferring with players Robert Kau, Damien Rocha, Harry Kahuawui, George Malama, and Ed Loui.[57]

Talented Asian Pacific Islander athletes competed for UH in the 1940s and 1950s. Among these were Fred Furukawa and Willie Lee. In the early 1950s, Furukawa and Bill Lee formed an impressive front court dual for a UH team, which trekked to the Pacific Coast in December, 1953. Lee, for example, scored twenty-four points in leading UH to an upset victory over Washington State. Lee stood at 6 ft. 5, while Furukawa was 6 ft. 4. Both were products of Farrington High School in Honolulu. Sometimes called Korean by the mainland press, sometimes Chinese, Lee eventually coached basketball in Honolulu, while Fu-rukawa coached college basketball and tennis in California, most particularly for Sacramento State. In the late 1990s, Native Hawaiian Alika Smith combined with mainlander Anthony Carter to form for the University of Hawaii what *Sport Magazine* called the best backcourt in the Western Athletic Conference. A few years, five foot four inch Lance Takaki suited up for UH. He told Cindy Luis of the *Honolulu Star-Bulletin,* "I didn't come out thinking I'd play a whole lot. But there is a sense of pride, being the one local kid. Even getting in for just a minute ... you have to swallow your pride just to be in the (score) book."[58]

The University of Hawaii, Hilo, has also suited up fine players of Asian Pacific Islander ancestry. For example, guard Alex Cabagnot was named Pacific West Conference Player of the Week in February, 2005. Born in the Philippines and raised in Los Angeles, Cabagnot was not only one of his team's top scorers but was a conference leader's in assists.[59]

NBA players of Asian Pacific American ancestry have included Raymond Townsend, Rex Walters, Corey Gaines, and Wallace Rank. Hailing from San Jose, Raymond Townsend possesses Filipino ancestry. He starred as a guard on some fine UCLA teams in the 1970s. He then played in the NBA with the Gol-den State Warriors. Townsend, subsequently, coached high school basketball in Santa Clara County and presently runs a popular youth basketball program. Rex Walters is another Californian from San Jose, but of part-Japanese ancestry. As a youth, he played for the San Jose Zebras. After attending and playing basket-ball for De Anza Community College in Cupertino, California, Walters starred as a guard for the NCAA Champion University of Kansas five. Walters later played in the NBA for the New Jersey Nets, Philadelphia 76ers, and Miami Heat before heading to a career as a college basketball coach. Corey Gaines, part Jap-anese and part-African American, played for the New York Knicks, while Sa-moan American Wallace Rank also competed in the NBA.[60]

In recent years, men's college basketball has attracted skilled athletes of Asian Pacific Islander ancestry. Jason Kapona possesses Pacific Islander ance-stry and the basketball skills to help lead UCLA in the late 1990s and early 2000s. Kapona, as of this writing, is playing in the NBA. At Cal, Kirk Kim suited up, but played infrequently in the 2000-2001 season. Hawaiian Kawika Akina stood out for Northern Arizona University as a point guard in the late 1990s. Born in Fiji, 6 ft. 9 inch Mekeli Wesley did a fine job in the front court for BYU after graduating from Provo High School in Utah. Stanford's exciting backcourt in the early 2000s featured an athletic guard named Julius Barnes, who is part-Samoan. While not a regular, Jason Haas, who possesses Korean ancestry, also played for Stanford in the early 2000s. In 2004, Derrick Low be-came Washington State's starting point guard as a freshman. Low had been an all league player for four straight years as a Honolulu prep star. Against national powerhouse, Arizona, the freshman Low scored thirteen points, making four out of four three point attempts, in leading the Cougars to an upset. Two years later, Low helped lead Washington State into its first NCAA appearance in years.[61]

Moreover, several Filipino American players have competed professionally for the Philippines Basketball Association (PBA). During the 1998-1999 season, for example, Paul Asi Taulava, a six foot ten inch center of Filipino-Tongan ancestry made a stir in PBA circles, as did other Fil-Am performers such as Eric Menk, Andy Seigle, Jeffrey Cariaso, Danny Seigle, Jonathan Ordonio, Noy Castillo, and former University of Texas standout Sonny Alvarado. Taulava was born in Tonga to a father of Tongan and Ilocanan descent and a Filipino mother. He told the press, "I was born poor. There were times when I had to skip meals in my early years in the United States where I grew up."[62]

Granted there have not been too many individual American professional basketball stars of Asian Pacific ancestry. Around 1940, however, a San Francisco-based Chinese American team toured the United States for pay. The Hong Wah Kues were formed in 1939 by a white businessman, who believed that an all-Chinese basketball team was marketable as a novelty. The team consisted of about six players packed into either a Plymouth Sedan or a station wagon with their coach. Among the players wearing a Wah Kue uniform were George Lee, Albert Lee, Robert Lum, Albert F. Lee, Douglas Quong, Fred Gok, and Chauncy Yip. The Wah Kues, otherwise known as the Great Chinese Warriors, were paid about $200 a month each and played in towns mainly situated in the American Midwest. Even though Gok, at five feet ten and one-half inches stood as the quintet's tallest player, the Wah Kues won more often than they lost. In Cincinnati and other cities and towns, they performed on the same card as the Harlem Globetrotters. On one particular night in Cincinnati, Robert Lum dazzled the Midwestern crowd with his ball handling and shooting skills.[63]

In order to market them as exotics, their European American promoters compelled the Wah Kues to speak only Chinese while playing. Fans, however, often called the Wah Kues "chinks" and expressed other racial epithets. Gok recalls, "They told us to talk Chinese only on the court, so we make the spectators laugh. So they don't understand what <we> say, you know... And you could be telling them to go someplace and they don't know the difference. You get back at them." Meanwhile, newspapers referred to the Wah Kues as "the laundry men" or a "group of tiny Oriental rug cutters." One Midwest newspaper described the Hong Wah Kues as "the Chinks <who> flashed a snappy and deceptive passing attack."[64]

In the 1990s and early 2000s, a number of fine female college players emerged on the mainland and Hawai'i. One of the most talented had been six foot four inch center/forward Naomi Muliatolopele. A Samoan American and niece of Manu Tuiososopu, Muliatolopele helped Stanford achieve high national rankings in women's college basketball and played professionally for the Seattle Reign of the defunct American Basketball League. A few years later, the versatile Lindsay Yamasaki joined the Lady Cardinal. In the late 1990s, Arizona State's Michelle Tom saw plenty of action at point guard after transferring to the Tempe, Arizona campus from the University of South Florida. At the same time, Filipina Jackie Montalban departed Chula Vista, California, to play guard for West Point. Yuriko Jung, Kiyoko Miller, Leslie Sotero-Higa competed for University of California, Irvine, USC, and California State University, Fullerton respectively in the late 1990s. At nearby UCLA, Natalie Nakase stood out as a point guard in the early 2000s. In 2005, she was the only Asian American playing in the professional National Women's Basketball League as she started at point guard for the San Jose Spiders. Selena Ho was another good point guard, competing for the University of Pacific in the late 1990s and early 2000s. In 2001, sportswriter Ethen Leiser found her playing in the San Francisco Bay Area Pro-Am League. Competing in the same summer league was Maya Fok, a "hyperactive, hustle-till-you-drop point guard" who suited up for the University of San Diego. Oregon State's Leilani Estevan was a fine guard in the early 2000s. Possessing Samoan ancestry, the daughter of a UPS worker told the press she wanted to visit Samoa one day. At Boise State, Hawaiian Jody Nakashima played guard in the early 2000s. Meanwhile, exciting point guard Corrie Mizusawa led St. Mary's of Moraga when the Michelle Sasaki Jacoby team got into the NCAA tournament and lost valiantly to perennial powerhouse Tennessee. Mizusawa subsequently transferred to Oregon and helped the Ducks gain a rare NCAA berth in her senior year. In Division III women's basketball, Man-Khoi Nguyen, played guard for Haverford College in 2005, along with five foot three inch Bea Chang.[65]

As one might expect, the University of Hawai'i's women's team has possessed more players of Asian Pacific ancestry than other Division I schools. In the late 1990s, point guard BJ Itoman sparkplugged a winning Wahine basketball team. According to the *Honolulu Star-Bulletin's* Cindy Luis, "Blythe Jean "BJ" Itoman was a home-crowd favorite and an opponent's nightmare." Luis quoted Itoman's coach, Vince Goo, who declared, "The crowd likes her because of how hard she plays...She's the No. 1 enemy for opposing players and the least liked by opposing coaches because of all the problems she causes defensively." A few years later, forward Hedy Liu, a Hawaiian of Samoan ancestry, starred for Goo's five.[66]

Crossing the Sidelines

Asian Pacific American basketball players possessing a variety of skill levels have competed with and against non-Asian Pacific American players since the early 1900s at which time the *San Jose Mercury* pointed out that competing for Fremont Grammar School in San Francisco was "a young Japanese student." In 1912, the *San Francisco Evening Post* declared that "Fujita, the plucky little

Japanese" played forward for Lowell High School. That same year, the Kalihi girls basketball team beat the Palama Settlement House team, 39-23. Playing for the winners were A. Sing, L. Kekai, F. Kekai, and L. Akea, while the opposition included athletes such as Mabel Doo and L. Akana. In 1914, Lincoln school in Honolulu suited up Tai Loy. Achoy Ahou coached the Maui girls' basketball team, on which Jennie Kalekui played guard. A few years later, Eliza Kamaka played for Papaikou in Hilo, while Clem Akina took to the court for the Hilo Yacht Club team. In 1917, Hannah Lee Kwai competed for Honolulu's Normal Hookipa squad. In 1919, Fred Koba played for San Francisco's Poly High School's 110 pound team. [67]

In the early 1920s, a squad called the Hawaiian All Stars toured the U.S. mainland. Its members included players of Japanese, Chinese, Native Hawaiian, and haole ancestry. One of the squad's stars was another great all around Hawaiian athlete named Walter Mon Sin "Chocolate" Chung, who would subsequently carve out a career as one of Hawai'i's most respected physicians. On this Hawaiian multicultural roster were players such as Ernest Nolan, Abe Kaleikuu, Bunny Chung, Herman Clark, and Shig Matsuyama. Yet, according to the *Sacramento Bee*, "Chocolate Chung, a Chinese forward, is said to be the real star of the outfit, and has been making impressive showings in the games played by <the Hawaiian team> team."[68]

During the 1920s, Asian Pacific American competed for school teams throughout the American mainland. Chinese Americans George Yung and Stephen Chow represented San Jose High School in basketball. In the late 1920s, Kango Nagano and "Midget" Hirasa Sugimoto played lightweight basketball for the Salinas YMCA. In Montana, George Wong and Gar Ken Wong played grade school basketball in Helena. In New York City, a Nakagawa competed for Roosevelt High School.[69]

California witnessed several Asian Pacific Americans playing school basketball. In San Francisco during the 1930s, a Mini Ichiyasu played guard for Poly High School's varsity, while Hong Wong was named to the all-city third team from the same school. Francis Min Chin competed for Commerce and Walter Tong was, according to the *San Francisco Chronicle*, "a capable scorer" for St. Ignatius High School. Among the most notable lightweight players in San Francisco was Robert "Egg Foo" Lum, who attended Sacred Heart High School. Author Robert Christagu maintained that, "The Asian Americans at <San Francisco's> Lowell were among the benefactors of the city's exponent system for basketball competition. Assigned 'exponent' points based on age, height, and weight, players could enjoy the democracy of a system of basketball competition that eliminated towering players." Moreover, in the 1930s, Sal Jio, "a diminutive Japanese" competed in freshman basketball for San Jose State. Down in Los Angeles, Frankie Dong competed for Belmont High School. [70]

Hawaiian basketball involved a variety of Asian Pacific Americans in the two decades before World War II. Soo Sun Kim was a top player for McKinley High School in 1928. William "Spike" Nakayama suited up for the Bishop's Trust five in 1933. Tuck Chong starred on the Palama five, coached by Dr. Clarence Lee Chong, while Norman Oda coached Maui's Lahaina quintet. Chew Chong Chin, Kan Chong Yuen, Gene Moriguchi, and Yim Pui competed for the Nuunu Speedsters, coached by Hong Wai Ching. The talented and versatile Ted Nobriega coached the AAU Vagabounds. The University of Hawaii team typically played local fives such as Palama. Unsurprisingly, Tommy Kaulukukui was one of the better UH players in the 1930s. Kaulukukui's mastery of basketball as well as football and baseball inspired sportswriter Andrew Mitsukado to call him "the greatest athlete to come out of Hilo." On the female side, Bernice Namaka and Ruth Ahuna competed in Honolulu.[71]

A son of a Chinese immigrant auto mechanic father and a Native Hawaiian mother, Ah Chew Goo became the scourge of Hawaiian high school basketball during the 1930s, before he played with and against visiting basketball stars such as Hank Luisetti and the Harlem Globetrotters. Andew Mitsukado wrote of Ah Chew Goo, "He did everything with the ball except make it talk back to him." Hank Luisetti claimed that Goo could play with any college team because of the Hawaiian's ball handling skills. Vince Goo reported that his father so impressed the Harlem Globetrotters in the 1940s that they did not want to face him again and that the Globetrotters' coach, Abe Saperstein, wanted to sign him. [72]

Hilo-born Ung Soy "Beans" Afook was another pioneer of Hawaiian basketball during the middle of the twentieth century. Afook coached the Hilo High School boys basketball team for several years, mentoring, in the process, Ah Chew Goo and Jimmy Yagi, who started the University of Hawai'i, Hilo, men's basketball program. Moreover, his high school team won several territorial championships. In 1949, Afook, "the builder of champions" retired as head basketball coach for Hilo High School.[73]

On the eve of internment, Japanese Americans were sprinkled on West Coast squads. In Portland, St. John's High School suited up a forward named Tokomoto and Harold Ito played for Multnomah College. In Seattle, Bill Yanagimashi competed for Garfield High School along with Chinese American cagers, Phil Mar Hing and Al Mar. A Midge Kojimoto played in San Francisco on Commerce High School's varsity squad with a young man possessing the surname of Wong. A Yoshimura competed for San Francisco's Mission High School's lightweight team. Otto Oshida shone, according to the *San Francisco Examiner* as a "diminutive star" for the San Francisco Junior College five. [74]

During World War II, Asian Pacific Americans of both sexes crossed cultural borders to compete for an assortment of basketball teams. Ruth Chan Jang recalled for Judy Yung that she played for a WAC squad in Georgia: "I was the only Chinese on the basketball team and all the other teams we played were white...I was very active and loved playing basketball."[75]

In the immediate post-World War II years, players of Asian Pacific ancestry seemed to compete more often than ever with players from other racial and ethnic groups. During the late 1940s, San Francisco's Commerce High School suited up Henry Chin, who ranked among the highest scorers in the city. Harry Mock starred for Commerce High the following year. One of Mock's teammates was the great K.C. Jones. Meanwhile, Helen Wong led a Star of the Sea High School team in San Francisco, on which Lillian Ong played in 1951. Susumi Kashuwagi played for Ballard High School's varsity basketball squad in Seattle during the 1945-1946 season. Seattle's Garfield High School suited up Jim Hino a few years later. Also in Seattle in the fall of 1949, seven players from the American Legion's Cathay Post joined forces with seven players from the Nisei Veteran's Committee to represent their city in the National All Oriental basketball tourney scheduled later in the year in San Jose. In Los Angeles, Herb Isono was a standout forward for University High School. In Northern California, George Goto stood out for Placer Junior College. The *Pacific Citizen* asserted that Goto was "probably the first six-foot Nisei player to come along since Ted Obashi." A son of a father who owned a fish market in Placer County and a mother who cooked for a boarding house, Goto, subsequently, played a bit off the bench for Stanford. Near Portland, Jimmy Tsugawa stood out for Beaverton High School. In Denver, the great Nancy Ito also played basketball. According to the *Pacific Citizen,* she was a leading scorer for the Denver Hudsonettes, a team which took on men's squads. In one game, she scored twenty-two points as the Hudsonettes beat the Sedalia Booster's male quintet, 36-28. [76]

The inception and brief existence of the National All-Oriental basketball Tournament deserves greater discussion. According to a *Seattle Post-Intelligencer* sportswriter, Jack Heuing, two of Seattle's Chinese Americans residents merited credit for getting the tournament started. After World War II, Art Louie ran a sporting goods store in Seattle, while Phil Mar Hing was a standout local Chinese American basketball player. Both believed in the importance of building bridges between Seattle-area Chinese and Japanese American communities. Louie apparently told Heuing that ill-feelings between Chinese and Japanese Americans ran high before the war. A Chinese American basketball team had actually entered and won a tournament promoted by Seattle Japanese Americans. The Chinese American five went on to another Japanese American tournament held in an unnamed Pacific Northwest city where, Louie claimed, they were mobbed and forced to withdraw. In any event, Louie now hoped basketball could bring Chinese and Japanese Americans closer together. He told the press, "Basketball is a game close to the hearts of all of us and we thought it would be an excellent means of demonstrating our mutual citizenship."[77]

The *Seattle Post-Intelligencer* seemed to hail the advent of the first All-Oriental Basketball Tournament in late December, 1947, as well as the second tournament staged in Seattle the following year. The headline to the previously mentioned Heuing article read, "Democracy in Action." One of the teams invited to compete in the tournament was the Hawaiian Nisei All-Stars. The Hawaiians were greeted upon arrival in Seattle by the city's mayor and other dignitaries. A photo in the *Post-Intelligencer* shows the Nisei All-Stars presenting Seattle's mayor with a lei. The mayor, in turn, is quoted as quipping, "All I need now is a grass skirt." A few days later an article, seeking to promote the upcoming tournament, appeared in the *Post-Intelligencer*. The article declared, apparently in reference to the presumed small stature of the athletes involved, that the "Oriental tourney" was "<a>ppropriately called the season's biggest little tournament." After the tournament started, Royal Brougham, a *Post-Intelligencer*, columnist, announced: "Athletics knows no race, color, or creed and there was nothing but the best sportsmanship when Japanese, Chinese, and Hawaiian teams from all over the Pacific played their basketball tournament this week." A year later, Brougham echoed those sentiments when he asserted that the "National Oriental-American basketball tourney <was an> athletic event fostering good will."[78]

In December, 1949, the *San Jose Mercury* also appeared pleased that San Jose State College hosted the third tournament and eager to promote the cause of the local favorites, the San Jose Zebras. As in Seattle, however, the arrival of the Hawaiian AJA team assumed center stage at the outset. San Jose city and San Jose State college officials greeted the Hawaii All Stars at San Jose's Civil Auditorium. The Hawaiians, for their part, conferred upon city officials a gift from the mayor of Honolulu.[79]

As for the tournament itself, the San Jose *Mercury* promised before the games started that "<s>ome of the most colorful basketball games of the local season" will take place   Indeed, the *Mercury* writer used "colorful" three times in the article to describe the basketball that would be played by the Asian Pacific American athletes. Undoubtedly, the sportswriter meant well, but applying the word "colorful" so often to depict Asian Pacific American athletes and athletic competition served to exoticize as well as praise them. Nevertheless, according to the *Mercury*, spectators at the tournament would get a chance to see "<o>ne of the most outstanding sports events in the history of San Jose." Several fine basketball players, with impeccable high school and even college careers, such as Raymond Saito who made Wyoming's all prep team, would appear for the Seattle Oriental All Stars. Moreover, Zebra standout T-Bone Akizuki, a "great favorite with local court fans" would also take to the court.[80]

Also after World War II, Asian Pacific Islanders competed on barnstorming quintets. In 1946 and 1947, a Hawaii All-Star squad toured the American
mainland. Paul Kim, Harry Chang, Peter Chun, Tom Harimoto, a 442nd veteran,
played regularly for the barnstormers. After winning a game in the Midwest, a
local paper asserted, "The islanders impressed with slick ball handling, plenty of
drive and a skilful passing technique." Meanwhile, a team called the San Francisco All-Nations was formed. This squad toured with the Harlem Globetrotters
and a five called the Los Angeles Red Devils, which featured Jackie Robinson.
A crowd of 3,000 people packed San Jose's Civic Auditorium to see the All
Nations team play the Harlem Globetrotters. Among the players performing for
All Nations were a Liu and a Wong. The Globetrotters won 44-25, but, according to the San Jose *Mercury*, took the game seriously until five minutes re-
mained in the game. Nearly a year later, Robinson led the Red Devils to a victo-
ry over the All Nations five in Los Angeles, 37-29. Yuen, Wong, and Robert
Lum played for All Nations. According to a San Francisco *Chronicle* article, the
All Nations five was "paced by the Grant Avenue sharpshooter, diminutive
Bobby Lum.[81]

An engaging example of basketball as a bridge across cultural divisions derives from a basketball clinic run by Hank Luisetti and sponsored by the *San
Francisco Examiner* for several years in post-war San Francisco. The attendees
were children and teenagers, males and females, ranging from eight to eighteen
years of age. Since the *San Francisco Examiner* after all sponsored it, the daily
assigned sportswriters such as Bob Brachman to write promotional pieces before and during Luisetti's clinic.

Whether any African American or Latino/a youths attended the clinic is not
clear. African American standout Don Barksdale, however, joined other top
flight Bay Area adult basketball players in helping Luisetti coach the attendees.
Brachman and other Examiner journalists, moreover, detailed Chinese American
interest in the clinic in the late 1940s and the performances, in particular, of Helen Wong.

Several days before the clinics started in the late 1940s, Brachman wrote
unsurprisingly that Luisetti's clinic had attracted plenty of interest from various
community teams in and around San Francisco. Before the 1948 clinic got under
way, Brachman said that about 125 girls had registered. Among them were a
good number "of girls…from Chinatown where sport is having a big boom." In
particular, Maureen Chan from Commerce High School and Elizabeth Chong
from Star of the Sea High School were expected to enroll along with Helen
Wong. Brachman declared prior to the 1949 clinic: "As usual one of the most
enthusiastic groups is the gang from the St. Mary's Boy's Club." Club Director,
Hank Wong, according to Brachman had requested one hundred entry cards.

About a week later, Brachman pointed out that Cynthia Wong from the Catholic
Chinese Social Center wanted to enroll "our girls from the St. Mary's Chinese

basketball team." According to Brachman, "that means sensational Helen Wong, who coaches the Chinese girls will be in there pitching." The year earlier, Brachman wrote, "Helen gave an amazing exhibition of shooting when she sank 49 of 52 shots, including 32 straight free throws in an informal contest with Luisetti."[82]

During the course of the 1948 clinic, Brachman wrote that Helen Wong, "the young Chinese miss" put on a shooting exhibition that amazed Luisetti and other onlookers. Former All American Jack Nichols, who was helping Luisetti run the clinic, said, "I've seen a lot of girls shoot a basketball...but in all my life I've never seen any girl shoot like that." Another *Examiner* reporter, Don Selby, raved about Wong's "easy, co-ordinated style of ... shooting" and maintained, "She could put many men cagers to shame in that department." Reporting from the 1949 clinic, Brachman affirmed that of all the basketball students only Helen Wong seemed to master the one handed push shot, which Luisetti had used to as a basketball pioneer. Wong, furthermore, "is perhaps the most graceful student in the school." At the end of the camp, Helen Wong won the award as best shooter among the 16 year old and older girls—an award which escaped her a year earlier when she was upset by a European American youth. Elizabeth Chong, who attended Star of the Sea High School with Wong, came in second among 14 and 15 year old girls. And Berkeley High's Billy Wong won the award for 15 and 16 year old boys. [83]

Cross-cultural Hawaiian fives competed with less diverse mainland fives in the 1940s and 1950s. In 1944, Rose Kaulukukui starred in women's basketball in Honolulu. In 1949, Gwen Kam, Louise Kipi, Bobbie Dela Cruz, Dorothy Dung and Annette Akana competed in the Hawaii Senior Girls' League. In 1951, Ruby Kalama, Miriam Wong, and Doreen Leong played on a Honolulu women's team. A few years later, St. Mary's of Moraga sent a basketball squad to the Hawaiian Islands. Among the teams St. Mary's opposed was an independent five sponsored by Universal Ford. The mainland team won, 63-44, but the Hawaiian team suited up players such as Chico Miyashiro, George Malama, John Honda Holi, and Wally Tome.[84]

In the 1950s and 1960s, Chinese and Japanese Americans competed on several American mainland teams. During the early 1950s, Jimmy Yokota illuminated junior college basketball in California when he competed for Placer Junior College. .In Seattle, Ken Sakamoto played for O'Dea High School. Around the same time, Junior Singh starred in basketball for San Bernadino Junior College. Yosh Kumagai was a top scorer for Palo Alto High School, while Howard Lum led Hollister Junior College in scoring and Kaz Shinzato achieved all-city status as a guard in Los Angeles. In Sacramento, Tom Takahashi played for the State's Department of Architecture five which competed in a basketball tournament sponsored by Aerojet Company in 1957. In 1965, Barry Ng was "a high scoring center" for Newark High School in California's Alameda County.

Four years later, Chinese American Ronde Deere won the *San Francisco Examiner's* Player of the Week Award after scoring twenty-three points for Galileo High School against Mission.[85]

Since the 1940s, high school, club, and college basketball has allowed some Asian Pacific Americans coaches to cross racial and ethnic borders. In the late 1940s, Hawaiian basketball legend, Ah Chew Goo, coached the Bank of Hawaii five and Bert Chan Wa coached a team representing the Liberty House. Ah Chew Goo and Bill Choy, furthermore, conducted basketball clinics for the YBA in Honolulu after World War II. In 1951, Goo coached a Hawaiian all-star team that played the Harlem Globetrotters in Honolulu. Playing for Ah Chew Goo were Bill Choy, Alvin Chang and Sunny Lee. In the mid-1950s, Ah Chew Goo coached for the University of Hawaii. Bert Chan Wa also coached the National Supply Company's basketball team, which represented, by the way, a store that Chan Wa managed. And Chan Wa headed UH's basketball program in the late 1940s. Walter Wong was another highly regarded Hawaiian coach. In 1947, Wong coached Whitey's Athletic Club five, which competed in Honolulu's Senior Basketball League. On Kauai, Akio Kubota coached the islands' boys' high school team in 1950. The highly respected coach of the University of Hawai'i women's basketball team, Ah Chew Goo's son, Vince Goo, coached plenty of male high school basketball on the islands in the 1970s. In Oakland in the 1970s, Dave Shigematsui was a very successful Nisei coach for the Carlmont High School varsity. During the same decade, Doug Kagawa, who starred for the Berkeley High School varsity five, coached at Albany High School. In the late 1990s, Wade Nakamura was a successful girls' basketball coach for Homestead High School in California's Silicon Valley.[86]

The versatile Bill Kajikawa pioneered as the head basketball coach at Arizona State after World War II. In 1948, Kajikawa became Arizona State's head basketball coach. And when Kajikawa brought his team on a East Coast trip during the 1949-1950 season, Vince Johnson, a sportswriter for the *Pittsburgh Post-Gazette* declared, "Basketball fans... blinked with surprise when wiry, amber skinned Bill Masao Kajikawa made his appearance with the Arizona State team in the Gardens." In 1949, Kajikawa recruited Arizona State's first African American basketball player—John Burton. Kajikawa led the Wildcats to five league upper division seasons. Ned Wulk, who replaced Kajikawa, said of his predecessor, "Bill is one of a kind in athletics...and one of the positive kinds He has the unusual quality of being interested, involved and concerned about everyone around him, be it player, fellow coach or anyone else."[87]

Almost as multi-talented as Kajikawa, Buck Lai, Jr., became LIU's head basketball coach in the mid-1950s, helping to revitalize the sport on the Long Island campus after the infamous gambling scandal struck it down as a big time power in the early 1950s. After World War II, Lai assisted Clair Bee, one of college basketball's most renowned coaches. Moreover, Lai seemed to serve as a public relations person for Bee and the powerful LIU basketball team.[88]

The gambling scandal that took down the LIU basketball program and forced Clair Bee's resignation was a blow to Lai. The Hawaiian ballplayers' son told the press that he was very close to many of the LIU basketball players involved in the scandal and was stunned that there could have been a problem. Lai considered the option of leaving LIU and retire from coaching. However, he declared he could not give up on a school that had been a prime part of his life since 1937. As LIU's new basketball coach, Lai called the effort to breathe life into a defunct basketball program, "Operation Rebound." Lai promised, however, that LIU would shun the limelight and Madison Square Garden.[89]

Lai coached LIU for six years and achieved a record of forty-four victories against thirty-nine defeats. As athletic director, he oversaw the transformation of the old Paramount Theatre in Brooklyn into a home gym for the LIU five, which had once called Madison Square Garden its abode before the gambling scandal. Lai, however, continued to assured the press that LIU would not return to big-time college basketball and its temptations.[90]

Dan Fukushima was one of the most respected high school coaches in the San Francisco Bay Area. Perhaps the first Nisei to coach high school basketball in California, Fukushima played for Montebello High School and Fullerton Junior College in the 1930s, as well as the Berkeley Nisei and the San Jose Zebras. His first coaching stint after graduating from Cal was for East Contra Costa Junior College. However, he stayed longest with James Lick High School in San Jose, where over twenty-two years, he stressed basketball excellence on the court as well as academic excellence as a classroom teacher in Journalism and English.[91]

Asian Pacific Americans coach in men's college basketball programs. In 2002, Jeffrey Hironaka was named head coach of the Seattle Pacific University male five. He had been an assistant at the university since 1991. Kirk Townsend, the younger brother of Raymond, has been an assistant for several top Division I programs over the last several years, including top-ranked Kansas University.[92]

As female participation in basketball grows in the 1990s and 2000s, we can find more women of Asian Pacific ancestry playing college, high school, middle school, and Amateur Athletic Union (AAU) basketball. For example, during the late 1990s Lindsay Yamasaki starred on the Oregon City High School basketball team, which was considered by many as one of the great powerhouses in high school basketball. Also a volleyball standout, Yamasaki became a local celebrity in Oregon City. She gave basketball clinics for young people and served as a grand marshal of an Oregon City anti-drug parade. The *Sports Illustrated* quoted the 6 ft. 2-inch forward on basketball: "I love how you can take charge of a game. I love that feeling when an opponent scores, and you're already running a fast break, and scoring at the other end. That's the best." Subsequently, Yamasaki did well for the nationally respected Stanford University women's basketball program and played a few years in the Women's National Basketball Association. (WNBA)[93]

Asian Pacific American female coaches have popped up in the high school, college and even professional ranks. In the mid-1990s, Da Houl became a full-time assistant coach for the University of Hawai'i's women's basketball team. A Cambodian native, Da Houl won the Orange County and Los Angeles Times Player of the Year award in 1983 while leading the Brea Olinda High School women's five in 1983. Da Houl, subsequently, went to the University of Hawai'i, where she played standout point guard and became team captain. After a successful stint as a high school coach in Southern California, Da Houl returned to her alma mater, where she helped Vince Goo in the area of scouting, weight training, and working with the guards. Meanwhile, Jennifer Omana served as the assistant head coach for the Haverford University's women's team in the late 1990s. A former point guard for Haverford, the Filipina American also helped establish in the tri-state area of Pennsylvania, New Jersey, and New York, The Filipino American Community Athletic Association that sponsored athletic competition for Filipino American youth of both sexes. In the professional ranks, Colleen Matsuhara became an assistant coach of the Los Angeles Sparks of the WNBA in 1997. A one time starting guard for Sacramento State, Matsuhara later joined the women's basketball coaching staffs of Long Beach State, Notre Dame, UCLA, and the University of Texas. As head coach, Matsuhara guided the University of California, Irvine (UCI) women's five. In 1995, Matsuhara's UCI squad reached the NCAA tournament for the only time in the university's history. When Matsuhara joined USC's staff, head coach Chris Gobrecht remarked, "Colleen has certainly been one of the pioneers of women's basketball on the West Coast." At California State University, Los Angeles, Marcia Murata coached for several years in the 1990s. A guard for Los Angeles State in the late 1970s, Murata became an assistant for her alma mater in 1984 before taking over the head coaching reins. In 2000, Michelle Sasaki Jacoby was named head coach of the St. Mary's of Moraga's five. Starring as a guard for the University of Pacific in the 1980s, Sasaki Jacoby previously served as an assistant at Washington State and Gonzaga, as well as St. Mary's.[94]

Buck Lai, Sr., was an early Asian Pacific Islander promoter of professional basketball. While still active in semi-professional baseball circles as a member of the Brooklyn Bushwicks, Lai headed in the early 1930s a barnstorming team of professional basketball players known as the Aloha Hawaiians. Like other barnstorming professional squads, the Aloha Hawaiians were merchandised on the basis of cultural stereotypes even though few of the players aside from Lai were actually Hawaiian. The Aloha Hawaiians, that is, played at least for awhile wearing grass skirts and leis. The halftime show of their games featured "a genuine hula dance" by a young woman named "Miss Likens." Lai's team was supposedly good. One press report claimed it had won thirty-three out of forty-one games while competing in the Midwest and the Northeast.[95]

Hawaiian Arthur Kim ranks as one of the more interesting Asian Pacific American entrepreneurs. Kim had been active in Hawaiian basketball circles for years as a player and AAU administrator. In 1944, Kim coached a team of Hawaii Senior Basketball All-Stars against a squad of top players representing the armed services stationed on Oahu. Francis Sing, James Koo, Harold Tome, George Lee, and Bill Choy were Asian Pacific Islanders playing for Kim. During the 1950-1951 season, Kim coached the Service Center 5 in Honolulu's University Invitational Conference. Playing for him were Hawaiian standouts such as Robert Kau, Ed Loui, George Makini, Larry Sato and Robert Wong. In the mid-1950s, Kim coached a team called the Hawaiian Surfriders, which went on the road to lose consistently to the Harlem Globetrotters in the mid-1950s. Five years later, Kim headed up a similar contingent of Globetrotter victims called the Hawaii 50 Staters. The mainland press referred to him as the "wily Art Kim." In 1961, Kim owned the Hawaii Chiefs of the fledgling and short-lived American Basketball League. The next year, Kim moved the franchise to Long Beach where it faced its demise along with the rest of the league.[96]

In 1967, the longer-lived American Basketball Association was formed. The ABA at least threatened the NBA's dominance of American professional basketball and featured great players such as Julius Erving, Rick Barry, and Artis Gilmore. Unfortunately, none of these great players competed for Kim's Anaheim Amigos in 1967. A mediocre team at best, the Amigos drew poorly and Kim lacked the financial resources to sustain the franchise. He consequently sold the Amigos to a Los Angeles businessman who transformed them into the Los Angeles Stars.[97]

Conclusion

When Asian Pacific people first started coming to the United States in significant in numbers, baseball dominated more of the sporting headlines in the United States than any other team sport. In many American communities baseball often labored as fragile bridge between native born Americans, on the one hand, and immigrants and their children, on the other. As new waves of Asian Pacific people migrated to the United States since 1965, basketball's popularity has risen as both a spectator and participatory sport. By the 1990s, basketball seemingly engaged the passion of significant numbers of young people whose parents have migrated to cities and towns such as Monterey Park near Los Angeles.

In the late 1980s and early 1990s, UCLA sociologist John Horton and several colleagues studied the interactions between Asian Pacific immigrants and their culturally diverse neighbors in Monterey Park, a small Southern California city that displayed considerable racial and ethnic tensions. One of the areas examined was participation in the youth basketball leagues held at the Monterey Park Sports Club during the 1988-1989 season. The researchers discovered that forty-five percent of the players, forty-seven percent of the coaches, and fourteen percent of the league commissioners were Latino. Twenty percent of the players were Anglo, while thirty-four percent of the players and fifty-seven percent of the commissioners were also Anglo. Asians comprised thirty-four percent of the players, nineteen percent of the coaches, and twenty-nine percent of the commissioners.[98]

To a significant degree Monterey Park basketball both reflected and hurdled the tensions existing in Monterey Park. At the beginning of the season, researchers noted that the Chinese immigrant families that were new to the league tended to sit apart from the others in the stands. By the end of the season, they interacted more with non-Asian parents of their children's teammates. Horton and his colleagues write, "Although newcomers and established residents sometimes fought each other in City Hall, in the Sports Club they were members of a team. The link between them was their children. The motive was support and interest in their development. Teamwork and volunteering structured cooperation."[99]

Regarding the other end of the basketball spectrum, Wat Misaka, however, expressed disappointment in 1994 that "the NBA is not recruiting or encouraging Asian Pacific Americans to be professional basketball players." Yet perhaps the movers and shakers of American basketball are not entirely to blame. Writing for *Asian Week*, Brian Liou lamented the lack of parental support for youthful Asian Pacific Americans bearing basketball dreams of NBA stardom. He maintained that to attain basketball stardom, "We'll need to filter out all our parents' open laughter as we divulge our hoop dreams. We need to convince our parents that the NBA can be a reality. We need our parents faith." Liou cites Rex Walters experience as evidence of Asian Pacific Americans shying away from taking their basketball talents to the limit. Walters told Liou, "It's almost like Asian Americans have a predetermined excuse....It's like saying 'I'm Japanese and I'm not going to grow, I'm not going to do this and I'm never going to <be> big enough and fast enough' and I think that 's all bullshit." Liou did not totally blame Asian Pacific American parents. He advised that Asian Pacific American "ballers" start playing with athletes from other racial and ethnic groups as opposed to "play<ing> with one another." Journalist Richard Lee, likewise, was not pleased with the progress Asian Pacific Americans have made in elite college and professional basketball. He wrote in 2000 that while "Asian American women are carving a deep niche at the Pac 10 level" the lack of Asian American professionals male disappointed him. However, he added hopefully: "Whether Asian Americans have been discouraged from participation because of family or friends who de-emphasized sports or because of the perceived lack of height and size, the landscape of college basketball is undergoing a change."[100]

Yet whether on community or school teams, Asian Pacific Americans have found ethnic strength and individual joy playing basketball, as well as bridges to other Asian Pacific American ethnic groups and non-Asian Pacific Americans. Basketball, moreover, has proven more accessible to Asian Pacific American females than many other major team sports. Some Asian Pacific American females, indeed, have discovered through basketball local and national recognition of their athletic prowess. They have been able to make clearer their claims to cultural citizenship.

However, a sport such as basketball still sparks perhaps unintentional racism. Filipino American journalist Emil Guillermo recalled attending a Stanford women's basketball game with his daughter and some of her friends during the 1998-1999 season. A great admirer of the Stanford women's basketball program, Guillermo was happily impressed with Lindsay Yamasaki's talents. Less happily, he noted in *Asian Week* that after the game some Stanford fans greeted Yamasaki, who helped lead her squad to victory, with "yo-yo talk." Guillermo explained that "yo-yo talk occurs when people who speak perfect English say the words 'yo-yo' at an increasingly fast pace in order to mimic Japanese." Guillermo lamented, "It was loud. It was clear. I was stunned. It wasn't subtle. The yo-yo talk was loud enough for all to hear."[101]

More recently, Asian Pacific Americans have been aroused by derogatory remarks about Yao Ming, made by Shaquille O'Neal and encouraged by America's contemporary sports media. An angry Irwin Tang challenged Shaquille O'Neal to "come down to Chinatown" to test his manhood since O'Neal had contested Yao Ming's toughness. Tang likened Yao Ming to Jackie Robinson, although he admitted that the talented center has not faced the vicious racism that confronted Robinson. And he likened Shaquille O'Neal to Ty Cobb, a white baseball great notorious as a race baiter. While O'Neal subsequently professed respect for Yao Ming's game, it would seem that the basketball landscape has not changed all that much for Asian Pacific Americans.[102]

Notes

1. Peter Levine, *Ellis Island to Ebbetts Field: Sport and the American Jewish Experience*, (New York: Oxford University Press, 1992), 27, 28.

2. *Chinese Digest*, May, June, 1938; *California Chinese Press*, December 20, 1940.

3. *Mind and Body*, December, 1916; *Los Angeles Times*, March 28, 1922; *Daily Palo Alto*, January 23, 1923.

4. Ma, *Oakland*, 54-55.

5. *Chinese Digest*, May, 1938.

6. *Ibid.*, October 1938; Marjorie Lee, "Building a Community," *Linking Our Lives*, (Los Angeles: Chinese Historical Society of Southern California, 1984), 107-110.

7. *Los Angeles Times*, March 27, 1937.

8. *Chinese Digest*, December 16, 1935; May, 1938.

9. *Ibid.*, December 16, 1935; October 30, 1936; November 27, 1936; January, 1937; February , 1937; *San Francisco Chronicle*, January 18, 1928; February 7, 1930; January 4, 1931; March 20, 1934; March 8, 1935; March 9, 1935; *Sacramento Bee*, February 1, 1923; *San Jose Mercury*, February 4, 1936.

10. *Hawaiian Gazette*, March 21, 1899; *Pacific Commercial Advertiser*, March 16, 1903; December 6, 1911.

11. Hop, "Contributions," 104; *Honolulu Advertiser*, March 3, 1935; *Honolulu Star-Bulletin*, March 3, 1936.

12. *Honolulu Advertiser*, March 3, 1935; March 14, 1935.

13. *San Francisco Chronicle*, January 20, 1916; John Christagu, *The Origins of the Jump Shot: Eight Men Who Shook the World of the Basketball*, (Lincoln, Nebraska: University of Nebraska Press, 1999), 38-39.

14. *San Francisco Chronicle*, February 12, 1930; March 18, 1934; *San Francisco Examiner*, January 10, 1934; *Buddhist Church*, 271; *Los Angeles Times*, January 26, 1939; April 12, 1939; April 13, 1939; Christagu, *Origins*, 38-39.

15. *San Jose Mercury*, January 17, 1934; January 18, 1934; February 10, 1988.

16. *Buddhist Church*, 219.

17. Kitano, *Japanese Americans: The Evolution of a Subculture*, (Englewood Cliffs, New Jersey: Prentice-Hall, 1976), 71

18. *California Chinese Press*, February 28, 1941; March 28, 1941; April 18, 1941; Lee," Building," 107-110.

19. *Pacific Citizen*, April 15, 1943.

20. *Korean Independence*, May 17, 1945.

21. *Philippine News*, January 10-January 16, 1974.

22. *San Jose Mercury*, February 2, 1988; *Pacific Citizen*, January 21, 1943; January 28, 1943; February 4, 1943; March 18, 1943; *Heart Mountain Sentinel*, December 31, 1943; January 8, 1944; Regalado, "Incarcerated," 437.

23. *San Francisco Chronicle*, March 16, 1949.

24. *Chinese Press*, January 7, 1949; January 14, 1949.

25. *San Francisco Examiner*, February 18, 1946; February 23, 1946; February 24, 1946.

26. *San Francisco Examiner*, January 9, 1949; March 16, 1950.

27. *Ibid.* March 3, 1950; March 5, 1950; *San Francisco Chronicle*, March 15, 1950.

28. *Chinese Press*, June 2, 1950.

29. *Pacific Citizen*, November 29, 1947; *Sacramento Bee*, March 21, 1946; *San Jose Mercury*, March 23, 1947; February 4, 1955; *Buddhist Church*, 219; *Nichi Bei Times*, January 1, 1973.

30. *Philippines Star Press*, January 28, 1946; *The Philippines Mail*, April 1948; *Philippine News*, January 10-January 16, 1974; *Honolulu Star-Bulletin*, September 15, 1948; October 9, 1948; November 2, 1948; November 4, 1948; April 1, 1950; May 12, 1951; *Seattle Post and Intelligencer*, December 31, 1948.

31. *Korea Independence*, October 30, 1946; *Honolulu Star-Bulletin*, April 1, 1950.

32. *San Francisco Examiner*, December 26, 1949; *San Jose Mercury*, February 6, 1950; March 3, 1950; March 4, 1950; *Honolulu Star-Bulletin*, November 3, 1948; November 5, 1948.

33. *Hawaii Herald,* March 3, 1950; March 8, 1950; March 11, 1950; *Pacific Citizen,* March 11, 1950.

34. *Hawaii Herald,* January 23, 1951; February 7, 1951; *Hawaii Herald,* February 13, 1954.

35. *San Francisco Chronicle,* March 2, 1953; *San Francisco Examiner,* March 1, 1950; November 29, 1950; March 1, 1955; March 4, 1955.

36.*East/West,* January 22, 1969; September 9, 1981.

37. *Ibid,* May 6, 1970; January 20, 1982; February 10, 1982.

38. *San Jose Mercury,* March 7, 1964; February 10, 1988; San Jose CYS Basketball Invitational Program, 2003.

39. *Rafu Shimpo,* March 21, 1972; *Nichi Bei Times,* June 13, 1993; *Hokubei Mainichi,* December 15, 1977.

40. *Rafu Shimpo,* July 17, 1974.

41. Naku, Jr. Manuel Romero, "Filipino Service Center," (MS Thesis, San Jose State University, 1974), 70.

42. *Rice Paper,* September, October, 1980.

43. *Ibid,.* 1981.

44. www.megaherz.njt.edu, accessed August 7, 1998.

45.www.asianhoops.com, accessed May 8, 1998; www. halcyon.com, accessed May 8, 1998.

46. Philana Wu, "Girl Got Game," *Asian Week,* January 5, 2001-January 11, 2001; San Jose CYS Program.

47.Parker Hodges, Channel 4000, November 16, 1998; Sam Le, "Hoop Dreams,"www.aaja.org, August 9, 2002; Ian Thomson, "Comiing to America," *Sports Illustrated,* December 25, 2000-January 1, 2001, p. 86.

48. Rachel Graves, "Asian Community Goes Wow For Yao," *Houston Chronicle,* June 21, 2002.

49. *Daily Palo Alto,* January 1, 1923; *Washington Post,* February 5, 1924; *San Francisco Chronicle,* December 20, 1932; *Nichi Bei Times,* January 1, 1973.

50. Dick Rosetta, "An Original 'Cinderella Ute' Heads to the Alamo Dome to Relive a Dream,"www.strib.com, accessed March 7, 1998; Zander Hollander and Alex Zachary. (eds.) *The Official NBA Encyclopedia,* (New York: Villard Books, 1989); U.S. Census Manuscripts, Ogden, Weber County, Utah,, 1930; Hugh Fullerton, Jr. "Today's Sport Roundup," *Helena Independent Record,* March 22, 1944, *Oxnard Press Courier,* March 25, 1947; *Washington Post,* March 27, 1944; Bob Considine, "On the Line," March 28, 1944.

51. Samuel R. Cacas, "The Professional: Pioneer Wat Misaka Reflects on Being the First," *Asian Week,* December 16, 1994.

52. *Ibid; Honolulu Advertiser,* July 25, 1947;*Pacific Citizen,* November 15, 1947; November 29, 1947;Louinn Lota, "Misaka is NBA's Forgotten Minority, *Los Angeles Times,* May 7, 2000.

53.Pacific Citizen, January 14, 1950; Gary Y. Okihiro, *Storied Lives: Japanese American Students and World War II,* (Seattle : University of Washington Press,, 1999), 92, 94, 95, 97.

54. *San Francisco News,* March 7, 1950.

55. *Chinese Press,* January 21, 1949; University of San Francisco vs. Marquette Football Program, November 20, 1949, Kezar Stadium, San Francisco, California; *Chi-*

nese Press, December 26, 1949; November 10, 1950; *San Francisco Examiner*, December 22, 1949; *New York Times*, December 22, 1949.

56. *Los Angeles Times*, January 17, 1942; January 24, 1942; *San Francisco Examiner*, December 11, 1949.

57. *New York Times*, February 18, 1947.

58. *Los Angeles Times*, December 10, 1953; *San Francisco Chronicle*, December 18, 1953; *Honolulu Advertiser*, January 28, 2000;
San Francisco Chronicle, December 10, 1953; *Sport Magazine*, April, 1998; Cindy Luis, "Mr. Short Stuff," *Honolulu Star-Bulletin*, January 31, 2002.

59. www.asianweek.com, February 18, 2005.

60. Cacas, "Professional,"; members.tripod.com/ˉblssooalo/ps-sports.html, accessed August 7, 2001.

61. Pete Newell Challenge Program, Oakland Coliseum Arena, December 29, 2000; www.nau.edu, accessed July 27, 2000; www.gostanford.com, accessed February 10, 2001; www. byucougars.com. accessed February 2, 2001;; www.wsucougars.com, accessed April 3, 2005; www.asianweek.com,, February 11, 2005.

62. *Philippine Daily Inquirer*, April 9, 1999.

63. *California Chinese Press*, December 20, 1940; March 28, 1941; Darra Akiko Tom, "Great Chinese Warriors Played for Fun, Money, " *San Jose Mercury*, September 9, 1996.

64. Tom, "Great Chinese Warriors;" Al Young, "Hoop Dreams." *A Magazine*, February/March, 1996.

65. www.asianweek.com, February 22, 2005; www.osubeavers.com, accessed February 11, 2001; Yukiya Jerry Waki, "St. Mary's Put Up Valiant Effort Against Lady Vols," www.nichibeitimes.com, March 20, 2001; www.haverford.edu, accessed April 11, 2005.

66. Richard Lee, www.hardboiled.com, accessed March 14, 2000; Cindy Luis, "Itoman is Big Trouble for Her Opponents, *Honolulu Star-Bulletin*, January 30,1997; Ann Miller, "Hedy Liu is 'Auntie Aloha, *Honolulu Advertiser*, March 3, 2000; Stanford Women's Basketball Program, January 28, 1999 and January 30, 1999, Stanford University; *Filipinas*, February 1998, p. 42; Ethen Leiser, "They Got Summertime Game," *Asian Week*, July 6, 2001-July 12, 2001; www. BroncoSports.com., accessed November 16, 2002.

67.*Pacific Commercial Advertiser*, January 7, 1912; January 28, 1912; April 13, 1912; March 3, 1914; January 19, 1915; June 9, 1919; *Honolulu Star-Bulletin,* September 1, 1915; January 13, 1917; *San Jose Mercury*. April 30, 1905; *San Francisco Evening Bulletin*, October 26, 1912; *San Francisco Chronicle*, January 25, 1919.

68. San *Francisco Chronicle*, February 3, 1923; *Sacramento Bee*, January 24, 1923.

69.Connie Young Yu, *Chinatown San Jose*, USA, (San Jose: San Jose: Historical Museum Association, 1991), 99; *New York Times*, February 22, 1928; *Helena Independent,* January 8, 1930.

70. *San Francisco Examiner*, January 12, 1934; San *Francisco Chronicle*, January 9, 1931; January 10, 1931; March 3, 1934; March 15, 1936; February 2, 1938; *California Chinese Press*, March 14, 1941; *San Jose Mercury*, February 8, 1936; Susan Zieff, From Badminton to the Bolero: "Sport and Recreation in San Francisco's Chinatown," *Journal of Sport History*, (Spring, 2000), 14; Christagu, "Jump Shot," 34

71.Cisco, *Hawai'i Sports*, 48; *Honolulu Advertiser*, March 2, 1933; March 2, 1935; March 3, 1935; March 19, 1935; March 22, 1935; *Honolulu Star-Bulletin*, March 11, 1936.

72. U.S. Census Manuscripts, Hilo, Hawaii, 1930; Dave Reardon, "UH Basketball's First AC Shares Gift With Others," *Honolulu Star-Bulletin*, September 9, 2001.

73. *Honolulu Star-Bulletin*, December 2, 1949; Cisco, *Hawai'i Sports*, 47.

74. *San Francisco Examiner*, February 17, 1941; February 21, 1941; *Seattle Post-Intelligencer*, January 5, 1941; *Portland Oregonian*, January 26, 1941; February 2, 1941.

75.Yung, *Documentary*, 492.

76. *San Francisco Chronicle*, February 16, 1948; January 17, 1950; *Chinese Press*, January 7, 1949; January 14, 1949; November 18, 1949.; *Seattle Post-Intelligencer*, January 6, 1946; *Pacific Citizen*, January 21, 1950; January 28, 1950; March 11, 1950; *San Jose Mercury*, January 3, 1951; U.S. Census Manuscripts, Placer County, California, 1930; *The Monitor* (San Francisco), March 16, 1951.

77. *Seattle Post-Intelligencer*, December 21, 1947.

78. *Ibid*; December 25, 1947; December 29, 1947; December 22, 1948.

79. *San Jose Mercury*, December 21, 1949.

80. *Ibid*, December 20, 1949; December 22, 1949.

81. *Ibid*, February 19, 1946; *San Francisco Chronicle*, February 24, 1946; *Los Angeles Times*, January 4, 1947; *Dixon Evening Telegram*, February 28, 1947; *Pacific Citizen*, August 16, 1947.

82. *San Francisco Examiner*, December 18, 1948; December 8, 1949; December 19, 1949; December 16, 1949.

83. *Ibid*, December 23, 1948; December 28, 1948; December 21, 1949; December 23, 1949.

84. *Pacific Citizen*, January 27, 1951; *Honolulu Advertiser*, March 14, 1944; *Honolulu Star-Bulletin*, November 14, 1949; January 30, 1951; *San Francisco Chronicle*, February 17, 1952.

85. *Pacific Citizen*, January 27, 1951; *Seattle Post-Intelligencer*, March 4, 1955; *Los Angeles Times*, March 10, 1955; *San Jose Mercury*, February 4, 1955; February 5, 1955; January 16, 1965; *Oxnard Press Courier*, September 25, 1955; *Sacramento Bee*, April 1, 1957; *East/West*, January 22, 1969.

86. *Honolulu Star-Bulletin*, March 17, 1947; September 15, 1948; January 1, 1949; April 6, 1950; January 22, 1951; *Hawaii Herald*, March 8, 1950; *Los Angeles Times*, December 12, 1956; Pacific *Citizen*, March 30, 1973; *Hokubei Mainichi*, December 14, 1977; *San Jose Mercury*, June 1, 2000.

87.*Pacific Citizen*, January 14, 1950; January 27, 1950; www.asuonline.com., accessed November 26, 2002.

88. *New York Times*, January 16, 1951.

89. Howard Tuckner, "Lai Wants No Neon Lights in L.I.U. Basketball," in *Ibid.*, December 11, 1956.

90. Gordon S. White, "LIU's Wandering Five Awaits Home," in *Ibid*, June 2, 1963; March 7, 196; www.liu.edu, accessed August 19, 2001.

91. Mark Lundstrom, "Coach Knew His Calling," *San Jose Mercury News*, November 30, 1998; *Nichi Bei Times*, January 1, 1973.

92. Ryan Foley, "Falcon Basketball Pre-Season Heats Up," *The Falcon*, November 20, 2002.

93. Ed McGregor, "Queen Bee." *Sports Illustrated*, March 2, 1998.

94. www. hawaii.edu; *Filipinas*, May, 1998; www.wnba.com, accessed May 22, 2000; www.calstatela.edu website, accessed May 11, 2000; www.smcgaels.com, accessed October 28, 2000; Aarne Heikkila, "USC to Hire New Women's Hoops Assistant, *Daily Trojan*, May 17, 2000.

95. *Washington Post*, January 28, 1934.

96.*Honolulu Advertiser*, March 12, 1944; *Hawaii Herald*, January 4, 1951; *Bennington Evening Banner*, August 27, 1955; *St. Joseph Herald*, November 18, 1960;www. geocities/~arthurth/Anaheim-Amigos.html, accessed April 7, 2000.

97.wwww. geocities/~arthurth/Anaheim-Amigos.html, accessed April 7, 2000.

98. John Horton, *et. al.*, *The Politics of Diversity: Immigration, Résistance, and Change in Monterey Park, California*, (Philadelphia: Temple University Press, 1995), 44.

99. *Ibid.*, 46.

100. Cacas, "Professional;"   Brian Liou, "Tall Order," www.asianweek.com, November 25, 1999; Richard Lee, www.hardboiled.org, March 14, 2000.

101. Emil Guillermo, "Two Modern Takes on Racism," *Asian Week*, December 3, 1998-December 9, 1998.

102. Irwin Tang, "APA Community Should Tell Shaquille O'Neal to 'Come down to Chinatown,'" *Asian Week*, January 3, 2003-January 9, 2003.

Chapter Six: The Duke and Aquatic Sports

Probably the most famous Hawaiian athletes during the first two decades of the twentieth century were George Freeth and the legendary Duke Kahanamoku. Both were expert competitive swimmers, who also helped popularize the sport of surfing in California and around the world during the 1910s. Much less is known today about Freeth, who died in Southern California during the catastrophic Spanish influence epidemic in 1918. Jack London introduced Freeth to mainlanders in his 1907 essay on surfing, "A Royal Sport." Freeth, moreover, was Hawai'i's top "fancy diver." However, in the years before his death, the part-Native Hawaiian Freeth became a popular and innovative figure in Southern California water sports. Freeth is generally credited with introducing surfing to middle class, white Californians, as well as the sport of water polo. In 1907, Freeth led the Venice water polo team to a state championship, while he helped the Redondo squads win state championships the next two years. The Los Angeles Athletic Club hired Freeth as a swim instructor and Henry Huntington employed him to teach surfing at the plunge and pavilion owned by the Southern California magnate in Redondo Beach. [1]

Freeth was often associated with Kahanamoku in the 1910s. In 1915, the *San Francisco Chronicle* maintained that he had often worked with Kahanamoku on the latter's swimming techniques. It added, "Freeth formerly held the all-around championships of the Hawaiian islands and at present is considered to be one of the best divers in the country." Moreover, Freeth had received a special congressional medal for his exploits in life saving. The Hawaiian claimed he had saved about 300 people from drowning. [2]

Whatever Freeth left undone in making California a mainland aquatic sports Mecca, Duke Kahanamoku more than finished. Surfing is a traditional sport of Native Hawaiians. White missionaries, with the backing of an increasingly powerful haole elite and Christianized Native Hawaiian leaders, managed to get surfing banned in Hawai'i in the 1800s. Yet the emerging Hawaiian tourist industry helped legitimate surfing in Hawai'i once again by the 1900s as a means of exoticizing and romanticizng the islands and its people. Kahanamoku surfaced as the Native Hawaiian who best represented surfing to vacation-minded mainlanders. In so doing, he symbolized Hawai'i to potential tourists as a primitive paradise with nearly all the conveniences of home. [3]

Born in Honolulu in 1890, Duke Kahanamoku was named after his father, who in turn was named after Alfred, the Duke of Edinburgh, who visited Hawai'i in 1869. A full-blooded Hawaiian and son of a police captain, Kahanamoku grew up in Waikiki. He first drew international attention as a competitive swimmer, who swam his way to Olympic gold for the U.S. at the 1912 Stockholm Olympiad. At the time, the *New York Times* gushed forth a "noble savage" description of Kahanamoku as "a giant, ebony-skinned native" and "a magnificent specimen of manhood."[4]

In 1911, Kahanamoku caught the attention of the American sports world when he stroked his way to a free style world record in Honolulu. The AAU professed skepticism over the authenticity of the record. It doubted that a swimmer, unknown on the American mainland, could have accomplished such a feat. Otto Wahle, a mainland AAU executive, advised that Kahanamoku come to the mainland and display his swimming talents. Kahanamoku expressed confidence he could convince doubting mainlanders as he confronted the Honolulu press after he had just brought in "an enthusiastic bunch of pretty tourists" from an afternoon of canoeing in Waikiki.[5]

Kahanamoku readied himself rigorously for the mainland. According to the *Pacific Commercial Advertiser,* "Duke has been in constant training of late--in fact he is in the water for hours each day. He has no bad habits and is always in perfect condition. Of late, he has been practicing turns which will be of value to him in the tryouts for they must be held in swimming tanks less than 100 yards in length."[6]

Kahanamoku and a white Hawaiian swimmer, Vincent Genovese, were dispatched on a tour of the American mainland. One reason was to convince the American mainland of the skills possessed by Kahanamoku and other Hawaiian swimmers. Indeed, Hawaiian promoters hoped that both Kahanamoku and Genovese would make the U.S. Olympic team. A second reason was to market Hawai'i to potential American mainland tourists and investors. It was important, according to the *Pacific Commercial Advertiser*, that a haole manage the tour to lend credibility to Kahanamoku's struggles to win over a suspicious amateur athletic establishment on the mainland. George Freeth was expected to manage the tour. However, a fellow named Lew Henderson was eventually assigned the task.[7]

Making the Olympic team, however, proved not so easy for the Honolulan. The mainland had produced many fine competitive swimmers. Kahanamokua was not used to swimming competitively in fresh-water pools, where making effective turns would prove vital. In Pittsburgh, Kahanamoku was seized with cramps after getting off to a great start. The press claimed, "Accustomed only to salt water and straightway courses, the confinement of an indoor pool worried the swimmers from Hawaii." Kahanamoku skill won over at least some of the skeptics. He made the Olympic team in March, 1912 as James Sullivan, head of the AAU, announced, "Boys, this man Duke is no false alarm. His wonderful performances on his first attempt at tank swimming conclusively shows this." Kahanamoku would, thus, stay with Lew Henderson's family in Philadelphia and receive training from the University of Pennsylvania's swimming coach.[8]

The mainland sporting press both praised and denigrated the Hawaiian swimmer as he prepared for the Olympics. The *New York Telegram* described Kahanamoku as a "tall, handsome, and dark-skinned athlete." It reported Kahanamoku's versatility as an aquatic athletic, but added, "It is in surf riding that he stands in a class by himself." As for competitive swimming, the "dusky champion" has excelled more because of his athleticism than his willingness to train. The *New York Herald*, likewise, depicted Kahanamoku as a novice when it came to the rigors of competitive swimming.[9]

Kahanamoku's race and ethnicity stirred some controversy. Some of the AAU's old guard wondered if Kahanamoku and Jim Thorpe could truly represent the United States because they were "natives." The *Washington Post* pointed out, "There has been some criticism as to whether the Hawaiian should compete as an American but it is pointed out that he is in exactly the same position as the Indian Ranji, who for years represented England in cricket."[10]

Kahanamoku's triumphs aroused support from Hawaiian islanders of various ethnic backgrounds. Before heading off to Sweden, Kahanamoku thanked Hawaiians for their support. He wrote the editor of the *Pacific Commercial Advertiser*, "I am very mindful of this splendid opportunity offered me and in the contests for which I am entered, will put forth my best efforts to win, and add to the athletic glory of the United States and Hawaii." Some Hawaiians living on the East Coast tendered Kahanamoku a "Hawaiian send-off" to Sweden. "Hawaiian musicians" played "Aloha Oe" as Kahanamoku's ship prepared to sail across the Atlantic. After he won his gold medal, the *Advertiser* insisted that he proved that America was not a weak, racially mongrel national—as some Americans and non-Americans had charged. Rather, "there is not a drop of diluted blood in his veins, yet he is a good a American as need be as he just proved to the chagrin of many of Anglo Saxon or Caucasian ancestry." About the same time, an editorial in the *Honolulu Star-Bulletin* applauded Kahanamoku's behavior on the ship taking the Olympic team to Sweden. Kahanamoku had entertained passengers in an impromptu vaudeville show and had become immensely popular among all those sharing the trip across the Atlantic with him: "'The Duke,' as they call him won friends by his modesty, his quiet determination, to win, his fine personal habits and his happy temperament, and such qualities as these are worth a thousand times more than his wonderful arm and leg muscles that drive him through the water at a rate never before equaled by a human being." Upon his return to Hawai'i, Kahanamoku triumphantly toured the various islands to thank all Hawaiians who supported him.[11]

Kahanamoku won over Australian followers of aquatic sports. In 1915, the *Pacific Commercial Advertiser* reported that the "Kahanamoku Kick" was converting Australians from the "Australian Crawl." Apparently, many Australian swim experts had been skeptical about Kahanamoku's skills despite his gold medal winning performance in 1912. Kahanamoku not only overcame such skepticism but "<g>eneral interest in swimming has received a big impetus in Australia as a result of the tour of Duke Paka <sic> Kahanamoku." Fred Williams, known as the Australian "father of sun-bathing," complimented Kahanamoku's ability to fit in with white Australians. He observed with more than a trace of racism, "One would not be surprised at seeing that in one of our own origin, but it was an eye-opener to find it so through in an island native, even though we know the Hawaiians were a cut above most of the aborigines of the Pacific."[12]

While hailed in Honolulu as a local hero, Kahanamoku still could be targeted by those in the press who were determined to racialize and exoticize him. In October, 1912, the *Honolulu Star-Bulletin* published a montage of illustrations signed by an artist named Randall. It displayed a lifelike drawing of the young Kahanamoku surrounded by various cartoons depicting him much the way racist illustrators depicted African American men on the mainland. Moreover, the point of the cartoons was to convey sympathy for Kahanamoku as he had to deal with Hawaiians of various ethnic backgrounds trying to take advantage of him. In 1913, the *Pacific Commercial Advertiser* lamented that Kahanamoku's head had gotten too big; that "he is embodied with the idea that he is invincible." In 1915, he was visiting Sydney, Australia, where he was generally a hit. Nevertheless, the *Pacific Commercial Advertiser* expressed some disappointment in his performances, lamenting that Kahanamoku would do better if he took his training more seriously: "But your island native will not work more than he can help. Besides, he looks upon swimming as a pleasure not a labor and takes it in that spirit."[13]

The sporting world would learn that swimming ranked as just one of Kahanamoku's aquatic talents. He was also a skilled and joyful surfer, who transported his knowledge of the sport to California and Australia. Indeed, despite the early efforts of Freeth, it has often been said that Kahanamoku taught the world to surf and, to many, he epitomized the sport until his death in 1968. In 1915, for example, California's neophyte surfers recognized their debt to Kahanamoku, who brought a surf board with him to his trips to the West Coast. According to one press report, "Wherever Duke appeared with <his board> a great crowd gathered on the beaches to marvel at the ease with which he stood upright and rode the bucking waves as skillfully as a cowboy a broncho.<sic> Everywhere he was besieged with pupils anxious to learn his methods and his skill with the board is already a popular legend in a dozen great resorts."[14]

Kahanamoku, moreover, garnered national publicity for his life saving skills. While training for the Olympics in Philadelphia, Kahanamoku saved a drowning man at an Atlantic City swim tank and a few weeks later, he and a companion pulled two men out of Schuylkill River. In 1914, tourist Addie Dunbar claimed she was saved twice in one day by Kahanamoku. At Waikiki, Kahanamoku had to drive away a shark bent on attacking her. Then, a few hours later, the Hawaiian saved her from drowning after her boat capsized. In 1925, Kahanamoku and his brother Sam helped save a crew of drowning fishermen off of Southern California's Newport Beach.[15]

Nevertheless, as a competitive swimmer, Kahanamoku remained one of the best in the world throughout the 1910s. World War I prevented him from repeating his Stockholm feats. However, at the age of thirty, Kahanamoku won a gold medal in the 1920 Olympiad. Meanwhile, Kahanamoku garneredAmateur Athletic Union (AAU) championships in 1916, 1917, and 1920.

While perhaps well meaning, the mainland press and American mainlanders in general frequently racialized and exoticized Kahanamoku. On Kahanamoku's first venture to the mainland, he was consistently asked to perform the hula. In 1913, a Philadelphia newspaper stressed the natural affinity Hawaiians such as Duke supposedly possessed with water, in general, and swimming, in particular. The article even declared that Hawaiians played tag with sharks and had trouble walking on land. Raymond Bartlett wrote in the *San Francisco Chronicle* in 1915 that Kahanamoku was "clear-eyed, lithe, and filled with a vigor that is born from long rambles though the scented surf of the islands seas." Two years later, Kahanomoku lamented to the mainland press about what the *Washington Post* termed as "two American mistakes." One mistake was the "prevailing belief that the 'Duke' prefix is a title." The other concerned the consistent mispronunciation of his last name. Kahanamoku insisted, "I never hear my last name pronounced twice alike by stranger. Most persons merely mumble it."[16]

Kahanamoku spent many years shuttling between Honolulu and Los Angeles, where he carved out a movie career of sorts playing Polynesian "natives." During one of his early visits to Los Angeles in 1914, a *Los Angeles Times'* sportswriter hailed Kahanamoku as the "world's greatest swimmer." Nevertheless, writer William A. Henry patronized Kahanamoku as "<a> child of the Pacific...easy going, good natured, <who> never worries." Henry, moreover, reported that Kahanamoku studied how to start under George Freeth's tutelage. Kahanamoku, Henry claimed, displayed a "childlike confidence in Freeth," the whiter looking Hawaiian.[17]

Because of his international fame, the possibility that Kahanamoku would voluntarily or involuntarily surrender his amateur status shadowed him. As early as 1913, it was feared that a house in Waikiki offered by Honolulu backers to Kahanamoku in gratitude for his Olympic achievements would professionalize the Hawaiian. That same year, the press reported that Kahanamoku was thinking about turning professional. A group of Australians wanted the "dusky paddler" to compete professionally so that he could "take on all comers" in Australia. A couple of years later, Hawaiians worried that if Kahanamoku competed in a outrigger canoe racing regatta he would lose his amateur status because a couple of professional baseball players were also competing. In 1916, the *Pacific Com-*

mercial Advertiser published a rumor that Kahanamoku was considering quit-
ting his amateur status to join a vaudeville circuit. Early in 1917, Kahanamoku
dived into the Pacific to salvage a case of bacon. The company that lost the case
offered the Hawaiian a side of bacon for his troubles although apparently if he
accepted he would be breaking AAU regulations. A clearer threat to his amateur
status emerged when he was offered a job in promotions for Hawai'i. Those
responsible for the job offer insisted that they did not try to recruit Kahanamoku
because he was an athlete but because they needed a Native Hawaiian and felt
the athlete filled their needs. Kahanamoku turned the job down, insisting it was
"not promising enough." In 1922, the Hawaiian was accused of professional-
ism for taking money for endorsing a surfboard varnish. However, the Hawaii
AAU insisted he was still an amateur as far as competitive swimming was concerned. Four years later, Kahanamoku was reportedly interested in competing in
the Los Angeles to Catalina Island race. Philip Wrigley, who owned Catalina
Island, offered $35,000 to the winner—a prize which worried the Hawaiian be-
cause he wanted to compete in the 1928 Olympiad.[18]

In Honolulu, Kahanamoku gained repute as an unofficial greeter to well-
heeled tourists. For example, a photograph published in the *Reno Evening Gazette* in 1950 showed Duke Kahanamoku welcoming Reno's Rotary Club president and presenting him with the "traditional Hawaiian lei of friendship." Kahanamoku, however, was not so well heeled himself as he operated a gas station in
Honolulu. A bittersweet Hawaiian-language song was written about the great
Hawaiian hero pumping gas for rich haole tourists. Kahanamoku, nevertheless,
need not be pitied. Indeed, he transformed his notoriety into political capital as
he was elected several terms as Sheriff of Honolulu County on both the Republican and Democratic Party tickets.[19]

Soon after Hawai'i became a state, famed Washington, D.C. correspon-
dent, Drew Pearson, reported that Republican U.S. Senator Hiram Fong wanted
Kahanamoku to run against Democrat Daniel Inouye for a U.S. Congress seat.
Fong believed that the Olympic swimmer was so popular on the islands that
Kahanamoku could thwart Inoyue's ambitions to eventually run against the Chi-
nese Hawaiian senator.[20]

Kahanamoku, moreover, almost single-handedly represented Hawaiian athleticism for American mainlanders until Herman Wedemeyer's rise to fame. In
1941, sportswriter Harry Grayson asserted that for Hawaiians swimming came
as naturally as walking. He added, "Hawaiians devote more time to sports than
any other people. The result is stalwart men averaging six feet in height and
keeping youthful vigor to an advanced age. You see 60-year-old Hawaiians with
snowwhite hair and the smooth, supple skin of a man in his 30s. Get a load of
Duke Kahanamoku. At 51, his speed in swimming 50 yards would surprise
you."[21]

While thirty-two years dead in 2000, Kahanamoku continued to garner
praise and honors. In 1999, Momi Kealana, mother of great Hawaiian surfer,

Rusty Kealani, said that Kahanamoku deserved *Surf Magazine's* honor as "surfer of the century:" "He exemplifies what being a Hawaiian is: generous and
humble." Another well known Hawaiian surfer, Rabbit Kekai, declared, "No
matter what he did, he spread aloha, and everybody absorbed that."[22]

From one perspective, Kahanamoku's story expresses the ability of sport to
convey certain gifted individuals across cultural barriers. From another perspective, however, it reveals sport's ability to help exoticize Hawaiians as fun loving, easy going, non-threatening, *poi* eating, musical people. It was not enough
to recognize Kahanamoku as a marvelous aquatic athlete and a generous person.
It was also important that people, especially white mainlanders, know that Kahanamoku ate *poi* and danced the hula with relish. In other words, because he
was Hawaiian, Kahanamoku was racially and culturally cordoned off from white
mainlanders.

Other Hawaiians, of diverse racial and ethnic backgrounds, excelled in
competitive aquatic sports. When Kahanamoku's swim team, the Hui Nalus
dominated a 1913 swim meet in San Francisco, his teammates included Native
Hawaiians surnamed Kaupiko and Kaawa. Moreover, Duke's brothers were excellent competitive swimmers. In 1923, Sam Kahanamoku and Charles Pung
starred in a Honolulu swim meet. In 1924, Duke and his brothers Sam and David
all qualified to compete in the Paris Olympics. Duke won a silver medal in the
100-meter free style competition, while Sam garnered a bronze medal. In the
1910s, the Portuguese Hawaiian George Cunha swam to championships for the
Olympic Club in San Francisco. According to Hall and Ambrose, however, the
sporting press often labeled Cunha as white in order to distinguish him from
Kahanamoku, although in Hawai'i the haole elite frequently excluded Hawaiians
of Portuguese ancestry from their ranks. In any event, the Kahanamokus were
not the only talented Native Hawaiians swimmers eighty-five years ago. At the
1920 Olympics, Pua Kealoha won a gold and silver medal. His brother, Warren,
was another swimmer of international repute. In the early 1920s, William Kahu-
anuii, the first Native Hawaiian who entered the U.S. Naval Academy, swam
competitively for the Annapolis school. Moreover, Walter Mon Sing Chung, the
aforementioned Hawaiian basketball player, turned to swimming while attending Chicago University in the 1920s and became a champion.[23]

Hawaiian swimmers excelled in the 1930s, 1940s and 1950s. Keo Nakama
might have gained Olympic honors, too. His greatest years as a swimmer, however, conflicted with the onset of World War II. Nevertheless, he won twenty-
six national tittles by the early 1940s, set a world record in the mile, and was a
dominant swimmer for Ohio State University. In 1944, readers of a wire story
learned that Nakama was a "Little Guy But Big Man In Big Ten Swim Meet."
Called "Ohio State's Hawaiian-born swimming star," Nakama "is only a little
fellow but he stood out as one of the biggest stars in the Western conference
swimming meet at Chicago," winning both the 220 yard and 440 yard free style.
And at the age of forty, Nakama became the first man to swim the twenty-seven

mile Molokai Channel. Nakama also served as head coach of the UH swimming team in the 1960s. Jose Balmores was a strong Filipino Hawaiian competitor in the late 1940s. A son of Filipino immigrants, Balmores' father, according to the U.S. Census manuscript was a railroad brakeman for a Maui railroad company. Charlie Oda, Johnny Tsukano, Bob Iwamoto, Bob Kumagai, Herb Kobayashi, Halo Hirose, Jimmy Tanaka, Chie Miyamoto, Harry Harukawa, and Keo's brother Bunnei were fine Japanese Hawaiian swimmers. At the 1948 Olympics, seventeen year old Thelma Kalama Aiu won a gold medal swimming a leg of the 400 meter free style. The same Olympics witnessed William Smith, another Ohio State University swimmer of indigenous ancestry, win two gold medals. The *New York Times* described Smith as a "ukulele strumming Hawaiian." In 1949, Honolulu's Evelyn Kawamoto joined Thelma Kalama Aiu on the AAU's All-American swimming team Moreover, the *Hawaii Herald* announced she was the AJA athlete of the year—a distinctive honor given the fact that Wally Yo-namine, Jyun Hirota, and other formidable Japanese American male athletes were around. The *Pacific Citizen* praised Kawamoto as "probably the greatest Nisei girl athlete in history." And *Sport* magazine asserted that "Evelyn Kawa-moto...and her able partner, Thelma Kalama, form one of the strongest freestyle duets in women's swimming." In 1952, Kawamoto won two bronze medals in the Olympics. The lesser known Doris Kinoshita, June Ogata, Winifred Kumazu and Julia Murakami were other talented Nikkei female Hawaiian swimmers after World War II. Mentored by Soichi Sakamoto, Joe Nishimoto, swam for the University of Oregon. [24]

The son of Japanese immigrants, Ford Konno ranked as one of the great American. swimmers of the 1950s. An Olympic gold medal winner in the 1952 and 1956 Olympics, he, too, attended Ohio State University. Konno gained at-traction as a teen-age competitor in Honolulu. While still a senior at McKinley High School, Konno was called by the *Pacific Citizen* a "sensational young Ni-sei" and "may be one of the U.S. answers to the challenge provided by Japan's Hironshin Furuhashi & Co." When he decided to enter Ohio State, his choice garnered national publicity. While swimming for Ohio State in 1954, Konno and Hawaiian teammate Richard Cleveland put on a dramatic display in a meet against Indiana University. Called the "lithe Hawaiian" Konno broke the world record in the 220-yard free style, while Cleveland tied his own world record in the 100-yard free style. Ford Konno's talents won him national attention from prominent American sports publications. Called Ford because his dad worked for a Ford dealership in Honolulu, he was the object of an article published in *Sport Life*. Written by Jack Clowser, the piece depicted Konno as the "small, smiling, 19-year old son of Hawaiian auto mechanic and Ohio State freshman." Moreover, in 1956, *Sport* named him as the top swimmer of the previous dec-ade. [25]

Konno's teammate at Ohio State and the Olympic swimming team was Yoshinobu Oyakawa, described by an Associated Press writer in 1952 as a "small, 18 year old freshman" at the Columbus, Ohio university. A gold medal-ist in the 100-meter backstroke in 1952, Oyakawa has been called the last of the "great 'straight-arm-pull" backstrokers." Significantly, Konno and Oyakawa were voted to co-captain the U.S. Olympic men's swimming team in 1956. Indeed, five of the AAU's All-American swim team in 1955 were Hawaiians of Asian Pacific Islander ancestry—Konno, Oyakawa, Cleveland, as well as Bill Woolsey and George Orekea.[26]

Making much of the Hawaiian success possible was Soichi Sakamoto, who taught science at Puuene School on Maui and taught swimming to countless Hawaiians in Maui's sugar cane field ditches. For example, Sakamoto trained Bill Smith in a Maui "irrigation pool." Later, after coaching some of the greatest swimmer in Hawai'i such as Oyakawa and Konno, Sakamoto was named Assistant Coach of the American men's swimming teams in 1952 and 1956. He also coached UH swimming from 1946 until 1961.[27]

While not as internationally famous as Sakamoto, Yoshi Segawa earned credit as an influential Hawaiian swim coach. Coaching out of the Nuuanu YMCA in Honolulu, Segawa helped develop important Hawaiian swimmers such as Herb Kobayashi, Ford Konno, and Evelyn Kawamoto.[28]

After his swimming career ended, Bill Smith coached swimming on the islands for years as well as serving as head director of Honolulu's life guard program. Smith coached the K-Bay Swim Club at the Kaneohe Air Station in the 1970s. He also coached at the Kamehameha Swim Club for twenty years. Kaili Chun was one of Smith's top swimmers. At one time, she was ranked number one nationally in the 100-meter backstroke.[29]

Clearly, Hawaiian contributions to competitive swimming have been immense. Yet George F. Lineer, who wrote about competitive swimming and diving for the *San Francisco Chronicle* in the 1930s and 1940s, expressed ambivalence toward Hawaiian swimmers. When a contingent of Hawaiian swimmers arrived in San Francisco to compete at a meet held at the famed Fleischacker Pool, the headline to a Lineer article read, "Hula Land Stars To Race." Lineer pointed out that "the only full blooded Hawaiian" racing would be Lulu Kea, "a smallish 14 year old." One of the leading Hawaiian swimmers was on hand, according to Lineer. He was Barney Pung, the "Chinese delegate from Hawaii."[30]

For the next day's edition of the *Chronicle*, Lineer noted with apparent respect the multicultural character of the Hawaiian swim squad:. "Where else in the world," he asked, "can you see a relay team composed of Chinese, Japanese, and Hawaiian swimmers?" They were good, too. Regarding the Hawaiian relay team, Lineer declared, "So good is this trio that an *American* team beat them by less than a foot recently in Los Angeles."(emphasis mine.)[31]

Ten years later, Lineer continued to dispatch mixed signals regarding Hawai'ian swimmers. He declared that Hawaiian swimmers were undoubtedly talented, but they seemed to lack the necessary drive to push them to the top of their sport. This lack of drive was somehow typical of Hawaiians in general. Lineer wrote, "Nature has endowed Hawaiians with brilliance in all departments with the possible exception of ambition." The Hawaiian coach Soichi Sakamo to, Lineer admitted, was ambitious enough to push his swimmers to competitive heights.[32]

Other Hawaiians who excelled in aquatic sports were Noble Kauhane, Bill Napihaa, Peter Okumoto, Chris Woo, Rachel Kealaonapua O'Sullivan, Ah Kin Yee, Mark Foo, Sunny Garcia, Derek Ho,and Hiromi Hasegawa. In 1919, Kauhane and Napihaa not only starred for the St. Mary's Gaels football team, but the "dusky Hawaiians," according to the *Oakland Tribune*, also swam for the college. In 1940, Okumoto swam for Stanford. Woo was an Olympic swimmer in 1976. Kealaonapua O'Sullivan won the bronze medal in the three-meter diving event at the 1968 Summer Olympics. In so doing, she became the first Hawaiian to win an Olympic medal in diving. She, subsequently, became a noted diving coach at Iolani High School in Honolulu. In the early 1960s, *Sports Illustrated* writer Coles Phinzy documented the surfing talents of a 62 year old Ah Kin Yee. Tragically, Mark Foo, a world class surfer died while braving the often perilous surf at Half Moon Bay in California in the 1990s. More fortunate, Sunny Garcia, who possesses Chinese, Hawaiian, and Filipino ancestries, emerged from a tough working class, West Oahu neighborhood to become a world class surfer. Derek Ho, a masterful professional surfer, served as Garcia's father figure. Hiromi Hasegawa, meanwhile, surfaced as one of the world's finest women surfers after riding the waves of Oahu's North Shore for ten years.[33]

Rell Kapoiloka-ehukai Sunn developed into one of the most famous female surfers in the world in the late 1900s. One of the first female lifeguards for the City and County of Honolulu, Sunn competed effectively against males for years. In 1997, she died after a fourteen-year battle with breast cancer, but not before leaving behind a legacy which transcended surfing and embraced active community involvement. Writer Greg Ambrose declared, "Sunn was the living embodiment of aloha when that spiritual force has increasingly become a commodity to create commerce. She exuded a warmth that convinced all she met that they had a friend for life." Ambrose, furthermore, pointed out that Sunn had helped to create a women's professional surfing circuit, "and her success as a competitor allowed generations of local girls to dream that they could turn their love of the ocean into a rewarding career."[34]

Sunn, in many ways, was a true heir of Duke Kahanamoku. A *Honolulu Weekly* article on the twenty-fourth reunion of the Kuhio "beachboys" shows that Kahanamoku's legacy still lingers along Hawaiian shores. Writer Rick Valdez called the Kuhio "beachboys" an "original hui, whose godfather was Duke Kahanamoku." Eighty-two year old Rabbit Kekai was at the reunion. Still giving surfing lessons at Waikiki, Kekai remembered that Kahanamoku taught him valuable "waterman skills." Kekai recalled, "He always gave aloha with a smile. That's the Duke, and that's what I was taught." While often patronized by haoles, the beachboys did not regard themselves as servants to white tourists wanting to learn how to surf and paddle a canoe in order to get a taste of local culture. According to canoe paddler Jo-Jo Keanu, the beachboys have regarded themselves as highly trained, skilled and proud artisans of the Pacific waves.[35]

On the mainland, people of Asian Pacific Islander ancestry achieved considerable success in competitive aquatic sports despite the disadvantages they faced. Among these disadvantages were the systematic efforts on the part of public and private swimming pool operators to discriminate against them. We have already examined how such discrimination affected the careers of divers Sammy Lee and Vicki Manalo. But there was also the case of Japanese Americans in Fresno, California—a place where access to a swimming pool would be especially nice during the warm summers that embrace California's southern Central Valley. In the 1920s, nevertheless, the Fresno YMCA denied Japanese Americans swimming pool privileges. Nor were any of the public swimming pools in Fresno opened to Japanese Americans. [36]

White mainlanders who followed aquatic sports knew before World War II that people of Asian Pacific Islander ancestry could swim well competitively. Hawaiian swimmers were well known at least in Pacific Coast sporting circles. The 1932 Summer Olympics held in Los Angeles launched the competitive swimming skills of Japanese athletes onto the world sporting stage. The Japanese swimmers, who won their share of Olympic medals, seemed to reinforce Japanese American community pride, while provoking both respect and contempt from white followers of the Olympics. David Welky, for example, writes that the *Seattle Japanese-American Courier* consistently published positive reports of Japanese athletic achievements at the Los Angeles Olympiad: "The *Courier* believed that Japan's sportsmanship and goodwill would earn the respect of the world.' In particular, the paper hoped that the Olympics would give Americans a chance to learn 'the true character of the Japanese people,' thus leading to peace and friendship between the two nations."[37]

The same 1932 Summer Olympics also inspired the athletic ambitions of a young Korean American named Sammy Lee, whose immigrant parents ran a grocery store in Los Angeles. Born in Fresno, the adolescent Lee's diving abilities were recognized and nurtured in Los Angeles by a local African American athlete named Hart Crum. According Mary Paik Lee, Sammy Lee's parents also encouraged their son's educational and athletic objectives. Life was not always easy for the Lees. When they moved to Los Angeles, they immediately ran into anti-Asian bigotry. Lee told an oral historian,

> My sisters tell me that when my father tried to move to Sunset Boulevard, we stayed only about a week. The people did not want Asians living on Sunset Boulevard. We lived in the back and had the grocery store in the front, and I wondered, "Well, gee, we're moving again," and we moved to Highland Park. But the irony of ironies, in 1984 they were putting in plaques of famous Olympic athletes, and here, almost diagonally across the way from where we were asked to leave, is my star. My sister reminded me that there were pickets, "No Chinks, no Japs," in Highland Park on York Boulevard. [38]

Despite the difficulties of getting pool time at the Brookside Pool and despite the racial slurs he heard, Lee became one of the greatest divers ever. Meanwhile, he found time to pursue a medical career upon graduation from Occidental College in Los Angeles and the University of Southern California's medical school.[39]

While a doctor in the U.S. Army, Lee won Olympic gold medals in 1948. The *San Francisco Chronicle's* Art Rosenbaum declared during the 1948 summer Olympiad that "Bill Smith, Hawaiian-American water wizard from Honolulu and Ohio State and Lieutenant Sammy Lee, a little Korean from Los Angeles kept the United States rolling along the aquatic path to victory today." Lee told the press that his triumph at the 1948 Olympics stoked his American patriotism, "I can't begin to tell you what that did to this 'Oriental" from Occidental. It's so wonderful being an American." Indeed, Lee represented himself as an ardent American cold warrior. In an article by Rube Samuelson, Lee related how he had been approached by Syngman Rhee to represent South Korea in the 1952 Olympiad. Since Rhee, the fervently anti-Communist leader of South Korea, had been a boyhood friend of Lee's father, the diver was both honored and tempted. Samuelson wrote:

> United States citizens with generations of American forebears behind them, probably will not realize the complexities of the situation. With his father and mother providing the bridge between the Asian world and ours, that is just about as close as next door. Roots go deep and ties are strong. It would be an honor to represent their country, Korea. And Rhee's offer provided for all expenses to be paid, not only for the athlete himself, but for his wife as well.

Lee said no. His love of the United States, he maintained, ran too deep to represent even anti-Communist South Korea.[40]

In 1952, he repeated his Olympic triumphs. The next year, he became the first Asian Pacific American to win the prestigious James E. Sullivan Award—an award bestowed upon the finest amateur athlete in the United States. The Sullivan Award's citation read in part: "The trail of international freedom made by Dr. Sammy Lee is as lengthy and encircling as the equator." Yet despite his athletic accomplishments and the fact that he was an Army veteran and physician, Dr. Sammy Lee and his young family encountered housing discrimination in Southern California during the early 1950s. Ironically, it would seem, Lee was invited to a White House summit on encouraging athletic competition in the United States in 1955. Among the others in attendance were Bill Russell and Willie Mays.[41]

Vicki Manalo Draves was born in San Francisco. As mentioned earlier, her father was Filipino and her mother was born in the United Kingdom. She grew up in San Francisco's working class south of Market district and saved pennies for street car rides to public swimming pools, where she could practice as a youth. While fearing discrimination because of her Filipino ancestry, Vicki Manalo received considerable encouragement from Sammy Lee. Meanwhile, she attended Commerce High School in San Francisco, as well as San Francisco Junior College. During World War II, the U.S. Government employed her in San Francisco.[42]

By the end of World War II, Vicki Manalo was considered one of America's most skilled female divers. George Lineer, called her "<t>he petite dark eyed...diving queen." Another *San Francisco Chronicle* sportswriter, Bill Leiser referred to Manalo as "pretty and dark with a shy friendly smile and not like anybody you ever knew. She is 18 years old, looks 13, normally and on the diving board, they say, she looks like a little baby doll." [43]

In 1944, Manalo won her first national diving championship. She, meanwhile, performed for Oakland's Athens Club team, coached by Lyle Draves. In 1945, she resigned from the Athens Club team after Draves was fired. In 1946, Manalo married her former coach and then competed out of Pasadena under her married lastname of Draves. At the 1948 Olympics, Manalo Draves became the first woman to win both the platform and high diving competitions. As she achieved a diving gold medal winning performance in the Olympics, Art Rosenbaum of the *San Francisco Chronicle* summed up what many of her contemporaries thought of her: "<Draves is>about as big as a minute physically, but with the outsized heart of a champion." Similarly an AP story gloated, "A little, brunette beauty from Pasadena, Mrs. Victoria Manalo Draves made Olympic diving history today....." That Manalo Draves won the gold in platform diving did not surprise many. However, that the "agile little athlete" copped the Olympic championship in the springboard was an upset. Southern California's prestigious Helms Athletic Foundation, moreover, named her amateur athlete of the year for 1948. Manalo Draves, subsequently, performed professionally for an Aquacade produced by Bing Crosby's brother, Larry. Buster Crabbe, a magnificent Olympic swimmer who moved on to become a movie Tarzan, also performed in the Aquacade. Somewhat condescendingly, he told the press that "girls who have had Vickie Draves' success can be impossible. But Vickie--she's one of the sweetest girls I've ever had the pleasure of working with." [44]

Vicki Manalo Draves eventually retired from the diving scene, but Sammy Lee, despite his professional duties, remained involved as a coach and mentor to future Olympic greats such as Patty McCormick, who dominated female diving in the 1950s and Olympic diving champion Bob Webster in the 1960s. Lee, furthermore, helped build international bridges by coaching swimming in India in the mid-1950s. More recently, Greg Louganis owed much of his diving accomplishments to Sammy Lee's coaching. As a young man, Louganis moved into Lee's home in Santa Ana, California, and went to Santa Ana High School with Lee's son. [45]

Part Samoan, Greg Louganis turned into one of the most controversial and accomplished athletes possessing Asian Pacific Islander ancestry. An orphan, Louganis took up competitive diving when he was ten years old. At sixteen, he won a silver medal at the 1976 Olympiad. The U.S. boycott of the Moscow

Olympics in 1980 forced Louganis to wait another four years to go for the gold again. Still, he won gold medals in both the 1984 and 1988 Olympics. Before entering the 1988 Olympics, Louganis learned he was HIV positive. While diving in the 1988 Olympics, Louganis cut his head against the platform. The fact that his blood entered the pool stirred considerable controversy upon Louganis's announcement of his malady. Critics condemned Louganis as incredibly irresponsible, if not immoral. Unbowed, Louganis, declared that he was gay; a declaration that did not sit well with a sporting world that preferred its athletes heterosexual or sexless. Sadly, the controversy split Lee's partnership with Louganis. Lee insisted that he knew Louganis was gay and was not personally concerned. However, he was hurt that Louganis was not straightforward with him and subsequently became too public about his sexual orientation. Lee believed that such outspokenness would hurt Louganis' career. During the 1990s, Louganis became an articulate spokesperson on behalf of gay and lesbian causes, as well as a persistent battler against AIDS.[46]

In 2004, Kimiko Soldati dived for the American Olympic team. A daughter of a father interned in World War II, Soldati first became a competitive athlete as a gymnast in Texas. Using her gymnastic skills, she became one of the best divers in the United States.[47]

While not Olympic gold medal winners, other Asian Pacific Americans have competed in swimming and diving on a variety of levels. In 1926, a swimmer surnamed Tanaka competed for the University of Wisconsin. The incredibly versatile Art Matsu coached the William and Mary swim team in the late 1920s. In 1930, Nakayama competed for Stanford. Five years later, an athlete surnamed Tamura swam for Lodi High School in California. In 1950, Tak Iseri stood out as a competitor for Sacramento's YMCA. Mike Wong swam for Stanford's varsity team in 1957. Several years later, Jessica Tong competed on the Stanford team which won the NCAA championship in 1994. During the early 2000s, Iris Nishimoto fought back from a near fatal auto accident injury to become a fine swimmer for San Francisco State. In Southern California, Dave Mayekawa swam for USC in the early 1970s. In 2005, Chelsea Nagata and Randall Tom were top swimmers for the University of California, Irvine.[48]

Asian Pacific Americans have achieved prominence in Synchronized swimming. Margot Thien competed in the sport in the 1996 Summer Olympiad at Atlanta. Kristine Lum of the Santa Clara Aquamaids gained attention in the late 1990s as not only a fine performer, but one of the few, if any synchronized swimmers, competing with a male partner.[49]

Asian Pacific Americans have participated in a wide variety of other water sports. We have already noted Duke Kahanomoku's skill in water polo and outrigger canoe racing. In 1915, he was a crew member for the Honolulu's Myrtle Club in a regatta, while his brother David competed with the Honolulu Club. .In 1940, he raced a yacht called the "Haupala." In the early 1950s, George Morimoto and Yorio Aoki competed as outboard racing drivers in the Sacramento area.[50]

In the 1990s, dragon boat racing became popular among Bay Area Asian Pacific Americans. Bert Elijeria in *Asian Week* quoted Juliane Tjan, a resident of Foster City who brought along her sons to watch their father row for the Bank of Canton team. She told Elijeria, "It's a nice outdoor activity, good exercise, and people are having fun." Tjan added that the sport helped Asian Pacific Americans to compete athletically, while breaking down a stereotype: "It's good to get out of the stereotype that Asians are not just working and studying [all the time]; they can engage in athletics too."[51]

The sport drew females as participants. Elijera interviewed Dorothy Chung Yeung, who captained the Women Warriors for the Elderly team. She told Elijeria that the sport was "virtually gender-free." Yeung noted, "Anyone can compete...This also encourages people to exercise and help charities." Filipino American Emmie Yang said that her Asian Pacific ancestry was a factor in her taking up the sport. A Bank of America executive at the time, she explained to Elijeria that dragon board racing was "a predominantly Asian sport and you'd want to expand it and have it become a prominent sport." Competing for the Bay Area Dragons club, Yang declared that she learned team-building skills and "*i*t makes you more extroverted in terms of reaching out to people in the Asian Pacific American community."[52]

Conclusion

While certainly encouraging racialization and exoticization, aquatic sports have afforded numerous Americans of Asian Pacific Island ancestry not only the opportunity to participate but excel. Aquatic sports granted the world the first Asian Pacific Islander American superstar in Duke Kahanamoku. The first Pacific Islander to win an Olympic gold medal, Kahanamoku subsequently pioneered the popular sport of surfing. *Surf Magazine* quite properly recognized him as the greatest figure in twentieth century surfing history. Later, *Sports Illustrated* published a survey in which Kahanamoku was named Hawai'i's most important athlete of all time.

Aquatic sports allowed other Americans of Asian Pacific Islander ancestry to accomplish significant sports "firsts." In 1948, Korean American diver Sammy Lee became the first Asian Pacific American to win an Olympic gold. At the same Olympiad, sport history was made by Vickie Manalo Draves who achieved the distinction of being the first woman of Asian Pacific Islander ancestry to win an Olympic gold medal.

Indeed, aquatic sports inspired Asian Pacific Islander Americans of both sexes to gain world class athletic status. Great male aquatic athletes have included Ford Konno, Greg Louganis, and Keo Nakama. However, magnificent female athletes have included Thelma Kalama, Evelyn Kawamoto, in addition to the beloved and courageous Rell Sunn.

Notes

1. Kevin Starr, "The Sporting Life," *California History*, 63 (Winter, 1984), 31; Jack London, *Learning Hawaiian Surfing: A Royal Sport at Waikiki Beach* (Boom Enterprises: Honolululu, Hawai'i, 1983); *Pacific Commercial Advertiser*, December 27, 1911; February 7, 1912.

2. *Honolulu Star-Bulletin*, March 8, 1915.

3. Sandra Kimberley Hall and Greg Ambrose, *Memories of Duke: The Legend Comes to Life*, (Honolulu, HI: The Bess Press, 1995.); *Pacific Commercial Advertiser*, December 24, 1911.

4. Zia and Falls, *Notable Asian Americans*, 143.

5.*Washington Post*, June 13, 1913; *Pacific Commercial Advertiser*, November 18, 1911.

6. *Pacific Commercial Advertiser*, January 14, 1912.

7. *Ibid.*, December 27, 1911; January 8, 1912; January 18, 1912.

8. *Hawaiian Star*, March 5, 1912; March 9, 1912.

9. *Pacific Commercial Advertiser*, May 15, 1912.

10. Hall and Ambrose, *Memories of Duke*, 4; *Washington Post*, July 10, 1912.

11. *Pacific Commercial Advertiser*, June 10, 1912; July 8, 1912; October 3, 1912; *Honolulu Star-Bulletin*, July 10, 1912.

12. *Pacific Commercial Advertiser*, March 3, 1915; April 2, 1915.

13. *Ibid.*, November 8, 1913; January 29, 1915; *Honolulu Star-Bulletin*, October 2, 1912.

14. *Honolulu Star-Bulletin*, August 14, 1915.

15. *Pacific Commercial Advertiser*, May 16, 1912; *Atlantic Constitution*, March 28, 1914; *Elyria Chronicle Telegram*, August 27, 1925.

16. *Pacific Commercial Advertiser*, March 31, 1912; *Honolulu Star-Bulletin*, February 18, 1913; San Francisco Chronicle, July 12, 1915; *Washington Post*, February 4, 1917.

17. Hall and Ambrose, *Memories of Duke*; 58-92; *Los Angeles Times*, December 10, 1914.

18. *Honolulu Star-Bulletin*, June 17, 1913; January 20, 1917; January 25, 1917; *Washington Post*, October 26, 1913; May 18, 1922; *Pacific Commercial Advertiser*, September 13, 1915; September 8, 1916; *Elyria Chronicle Telegram*, September 3, 1926.

19. *Reno Evening Gazette*, December 18, 1950; Zia and Falls, Notable *Asian Americans*, 144-145; Hall and Ambrose, *Memories of Duke*, 106-107.

20. Drew Pearson, "Washington Merry Go Round," *Chillicothe Constitution*, October 14, 1961.

21. Harry Grayson, "Mainland Sports Flourish in Hawaii," *Helena Independent*, January 26, 1941.

22. Greg Ambrose, "Duke Kahanamoku, is Selected by Surfer Magazine as the Surfer of the Century," *Honolulu Star-Bulletin*, July 29, 1999.

23. *Honolulu Star-Bulletin*, July 15, 1913; *San Francisco Examiner*, June 2, 1916; *Atlanta Constitution*, February 13, 1921; *Washington Post*, January 7, 1923; *Indianapolis Daily Star*, May 13, 1923; December 10, 1949; Hall and Ambrose, *Memories of Duke*, 13; www. alohafame.com, accessed November 13, 1999.

24. *St. Joseph Herald*, February 23, 1944; U.S. Census Manuscripts, Wailuki, Maui, 1930; Okhiro, *Storied Lives*, 92; *Pacific Citizen*, August 16, 1947; www.alohafame.com, accessed November 13, 1999; Cisco, *Hawai'i Sports*, 294, 295;

Honolulu Advertiser, July 30, 1947; *Pacific Citizen*, January 28, 1950; *Sport*, July 1951; Blue Book of *College Athletics, 1966-1967*; *New York Times*, July 11, 1948; *Hawaii Herald*, January 1, 1950; January 1, 1951; February 15, 1951; *San Francisco Chronicle*, July 18, 1950; Harold Rosenthal, "Buckeyes From Alohaland," *Sport Life*, Feb. 1953.

25. *Pacific Citizen*, March 11, 1950; *Bridgeport Telegram*, September 2, 1951; Jack Clowser, "Konno on the Go!" *Sport Life*, June, 1952; Rosenthal, "Buckeyes;" *Honolulu Advertiser*, February 13, 1954; Ed Fitzgerald, "Top Performers of the Decade," *Sport*, September, 1956.

26. *Newport Daily News*, July 7, 1952; *Sports Illustrated*, December 12, 1955; June 13, 1956; Rosenthal, "Buckeyes."

27. Clyde Matusoka, "Bill Smith," www.hawaiiswim.org, accessed October 9, 2001; Cisco, *Hawai'i Sports*, 294, 295.

28. *Pacific Citizen*, March 11, 1950.

29. Matsuoka, "Bill Smith."

30. *San Francisco Chronicle*, July 9, 1938.

31. *Ibid*, July 10, 1938.

32. *Ibid*, February 6, 1948.

33. www.alohafame.com, accessed November 21, 1998; *Oakland Tribune*, September 12, 1919; *Honolulu Star-Bulletin*, April 22, 1940; Coles Phinzy, "Riders of the Surging Sea," *Sports Illustrated*, February 18, 1963; Sullivan, "Killer Waves," *Sport*, Oct. 1997; Chelsea J. Carter, "Women Surfing Makes Splash," AP Online, July 29, 2000; Cisco, *Hawaii*, 296; Kostya Kennedy, "All the Rage," *Sports Illustrated*, April 23, 2001.

34. Greg Ambrose, "Makaha's Maiden's Aloha Immeasurable," *Honolulu Star-Bulletin*, September 29, 1999.

35. Ric Valdez, "Still on the Beach," *Honolulu Weekly*, December 25-December 31, 2002.

36. Strong, *Second Generation*, 25.

37. Welky, "Mermaids' Richard D. Mandell, *Sport: A Cultural History*, (New York: Columbia University Press, 1984), 216.

38. U.S. Census Manuscripts, City and County of Los Angeles, 1930; "An Olympian Oral History, Sammy Lee," interview by Dr. Margaret Costa, , edited by Carmen Rivera, (Los Angeles: AAFLA, 1999.)

39. Mary Paik Lee, *Quiet Odyssey: A Pioneer Korean Woman in America*, edited and introduction by Sucheng Chan, (Seattle and London: University of Washington Press, 1990), 107; Larry J. Tazuma, "The Autobiography of Greg Louganis According to Sammy Lee," *Yolk*, June 30, 1995.

40. Rube Samuelson, "Diving Doctor," *Sport Life*, February, 1953, p. 31

41. Lee, *Quiet Odyssey*, 159; *San Francisco Chronicle*, August 5, 1948; Samuelson, "Diving Doctor"; *The Asian Student*, January 8, 1954; *Sports Illustrated*, July 25, 1955.

42. *San Francisco Chronicle*, September 4, 1943; *Filipinas*, January, 2000;

43. *San Francisco Chronicle*, September 4 1943; September 18, 1943.

44. Zia and Falls, *Notable Asian Americans*, 72; *San Francisco Examiner*, April 6, 1945; *San Francisco Chronicle*, August 4, 1948; August 9, 1949; *Los Angeles Times*, August 6, 1948; August 7, 1948; *Filipinas*, January 2000.

45. Campbell, "Indian Girls," *Sports Illustrated*, November 23, 1955, p. 19; Tazuma, "Lee."

46. Tazuma, Lee.

47. www.usolympicteam.com, accessed April 26, 2005.

48. *Appleton Post-Crescent*, December 13, 1926; *Washington Post*, January 12, 1928; *San Francisco Chronicle*, March 2, 1930; *Sacramento Bee*, June 3, 1935; *Pacific Citizen*, February 18, 1950; *San Francisco Examiner*, May 5, 1957; Stanford v. USC, Football Program, Stanford Stadium, October 15, 1994; Brian Kluepfel, "Iris, the Comeback Kid, Bids SF State Good-Bye," www.asianweek.com, February 28, 2003; February 4, 2005; *Rafu Shimpo*, March 25, 1972;

49. *Asian Week*, July 19-July 25, 1996; Gina Arnold, "Synch Different," *Metro*, September 10-16, 1998.

50. *Honolulu Star-Bulletin*, September 15, 1915; *Honolulu Advertiser*, April 20, 1940; *Sacramento Bee*, June 26, 1953.

51. Bert Elijera, "Paddling to Popularity, *Asian Week*, October 3-October 8, 1997.

52. *Ibid.*

Chapter Seven: From Tiger to Michelle

Few American sports figures in recent years have attained as much media focus as golfer Tiger Woods. Barely in his twenties when he turned professional in the mid-1990s, Tiger Woods was predicted by many to change golf history, and by some to even change human history. Quite a burden, one must say, for a young man to shoulder. What made the Tiger Woods story so compelling, despite Mark Twain's wry observation that golf is a good walk spoiled, was that he possessed not only considerable skills and magnetism, but that he excelled as a non-white in a sport that has long been dominated by whites.

As a person of color, Woods inspired many other people of color and has gotten enormously wealthy in the process. *Sports Illustrated* writer, Rick Riley, declared in the late 1990s that Woods could "find...positives all around him, like in the new, throbbing gallery he is inventing, school teachers and Little League teams and whole black families, like the McCorveys of Merrit, Georgia, the kind of family that golf never saw except waiting outside the caddie tents." According to Riley, Carolyn McCorvey contended, "They used to say this was a white man's sport...Well, not anymore. They used to say it was boring, too. But not with all the money this young man is making."[1]

Possessing Thai, Chinese, as well as Native American and the more widely recognized African American ancestry, Woods' racial and ethnic identity became contested terrain. Media critic Karl Yamada decried the mainstream media's tendency to ignore or downplay Woods' Asian background. It seemed to prefer, Yamada complained, to cast Woods in the role of "a black hero." Meanwhile, Yamada pointed out, Woods was not entirely happy with the emphasis placed upon his African American roots, claiming that to describe him as an African American insulted his Thailand born mother. Yet, in *Sport*, journalist Jeff Weinstock urged Woods to "get smart." In America, "you can't be a little black any more than you can be a little bald or a little broken." [2]

Nevertheless, Asian Pacific people have had as much right to claim Woods as an athletic role model as any other group. However, in sports such as golf, as well as tennis, gymnastics, swimming and diving, ice skating, horse racing, rodeo riding, speed skating, volleyball, ice hockey, table tennis, weight lifting, pool, bowling, and track and field, Asian Pacific American athletes have long stood out and in a few cases reached super stardom. Before Tiger Woods, Jackie Liwai Pung and Michael Chang achieved fame. Today, Woods has to share the stage with Apollo Ohno , Michelle Kwan, and Jeanette Lee.

Tennis

Tennis has served Asian Pacific Americans well as both a recreational and a competitive sport. Most of us know Michael Chang as one of the top professional tennis players in the world during the late 1980s and 1990s. But all sorts of people of Asian Pacific Islander ancestry have been playing tennis for decades.

In the late 1800s and early 1900s, athletic Asian Pacific Islanders in Hawai'i frequently took up tennis. In 1899, the *Hawaiian Gazette* reported on two female tennis players of Native Hawaiian background, Kamehameha student Maggie Anahu and Helen Desha. In 1912, the *Pacific Commercial Advertiser* claimed that the Japanese YMCA in Honolulu was trying to lease a plot of ground in the city large enough to construct two tennis courts. The daily proclaimed that Japanese Hawaiians had shown substantial enthusiasm for the sport. In the late 1910s, an athlete surnamed Fujiokimura was one of the better tennis players in Honolulu.[3]

By the second decade of the twentieth century, followers of tennis in the United States not only noticed that fine tennis players from Japan challenged people of European ancestry in competitive tennis but that a good number of people of Japanese ancestry in America were playing tennis. In particular, the *San Francisco Examiner* noted in 1916 a player with the surname of Mikami starring in Japanese American tennis circles in Southern California.[4]

During the 1920s and 1930s more Americans learned that tennis players of Japanese ancestry could compete effectively. In Hawai'i, Tokuku Moriwake won several championships.. In 1923, a Japanese tennis star arrived in San Francisco to warm up for the Davis Cup tournament. The *San Francisco Chronicle* described the tennis player as the "Little brown net wizard." He was greeted by Bay Area tennis players and "members of the local Japanese colony" before playing against S. Yoshokawa, called the junior tennis champion of San Francisco. Meanwhile, a player called Zeno Shimidzu competed out of New York City and became one of the best male performers in the country. In 1925, according to the *Chronicle*, Willie Shimizu represented the San Jose Tennis Club in a San Francisco tournament. In the mid-1930s, George Tanaka lettered in tennis for the University of California.[5]

Chinese Americans on the American mainland were seemingly less impressed with tennis than their Japanese American counterparts. However, in 1916, Chinese American students at Stanford and the University of California assembled tennis teams. In 1927, Thomas Chinn pointed out, San Francisco's Chinatown got its first tennis court. Apparently, much of the community was more amused than inspired. Not many could figure out who could afford a tennis racquet or why a lopsided court held much attraction. By the 1930s, Chinese Americans in and out of San Francisco became more involved in tennis. In 1935, the *Chinese Digest* reported that tennis had developed an enthusiastic following in San Francisco's Chinatown: "Tennis, a sport considered a silly game a few short years ago by many young Chinese is one of their most popular games today. Enthusiasm grew by leaps and bounds, to such an extent, in fact, that several ardent racket wielders put their heads together and held a conference." The result was the Chinese Tennis Association, headed by dentist Theodore C. Lee. In 1937, Lee reported that in San Francisco's Chinatown "a player cannot even hope for a set of singles at the ungodly hour of 5 AM, because tennis is so popular." [6]

San Francisco dailies such as the *Chronicle* and *Examiner* reported on Bay Area Chinese American tennis in the 1930s. In 1933, a Chinese Doubles Tennis Tournament was held in San Francisco. In 1935, the *San Francisco Examiner* noted: "And now we have a Chinese tennis player coming to the fore...11 year old Henrietta Yung—main attraction at a series of exhibitions for the Chinese community." [7]

Chinese Americans outside of the San Francisco Bay Area engaged in tennis. In 1933, the Chinese Bees competed in the Honolulu Tennis League. Henry Wu played tennis for Reed College of Oregon in the mid-1930s. The *Chinese Digest* in 1939 reported on a tennis team of Chinese Americans in Santa Barbara. In Hawai'i, Chinn Sunn emerged as one of the greatest tennis players in Hawaiian history. His career spanned the decades of the 1930s to the 1960s and included over 150 titles. Another fine Hawaiian player of Chinese ancestry was S.H. Loui, who eventually coached tennis at the University of Hawai'i and in the late 1940s was reportedly one of only two Chinese Hawaiian CPAs. Dooley Kam was a veteran Chinese Hawaiian tennis star. In the early 1950s, Hawaiian Wallace Kau competed for Michigan State. In Washingon, Joyce Yee was called Seattle's best young tennis player in 1961. [8]

The Great Depression years and after also witnessed participation in tennis among Filipino Americans. The Filipinos participated in the Honolulu Tennis League. That same year, the Catholic Filipino Tennis Club was active in San Francisco. One contemporary study reported that in Los Angeles sixty Filipinos played tennis as members of the Filipino Tennis Club, the Laguna Lawn Tennis Club, the Luna Tennis Club, the Tandy Tennis Club, and the Filipino Catholic Tennis Club. In 1939, the Filipino Tennis Club in the San Francisco Bay Area lost a match with the Chinese Tennis Club. At the Northern California Indoor Tennis Championship tournament held at San Francisco's Palace of Fine Arts in 1941, the *San Francisco Examiner* observed that one of the competitors was "Billy Madamba, city Filipino champ." In 1942, he played tennis for San Francisco State. In the early 1950s, Filipinos in California formed the Filipino Tennis Club of Northern California and a Filipino Tennis Club in Pasadena. Nearly thirty years later, an All-Filipino Tennis Tournament was staged in Washington, D.C. [9]

During and after World War II, tennis remained an important contributor to Japanese American community endeavors, as well as a way for individuals to advance athletically. While in camp, interned Japanese Americans held tennis tournaments. In 1947, the *Pacific Citizen* publicized the appearance of Japanese Hawaiian tennis star, James Kawaoka, on the American mainland. That same year the JACL weekly reported that PFC Yukimasa Shiaki of Hawaii won the Ninth Corp Tennis Tournament in Japan by upsetting the favorite. In 1955, Boyd Smith of the *Seattle Post-Intelligencer* wrote about "wiry little Art Kono of Garfield High School." During the early 1960s, Yoshi Misegishi played some fine tennis for Stanford. In the 1970s, Ann Kiyomura of San Mateo, California emerged as one of the top female tennis players in the world. Among her great victories was an upset win over Virginia Wade, an all time great tennis pro from the United Kingdom. Kiyomura played professionally with the magnificent Chris Evert for the Los Angeles Strings of the World Team Tennis League. [10]

Chinese Americans such as H.K. Wong helped keep the love of tennis alive in places like San Francisco's Chinatown. A Chinatown furniture dealer and journalist, Wong's prestige in tennis surpassed his community. Wong was a lifelong supporter of athletic organizations in Chinatown, but his main love appears to have been tennis. He served as director of the Chinese Tennis Club from 1935 to 1985. Moreover, in 1949 Wong became the first Chinese American elected as president of the Northern California Tennis Association. The San Francisco Chinese Tennis Club competed effectively against other Asian Pacific American community squads. In 1937, it downed the Los Angeles Chinese team in a series of matches at San Francisco's Palace of Fine Arts. In 1950, the *Chinese Press* proudly reported that the San Francisco Chinese Tennis Club team beat a squad of Bay Area Nisei in Berkeley. [11]

San Francisco's Chinatown hosted an annual tournament, variously called the Pacific Coast or National Chinese Tennis Tournament. Entries arrived from Shanghai, New York City, Canton, and Honolulu. In 1945, Private First Class Ben Chu won the male title after serving thirty months in the South Pacific. Los Angeles' Florence Jue took home the female crown. Gordon Chun of Shanghai and Arizona's George Leong garnered the men's doubles championship, while Jue and Wing Git Jue won the women's doubles title. Among the leading participants in 1950 was Gene Louie of Oakland. At about the same time, teenager Helen Wong developed into one of the best young women tennis players in the United States. Mentioned in a previous chapter as a basketball whiz, Wong represented the U.S. in the Junior Davis Cub and Wightman Cup tournaments. In 1950, she won the National Chinese Tennis singles' title for the fourth straight year. While no Althea Gibson, Wong was at least one of the best female tennis players in California. She and Patricia Hoang won the doubles' title, while she and Bill Lum won the mixed-doubles title. Lum and Peter Lee won the males' doubles. Gene Louis took home the men's crown. In 1958, Willie Chan of Singapore by way of UCLA won the singles crown by defeating Hawaiian Roger Hing. Carol Lum, a seventeen year old Hawaiian, beat San Francisco's Jackie Yee for the women's crown. Ten years later, Marcie Louie, who at 13 was the youngest athlete to win a championship at the venerable tournament, reigned supreme in the women's competition.[12]

In the late 1960s and 1970s, the four Louie sisters competed for tennis glory. Marcie and Maureen were probably the most talented. In 1969, their father, Ronald, pulled Marcie out of the state juniors' championship, complaining that line calls consistently went against his daughter. Nevertheless, Marcie Louie ranked eventually as the fifth best woman tennis player in the world in the 1970s and once beat famed Margaret Court. Maureen "Peanut" Louie won fourteen national titles by the time she was sixteen. In 1978, *Sports Illustrated* quoted Maureen Louie as explaining why she turned pro at eighteen was because, "I hate homework." Meanwhile, tennis helped maintain the San Francisco Bay Area Chinese American community. The San Francisco Parks and Recreation sponsored free tennis clinics in Chinatown in 1981. In the summer of 1982, for example, the San Francisco Chinese Tennis Club sponsored an annual fund-raiser tournament at San Francisco State University. Proceeds were targeted for the Chinatown North Beach Family Planning Services. In 1983, *East/West* reported that Mitchell Gee starred on Lowell High School's tennis team. Two years later, the Chinese for Affirmative Action held a fundraising tennis tournament at Oakland's Chabot Racquet Club.[13]

During the 1980s, the biggest news coming out of Chinese American tennis was the play of Michael Chang. Born in Hoboken, New Jersey, Michael Chang was raised by parents who were both research chemists. After the young Chang displayed an awesome talent for the sport, his family moved to Southern California largely so that Michael could play tennis the entire year. In San Diego, Chang won his first title as a twelve-year-old. In 1988, the sixteen year old Chang turned professional. Called the "undersized warrior with the heart the size of a watermelon," Chang ranked as one of the top male tennis players in the world by the 1990s. And even after he fell in world rankings, Chang seemed more popular and well known in Asia than in the United States. This is particularly true in Hong Kong. A part of the reason why is that he did considerable endorsement work for Procter and Gamble and Reebok in Asia, as well as for

other multinational corporations. In the late 1990s, *Asian Week* journalist Bill
Wong noted Chang's popularity in places like Hong Kong. He wrote, "Michael
Chang has been the rarest of species; a Chinese American athlete of world re-
nown, consistently ranked among the top 10 men's tennis professionals." Wong
described Chang as "a fierce competitor. Although relatively undersized compared with other tennis professionals, he maximizes his skills." Chang, according to Wong, was a role model: "Off the court, he's ..., modest, humble, not
force-feeding his devout Christianity. He is enough of a crossover commodity
that he endorses a number of products to a mainstream American audience."
Michael's brother, Carl, served as his coach and in 1997 *Tennis* magazine
named him as coach of the year. Previously, Carl played for the University of
California.[14]

Less publicized than Chang's exploits was the tennis comeback of Helen
Wong Lum. Illness had kept her off the courts for years. But in 1988, she won
the U.S. Tennis Association's Women's Age Division 55 Championship. She
also garnered championships in her division's National Indoor and Hardcourt
tournaments. In the 1990s, the USTA ranked Wong Lum as the best women's
tennis player in the over sixty category.[15]

Cecil Mammit, a Filipino American who subsequently turned pro, com-
peted for USC in the 1990s. In 1999, Mammit gained notoriety for defeating
Michael Chang in order to get into the finals of San Jose's Sybase Open. *Asian
Week* acknowledged that when Chang met Mammit it was the first time since
Chang met Hawaiian Tommy Ho in 1993 that Asian Pacific Americans played
one another in an American Tennis Professional (ATP tournament. Several
Asian Pacific Americans from San Francisco's Washington High School served
as ball boys and ball girls. Mammit told the press, "I was warming up and
looked around the court and saw every ball kid was Asian. That sure made me
grin."[16]

In recent years, several young women and men of Asian Pacific Islander
ancestry have competed in college tennis. In the 1980s, Laxni Poruri, a talented
athlete of East Indian ancestry, competed for Stanford's women's team in the
1980s before going professional. Jason Yee played for Stanford in the late
1980s. In 2000, Alex Kim won the NCAA men's single's championship as a
Stanford undergraduate. A few years later, Amber Liu became an NCAA champion for Stanford.[17]

Meanwhile, Filipino American Rex Ecarma coached tennis at Louisville
University. Both he and his brother Reggie were standout players for Louisville.
In 1988, he was named head coach of Louisville's tennis program; thus becoming one of the youngest Division I coaches in the nation. In 2000, Ecarma was
named coach of the year by the Conference USA. That same year, the Filipino

Medicine Association of Kentucky and Indiana bestowed upon the Louisville native the Distinguished Filipino-American Award. [18]

In the related sports of table tennis and badminton, Asian Pacific Americans have achieved significant recognition. Hack Ong, described by the *San Francisco Examiner's* Prescott Sullivan as a "small Chinese" won California's badminton crown in 1937. In 1969, *East/West* hailed the accomplishments of "Richard Ng, triple badminton champ from City College of San Francisco." In 1981, an *East/West* piece on table tennis in the San Francisco Bay Area reported on the California Table Tennis championships. It noted that many of the participants were Asian immigrants and relatively recent arrivals in the United States. Largely trained in China, these athletes had, according to Richard Springer, decidedly improved the level of table tennis in the United States. Among those participating were Henry Low and Quang Do. While both were great players, trained in China, Do had previously ranked as the second best player in Vietnam. Meanwhile, Angelita Rosals, who possessed Filipino and Sioux ancestry, emerged into a national champion in the 1970s and 1980s. In 1996, Rosals was elected to the United States' Table Tennis Hall of Fame. [19]

Several Asian Pacific Americans gained places on the 1996 U.S. Olympic table tennis team male and female teams. Indeed, the entire female contingent consisted of Asian Pacific Americans Wei Wang, Amy Feng, and Lily Yip. David Zhuang competed for the male team. Representing the U.S. in badminton at the same Olympics was Kevin Han. In 2000, Michelle Do, Yunghua Chen, Gao Jun, and Khoa Nguyen represented the U.S. in the Olympiad. [20]

Table tennis and badminton have also helped reinforce community ties. In the 1930s, the Filipino Christian Association of Southern California formed a ping pong club with thirty members. Ethen Leiser observed the popularity of table tennis among Chinese Americans in San Francisco. He quoted sixty year old Sam Lee remarking, "I do it for the exercise and for better health,"…Plus, it's hard to get injured. When you play basketball, somebody can hit you and you can get hurt." [21]

Golf

Long before Tiger Woods made golf history, Asian Pacific Americans, of varied skill levels, played golf. Back in the 1920s, Charley Chung was a professional golfer from Hawai'i. According to the *San Francisco Chronicle*, Chung played out of the Honolulu Country Club and was not the only stellar Hawaiian golfer of Chinese ancestry. Chung, when interviewed, mentioned that his old brother Sam, Alex Kong, and Guinea Kop were all fine Chinese Hawaiian golfers. Chung, the *Chronicle* maintained, "financ<ed> his own trip to the states."

The *Chronicle* reported that Chung, "talks perfect English." Yet " '<a>t a country club one has to,' laugh's China's champion." In the 1930s, Honolulu sportswriter Loui Leong Hop boasted that Chinese Hawaiians were spirited and accomplished golfers. He maintained, "Former caddies, they now are territorial champions." Aside from Guinea Kop, he mentioned Francis Maru Hong and Apau Kong as two of the finest Hawaiian golfers around.[22]

However, European Americans found it easier to think of non-white Hawaiians as caddies as opposed to competitors. One white mainland golfer, Charles "Chick" Evans, extolled Japanese and Native Hawaiian golfers in a 1916 piece published in *American Golfer*. These caddies wore little but trousers and a shirt. Thus, they could splash around ponds and irrigation ditches to locate missed struck balls. They were, according to Evans, "unusually enthusiastic and interested in the game." Evans added that he was pleased with a "Hawaiian boy" caddying for him at a golf tournament at San Francisco's Pan-Pacific Exposition. Hawaiian caddies, according to Evans, earned fifteen cents for nine holes and twenty-five cents for eighteen. Tipping, apparently, was forbidden.[23]

On the mainland, golf attracted less support from Chinese Americans before World War II than from mainland Japanese Americans. In 1935, the *Chinese Digest* noted that Thomas Leong "is an enthusiastic golfer, one of a few local Chinese who is really interested in this particular sport." In 1928, the *San Francisco Chronicle* reported on Japanese American golf in California. It claimed that in Los Angeles, Japanese Americans had formed a golf club called Yogi Oki, which, the *Chronicle* asserted, meant, "Get Up at 4 AM." There were, according to the *Chronicle*, about 400 Japanese Americans golfing actively in California. The best apparently was A.G. Sato, from Salinas. Sato, the *Chronicle* maintained, ranked as the first Japanese American to engage in California championship competitions with white golfers. Sato even competed in the Los Angeles open in 1932, after the "little Japanese star" won San Francisco's city championship in 1931.[24]

Indeed, Japanese Americans played plenty of golf in Hawai'i and the American mainland. A story published in the *Washington Post* reported in 1915 that "four Japanese merchants of New York rank among the best golfers enrolled as members of the North Mersey Country Club." T. Aoki, H. Yoshida, K. Ichinomiye, and S. Nomura had been playing golf for about a year. Nomura explained, "Golf is a wonderful game...We are fascinated by it and play it whenever we get a chance." In 1923, the Japanese Consul-General in Honolulu offered a gold cup to the winner of golf tournament for Japanese Hawaiians. In 1933, the *Sacramento Bee* reported that a Northern California Japanese American golf tournament was to be held in California's state capital. Golfers from Salinas, Fresno, Stockton, and San Francisco would participate. Such an undertaking deserves notice. Californians of Asian Pacific had long been excluded or made to feel unwanted at public golf courses, as well as tennis courts and swimming pools. Until 1924, according to one researcher, public golf courses and tennis courts had banned Japanese American players. By the 1930s, these bans were reputedly lifted. Another researcher suspected, however, that into the 1930s Japanese American golfers avoided problems by golfing at the crack of dawn and passing up the public links on Sundays and holidays when they might encounter whites.[25]

The enthusiasm of at least some Japanese Americans for golf endured the concentration camps. Internees at the Manzanar camp, somehow, staged a golf tournament. And after the war, the San Jose *Mercury* reported that Sal Jio, a "San Jose Japanese" had shot a hole in one at a local golf course. Jio was playing with "three other Japanese" at the time. In 1947, Ted Murata and Yukio Kashiwa represented the Hawaiian Islands at a national public links tournament in Minneapolis. Two Japanese American organizations in Chicago—the Enterprisers and the 20 and 5 Club were represented by golf teams. In California, the East Bay JACL held a golf tournament at Berkeley's Sinclair Park. Moreover, the Hawaiian Japanese Golf Club was active in the early 1950s. In Minnesota, the Twins City JACL held a golf tournament in 1950. In 1953, the Lakers, a Nisei organization in Chicago, had established a golf club.[26]

Filipino Americans showed up on golf courses on the American mainland and Hawaiian Islands. In the early 1930s, the Filipino Golf Club was established in Chicago. Twenty years later, it was still in existence. In 1952, Dionicio C. Perez, a civilian mechanic at McClellan air force base near Sacramento, won the San Joaquin Valley's Men's Handicap tournament.[27]

Meanwhile, Hawaiian Jackie Liwai Pung became perhaps the most prominent golfer of Asian Pacific American ancestry before the 1990s. Her father, Jack, was a touring Hawaiian musician when he met her mother in Memphis, Tennessee. The couple settled in Hawai'i, where Jackie Liwai was born and learned golf from her father. In 1930, the U.S. Census described her as a Caucasian-Hawaiian, with a Native Hawaiian father who then worked as a nurse and a European American mother. In 1941, sixteen year old Jackie Liwai married Barney Pung, one of Hawai'i's finest swimmers.[28]

During the 1940s, Pung surfaced as one of the best female golfers in the world. As an amateur, she was named by the *Los Angeles Times* as women's golfer of the year in 1948. In 1952, she won the Women's National Amateur tournament. Subsequently, she turned professional and joined the Ladies Professional Golf Association. (LPGA). While touring with the LPGA, Pung won twelve tournaments. In 1955, she made 5,000 dollars by copping the Jacksonville Women's Open.[29]

Pung's Hawaiian background was neither concealed by her nor ignored by the mainland press. When Pung won the U.S. Women's Amateur Open in 1952, she performed an impromptu hula which earned her a reprimand from the United States Golf Association. One *Sports Illustrated* writer called her "the good natured Hawaiian."[30]

In reality, Pung had plenty of reasons not to be so good natured. In publicizing that the Hawaiian had joined the LPGA tour, Jeanne Hoffman of the Los Angeles Times noted Pung's difficult financial situation. The *Times'* paid her way to the mainland to accept an award. This gave her a chance to enter the LPGA tour, although she was going to have to do well in order to finance her way back home to Hawai'i. Determined to excel, Pung told Hoffman, "I know I'm sort of a freak in golf. I'm fat. I'm Hawaiian. I'm a housewife with two kids. But I can play golf!" Hoffman agreed, adding that Liwai Pung was the most colorful golfer athlete to grace women's golf in many years. [31]

The perils of women's professional golf were played out in Pung's career as she suffered from a nervous breakdown in the mid-1950s. Journalist Paul Gardner indicated that financial problems added considerably to the stress of the LPGA tour for Liwai Pung. Gardner wrote that the "the affable Hawaiian" was the only mother who had to provide for teenage daughters on the LPGA tour. Her husband labored in a blue-collar job for an oil company. Thus, he could not be counted upon for much financial assistance. Meanwhile, women professionals such as Pung did not make all that much money themselves. Pung explained, "Whatever happens....it costs about $200 a week to live before a penny comes in. I don't know why I go on the tour each time--I say I never will again--and then I do." The most money Liwai Pung had made as a pro as of 1958 was $10,000 in 1953 and the most she had netted was $2,000.[32]

After Pung's breakdown, she and her family settled in San Francisco. There, she invested in a "Polynesian" restaurant, which went under. She was forced to go on the tour again. In 1957, Pung staged a comeback—of sorts. She had apparently won the U.S. Women's at the Wing Foot club in Mamaroneck, New York. Then, the unthinkable happened. The prestigious title was taken away from her on a technicality. Moreover, she not only lost the $1800 prize money but was suspended from competition entirely. What was the grievous crime committed by Pung that offended the golf gods? Pung and her partner, Betty Jameson, had mistakenly written down the wrong scores on the fourth hole, even though this error did not affect the final results. Paul Gardner wrote, "Technically correct, the disqualification seemed unfair under the circumstances." The spectators agreed. They took up a collection Everybody chipped in. Reporters notoriously blasé dipped into their pockets. Society matrons wrote out checks. Teenagers handed over part of their week-end money. It was a deluge, and a vote for the underdog. In the end, $3,400 was collected."[33]

Pung continued to be one of the better professional golfers in the LPGA. However, victory in the Women's Open eluded her. After retiring from the LPGA tour, Pung seems to have settled down to a life of contentment and achievement. She coached women's golf at the University of Hawai'i in the 1980s. And she established the Jackie Pung Golf Academy on the Big Island. When Pung turned eighty in the early 2000s, Ben Wood of the *Honolulu Star-Bulletin* observed that she was still teaching golf and had, in fact, been named one of the top fifty golf instructors in America by *Golf for Women* magazine.[34]

Hawaiian golf, unsurprisingly, proved more inclusive for Asian Pacific Islanders than on the mainland. In 1950, Kammy Lau served as tournament chair for the Hawaiian PGA, while Guinea Kop served as treasurer. Hawaiian men such as Jimmy Ukauka and Ted Maklanena played professionally after World War II. Hailing from Hilo, Ukauka often competed in the Los Angeles Open. In 1953, the *Los Angeles Times'* Paul Zimmerman observed Jackie Pung following Ukauka on a Los Angeles Open round in early 1953. Zimmerman lamented that Ukauka could have used Pung's help as he shot a horrendous eighty-three. Maklanena started as a caddy, but became a Professional Golf Association (PGA) tournament victor in 1966. At that time, he defeated the great Doug Sanders to win the Hawaii Open. Before that he battled golf immortals such as Gary Player and Jack Nicklaus on his way to a third place showing in the 1963 Canada Cup.[35]

In 1959, the USGA Journal and Turf Management magazine noted that Violet H. Goo, "a little Hawaiian housewife" had been chosen as president of the Hawaiian Public Links Association, founded by Thomas Ching. She, accordingly, became the only woman to head a USGA organization. Goo, the magazine observed, was very active in the Chinese Hawaiian community.[36]

Tommy Yee was a San Francisco Bay Area professional in the 1950s. The *San Francisco Chronicle's* featured Yee in a piece not entirely complimentary to Yee or the city's Chinese community. Yee, according to Will Connolly, was a World War II veteran who suffered a severe wound. Yee rehabbed through golf and became quite good at the sport except in the crucial area of putting. Connolly wrote, "You'd think a Celestial with a delicate touch would take the easy drop-ins from five feet away. But no, putting is the worst part of the Chinese game." Claiming that Yee's backers came from Chinatown's most prominent leaders, Connolly added, "The Six Companies will have something to say about this. Unless Tommy Yee learns to putt, they are liable to withdraw their support."[37]

Several top-flight golfers of Asian Pacific ancestry have been competing professionally in recent years. While born in Fiji of East Indian ancestry, Vijay Singh lived in Florida when he won the United States PGA tournament in 1998. Thus *Asian Week* felt free to hail Singh as the first Asian Pacific American to ever win that prestigious tournament. The same article also lauded the tremendous golf skills of Korean female champion Se Ri Park, but noted that Thai American Jenny Chuasinporin contested Park hole after hole in the 1998 U.S. Women's Open. *Sports Illustrated* displayed a photo of Chuasiriporn sinking a forty-four foot putt—a photo captioned "Fit To Be Thai-ed." A daughter of Thai restaurant owners in Maryland, Chuasinporin's competed on the Duke University golf team, while her brother, Joey, golfed for Penn State University. Grace Park, who golfed for Arizona State University and won the U.S. Women's Amateur Championship in 1998, deserves attention. So does Dorothy Delasin a golfer of Filipino ancestry who won the California Women's Amateur Championship in 1996 as a teenager and more recently won the U.S. Women's Amateur Championship in 1999. [38]

Delasin, subsequently, turned professional against the advice of the LPGA which maintained she was too young. Insulted, Sonny Delasin took Dorothy to the Philippines to attain financial backing. The National Golf Association of the Philippines held a benefit tournament for Delasin. However, none of the bigger names in Filipino golf showed up. The Delasins left the Philippines with enough to support Dorothy for the first months of the 2000 tour. After a few months, the nineteen year old from Daily City, California, began to win money. In the late summer of 2000, she won her first LPGA tournament when she took the Giant Eagle Classic in Howland, Ohio. [39]

Born in Lubbock, Texas, Delasin spent most of the first five years of her life in the Philippines. In 1985, her father, Sonny, and mother, Selve, moved to Daily City, which is situated just south of San Francisco and has possessed a substantial Filipino American community. As a driving range attendant in the Bay Area, Sonny Delasin not only fell in love with golf but became good enough at it to become a teaching professional. He also taught his daughters Dorothy and Divina to become masterful golfers. and caddied for Dorothy when she won her first LPGA tournament. As a result of Delasin's come from behind victory in Howland, she won $150,000, quite a difference from Jacki Liwai Pung's day, and signed a contract with Sports Alliance, a New Jersey sports management firm. She also rose to the ranks of the twenty-second highest money winner in the LPGA for 2000. Grace Park, who had also turned professional, ranked thirteenth.. Meanwhile, Delasin "became," according to an *Asian Week* article, "an even bigger champion to Filipino American parents everywhere when she announced that she would use the $150,000 first place prize to buy her parents a new home in Daly City, not too far, she said, from the modest and cramped apartment in which they presently live." [40]

In 2001, an eleven year old Hawaiian caught the attention of *Sports Illustrated*, which featured her in its "Faces in the Crowd" section. Michelle Wie became the youngest winner of Hawai'i's Jenni K. Wilson Invitational Golf Tournament. She had also become the youngest person and first female to qualify for the Manoa Cup competition. Moreover, Hawai'i's governor, Ben Cayentano, had issued a proclamation in her honor. The Korean American youngster told the press she wanted to compete in the PGA rather than the LPGA and admired Korean and Korean American women golfers such as Se Ri Park, Grace Park, and Mi Hyun Kim, but respected Tiger Woods the most. Capable of drives of 270 yards, Wie was acquiring heady tributes such as the one articulated by Hawaiian golf expert, Sean Lunasco: "She is like the Tiger Woods for Hawaii...She put women's golf in Hawaii on the map."[41]

Two years later, Wie was able to reach the finals of the Hawaii Pearl Open, a match tournament in which she was the only female. *Asian Weekly* declared, "Wie isn't like most 13-year-old girls you run into. She's nearly six feet tall, hates the mall, thinks boys are annoying and can rip a golf ball nearly 300 yards." Wie was born in 1989 to Korean immigrant parents. As she gained fame, her father, coach and caddy was a Professor of Transportation at the University of Hawai'i, Manoa, while her mother was a Honolulu realtor. Michelle attended Punahou and was expected to stick to her studies until she reached eighteen, at which time she would join the LPGA or even the PGA. However, by fifteen she had already impressed the golf world for her potential as she entered elite men's tournaments on the mainland and came close to making the cuts. The pressure to enter the professional ranks became too great as lucrative endorsement packages were dangled before Michelle and her family. In the fall of 2005, she turned professional well before she graduated from high school. Yet, as of this writing, Wie still has a long way to go before she becomes as dominant among women golfers as Tiger Woods became among male golfers.[42]

Few golfers of any ethnic background have attained the stature of Tiger Woods. As Woods began his professional career in 1996, his racial and ethnic identification became a source of conflict. His mother Tida, who possessed Chinese and Dutch as well as Thai ancestors, told the press that she was angry that her son had been called "The Great Black Hope" and asserted, "to call Tiger black is to deny my existence." Meanwhile, Tiger's father Earl was apparently marketing his son as African American in the United States and Asian in Asia.[43]

Woods, while often criticized for a lack of social consciousness, does show an awareness of what he represents to millions of people. In 1998, he established a foundation that set up golf camps in America's inner cities in order to promote both the sport in unfamiliar territory and racial harmony.[44]

While far from the heights reached by Tiger Woods, Will Yanagisawa is another American of Asian Pacific Islander ancestry who golfs professionally. The Californian won the Hawaii Pearl Open in 2005.[45]

Amateur golf has seen a significant number of Asian Pacific Islander participants in the last thirty years. In 1989, Laura Saiki and and Tracy Nakamura golfed for USC's women's team. Sixteen year old Jeong Min Park was featured in 1991 in *Sports Illustrated* "Faces in the Crowd." The young resident of Alameda had made Junior All-American as a golfer. In 1994, Will Yanigisawa played on a NCAA championship team at Stanford along side notable future professionals Notah Begay and Casey Martin. A daughter of Korean immigrants, Jae Jean Ro competed for Stanford's women's team in the late 1990s. In 2000, He Jin Koo of Guam and Natalie Nakamura of Hilo played for USF's women's golf team..[46]

Asian Pacific Americans formed ethnic-based golf clubs after World War II. Journalist Ethen Leiser has pointed out that during the 1950s a nation-wide Federation of Chinese Golf Clubs was established in response to the racial segregation Chinese American golfers confronted. In Sacramento, the Chinese Golf Club was formed in 1947. In 1958, Earl Wong was elected president to succeed Dr. Courtland Chow. Johnson Fong was named tournament Chairman and Jack Seid, assistant tournament chairman. Mrs. Thomas Chan was named captain, Mrs. Mee Lee, women's tournament chair and Christine Owyang, handicapper In 1969, the Chinese Golf Club threw a tournament with male and female participants from Washington to Hawai'i. In the meantime, Japanese Americans in the Sacramento area organized the Kagero Club, which held an annual medal play tournament. In 1957, Kel Maruyama won the tournament. In 1968 *East/West* noted the existence of the Sacramento Chinese American Women's Golf Club. At about the same time, the Oakland Chinese Golf Club, in its second decade of existence, had 180 men and twenty-five women as members. Sacramento, it would seem, was a beehive of Chinese American golf in the late 1960s. Six years later, the *Philippine News* published a report on the Filipino American Golf Association that was active in the Seattle-Tacoma region. [47]

Bowling

In 1902, a Fresno bowling alley operator hired several Japanese immigrants to labor as pinsetters. Consequently, the young white boys hitherto employed as pinsetters went out on strike. Many of the white bowlers, who had been patronizing this alley, stayed home or found something else to do with their lives out of sympathy for the white pinsetters. In general, however, the Asian Pacific American experiences with bowling have been happier. [48]

During the early 1900s, Hawaiian bowling teams and leagues included participants of Asian Pacific Islander backgrounds. Henry Yap bowled for the Chamberlain Colts of the YMCA League in 1915, while B. Kaumehelwa and L.B. Kaumehelwa bowled for Puuene. A bowler surnamed Sing competed for the Printer's squad in Honolulu. And in early 1917, an All-Chinese bowling team competed in Honolulu. The players were surnamed Young, Sing, Ho, Yap, Ching, and Pung.[49]

In 1938, the *Chinese Digest* declared that "more and more of young Chinese are going in for bowling in New York, Philadelphia, San Diego, and other cities." Philip Lowe and Bill Wong, the *Chinese Digest* added, had just opened a "Chinese bowling alley" in San Francisco. Twelve years later, H.K. Wong wrote in the *Chinese Press* that "<o>ne of the fastest growing and most popular sports in Chinatown is bowling. Most any night you can see them, young and old, both sexes, heaving the ball down the maple way." [50]

Despite the joy many Chinese Americans and other Asian Pacific Americans found in bowling, they ran into discrimination. In 1946, the Chinese American Girls bowling team had been banned from league play in Los Angeles. Apparently, the ban was based upon a Women's International Bowling Congress (WIBC) rule that permitted only white members. The Chinese American bowlers were Margaret Kwong, Julie Wong, Olga Wong, June Joe, and Gladys Quan. They protested the ban by appealing to the Chinese Consul General in Los Angeles and declared that they had husbands and close relatives who had fought against the Axis powers during World War II and they deserved respect and equal treatment. The WIBC, moreover, had also refused to sanction a Hawaiian team, which included players of Asian Pacific American descent.[51]

Asian Pacific American male bowlers faced similar problems. In 1947, a multi-ethnic Hawaiian bowling team traveled to the mainland to campaign against the American Bowling Congress's policy of racial discrimination. Among those departing the islands were Stan Lai, Ray Ogata, Tad Nagasawa, and Eddie Matsueda. The *Pacific Citizen* identified Nagasawa as a 442nd vet who had only taken up bowling since the end of the war but had nevertheless won a Honolulu city championship. [52]

Meanwhile, the United Auto Workers agitated against the ABC. The instigating factor was the ABC's refusal of membership to a CIO team in Wisconsin. Participating on this team was Gin Wong, a World War II veteran and autoworker.[53]

A few years later, E.S. Matsui, secretary of the Oahu Bowling Association, protested to the *Honolulu Star-Bulletin* about the ABC's discriminatory policy. Matsui wrote in a letter to the editor: "It was for the elimination of such racial discrimination that Hawaii's 100th and 442nd Battalions and those of other racial extractions gave their lives and blood in the last war." Early in 1950, New York City was the site of an Interracial Bowling Exhibition. Nisei bowlers such as Hubie Nakanashi, Frank Kawakami, Sogi Uchida, Tosh Yoshimura, Fred Miyasato, Frank Yoda, Beth Fujimoto and Alice Kono participated.[54]

The JACL condemned ABC's white only policy. Hito Okada, a JACL officer, applauded the *New York Journal* for canceling an ABC tournament which the daily sponsored. Moreover, the JACL sponsored a tournament of its own, available to non-whites. Okada declared, "We regret that we have to sponsor a segregated tournament of our own, and we hope to see the day soon when bowling will attain the stature of all other national sports by recognizing a person upon the basis of his ability rather than whether or not he chose the right parents..." Indeed, the JACL became a charter member of the National Committee for Fair Play in Bowling and sponsored a tournament in which non-white and allied white bowlers would compete.[55]

Discrimination against Asian Pacific American bowlers persisted. In January, 1950, Seattle sportswriter Royal Brougham criticized the ABC's exclusion of Nisei bowlers in the Boeing Aircraft League. Kenneth Doji, a Hawaiian bowler of Japanese ancestry, tried in 1950 to enter a tournament sponsored by the ABC in Wisconsin. Doji was excluded, because of the "white only" clause in the ABC's rulebook.

Meanwhile, the ABC and the WIBC faced so many lawsuits regarding its white only clause that they eliminated the ban on bowlers of color. The JACL praised the ABC's decision and hoped that JACL leagues would join the organization. Chinese American bowlers, however, assumed a wait and see approach. The *Chinese Press* noted, for instance, that white bowlers from San Francisco, Los Angeles, and Sacramento ranked high among the most vociferous supporters of the whites only ban. In July, 1950, the ABC invited the San Francisco Chinese Bowlers Association to join. By the 1960s, Asian Pacific American bowlers were regularly involved in ABC and WIBC sanctioned tournaments. Hawaiian Hiroto "Hiro" Hirashima, after years of struggling against racial segregation in professional bowling, became the first person of color elected to the ABC board of directors in 1963. Hirashima, subsequently, became the first person of Japanese ancestry inducted into the ABC Hall of Fame. In 1964, Bob Nagagiri, Harry Oshiro, and Ken Taniguchi were participating in an ABC-sanctioned tournament in Oakland. [57]

Post-war Japanese Americans put in a great deal of time at their local bowling alleys. In the late 1940s and 1950s, Nisei leagues sprang up wherever Japanese American communities were significant. Salt Lake City was the site of a JACL sponsored women's league in 1947. Aoki Produce, Sage Farm, and Dawn Noodle were some of the teams competing. Sportswriter Larry Tajiri was one of the best male bowlers in Salt Lake City, in which male Nisei teams representing Main Jewelry and Appliance, Dawn Noodle, Doi's Cleaners, Pagoda, and Gil's Service took part. The *Pacific Citizen* pronounced Chiyo Tashima as "probably the best Nisei girl bowler in the country." Hailing from Los Angeles, Tashima averaged an impressive 160 a game. Eiko Watanabe was another talented female bowler from Los Angeles. Watanabe starred for a team called the Los Angeles Debs. In 1949, Nisei Mixed Foursome Leagues were active in San Jose. A Chicago Nisei Bowling League existed in Chicago in 1950. The Denver Denaro Bowling team and Salt Lake City's Okada Insurance Company proved to the *Pacific Citizen* in the spring of 1950 that "<d>espite the restrictions imposed by the UnAmerican Bowling Congress, Nisei bowlers are participating in more and more local tournaments." Moreover, Utah's Jack Aramaki competed in some ABC-sanctioned tournaments, while Fumio Hangai of Minneapolis held an ABC membership card. In Stockton, California Jimmy Kimura won 500 dollars at the El Dorado Bowl's Fourth Annual Classic. According to the *Pacific Citizen,* this was the most money ever earned by a Japanese American bowler, beating the record of Tok Isikawa who took home 400 dollars from a Los Angeles tournament in 1949. In Seattle, three Nisei bowlers participated in the Men's Bowling Association Tournament in 1955, while Akio Yanigihara competed for the University of Washington's bowling team. Meanwhile, Fuzzy Shimada emerged as a nationally respected bowler out of San Francisco in the 1950s. Early in 1956, San Francisco's Downtown Bowl staged its sixth annual Northern California Nisei Tournament. One of the winners was a San Jose woman named Happy Taketa, who garnered the singles title with 130 points a game average. Furthermore, San Francisco's Nisei had been competing in an International League, which consisted of teams of players possessing Italian, German, French, Scandinavian, British, Irish, and Chinese ancestries. In San Jose, Sayo Tagami was a top female bowler in the late 1950s and early 1960s, while few women bowlers in Southern California were better than Judy Sakata. In Honolulu, an AJA Novice Bowling League competed at Waialae Bowl in 1964. Several years later, the Japanese American newspaper, *Rafu Shimpo*, devoted whole columns to bowling among Southern California Japanese Americans.[58]

Other Asian Pacific American bowlers shined as individuals or as representative of community organizations. In 1947, the *Pacific Citizen* observed that Chinese and Korean bowlers participated in Los Angeles's Nisei Men's Leagues and that, in particular, Bowman Chung was a leading member of the JACL squad. In 1950, Henning Chin and Philip Wong were among the top bowlers in the Fresno Nisei League, while bowlers of Chinese, Filipino, and Japanese ancestry competed in Stockton's Oriental League. In San Francisco, Julia Wong was a leading competitor for the Kikkoman Shoyu team. In 1953, Steve Wong was considered one of the top amateur bowlers in the San Francisco Bay Area. Six years later, the *San Francisco Chronicle* noted the participation of San Francisco's Chinese Americans in a mixed foursome league at a bowling alley on Broadway and Van Ness. Ruby Chong, a professional bowling instructor, received attention from the *Chronicle*'s Will Connolly in 1962. Connolly wrote that Chong got publicity because "of her Oriental extraction." She told Connolly that "in San Francisco and Oakland, the Chinese, Japanese and Filipino athletes are no novelty...In Florida and other places back East, we are considered exotic." Six years later, *East/West* asserted that the WIBC had certified that the 784 Chong bowled at Golden Gate Lanes in El Cerrito was the highest ever by a woman. In 1947, Sam Tamayo, Seattle's "Filipino American" bowling star won the Northwest Nisei Bowling Tournament in his home city. Filipino Americans were fervent bowlers in Chicago in 1953. Vince Illustre wrote the *Fil-America Advocate* that the Cebu Club and the Filipino Post No. 509 of the American League were represented by bowling teams. In 1975, the Fil-Am Lions Club sponsored a bowling team.[59]

Volleyball

Volleyball has long attracted Asian Pacific Americans of varied skill levels and diverse backgrounds. In 1915, Ed Kam and Sung Bung Sam competed for the Sherman Club Volleyball team in Honolulu. Recall that back in the 1930s, Filipino Hawaiian workers considered volleyball their favorite sport, because it was relatively easy and inexpensive to play. One of these workers, Emigdo Cabico, told oral historians that during the 1930s, "In each camp we have volleyball...Baseball, volleyball—that's the only recreation we have <at the time. >" Indeed, Filipinos who brought their love of volleyball to the Hawaiian Islands also introduced the game's first great innovation—the spike, which was also known as the "Manila Bomb." One observer noted in the mid-1930s that Filipino agricultural workers played "sipa or fast volleyball" at Honolulu's Aala Park. In Northern California in 1933, Salinas was the site of a match between the Cebu Club of California and the Tanay Club of Oakland. The *Philippine Mail* declared that the two teams included some of the finest Filipino volleyball players in the world. As it turned out, a nice crowd of 1200 watched the two teams battle to a controversial draw. Back in Hawai'i, a *Honolulu Advertiser* photograph published in 1935 shows girl volleyball competitors. Among them were young athletes such as Florence Halemano, Ruth Anae,, Eleanor Hiram, Annett Akau, Lee Pae, Alan Akeo, Jennie Kepilino, and Sara Kauhane.[60]

On the East Coast, male laundry workers in Boston's Chinatown often found, according to the one of them, that life was mostly "a matter of no time and no money." These laundry workers sought refuge in the Chinatown Y, where they engaged in table tennis, but mostly volleyball. To one of these laundry workers, Henry Oi, volleyball promoted a sense of community among these laundry workers. Eventually, they started playing games against volleyball players representing Chinatowns in New York City, Providence, and Newark. While competition was important, Oi recalled, these games and a venerable North American Invitational Chinese Volleyball Tournament (NAICVT) which these games sired, helped bridge the geographic and class differences among Chinese Americans on the East Coast in the 1930s and 1940s.[61]

Fifty and sixty years later, volleyball remained an important contributor to Chinese American community building. According to the NAICVT website, "by bringing young people back into Chinatown from the suburbs." The website continues:

> Asian youth growing up in the suburbs are in some ways
> as isolated as the laundry workers of an earlier generation.
> Though youth today may be more integrated into the sur-
> rounding culture, they may be cut off from their Chinese herit-
> age and the people who make that heritage come alive.

In 1984, the NAICVT was held in San Francisco's Chinatown. Forty-two teams from all over the United States and parts of Canada competed at Commodore Stockton School and the Chinese Playground. By this time, the participants were no longer substantially laundry workers, but many restaurant workers, who had to overcome their relatively unusual shifts in order to get practice time and games into their overwhelmingly busy schedules. Also by this time, female teams were allowed to enter the tourney, although there admittedly was some opposition. Indeed, among the winners was a female team representing the Methodist Church in San Franicsco.[62]

Twenty years later, *Asian Week* promoted the tournament in San Francisco. Journalist Allison Lee informed readers that at least two-thirds of a participating team had to be 100 percent Chinese. The rest had to possess at least some Asian ancestry. Lee described the tournament as a "<u>niquely Chinese form of volleyball" played with nine on a side and involving hundreds of athletes from Boston, Washington, D.C., New York City, and Toronto. A Labor Day parade from Fishermen's Wharf to Chinatown, wrote Lee, kicked off the tournament. Lee maintained, "Colorful Chinese flags, dragon dancing and team cheers brought this parade to life. Adding to the spectacle was the fact that those in the parade were some of the tallest APA men and women ever seen, many of them six feet or over."[63]

Other Asian Pacific American volleyball leagues and tournaments were organized on the mainland. During World War II, a volleyball league was formed for women at the Roher concentration camp in Arkansas. In 1981, the Queens Cup Volleyball tournament took place at San Francisco's Chinatown.[64]

In the 1950s, volleyball enthusiasts began to note that the Hawaiian Islands bred top-notch players. In 1956, Honolulu's Central Y's squad of male athletes won second place at the United States Volleyball Association tournament at Seattle. One of the Central Y's biggest stars was Longy Okamoto, a barefoot setter. After his playing career ended, Okamoto became an outstanding coach of youthful female Hawaiian players and helped pioneer wahine volleyball on the islands.[65]

Meanwhile, a number of Asian Pacific Americans emerged as excellent high school, college, and professional volleyball players. Many of these fine athletes were females. Hawaiian Pete Velasco rose from working class origins to become captain of the U.S. Olympic Volleyball team in 1964. In 1968, Fanny Hopeau joined the female U.S. Olympic Volleyball team. In the process, she became a wahine trailblazer. In 1976, Mel Nishita served as co-coach of San Jose State's volleyball club. In California's Central Valley, Annette Hirata and Kathy Sumamoto were all-conference players for Reedley High School in 1977. Liz Masakayan was born in Quezon City in the Philippines. She first gained notoriety in volleyball circles as a standout player for Santa Monica High School. Masakayon, subsequently, went to UCLA, where she became an All-American volleyball player and UCLA's female athlete of the year. In 1984, she was a member of the U.S. Olympic Volleyball Team. Since then she turned professional and hit the professional beach volleyball circuit. In 1996, Masakayon was voted the best hitter in the Women's Professional Volleyball Association. Lucy Hom was born in Hartford, Connecticut. Yet like Masakayon, she went to Santa Monica High School and UCLA. Since leaving UCLA, Hom played professional beach volleyball for over eleven years. Nicknamed the "sand flea," Hom became a mechanical engineer and an activist in the Organization of Chinese Americans. Santa Monica, which seemed to have served as a North American volleyball capital in the late twentieth century, was Lianne Sato's hometown. She played volleyball at San Diego State, however, before transferring to the University of California, Santa Barbara. Sato competed on both the 1988 and 1992 U.S. Olympic teams. Marlon Sano coached women's volleyball in the 1980s and 1990s for such institutions as Utah State. Prior to that he was an assistant women's volleyball coach for the American Olympic team in 1984. In 1993, Guy Takashima was named Division III girls volleyball coach of the year as he guided a South Torrance High School squad in the Los Angeles area. Yoko Zetterland competed on the 1996 female Olympic team. Born in the U.S. of a Swedish father and Japanese mother, she was raised and became a fine volleyball in Japan. In fact, she became an outstanding setter on the Japanese nation team before seeking a permanent home in the country of her birth. [66]

In recent years, the University of Hawai'i's, wahine volleyball team has surfaced as one of the nation's powerhouses. Moreover, in the 1990s, Hawai'i's sports fans truly embraced wahine volleyball; attending women's volleyball games in numbers that went unmatched on the mainland. Coached by David Shoji, the team has featured multi-ethnic, multi-racial rosters with such players as Nalani Yamashita from Colorado Springs, Colorado, Robyn Ah Mow, from Honolulu, Teresa Crawford, an African American from Michigan, and Angelica Ljungquist from Sweden. In the late 1990s and early 2000s, UH suited up athletes such as defense specialist and Kamehameha grad Aven Lee.[67]

Asian Pacific American women continued to star in college and international volleyball into the late 1990s and beyond. UH did not suit up the only top notch female volleyball players on the islands. In 1996, Nue Chang was an ex cellent defender for BYU-Hawaii. A look at the 1997 Women's All-American team will reveal a number of Asian and Pacific Islander names. The University of Hawai'i's nimble setter Robyn Ah Mow was named to the Division I first team, along with Fiona Nepo, a great Samoan Hawaiian athlete who competed for the University of Nebraska. Christine Kalewuawehe from Central Missouri State was a Division II All American along with University of Nebraska-Kearney's Danielle Shum and Barry's Cindy Yuan. Liu Jun from Northern Michigan was honored as Division II player of the year. Christine Chi, from the University of California, San Diego, was a Division III All American. Two years later, Hawaiian Brandy Mamizuka was named Idaho's NCAA woman of the year for her performance as a star volleyball player for Boise State. A little to the east, Leslie Tuiasosopo was an all-PAC 10 player for the University of Washington. A daughter and sister of famed Husky football players, Tuiasosopo later became an assistant coach for her alma mater. Michelle Quon stood out as a defense specialist for UCLA in the late 1990s. Her coach described her as "the best pure defense player" ever at UCLA. At Stanford, Debbie Lambert, an Hawaiian possessing Korean ancestry, stood out for Stanford's powerful volleyball team. Also playing for Stanford in the late 1990s were Lindsay Kagawa and Lindsay Yamasaki, whose athletic talents were scarcely limited to basketball. Indeed, Yamasaki was good enough to be named to the World University Games in Bejing in 2001 and helped the U.S. win a gold over China. Hawaiian-born Logan Tom was an even better volleyball player for Stanford. In 2001, Tom led Stanford to an upset victory over Long Beach State University in the NCAA finals. Tom attained twenty-five kills, twelve digs, and five blocks, in the process. Mel Tom's daughter, Logan Tom achieved All-American honors and a place on the U.S. Olympic team.[68]

Asian Pacific Americans had much to cheer, as well, when it came to male volleyball stars. Eric Sato competed professionally in the middle and late 1990s. Mike Lambert, Debbie's brother, was an All-American at Stanford before competing on the American Olympic team. Kevin Wong and Eric Fonoimoana won Olympic gold as beach volleyball partners in 2000. Wong, a six foot seven inch Hawaiian graduate of UCLA, told the press that he got into volleyball because in Hawai'i, "volleyball is a pretty big sport." A University of California, Santa Barbara grad, Fonoimoana had won a pro volleyball "King of the Beach" title in 1998. And Scott Wong participated in Bejing as part of the 2001 World University Games.[69]

However, it has not just been Olympic stars and All-Americans who have found joy in volleyball. In 2001, *Asian Week* writer Ethen Leiser depicted the experiences of Asian Pacific American women participating in the Women's Volleyball League at San Francisco's Kezar Pavilion. Fifty-three year old Sharon Yasukawa told Leiser that Asian Pacific American competitors like herself were not the tallest athletes on the court but they were good setters—"very fast and low to the floor. They have great defensive skills." Thirty year old nurse, Angi Pong, enjoyed the competition. A former high school player, she observed, "It's like stress relief for me."[70]

On Ice

Probably no sport is more associated with Asian Pacific American women than competitive ice-skating. In the 1990s, Kristi Yamaguchi and Michelle Kwan helped shape female ice-skating into one of the most watched and talked about sports in North America. As we will explore more in the next chapter, one can find a downside to the close association between Asian Pacific American female athletes and ice-skating. But very clearly, champion ice skaters, regardless of race, ethnicity and gender, typically deserve respect as supreme athletes, who have endured years of monotonous practice hours, as well as painful injuries.

As early as the 1960s, Asian Pacific American women were winning ice skating titles. In 1963, Lynn Yonekura, was described by *Sports Illustrated* as a "a lithe, statuesque 14-year-old from Berkeley." The straight A student had just won the Pacific Coast Junior Ladies Figure Skating Championship. In 1965, Christy Ito garnered her third consecutive Northwest Pacific Novice Championship in the "Ladies Division." Ito had just been figure skating for three years. Vera Wang, the famed dress designer, first gained national attention as an ice skater. In 1968, *East/West* reported that the Sarah Lawrence University freshman had won the North Atlantic Figure Skating championship at West Orange, New Jersey. [71]

Tai Babilonia and Elizabeth Punsalan were pioneering ice skaters of Filipino ancestry. Babilonia's father was a Filipino American detective with the Los Angeles Police Department, where her mother was largely African American. In the late 1970s, Babilonia and her partner, Randy Crawford, were considered the best ice skating pair in the world and favorites to win the 1980 Olympic gold medal in the pairs competition. Sadly, Crawford was injured while training for the Olympics. He and Babilonia were forced to skip the Olympics. The *Philippine News* hailed the pair despite the fact that Olympic gold eluded them in 1980. In an editorial, the *News* dispatched "Kudos to a Golden Couple" and asserted that Filipino American "hearts went out" to Babilonia and Crawford. The weekly admitted "it might have sent our spirits soaring to cheer one of our own in the Winter Olympics." Still, because they offered "respite from the world's graver calamities the magic of Tai and Randy deserve a gold medal." Yet even though they had to surrender their dreams for Olympic gold, Babilonia and Crawford continued to skate professionally into the late 1990s. As for Punsalan, her father was Filipino and her mother, Irish American. She and her partner,

Jerold Swallow won the American ice dancing championship five times before turning professional in the late 1990s.[72]

In the early 1980s, Tiffany Chin emerged as one of the best ice skaters in the world. In an interview with *East/West*, the then sixteen-year-old Chin said she loved ice skating because "<i>n ice skating you get a feeling of freedom out there...It's like there are no boundaries. You can glide and go as fast as you can, whereas in other sports, you have boundaries." Born in Oakland, California, but raised in San Diego, Chin placed fourth in the ice skating competition at the 1984 winter Olympics. In 1985, she won the U.S. national title. In the 1990s, Chin skated professionally both in the Ice Capades and competitively.[73]

Defining female ice skating for many fans in the 1990s has been Hayward, California native and Japanese American Kristi Yamaguchi. From 1983 to 1990, Yamaguchi skated pairs with Rudy Galindo. Then, she turned to individual skating. In 1994, Yamaguchi did much to return a little bit of grace to a sport somewhat sullied by the Kerrigan-Harding scandal. That year, she won the Olympic gold medal. Yamaguchi, as a supremely masterful and hard working ice skater, as well as a major endorser of a whole host of products and causes, seemed to symbolize the Model Minority thesis that has been applied to Asian Pacific Americans. In the next chapter, we will examine the Model Minority thesis more carefully.

Southern Californian Michelle Kwan has not, as of this writing, duplicated Yamaguchi's gold medal winning Olympic performance. She came close. In 1998, for example, she garnered a second to fellow American, Tara Lipinski's, first. Kwan, however, won several national and world titles to perhaps compensate for losing Olympic gold. Also in 1998, Kwan maintained that after winning the world championship in Minneapolis, she was gripped by both patriotism and love of her sport: "When I stepped on the ice, I saw the American flags and banners and I wanted to give the audience the joy and freedom that I have on the ice." Moreover, Kwan emerged as a symbol of Asian Pacific American pride. The usually unsentimental Emil Guillermo wrote in 2002, "If there was a lead dragon on our collective Lunar New Year parade it is the diminutive Michelle Kwan."[74]

Naomi Nari Nam, who hailed from Irvine, California, tried to compete with Kwan and Lipiniski for national honors. In 1999, the thirteen year old Southern Californian placed second in the U.S. figure skating championship. Five years later, Beatrice Liang reached for international honors as a figure skater.[75]

Interestingly, in Disney's *Mighty Ducks II* the one Asian Pacific American character is a young man named Kenny Woo, who is an Olympic gold medal figure skater turned into a hockey player just in time to help the U.S. national team win a Junior Olympics gold medal. Woo, we find out, can dazzle the opposition with his skating finesse. Eventually, an African American who learned street hockey in South Central Los Angeles teaches Woo to compete in a more physically aggressive manner instead of just "mincing" around the ice rink.

Fortunately, the real world eludes stereotypes. There are, indeed, some very exceptional hockey players of Asian Pacific ancestry—hockey players who have shined in the tough world of the National Hockey League. Paul Kariya, for example, is a Canadian of Japanese ancestry who has developed into one of the best NHL players of all time. Richard Park is less well known. Born in Seoul, Korea, Richard Park has won fans wherever he has played professional hockey. While with the NHL Philadelphia Flyers, Park impressed one fan with "his...integrity, dignity and his worldly eloquence... His sense of dedication to the game and more to achieving excellence in himself is remarkable and explicatory considering the fact that the Park's family ride to success was not an easy one."[76]

Park came to the United States with his family in 1980. While still young, he seems to understand that he is considered something of an anomaly in the world of sports. He admits that racism shadows his travels through the world of North American professional hockey:

> It's (racism) around when you're younger, you know from lack of awareness in kids, but as you get older guys are more aware and they are much more mature about the situation. Especially nowadays there is such a growing number of different nationalities playing this game that you'd be foolish to pinpoint one and make them stand out for a particular reason. I think it's really good for the game to become multicultural. It nice to see kids of color come up in this game.[77]

In 2000, the NHL offered two Asian Pacific Americans a chance to become sports entrepreneurs. Charles Wang, president of Computer Associates, and Sanjay Kumar, chief operating officer for the same firm, bought the New York Islanders. Previously, they had wanted to buy a NBA team and bring it to Long Island. However, they settled for the Islanders, admitting that they did not know much about professional hockey.[78]

Two fine American winter Olympic athletes of Asian Pacific ancestry emerged in 2002. In amateur hockey, Julie Chiu showed that not all Asian Pacific American women get on the ice to figure skate. Chiu was a forward on the U.S. Women's Olympic team that won Olympic gold in 2002. Just in time for the 2002 Winter Olympiad, Apollo Ohno surfaced as a world class speed skater and eventual gold medal champion. *Sports Illustrated's* S.L. Price declared, "a diamond stud in his ear, a whiff of scandal in his wake," Ohno was not the typical American winter Olympic athlete. His father, Yuki, was a Japanese native and hairdresser who raised the often tempestuous Apollo on his own.[79]

Gymnastics

Like ice skating, gymnastics is a sport significantly associated with Asian Pacific athletes—especially female Asian Pacific athletes. In the late 1990s, a teenager from California named Amy Chow attracted a great deal of attention. In 1995, Chow won a gold and a bronze medal at the Pan American games. In 1996, she made the well-publicized U.S. Olympic gymnastic team. Chow did not win any individual medals, but her performances took little off the luster attached to American female gymnastics. Indeed, after the Olympics ended, the gymnastics club in which Chow trained was flooded with applications and the Chow family flooded with offers from agents. [80]

Other Asian Pacific Americans, male, as well as female, have excelled in gymnastics. Makudo Sakamoto competed for USC and the United States men's team in 1963. In the early 1960s, Rich Chew was a fine gymnast for San Jose State College. In the 1970s, he served as coach for the San Jose State gymnastics team. Up at Stanford, Sadao Hamada coached gymnastics for years at Stanford. In 1997, Candace Kwok captained the University of California's women's gymnastics' squad. In the late 1990s, Yoichi Tomita was named developmental coach of the U.S. Men's Olympics Gymnastics team. A native of Japan and U.S. citizen, Tomita competed at one time for Long Beach State University. [81]

Running and Riding

One of the most popular American spectator sports in the late 1800s was pedestrianism, best described as a form of marathon walking races. The competitors, typically professional and culturally diverse compared to athletes in most other sports at the time except prize fighting, were usually colorfully attired and like latter day professional wrestlers, often seemed more inclined to entertain than anything else. The promoters followed the legacy of the great American showman of the nineteenth century—P.T. Barnum. In other words, they seemed determined to get people to pay good money to see that which was widely considered wondrous and bizarre.

In 1880, the *Sacramento Bee* reported on a "walking match in San Francisco." Among the participants were "a number of Chinamen." The promoters clearly hoped these Chinese athletes would attract the curious. Still, according to the *San Francisco Chronicle*, the Chinese "peds" dropped out of the race before it ended. Given California's powerful anti-Chinese tendencies, a victory for any of the Chinese participants would have, indeed, been an upset. [82]

By the 1900s, pedestrian races were replaced in the public's heart by amateur and often less festive track and field meets. Nevertheless, the Fourth Annual Kalakaua Avenue Walking Race was apparently a big deal in Honolulu in 1911. Among the participants were K. Kahalewai, Anton Kaoo, John Hau, and Sam

Hop, who managed the traveling Hawaiian ball team in 1913 and 1914. A Japanese language newspaper in Honolulu offered a special prize to the Nikkei who finished first. In addition, the Native Hawaiian who finished first among other Native Hawaiian entrants would receive a special prize as would the best Chinese Hawaiian walker.[83]

Track and field meets received plenty of publicity in early twentieth century Honolulu sports pages. The great Chinese Hawaiian ballplayer, En Sue Pung, was also a notable high school sprinter in turn-of-the century Honolulu. Tom Kaulukukui wrote that he and haole athlete A. Castle, had developed a steamy rivalry for the title of Honolulu's fastest teenager. Castle sprinted for the private Punahou school while En Sue Pung represented the public Honolulu High School. Apparently, the Chinese Hawaiian proved superior in the 100 yard dash, while Castle took honors in the 220.[84]

En Sue Pung's teammate Buck Lai Tin was not only one of Hawai'i's best baseball players, but one of its track and field performers. As a teenager, he set Hawaiian records in the 100-yard dash and the long jump. In the former, he sprinted the distance in 9.5 seconds and leaped twenty-three feet and eight and one-half inches. In 1912, a benefit track and field meet was held in Honolulu to raise funds to support Duke Kahanamoku''s first trek to the mainland. Lai Tin won the 100 yard dash, while another fine Hawaiian baseball player, Andy Yamashiro, took second. Aside from participating in sprints and the long jump, Lai Tin also was a shot putter for McKinley High School in Honolulu.[85]

Lai Tin represented the Chinese Athletic Union (CAU) at a Chinese Hawaiian track and field meet held in February, 1912. Other CAU athletes included fellow Hawaiian Traveler ballplayers such as Ah Toon and Sing Hung Hoe. Chinese Hawaiian athletes also represented the Beretania Mission, the Chinese Athletic Club, and Mon Lan School. Notable Chinese Hawaiian athletes such as Apau Kau and Vernon Ayau served as field judges, while Ensue Pung was a starter.[86]

Early in 1913, Lai Tin, Ensue Pung, and Sing Hung Hoe were successfully barred from an AAU meet in Honolulu because they were accused of being professional ball players. The athletes denied the charges, claiming they played baseball out of love for the sport. Subsequently, Hoe admitted that the players received money as Hawaiian Travelers but only twenty-five dollars a month for incidentals. Hoe argued that other Hawaiian baseball players were allowed to participate in the AAU meet even though they received shares of gate money for playing in Hawaii.[87]

Other Asian Pacific Islander athletes did well in Honolulu track and field meets in the early decades of the twentieth century. Before the turn of the twentieth century, Harry Hapai was a well known hurdler in Honolulu. In 1911, the *Pacific Commercial Advertiser* noted Tsukumoto, a "Japanese long distance runner" who worked on a plantation near Honolulu. The Honolulu daily also hailed Anton Kaoo, the "Wailea horse" and the "champion Island runner." The *Advertiser* maintained that Kaoo had been competing for over a quarter of a century. It added, "Although there is a good deal of gray stubble in his beard, the old runner of the Monarchy, the Republic and finally of the Territory, is still in the game and looks to be as strong as ever." Kamehameha's Frank Kanae set a Hawaiian discuss mark of ninety-five feet and 8 inches in 1913., while teammate George Mahoha was called the "speed marvel of Kamehameha." At a Honolulu AAU event, D. Takeuchi won the long jump, while Kamehameha's Benjamin Mill won the 440 yard race. Participating on the Punhou track and field team in 1914 were Lum Kita Wai and Kong Tim Hong. D. Kaopula and S. Kauku participated for the Kalihi Boys Track team in Honolulu in 1915. Chun Lee Puck was the best long distance runner for Mills School in 1916. Wah Kai Chang, the *Chicago Tribune* reported, hailed from Hawai'i and was training as a distance runner for the University of Chicago in 1915. Chang, moreover, was named captain of the sophomore track team and starred at the Chinese Student Conference track meet at Wesleyan. [88]

Another Chinese Hawaiian, Tin Luke Wongwai, became a standout sprinter with the University of Kansas track team in the 1920s. Prior to heading east to Kansas, Wongwai had run for the University of Hawai'i's track team. In 1922, the *Reno Evening Gazette* published a wire story, headlined "Chinese Racer To Meet Paddock." Charley Paddock was a magnificent USC sprinter who was slated to participate in an AAU meet in Honolulu. Tin Luke Wongwai was described as a "slim American Chinese student." When he arrived in Kansas, Wongwai was hailed by the mainland press. A wire story published in Ohio's *Elyria Evening Telegram* was accompanied by a photo of Wongwai in a University of Hawai'i uniform and declared, "Track experts who have seen Tin Luke Wongwai in action on the cinder path believe that the University of Kansas freshman will attract attention in collegiate circles when he is eligible to compete a year hence." The article added that Wongwai was born in Hawai'i and an American citizen. And while Wongwai may not have been a world beater as a sprinter on the mainland, he seems to have been more than competent. In a 1925 indoor meet at the Kansas City Athletic Club, he took third in the fifty-yard dash.[89]

Meanwhile, mainland Chinese Americans became active in track and field. In 1920, San Francisco's Chinatown YMCA staged its first annual track meet at Golden Gate Park. Among the organizations sending athletes to the meet was the nearby Berkeley Chinese Athletic Club. Sixteen years later, Ronald Ong starred in the eighty pound division, winning the fifty and seventy-five yard dash competitions.[90]

Athletes of Japanese ancestry demonstrated an interest in track and field. An athlete with the Japanese surname of Aoki ran track for Lowell High School's 100-pound squad in 1912. In 1922, Mitsuye Yamada won the standing

broad jump in his division at a meet in California pitting Cupertino and Sunny-
vale schools. In 1930, San Francisco's Golden Gate Park was the site of a thirty-
mile race. The *San Francisco Chronicle* reported that Victor Yoshakawa, a "local Japanese distance runner" won the race. Coming in second was Kosei Suzuki. In 1932, Lowell High School suited up Tad Fujimoto.[91]

Hawaiian and mainland athletes of Asian Pacific American background
stood out in track and field competition on the American mainland during the
1930s and early 1940s. In 1935, "little Kenji Marumoto" competed in the broad
jump for UCLA. Around the same time, Hawaiian Jim Kneubhl, described as
the "Samoan sizzler," sprinted for Stanford. Francis Wai not only played football for UCLA in the late 1930s, but also ran track. At a track meet won by the
Bruins, the *Los Angeles Times*, noted that the "Hawaiian lad" was an upset victor in the sprints. In 1941, the San Francisco Examiner's Bob Brachman identified Salinas Junior College track standout, Claudio Scott, as a "Hindu Filipino."[92]

During the post-World War II years, American athletes of Asian Pacific
ancestry have excelled in track and field as well as distance running and walking. After World War II, Hawaiians Norman Tamanaha and Takeo Takushi ran
in the Boston Marathon and San Francisco's Cross City Run. Several years later,
Japanese American Michiko Gorman ran in the Boston Marathon. George Uye-
da was a top long jumper for UH in the late 1940s. Meanwhile, Henry Aihara
gained a reputation as "the top Nisei athlete." As a high school senior, he ran
track for New Trier High School in Illinois. In 1945, he starred for the University of Illinois' freshman track team. He, subsequently, transferred to USC, where
he became co-captain and the Pacific Coast Conference's best long jumper. Aihara also toured with a U.S. national team that went to Scandinavia, winning
seven of nine events. In 1950, Bob Watanabe sprinted for UCLA. Previously, he
had run a 100-yard dash in 9.6 seconds in order to win the U.S. Army's Far
Eastern championship in 1947. Junior Singh starred in the high jump for San
Bernadino Junior College in the mid-1950s. Around the same time, Hawaiian
Lenny Chang ran track for Western Reserve.[93]

In more recent years, Asian Pacific American have participated in a wide
variety of track and field, as well as running events. During the late 1960s and
into the 1970s, Chi Cheng of Crown City, California won the AAU women's
pentathlon. A native of Taiwan, Cheng had represented her homeland at the
1964 Olympiad. In the 1960s and 1970s, Japanese American Ken Matsuda
coached track and field for USC after a career as a shot putter and football player for San Jose State. Matsuda, in 1972, told an audience at a Nisei banquet that
athletes "have a place in society because they become leaders of tomorrow when
they retire their spikes after high school or college career." Meanwhile, Terry
Hazama competed for Fresno State as 440 yard hurdler in the early 1970s. In the
1980s, New York City born Tracy Wong starred as a female distant runner for

Texas A&M. Prior to attending Texas A&M, Wong stood out as a prep distance runner in Nevada. According to *East/West*, Wong became the first female named "prep of the week by the *Nevada State Journal*. On the East Coast, Velma Wong was a hurdler for Brandeis University. In 1996, Shelia Hudson, a hapa of Korean and African American background, competed in the triple jump at the Atlanta Olympics. In 1998, Andy Leong coached track and field at Lowell High School in San Francisco. Born in Tielin, China Yueling Chin became the first woman of Asian descent to win an Olympic gold medal in track while representing China as a distance walker in 1992. Chin, subsequently, immigrated to the United States and became a citizen. In 2000, she represented the United States in the 2000 meters walk. In 2000, Samoan American Seilala Su'a was a formidable shot putter, as well as discus and hammer thrower for UCLA. Su'a also represented the United States at the 2000 Summer Olympiad. [94]

In 2005, Bryan Clay was dubbed "the future of the decathlon." Clay's mother is a Japanese immigrant, Michelle Ishimoto and his father is an African American, Greg Clay. His parents were divorced and Clay was raised in Hawai'i "under the strong influence of his mom's Japanese culture," according to *Sports Illustrated* writer, Tim Layden. Clay remembers, "We ate ozoni on New Year's Eve. My life was very Japanese." Clay wound up at Azusa Pacific in California, where he emerged as one of America's top decathlon athletes. [95]

Asian Pacific Americans have, moreover, established community running clubs and organized running events. The San Francisco Chinatown YMCA operated a "Fun Run" in connection with Chinese New Years in 1981. In the East Bay, an Asian Runners Club existed in Alameda County in the early 1980s. [96]

In the late 1800s and early 1900s, bicycle racing emerged as a popular spectator sport. California developed into one of the Meccas of bicycle racing. According to the *Los Angeles Evening Express*, the Fowler bicycle racing team had a Chinese racer named Ah Sam in 1895. Ah Sam, the *Evening Express* reported, wanted to head north to challenge the "champion Chinese rider from Oakland." On the Hawaiian Islands Asian Pacific Americans raced bicycles. Thomas Ah Chew competed as a bicycle racer in 1915. In 1940, Kasaumu Fujiyama was considered a top racer in Hawai'i. Other notable Hawaiian bicycle racers were Takashi Ishihara and Kotaro Miyasato [97]

Auto and motorcycle racing attracted the talents of some Asian Pacific Americans. In 1915, the Los Angeles *Times* claimed to have discovered "the only Chinese racing driver." Tong Tin was supposedly the name of this driver. And a photo of Tong Tin accompanied the *Times*' article. Tong Tin, the *Times* reported, sought to enter the Redondo Road Race in Southern California. After World War II, stock car racing was very popular in Honolulu. Ken and Masu Sakamoto ranked among the most favorite racers at the old Honolulu Stadium. Paul Yoshimura, Fred Kamai, George Akatsura,, and Clarence Moa also raced cars in post-World War II Honolulu. In the mid-1930s, Kazu Asazawa gained local fame as a motorcycle racer in the Sacramento. Asazawa, who also boxed as a flyweight, was provided with a bike by Frank Murray, manager of the Sacramento Speedways, for the athletes' debut as a rider.[98]

Asian Pacific American horse racing jockeys were relatively rare on the mainland until after World War II. However, on the Hawaiian Islands Kenji Ikeda was known as a "veteran Maui jockey" in 1940. And Paul Lau was one of Ikeda's rivals.[99]

In the mid-1950s, George Taniguchi surfaced as one of the better jockeys in the United States. In 1954, the man the *San Francisco Chronicle* described as "the 26 year old Nisei novice" was the leading rider at Golden Gate Fields near San Francisco. A wire story in December, 1954, announced that "Apprentice Jockey George Taniguchi" rode home five winners in one day and twelve winners in three days at Golden Gate Fields. The *Los Angeles Times'* Peter Petersen reported on Taniguchi in 1956 as he rode winning horses at the famous Santa Anita racetrack near Los Angeles. Depicted by Petersen as a "square jawed Japanese jockey," Taniguchi admitted that breaking into the ranks of professional jockeys was not easy. He quipped, "The market for Japanese was light." Taniguchi also recalled that the racing association had "told him to take a hike." He declared, "There has been fun poked at the horsemanship of the Japanese people. I want to show that with everything else equal we can do as well as the next person. It's meant something personal to me. It's helped me to keep going."[100]

Taniguchi also made his mark on the East Coast, although he unfortunately broke his collar bone on his first day as a jockey at Belmont Park. One of his biggest victories occurred in 1960 when he rode Papa's All to a victory at the Arlington Futurity. Taniguchi's career as a jockey lasted from 1954 to 1968. Then, he became a track steward.[101]

Since Taniguchi's debut, other jockeys of Japanese ancestry have done well. Ray Yaka and Mitchell Shirota joined Taniguchi at such horse racing venues as Golden Gate Fields and Bay Meadows. According to the *Nichi Bei Times*, Bay Area sportswriters would write about the "Japanese daily-double" when Yaka, Taniguchi, and Shirota won two or more races during the day. Thomas Nakagawa, John Kunitaki, Jason Iwai, and John Ishihara were notable Nisei jockeys as well. In the 1990s, Corey Nakatani ranks today among the better jockeys in the U.S.[102]

Asian Pacific Islanders are not generally viewed as rodeo riders or polo players. Still, Hawaiian Island ranches nurtured pariolos or Hawaiian cowboys. In the early decades of the twentieth century, Ikua Purdy became the king of the pariolas when he won a mainland rodeo champion in steer roping and tying. As for polo, the *Honolulu Star-Bulletin* reported in 1916 that Japanese Hawaiians on Maui were interested in organizing a polo team.[103]

Other Sports

American weight lifters of Asian Pacific American ancestry figured prominently in international competitions after World War II. During the 1948 Summer Olympics, the United States was represented by four weightlifters from Hawai'i. They were Richard Tomita, Richard Tom, Emerick Ishikawa, and Hal Sakata. Richard Tom was called Wah Sung Tom in a wire story, which declared that he had become an American Olympian by way of "Canton, China and Hawaii." Sakata, who won the national title in 1947, deserves some note. He earned a silver medal in the light heavy weight division. Later, he carved out something of a career performing as a professional wrestling villain. Sakata, subsequently, became famous as the cruel Odd Job in a James Bond movie during the 1960s.[104]

Born in Sacramento, Tommy Kono was perhaps pound for pound the greatest weight lifter of the 1950s. The son of cannery workers, Kono took up weight lifting as a teenager in a World War II internment camp. In 1952, Kono set two world records as a light weight in Copenhagen. Kono, however, needed to be weighed in the nude in order to qualify for the records. Officials who did not expect any records to fall failed to bring curtains designed to shield competitors while they were being weighed. Thus, officials formed a screen around the naked Kono as he weighed in. Called "the pocket Hercules," Kono won two gold medals in 1956 in weight lifting and in 1960 garnered a silver medal. According to journalist Pat Bighold, Kono turned down offers to perform in Mae West's Las Vegas Review in 1955, as well as roles in Japanese movies in order to keep his amateur standing. Instead, he earned money as an employee of California's Highway Department. By the end of his career, Kono had been nominated eight times for the prestigious Sullivan Award, broke twenty-two world records and six Olympic records, while standing out as the first and so far only person to hold records in four weight divisions.[105]

In 1961, Kono won a competition in Japan, prompting one mainland headline, "Kono Pleases His Ancestors." According to the AP wire story, "American muscleman Tommy Kono has fulfilled a family dream of setting a weightlifting mark in his ancestral homeland of Japan." Apparently, Kono's uncle from Hiroshima showed up to watch his nephew in action. Unfortunately, the uncle's attire of a kimono and clogs compelled the Imperial Hotel to withhold a room from him. Kono, subsequently, had to buy his uncle a business suit so that he could stay at the Imperial. The same wire story reported that coach Bob Hoffman declared that Kono's diet of seaweed and fish pastes helped keep the Japanese American weight lifter fit.[106]

After his active athletic career ended, Kono lived in Hawai'i, where he worked for the state department of Parks and Recreation as a physical fitness and sports section coordinator. Kono also found time to coach the first three .

women's national weight lifting teams. In 1987, the women's team took second place in the world championships. Kono admitted that he preferred coaching women, because they listened more than men.[107]

George Fujioka and Mits Oshima excelled as Asian Pacific American weight lifters in the 1950s. Hawaiian George Fujioka competed nationally for the featherweight crown in the 1950s. Mits Oshima was a training partner for Kono in the mid-1950s. Oshima was also a featherweight champion and record holder.[108]

Competing for the U.S. weightlifting team in the 1996 Olympics was Vietnamese American Thanh Nguyen. A three time, national champion by the mid-1990s, Nguyen explained to the *San Jose Mercury* the value of weight lifting competition to him: "The sport has given me the opportunity to grow and think about how you live out your life."[109]

While Tommy Kono, Sammy Lee, Vicki Manalo, and, to a lesser extent, Thanh Nguyen achieved Olympic stardom, the first Chinese American to represent the United States in the Olympics was Bob Chow, a U.S. pistol shooting champion. Chow was a member of the U.S. Olympics team in 1948. Indeed, Asian Pacific American men and women have excelled in shooting competitions. In 1954, Danny Wu competed in shooting for Cal. Two years later, Hawaiians Earl S. Iwata and John Kahoilua competed on a U.S. Army shooting team. Arleen Wong, a Stockton, California, police officer won many shooting ribbons in 1970. In the 1980s, a Hong Kong born, U.S. marine veteran, Sai Chiang, rated as one of the nation's best skeet shooters.[110]

Hunting and fishing clubs have long proven to be invaluable Asian Pacific American community organizations. In 1938, San Francisco's Chinese Americans had established the Chinese Sportsmen's Club for the community's lovers of hunting and fishing. San Jose's Japantown embraced a fishing club in 1941. In San Francisco, a Nisei Fishing Club operated in the late 1970s.[111]

A number of fine Asian Pacific American fencers have participated in local, national, and international competition. In 1936, Kimio Obata lettered as a fencer at Cal. In the early 1950s, Torao Mori fenced for the Los Angeles Athletic Club. Filipina American Josephine Regis fenced for San Francisco State in the early 1950s.. Japanese American brothers Roy, George, and Jon Nomomura won several national titles. San Francisco police officer Connie Louie was one of the top women fencers in the country in the early 1980s. In the mid-1980s, Elliot Chew was a top Stanford fencer. Jennifer Yu of California won the National Foils' championship in 1990. In 1996, Nhi Han Lee was a member of the U.S. Olympic team as a fencer. Peter Westerbrook, a hapa of African and Japanese American descent, was a top American male fencer in the late 1990s. In 2000, *Sports Illustrated* featured Lowell High School's Janet Ng for winning San Francisco's girls' foils title for the second straight time. Ng had to defeat teammate Christine Fong to win the championship. Possessing Taiwanese ancestry, Felicia and Iris Zimmerman represented the United States at the 2000 Summer Olympiad. Felicia and Iris, moreover, fenced for Stanford.[112]

Squash has engaged Asian Pacific American athletes. Chinese American, John Low, ranked as one of the best squash players in the U.S. The San Franciscan, according to the *Asian Week* in 1998, had won seventy-two titles in singles and doubles competition.[113]

The sport of billiards has attracted Asian Pacific American talent, energy, and time. In the 1930s, Kimrey Matsuyama won plenty of billiards matches in the United States. The *San Jose Mercury* called him the "diminutive Japanese cueman of New York." In 1936, "Jimmy Lee, Chinese player" became the Pacific Coast's Pocket Billiards champion. At this time, there are few, if any, better female billiards player in the world than the Korean American Jeanette Lee. A native of Brooklyn, New York, Lee has been ranked as the number one female billiards player for much of the last ten years.[114]

Journalist Paul Pratt describes Lee in *Asian Week* as "<a>n Asian beauty, dressed in a black, cleavage-baring spaghetti-strap lace top and matching slacks, devouring opponents with ease as she claims one championship after another." Lee has, according to Pratt, helped to feminize and glamorize the image of professional pool as white, working class, male, and unseemly. Lee apparently is not concerned about her image. She maintains, "There are a lot of women out there who feel you have to be overly tough in order to be respected...Men are allowed to be sexy. Michael Jordan is sexy, and that's OK. When a woman is sexy, it's, 'Oh, she's using sex to sell her sport.'" Commenting on Lee's "exotic looks and unparalleled skill" Pratt declares, " the Brooklyn-born Korean American not only changed the face of women's pool, quite literally, she revolutionized what was once considered very much a 'man's sport.'"[115]

Pratt credits Lee as something of a trailblazer for other women of Asian Pacific ancestry. Lee told him, "I was the only Asian when I came to the WPBA tour...I felt like it made me very special. It made me more recognizable. Everyone else was blonde, medium height, medium hair, you know, and here was this striking, long, black-haired Asian woman." Now, Lee believes, about 100 women of Asian ancestry are competing in professional billiards. Lee sees a transformation in the way women in sports are viewed, particularly in Asian Pacific communities. She asserts, "I see <the differences> way more these days, and not just with Asian Americans,"....I see it a lot when I'm traveling around the world. There are more women taking larger roles."[116]

Conclusion

In 1884, the *San Francisco Chronicle* published an article about a "group of Chinese <who> appropriate<d>a block of Powell to play a form of shuttlecock." According to the *Chronicle*, "The Chinese used their hands and feet to keep the corked object in the air. The object could hit the ground but once. If more the player who failed to strike it was out."[117]

Subsequent generations of Chinese and other Asian Pacific Americans have found joy and cultural citizenship in all sorts of physical exercise and competitive sports. The search has not always been easy. Bowling tournaments and tennis courts were often closed off to them. Many, because they needed to work and rest from their work, simply did not have the time for play or not enough money to buy even cheap golf clubs, tennis racquets, or bowling balls. Then there were others who were expected to watch the boys play.

Yet female athletes overcame expectations of what Asian Pacific American were expected to do by people inside and outside of their communities. Young women who grew up near San Francisco Chinatown's only playground in the 1930s often found playground supervisors encouraging them to engage in sports such as volleyball, basketball, and tennis. Helen Wong Lum, as we know, developed into one of the greatest athletes ever produced in San Francisco's Chinatown. After attending the College of Holy Names and USF, Wong Lum became a Physical Education instructor at Galileo and the College of Holy Names. Then she gained employment as the first Chinese American counselor at San Francisco City College, as well as a trustee for Chinese for Affirmative Action. Wong Lum did not seem to realize that she was too female and too Asian Pacific to overcome challenges and have fun through sports. [118]

Notes

1. Rick Reilly, *Sports Illustrated*, "Top Cat," January 18, 1997.

2. Karl Yamada' "Whose Triumph is Tiger Woods?" Channel A, October 2, 1996; Jeff Weinstock, "Get Smart," *Sport*, September 1997.

3. *Hawaiian Gazette*, March 21, 1899; *Pacific Commercial Advertiser*, June 15, 1912; *Honolulu Star-Bulletin*, December 15, 1917.

4. *San Francisco Examiner*, June 7, 1916.

5. Sakamaki, "Japanese Athletes," pp. 12-13; *San Francisco Chronicle*, May 2, 1923; *Daily Palo Alto*, January 10, 1923; August 18, 1925; *San Francisco Examiner*, May 3, 1936.

6. Chinn, *Bridging*, 271; *Mind and Body*, December, 1916; *Chinese Digest*, November 22, 1935.

7. *San Francisco Chronicle*, August 13, 1933; San *Francisco Examiner*, June 9, 1935.

8. *Honolulu Advertiser*, March 2, 1933; *Chinese Digest*, December 6, 1935; April 1939; *Honolulu Star-Bulletin*, June 4, 1951; *San Francisco Examiner*, June 29, 1961; East/West, September 30, 1981; Asian *Week*, August 11, 1983; *Chinese Press*, December 9, 1949.

9. *Honolulu Advertiser*, March 2, 1933; *Philippines Mail*, July 24, 1933; Catapusan, *Filipino Occupational*; Chinese *Digest*, May-June, 1939; *San Francisco Examiner*,

February 16, 1941; *San Jose Mercury,* May 8, 1942; *Fil-American Advocate, November 1952*; *Philippine News*, March 1-March 7, 1980.

10. *Manzanar Free Press*, August 13, 1944; *Pacific Citizen,* July 12, 1947; October 11, 1947; *Seattle Post-Intelligencer,* June 9, 1955; *Rafu Shimpo,* September 3, 1974; *Sports Illustrated*, September 4, 1978.

11. Chinn, *Bridging*, 271-272; *San Francisco Examiner*, June 3, 1937; *Chinese Press*, January 21, 1949; February 24, 1950. November 18, 1949.

12. *San Francisco Chronicle,* September 4, 1945; August 26, 1950; September 11, 1950; September 2, 1958; *New York Times,* May 2, 1955; *East/West*, September 11, 1968.

13. *East/West*, July 22, 1969; June 10, 1981; June 30, 1982; May 18, 1983; August 29, 1984; January 16, 1985; *Sports Illustrated*, October 16, 1978; Chinn, *Bridging*, 271-272.

14. Dave Higdon, "Good Old Days," *Tennis*, April 1997. Bill Wong, "Marlboro Man: Michael Chang's Smoky Image," *Asian Week*, May 30-June 4, 1997; *Tennis*, January, 1997.

15. Chinn, *Bridging*, 182; Philana Wu, "Girl Got Game," www.asianweek, January 5-January 11, 2001.

16. *Filipinas*, February, 1999; "New APA Talent Wows Tennis, Skating Worlds," www.asianweek.com, February 24, 1999.

17. Shankar Chadhuri, "East Indians," Ethnic Encyclopedia, 36-37; Stanford vs. San Jose State Football Program, Stanford Stadium, September 30, 1996; Sports Illustrated, June 12, 2000; www.gostanford.com, accessed April 26, 2005.

18. www.fansonly.com/school/lou, accessed July 9, 2005.

19. *San Francisco Examiner*, June 4, 1937; East/West, June 18, 1969; September 23, 1981; C. Richard King, *Native Americans in Sports* vol. 2 Sharpe Reference, Armonk NY, 2004,)262.

20. *San Jose Mercury*, September 29, 2000; November 15, 2000.

21. Catapusan, *Filipino Occupational*, 39; Ethen Leiser, "The Chinese Mystique," *Asian Week*, November 2-November 8, 2001.

22. *San Francisco Chronicle*, September 5, 1924; Loui Leong Hop, "Chinese Contributions," 104.

23. Charles "Chick" Evans, "The Oahu Country Club," *American Golfer*, (August, September, 1916).

24. *San Francisco Chronicle*, June 11, 1928; April 9, 1932; *San Jose Mercury*, January 10, 1932; *Chinese Digest*, November 15, 1935.

25. Washington Post, August 22, 1915; *Honolulu Advertiser*, January 4, 1923; *Sacramento Bee*, September 9, 1933; Mears, *Resident*, 361; Strong, *Second Generation*, 24.

26. *Manzanar Free Press*, July 19, 1944; *San Jose Mercury*, August 12, 1947; *Pacific Citizen*, August 16, 1947; August 23, 1947; March 24, 1950; *Honolulu Star-Bulletin*, May 11, 1951; *Fil-America Advocate*, June 15, 1953.

27. *Fil-America Advocate*, April 1, 1953; August 1, 1952.

28. U.S. Census Manuscripts, City and County of Honolulu, 1930; Paul Gardner, "Jackie Pung's Ordeal," *Sport*, February, 1958.

29. *Los Angeles Times*, January 4, 1953; March 8, 1955.

30. *Ibid.*, January 7, 1953; Cindy Luis, "One 'Bad Hole' Hasn't Spoiled Pung's Round," *Honolulu Star-Bulletin*, September 14, 1998; *Sports Illustrated*, July 7, 1958.

31. *Los Angeles Times*, January 7, 1953.

32. Gardner, "Jackie Pung's Ordeal," 38-39.

33. *Ibid.*

34. Luis, "One 'Bad Hole'"; *Honolulu Star-Bulletin*, December 2, 2001.

35. *Honolulu Advertiser*, January 31, 1950; *San Francisco Examiner*, January 10. 1949; *Los Angeles Times*, January 4, 1953.

36. *USGA Journal and Turf Management*, February, 1959.

37. *San Francisco Chronicle*, July 25, 1957.

38. *Asian Week*, August 20, 1998, p. 11; *Sports Illustrated*, July 13, 1998; Stacy Lovilla, "Par for the Course: A Winning Asian Presence," *Asian Week*, July 9, 1998; Esther Misa Chavez, "In the Swing of Things," *Filipinas*, September, 1997.

39. Rodel Rodis, " Dorothy Delasin's Birthday Gift," *Asian Week*, August 25- August 31, 2000.

40. *Ibid*; *San Jose Mercury*, August 3, 2000.

41. *Sports Illustrated*, August 12, 2000; Jaymes Song, "Michelle Wie Challenges Hawaii's Top Males, www.asianweek.com, June 15,2001-June 21, 2001.

42. "Thirteen-year-old Michelle Wie in Pearl Finals," *Asian Week*, February 14- February 20,2003; www.goldsea.com., accessed June 29, 2005.

43. *Asian Week*, October 17, 1996-October 23, 1996.

44. *Sport*, November, 1998.

45. www.asianweek.com, February 18, 2005.

46. *Los Angeles Times*, January 24, 1989; *Sports Illustrated*, December 23, 1991; Stanford vs. USC, Football Program, Stanford Stadium, October 15, 1994; www.gostanford.com, accessed May 11, 2000; www.usfcons.com, accessed January 17, 2001.

47. *Sacramento Bee,* April 1, 1957; December 20, 1958; *East/West*, January 3, 1968; July 17, 1968; May 21, 1969, *Philippine News*, October 16, 1974; "Ethen Lieser, "Golf Courses," *Asian Week*, September 7-September 13, 2000.

48. *San Jose Mercury*, March 29, 1902.

49. *Honolulu Star-Bulletin*, May 5, 1915; May 25, 1915; January 25, 1917, *Pacific Commercial Advertiser*, October 21, 1917.

50. *Chinese Digest*, February 1938; Chinese *Press*, November 24, 1950.

51. *San Francisco Chronicle*, February 15, 1946; *Pacific Citizen,* November 1, 1947.

52. *Pacific Citizen*, November 29, 1947.

53. *Ibid.*, November 1, 1947.

54. *Ibid.,* January 21, 1950; *Honolulu Star-Bulletin*, January 1, 1949.

55. *Utah Nippo*, February 24, 1950; *Pacific Citizen*, March 4, 1950.

56. *Pacific Citizen*, January 28, 1950.

57. *San Jose Mercury,* March 15, 1950; March 4, 1964; *Utah Nippo*, May 17, 1950; *Chinese Press*, May 19, 1950; July 14, 1950; www. alohafame.com., accessed February 23, 1998.

58. *San Jose Mercury*, July 26, 1953; May 18, 1954; February 16, 1960; *Pacific Citizen,* October 11, 1947; October 24, 1947; November 1, 1947; December 17, 1949; *January* 7, 1950; February 8, 1950; February 25, 1950; March 4, 1950; *Seattle Post-*

Intelligencer, March 9, 1955; April 15, 1955; San *Francisco Chronicle,* September 2, 1955; January 21, 1956; January 22, 1956; January 23, 1956; *Los Angeles Times,* January 15, 1964; *Honolulu Advertiser,* April 4, 1964; *Rafu Shimpo,* September 6, 1974.

59. *Pacific Citizen,* July 12, 1947; November 1, 1947; February 18, 1950; February 25, 1950; *Fil-America Advocate,* January 15, 1953; *San Francisco Chronicle,* March 9, 1953; June 25, 1959; January 22, 1962; *East/West,* May 8, 1968; *Philippine News,* May 28, 1975.

60. *Pacific Commercial Advertiser,* March 19, 1915; Carioga, *Filipino.* 89; *Philippine Mail,* September 25, 1933; October 30, 1933; *Honolulu Advertiser,* March 7, 1935; Michi Kodama-Nishimoto, Michi, et. al. *Hanahana: An Oral History Anthology of Hawaii,* (Ethnic Studies Oral History Project, University of Hawaii, Manao, 1984), 124; Velasco, 106; Dean Chatwin, *Wahine Ball: The Story of Hawai'i's Most Beloved Team,* (Honolulu, HI: Mutual Publishing, 1997), 4.

61. www. naicvt.fromthe. net, accessed March 12, 1998.

62. Ibid; *East/West,* September 5, 1984.

63. Allison Lee, "Chinese American Volleyball Tournament Comes to San Francisco," *Asian Week,* September 13-September 19, 2002.

64. Regalado, "Incarcerated," 436; *East/West,* January 28, 1981;

65. Chadwin, *Wahine,* 5.

66. *Spartan Daily,* February 26, 1976; *Hokubei Mainichi,* December 13, 1977; www.alohafame.com; www.volleyball.org; *Volleyball Monthly,* May, 1991; March, 1993; December, 1999; *Asian Week,* December 11, 1992.

67. www. hawaii.edu, accessed May 7, 1998; Chadwin, *Wahine,* 5.

68. *Volleyball Monthly,* November, 1996; www.starbulletin.com, September 3, 1999; UW website; www.uclabruins.com, accessed November 24, 2002; Chadwin, *Wahine,* 39; Stanford vs. University of California, Volleyball Program, Maples Pavilion, Stanford University, October 9, 1998; www.goldsea.com, accessed June 29, 2005; *Asian Week,* December 21, 2001-December 27, 2001.

69. *Volleyball Monthly,* November ,1996; *Asian Week,* September 14, 2000-September 20, 2000; *San Jose Mercury,* September 10, 2000; www.starbulletin.com, August 21, 2001.

70. Ethen Leiser, "The Spikes and the Kills of a Purple People Eater," *Asian Week,* November 8, 2001-November 15, 2001.

71.*Sports Illustrated,* February 4, 1963; January 11, 1965; *East/West,* January 20, 1968.

72. *Philippine News,* February 23, 1980-February 29, 1980; March 15, 1980-March 21, 1980; *San Jose Mercury,* April 4, 1998; *Filipinas,* January, 2000;

73. *East/West,* June 20, 1984, p. 3; www. kan.org, accessed October 6, 1997.

74. *San Jose Mercury,* April 4, 1998; Emil Guillermo, "She's Our Kwan," *Asian Week,* February 22, 2002-February 28, 2002.

75. www.asianweek.com, February 24, 1999; February 4, 2005.

76. Carol Williams-Dahlgren, Interview with Richard Park, www.phantoms @all-sports.com, accessed July 9, 2005.

77. Ibid.

78. www.asianweek.com, May 4, 2000.

79. *Asian Week,* December 21, 2001-December 27, 2001; S.L. Price, "Launch of Apollo Ohno," *Sports Illustrated,* February 4, 2002.

80. Jody Meacham, "Life after Gold," *San Jose Mercury*, November 13, 1996

81. *San Jose Mercury*, March 12, 1964; Jody Meacham, "Life after Gold, November 13, 1996; *Nichi Bei Times*, January 1, 1973; *Spartan Daily*, February 24, 1976; Stanford vs. Washington State, Football Program, November 14, 1992; *Asian Week*, November 20, 1997; Janet Dang, "A Graceful Coach," *Asian Week*, September 17-September 23, 1998.

82. *Sacramento Bee*, June 25, 1880; *San Francisco Chronicle*, June 28, 1880.

83. *Pacific Commercial Advertiser*, January 15, 1911; December 16, 1911.

84. Kaulukukui, *Development*, 24.

85. Everington, "Buck Lai;" *Pacific Commercial Advertiser*, January 22, 1912; March 15, 1912.

86. *Pacific Commercial Advertiser*, February 16, 1912.

87. *Honolulu Star-Bulletin*, February 25, 1913; February 28, 1913.

88. *Hawaiian Gazette*, January 22, 1897; *Pacific Commercial Advertiser*, December 4, 1911; December 7, 1911; March 8, 1914; March 15, 1914; November 22, 1916; *Honolulu Star-Bulletin*, March 3, 1913; March 5, 1913; June 3, 1915; September 22, 1915; *Washington Post*, January 31, 1915; *Chicago Daily Tribune*, January 25, 1912.

89. *Reno Evening Gazette*, March 29, 1922; *Elyria Evening Telegram*, April 25, 1924; *Chicago Daily Tribune*, February 8, 1925; Smith, *Americans in Process*, 246.

90. Chinn, *Bridging*, 116-117; *San Francisco Examiner*, May 11, 1936.

91. *San Francisco Evening Post*, October 4, 1912; *San Jose Mercury*, May 3, 1922; *San Francisco Chronicle*, January 20, 1930; April 9, 1932.

92. *San Francisco Chronicle*, March 24, 1935; *Los Angeles Times*, March 20, 1938; March 15, 1935; *San Francisco Examiner*, March 5, 1941.

93. *Chicago Daily Tribune*, May 8, 1944; *Pacific Citizen*, August 16, 1947; February 18, 1950; March 4, 1950; *Los Angeles Times*, March 10, 1955; *Honolulu Star-Bulletin*, May 9, 1956; Pamela Cooper, *American Marathon*, (Syracuse: Syracuse University Press, 1998), 110;

94.. *East/West, August 28, 1968*; May 9, 1979; April 13, 1983; *Los Angeles Times*, April 23, 1972; *Nichi Bei Times*, September 10, 1972; *Rafu Shimpo*, March 29, 1972; August 28, 1972; Asian Week, May 20-May 26, 1997; September 14, 2000-September 20, 2000; *San Francisco Chronicle*, November 6, 1998; Zia and and Falls, *Notable Asian Americans*, 28.

95. Tim Layden, "While You Weren't Watching," *Sports Illustrated*, August 22, 2005.

96. East/West, February 11, 1981; April 29, 1981.

97. *Los Angeles Evening Express*, April 6, 1895; *Honolulu Star-Bulletin*, February 23, 1915; *September 3, 1940*.

98. *Los Angeles Times*, January 15, 1915; Suehiro, *Honolulu Stadium*, 124; *Sacramento Bee*, June 10, 1935; *Honolulu Star-Bulletin*, May 5, 1956.

99. *Honolulu Star-Bulletin*, September 3, 1940.

100. *Indiana Evening Gazette*, December 10, 1954; *Los Angeles Times*, January 8, 1956; *San Francisco Chronicle*, December 8, 1954.

101. *Seattle Post and Intelligencer*, April 22, 1955; *Nevada State Journal*, July 31, 1955; *Nichi Bei Times*, January 1, 1973.

102. *San Francisco Examiner*, September 22, 1963; *Nichi Bei Times*, September 15, 1972; January 1, 1973.

103. www.alohafame.com, accessed June 7, 1998; *Honolulu Star-Bulletin*, December 19, 1916.

104. *Pacific Citizen*, August 16, 1947; *Bridgeport Sunday Post*, August 15, 1948; *Honolulu Star Bulletin*, August 31, 1948.

105. Franklin Ng, ed. *The Asian American Encyclopedia*. (Toronto, Marchall Cavendish, 1995); www.alohafame.com; *Washington Post*, October 14, 1952; *Los Angeles Times*, December 3, 1961; *Honolulu Star-Bulletin*, September 30, 2000.

106. *San Francisco Examiner*, June 19, 1961.

107. *Honolulu Star-Bulletin*, September 30, 2000.

108. *Ibid.*, June 9, 1951; *San Jose Mercury*, February 5, 1955.

109. *San Jose Mercury, The West Magazine*, July 14, 1996.

110. *Chinese Press*, January 28, 1949; *Coshocton Tribune*, August 31, 1956; *The Asian Student*, January 15, 1961; *East/West*, February 4, 1970; March 18, 1981; September 23, 1981; *Asian Week*, July 19-July 24, 1996; March 26, 1998-April 1, 1998, p. 8.

111. *Chinese Digest*, December 13, 1938; New World Sun 1941; *Hokubei Mainichi*, December 7, 1977.

112. *San Francisco Examiner*, May 3, 1936; May 20, 1951; *Fil-American Advocate*, June 1, 1953; *Nichi Bei Times*, January 1, 1973; East/West, March 18, 1981; Stanford vs. Arizona, Stanford Stadium, October 26, 1985; *Asian Week*, July 19. 1996-July 24, 1996; May 20-May 27, 1997; *Sports Illustrated*, July 24, 2000; San Jose Mercury, September 10, 2000; www.gostanford.com, accessed April 25, 2005; Andrew Shaw and George B. Kirsch, "Fencing," *Ethnic Encyclopedia*, 153.

113. *San Francisco Examiner*, June 4, 1937; *East/West*, June 18, 1969; Asian Week, July 19-July 25, 1996; 1998.

114. San Jose *Mercury*, January 12, 1934; *San Francisco Chronicle*, March 22, 1936; www.jeanetlee.com, accessed May 18, 1998.

115. Paul Pratt, "'Black Widow' Changes Face of Pro Billiards," www.asianweek.com, June 17, 2005.

116. *Ibid.*

117. San Francisco *Chronicle*, January 22, 1884.

118. *East/West*. January 12, 1983.

Chapter Eight: Asian Pacific American Sporting Experiences in a Comparative Perspective

Asian Pacific American sporting experiences share a great deal with those of other historically aggrieved racial and ethnic groups in the United States and around the world. To be sure, glaring differences exist among these groups. Yet the people in these groups have discovered that sports can both aid and hinder their efforts to defy stereotypes and assert cultural citizenship in their varied communities and nations.

"Invented Communities"

Through sports, Asian Pacific Americans have reinforced a sense of community in the face of racism and ethnocentrism. Moreover, perhaps sports have assisted the development of ethnic identities among Asian Pacific people living in America. One can see something like this occurring in the twentieth century among Filipino immigrants living and working on the American West Coast and Hawai'i. In the 1920s and into the 1930s, the people performing migrant labor or domestic labor services on the American West Coast were generally Filipino, when they were not Mexican. Very commonly these people were told that they were, at best, fit to serve European Americans. However, many prize fighting promoters discovered as well that Filipino immigrants were avid boxing fans and were, in particular, followers of Filipino boxers brought into the United States to challenge various American opponents. Numerous Pinoy boxers beat European Americans and non-European Americans with regularity and furnished a source of communal pride among marginalized and exploited Filipino workers, who came from different regions of Philippines and often asserted relatively little sense of Filipino nationality. Perhaps by following sports, Filipino immigrant boxing fans had been lured into trivial and potentially unhealthy diversions from political struggles against racism, colonialism, and exploitation. But scholars such as Benedict Anderson and C.L.R. James suggest more complicated ways to look at the relationship between sports and community empowerment. In so doing, they also suggest why Asian Pacific American sporting experiences connect to those of other aggrieved racial and ethnic groups in the United States and other societies. [1]

If political theorist Benedict Anderson is correct, nations are "imagined communities" and nationalism is the effort to build and sustain a sense of community among people who have little chance of seeing each other face to face. Sports have played an often underestimated role in nurturing "imagined communities" among exploited and colonized people of color. Historian and politi-

cal activist C.L.R. James chronicled the relationship between colonialism, nationality, race, and sport in his classic *Beyond a Boundary*; a book about cricket,
but as James reminded us constantly, it is much more than that. A Marxist, pan-
Africanist, and remarkably versatile scholar, James played and followed cricket
since his boyhood days in the predominantly black colony of Trinidad. His
Beyond a Boundary forcefully breaks down the stereotype of cricket as strictly
an elitist, white Englishman's sport. Indeed, the English colonizers brought their
love of cricket to the West Indies. They sought to use cricket as a way to Anglic-
ize as much as they thought possible the wealthier black West Indians. However,
even if cricket was intended as a helpmate for British colonialism, black West
Indians found in cricket multiple possibilities--some of which perhaps troubled
their colonizers.[2]

James and many of his fellow black cricket players honored the ethos of
fair play underlying cricket even if English colonizers nurtured that ethos. However, by playing well against whites and doing so within the framework developed by English Victorians, black West Indian cricket players maintained a
sense of pride in themselves and in their own way helped construct a bridge
connecting people of color throughout the British empire—a bridge which
linked the anti-colonial struggles of West Indian people to those of the equally
cricket loving East Indian people.[3]

From the playground and sandlot to the professional arena, sports can aid
the formation of racial and ethnic identities and communities. The famous stars
and teams often reflected and reinforced racial and ethnic pride, but so might the
lesser-known local athletes such as Willie Wong and the neighborhood teams
such as the San Francisco Chinese Saints. Ethnic community leaders, moreover,
often considered sports as important in resolving social problems disrupting
their communities.

Prominent Chinese and Japanese Americans frequently encouraged the
creation of athletic teams for both sexes. In the 1930s and 1940s, San Francisco's Chinatown avidly supported Chinese American basketball tournaments,
while West Coast Japanese Americans just as avidly backed community baseball
teams. An overwhelming need to assimilate into European American culture did
not seem to have been at work. Asian Pacific American communities in the
1930s and 1940s, like ethnic communities elsewhere, were sites of highly visible
poverty and criminal activities. To divert young people from gambling, street
gangs and substance abuse, organizations such as the Young Men's Buddhist
Association and the Young Women's Buddhist Association, accordingly sponsored the formation of baseball, basketball, softball, and football teams among
Americans of Japanese ancestry.

By the same token, Asian Pacific Americans did not necessarily savor the
isolation many must have felt from other Americans. Sports could, it was hoped,
help break down the barriers separating Asian Pacific American ethnic groups

from other racial and ethnic groups. The sustenance of Asian Pacific enthusiasm for sports, therefore, seems more explicable in terms of the concept of cultural citizenship rather than assimilation. The Asian Pacific American love of sports could also cut across class lines and embrace an offspring of relative affluence such as Michael Chang, but also bring solace and joy to exploited people of color such as the Filipino migrant workers laboring in Alaska and Hawai'i during the early 1930s. In *America is in the Heart*, Carlos Bulosan wrote a lyrical passage describing the freedom those workers experienced in playing baseball after work—when "trembling shadows began to form on the rise of the brilliant snow in our yard, and we would come out with baseball bats, gloves, and balls, and the Indian girls who worked in the cannery would join us, shouting huskily like men." Whether playing pool or an informal game of baseball or volleyball, Filipino workers constructed social spaces free, for a moment, from their work and their bosses.[4]

Community sporting practices have often been relatively accessible to female participation. Women of Asian Pacific ancestry have had to struggle against the stereotype of them as physically, intellectually, and emotionally passive. However, in numerous Asian Pacific American communities women eagerly played basketball and softball, as well as other sports. Remember that one of the best known amateur athletes in post-World War II San Francisco was Helen Wong, who excelled in both basketball and tennis.

"Star" athletes have seemingly reinforced community ties between members of racial and ethnic groups. Jackie Robinson and black heavyweight champion prizefighter Joe Louis glittered as visible symbols of many African American aspirations during the first half of the twentieth century. They demonstrated the kind of courage and dignity European Americans so often blindly ignored in the African American experience. While doing so, Robinson and Louis time and time again outperformed whites.

Renowned Asian Pacific athletes, therefore, have frequently become ethnic symbols. Filipino boxers such as Pancho Villa expressed and reinforced communal pride among the Pinoys during the early 1920s. Similarly, today many people of Asian Pacific ancestry have found special joy in the achievements of Tiger Woods, Jeanette Lee, and Michelle Kwan.[5]

Transcending Community

Of course, at present, we are used to the notion that the "superstars" of sport transcend community boundaries. We are also becoming used to the notion that many of our sports' idols might claim a different racial and ethnic identity than our own, while getting paid an obscene amount of money for playing games and advertising athletic shoes or breakfast cereals. Few can argue that sports have allowed a few black athletes such as basketball star Michael Jordan and former soccer star Pele to seemingly traverse racial barriers and become enormously admired and enormously wealthy. In the past and in the present, other athletes associated with aggrieved racial and ethnic groups have crossed cultural boundaries to become universally respected and frequently well paid. Prizefighters John L. Sullivan and Muhammad Ali could claim followings beyond Irish America and African America respectively. German American baseball star Honus Wagner was not just an idol to German Americans. And when Mexican Fernando Valenzuela pitched for the Los Angeles Dodgers more than Mexican and Mexican Americans rooted for him.

In the late 1900s, we began to see a number of American athletes identified as Asian Pacific gain stardom and transcend specific racial and ethnic communities. Tiger Woods comes to mind, because, in part he possesses no singular racial and ethnic identity. Yet, any number of athletes of Asian Pacific ancestry such as Junior Seau, Kristi Yamaguchi, Michael Chang, Jeanette Lee, Greg Louganis and Michelle Kwan can claim a spot among the best ever in their sports and followings that cross racial and ethnic lines.

However famous as well as wealthy many of these athletes have become, we should remember that some of the more moving stories in sports history revolves around the efforts of highly gifted amateur and professional athletes to endure and even contest racial and ethnic hierarchies. The German Jewish athletes who were denied places on Hitler's Olympic team come to mind. Of course, Jackie Robinson's experience is well known. Lesser known is the courage of another baseball standout, Henry Aaron, who faced down unspeakable racism as he chased and moved ahead of Babe Ruth's home run record. Lesser known still are struggles against racial discrimination waged by "Kid Lapulapu," Sammy Lee, Vicki Manalo, the Hong Wah Que basketball team, and a number of post-World War II Asian Pacific American bowlers.

That all sorts of people also cheered such struggles on is a reminder that star athletes might provide something of a common ground for people of different racial and ethnic groups. But even for lesser-known athletes, sports can span otherwise powerful racial and ethnic chasms. Athletic teams organized in the Hawaiian Islands have historically been more multi-ethnic and multi-racial than in other regions in the American empire. One can look at the all too unique rosters of Hawaiian football, basketball, and baseball teams in the 1920s, 1930s, and 1940s and note the Asian, Pacific Islander, Hispanic, Portuguese, and Anglo last names. Leading Hawaiian athletes such as Lang Akana and Herman Wedemeyer, moreover, possessed hybrid racial and ethnic backgrounds. Interestingly, as one scholar in the 1920s noted, Hawaiian society seemed relatively unconcerned when famous Chinese Hawaiian athletes such as Buck Lai Tin and Tin Luke Wongwai married European American women. Hawai'i, indeed, was arguably well ahead of the American mainland in using sports to enhance the cultural citizenship of the people represented by highly skilled athletes of Pacific Islander, Asian Pacific, and mixed ancestries.[5]

Sports, therefore, have permitted significant numbers of people of diverse Asian Pacific and non-Asian Pacific racial and ethnic groups to overcome racialized and ethnocentric assumptions developed about them. In many cases, sports have even helped link them as an "imagined community" prepared to battle racism, nativism, and colonialism. Sports have afforded opportunities for some Asian Pacific and non-Asian Pacific people to make money and achieve honors. They have given everyone of us wonderful stories of courageous struggles against bigotry and discrimination. However, if through sports, Asian Pacifc and non-Asian Pacific people have trekked across socially constructed boundaries to assert their cultural citizenship, then we should note that some people seem freer to move across those boundaries than others. Sadly, sports retain border guards, discouraging movement for some, while encouraging movement for others.

Sport and the Border Guard

In the United States, the sporting and recreational practices of immigrants and children of immigrants, Asian Pacific and otherwise, often provoked racist and nativistic responses. As industrial capitalism took root in the nineteenth century, immigrants were often seen as too inclined to patronize such "disreputable" activities as prize fights, dog fights, and, in the case of the Chinese, gambling halls and opium dens. Of course, class issues intertwined with the development of industrial capitalism to weigh heavily here--especially when it came to Sunday sporting and recreational practices, as well as the enforcement of vice laws. America's native born white Protestant elite clung tenaciously to the notion that Sunday Laws and vice laws would control ethnic workers. Its industrial capitalists often viewed Sunday Laws and vice laws favorably, because such laws supposedly bolstered a rested and sober work force, ready for fifty to sixty hours of labor from Monday through Saturday.

Into the twentieth century, people identified with varied racial and ethnic groups have been stereotyped as more interested in play than in work. Filipino immigrants, for example, while working incredibly hard to profit their California and Hawaiian employers were often labeled as incurably and excessively fond of partying, womanizing, cockfights, and prizefights. Often such stereotyping turned clearly racist, because it connected a person's interests with some kind of innate predisposition.

Today, people of African ancestry have to battle stereotypes of them as inherently talented in sports requiring speed and jumping ability. The battle, of course, is frequently joined by people of other racial affiliations and not made easier by some people of African ancestry who insist upon their natural superiority in sports such as basketball and track. Meanwhile, people of Asian Pacific ancestry have not typically experienced stereotypes acknowledging they possess unique natural athletic dispositions.

At one time, Asian Pacific people were lumped with other people of color as naturally inferior in most athletic skills. The early supporters of athletic competition in Europe and North America generally expressed little doubt that whites were more innately gifted athletes than non-whites and that some European-based groups were racially superior to Jews and other non-Nordic peoples. Indeed, for many, athletic competition revealed the truths advanced by Social Darwinists--that races existed and some races were fitter than others. Athletic competition, according to these racial ideologues, demanded intelligence, discipline, and "pluck," as well as coordination, speed, and strength. Non-whites might retain the latter two characteristics, but when it came to intelligence, discipline, and courage, they were lacking. Around the turn-of-the-twentieth century, almost lily white rugby and American football squads seemed to prove that time and time again to white supremacists.

Therefore, sports guided countless hands in drawing the color line in the United States and it helped rationalize European and U.S. imperialism in Asia, the Pacific, and elsewhere. To the extent that people of color displayed some ability to compete athletically, they were simply showing that they were "white inside" or, at least, making the effort to become white. The dominant racial ideology was scarcely disturbed at all. At the same time, some Europeans and European Americans who regarded people of color as not totally bound by their natures also considered sport as a civilizing tool. If East or West Indians learned cricket then those "natives" advanced one step closer to Western Civilization, while, hopefully, gaining new respect for their colonizers. In the Philippines during the early twentieth century, baseball was employed to "Americanize" Filipinos, a significant portion of whom had fought a protracted guerrilla war against U.S. rule. A.G. Spalding, moreover, praised the Japanese penchant for baseball, because it showed their admiration for cultural qualities esteemed by white Americans.

Within the United States, sports assumed a highly visible position in sustaining a racial hierarchy. Major League baseball and other professional baseball organizations affiliated with it barred African Americans from team rosters in the 1880s and backed "Jim Crow" until after World War II. While prominent as jockeys for many years, African Americans learned that by the twentieth century commercial horse racing had drawn the color line as well. Occasionally, during the late nineteenth century and early twentieth century blacks such as Paul Robeson might perform well for college football teams and some African American boxers were prominent. However, as Jeffrey Sammons points out, African American prizefighters faced substantial challenges in crossing the color line. Since prizefighting had been characterized by some as a true test of skill, courage, intelligence, and manhood, boxing champions stood as symbols of national and racial superiority. Consequently, black challengers to white American champions were widely perceived as threats to white and national superiority. If football was "the expression of the strength of the Anglo-Saxon...the dominant spirit of the dominant race," then boxing reduced this expression to individual terms.[6]

Significantly, black heavyweight champions such as Jack Johnson and Muhammad Ali signified an unapologetic awareness that they challenged white supremacy. Johnson, in particular, aroused white resentment and quests for "white hopes" to unseat him from his heavyweight throne during the 1900s and 1910s.

Non-black athletes of color have also faced discriminatory treatment in the world of sport. Some athletes of indigenous, Latin American ancestry, as well as Asian Pacific ancestry have reached the higher echelons of competitive sports. However, for decades, a racial ideology proclaimed all people of color as lacking the characteristics of true sporting champions. At the dawn of the twentieth century, American sportswriters expressed some surprise that prizefighter Ah Wing could manage adeptly in the boxing ring. He was associated with a racial and ethnic group whose members were perceived as generally lacking the white man's fortitude.

Recreational sports have illustrated too readily racial and ethnic hierarchies as well. Swimming pools and other recreational facilities were habitually cordoned off to Asian Pacific people as well as other Americans of color for decades. Moreover, Pasadena health officials ordered the Brookside Pool drained after "International Day"--the one day in the week in which young people like Sammy Lee or Jackie Robinson could use the pool.

In recent decades, the relationship between racial ideology and sport has been modified. The success of athletes of color in many competitive sports has, of course, weakened the argument that people of European ancestry are athletically superior. Instead, many of those involved in sports in one form or another argue that people of African ancestry harbor natural abilities which make them particularly proficient in sports that require a great deal of running and jumping; stereotypically basketball. On the other hand, it has also been claimed that people of African ancestry possess a natural tendency to fail at competitive water sports, as well as any sporting activity that requires intelligence, courage and endurance.

Whether supposedly complimentary or not and whether people of African ancestry internalize these assumptions about their athletic capabilities or not, it seems clear that sports remain a powerful racializing tool. In other words, historically and today sports can ascribe to a group of people certain characteristics that they presumably cannot change. Despite the evidence furnished by substantial numbers of physical anthropologists, sports continue to prove to some of us that race contains irrefutable scientific validity.

Asian Pacific people encounter racialization through sports. Most of us generally acknowledge that the lack of physical size possessed by significant numbers of Asian Pacific people diminish their inherent ability to excel in sports outside of ice skating, gymnastics, as well as perhaps golf and tennis. Does, however, the tendency on the part of some people of Asian Pacific ancestry to be smaller than people of European or African ancestries relate to racial or other factors?

One's height and weight is significantly determined by a combination of inherited and cultural factors. Diets low in calcium and carbohydrates will apparently limit size. For centuries, many Asian societies largely adopted such diets. As linebacker Dat Nguyen exemplifies, however, a modification in diet, as well as appropriate exercise, can alter the physique of a person of Asian ancestry. We also know that while some people of Asian ancestry have tended to be smaller than other people, they can display a variety of physical shapes and sizes. After all, how else can we explain Yao Ming?

Among the most interesting recent efforts to racialize Asian Pacific people in the arena of sports are those undertaken by leaders of China's athletic organizations. Scholar John Hoberman notes that Chinese officials have expressed concern about the ability of Chinese athletes to compete internationally. One official, Professor Tian Maiju, has argued that the racial composition of Asians makes it difficult for them to compete with people of African ancestry in several sports. Maiju, who has served as Vice-President of the Beijing Institution of Physical Education, declares that sprinting ability correlates with blood type and body type. Maiju writes:

> Seventy to 90 percent of blacks but only 30 percent of Asians, <Maiju> claims have blood type O and 'O-type people get excited every easily and that is why they make very good sprinters." In addition, 'black people have very good genetics. Compared with them, the people in Asia are very inferior. The buttocks the blacks have in very high position, the whites, a little bit lower. The Asians, even lower. Because of that muscles < in blacks> are longer, <and have> more power. That forms a very good lever.[7]

Thus while the scientific evidence for the racial categorization of people often seems flimsy at best, and ludicrous, at worst, sports have abetted racial formation. The consequences for people of African ancestry have been mixed despite the fact that numerous athletes of color have achieved fame and fortune. As sociologist Harry Edwards has long pointed out, the stereotype of blacks as naturally inclined toward athletics has more than likely persuaded too many African American youth from seeking careers more realistic than those of pro fessional athletics and more beneficial, in the long run, to themselves, their families, and communities. Just as seriously, the stereotype has often persuaded non-African Americans that if blacks are so naturally gifted athletically, then they are probably good for little else.[8]

Sadly, according to *Asian Week* journalist Brian Liou in 1999, too many Asian Pacific Americans agree with the stereotype shadowing African American athletic achievements. Liou complained that Asian Pacific American youth seeking to advance up the basketball hierarchy toward high school ball and beyond have often been diverted by parents lauding the inherent ability of African Americans to succeed at the sport. Liou wrote, "Parents immediately associate the African American majority within the NBA as both an indication that only blacks can dominate the sport and an affirmation that Asian Americans simply do not possess the athletic gift to succeed. Within our parents' eyes, we simply don't belong. Essentially, Asian American parents just prefer the security from a computer-fixing son than a hopeless, ball-hogging jock."[9]

The stereotype of Asian Pacific people as handier with computers than a ball is more likely less harmful, but, nevertheless, worth disputing. Moreover, this stereotype connects with the controversial Model Minority Thesis, which deserves mention at this time. Originating around 1965, the Model Minority Thesis has proven a useful weapon against social movements of people of color--social movements aimed at significantly changing the U.S.'s political and economic system. Forty years since its inception, the Model Minority Thesis still serves well in the battle against affirmative action and welfare programs, as well as efforts to politically empower low-income Americans.[10]

The essence of the Model Minority Thesis is that Asian Pacific Americans, especially those of South and East Asian origins, have made it in America despite the fact that they are non-whites, have often faced discrimination in the past, and, when immigrants, came to the America with little or no material capital. They have succeeded, the thesis proceeds, without the benefit of affirmative action or government welfare. Accordingly, if they can do it, so can African Americans, Latinos, American Indians, and those few, dysfunctional, and ungrateful Asian Pacific Islander people who continue to complain about unfair treatment.[11]

How have Asian Pacific people made it, according to the Model Minority Thesis? They have valued work above all else, except, perhaps, family. As young people, they do their homework rather than shooting hoops. The fact that many Asian Pacific American young people have become All American academics rather than All American athletes seems to corroborate the Model Minority advocates inside and outside of Asian Pacific communities.

In recent years, many scholars of Asian Pacific American experiences have powerfully condemned the Model Minority Thesis as a stereotype and, despite its friendly guise toward Asian Pacific people, as dangerous. This is not the place to examine these critiques in detail. What is relevant here is that the Model Minority Thesis imposes a racial identity on Asian Pacific Americans--a racial identity that ignores or belittles their experiences as car mechanics, nurses, artists, political and community activists, and athletes. And to the extent that the Model Minority Thesis might acknowledge Asian Pacific American athleticism, it more than likely will recognize the cheerful grace of a Kristi Yamaguchi rather than the aggressive defense of a B.J. Itoman. The point, of course, is not to demean Yamaguchi's considerable talents or her apparent decency as a human being, but to look beyond Yamaguchi and see the underrepresented athletic achievements of people such as Tiffany Roberts, Dat Nguyen, or Wally Yonamine.

The media often reinforces the image of Asian Pacific people in general and Asian Pacific Americans as alien to athletic competition. In 1999, a study of sports media in the United States analyzed 722 sports programming commercials. To support its contention that sports programming can shape racial attitudes, the researchers claimed that thirty per cent of white, Latino, and Asian Pacific American boys regularly watched sports programming, while forty-five percent of African American boys regularly watched sports programming. In addition, only fifteen percent of white boys, twelve percent of African American and Latino boys, and eleven percent of Asian Pacific American boys never watched sports programming. The study revealed that twenty-eight commercials displayed African Americans by themselves, three featured Latinos by themselves, and only two showed Asian Pacific Americans by themselves. Over half of the half of the commercials featured whites only. Sampling sports commentators for NFL, NBA, ESPN Sports Center, Professional Wrestling, and Extreme Sports the study found they were either European American or African American. No Latino or Asian Pacific commentator was observed.[12]

Educator Roy Saigo wondered in 1999 if coaches did not share in forming the image of Asian Pacific Americans as athletically underprivileged. Writing in *The Chronicle of Higher Education*, Saigo observed: "The United States seems to have accepted a sort of Newtonian law of talent" in that athletic and intellectual ability "cannot exist in the same person at the same time." Saigo maintained that Asian Pacific American youth seem to hold their own athletically at high school. "But," he added, "they disappear from the courts and fields when they get to college. How can it be that Asian Pacific Americans lose all their athletic ability in the summer between high school and college." Saigo wondered if coaches bought into the notion that Asian Pacific Americans were so obsessed with good grades that they could not commit themselves to the varsity squad.[13]

Today, we might see less in the way of overt racial and ethnic hostility in the sporting world. Yet such hostility or indifference to such hostility endures. In the mid-1990s, a Los Angeles radio personality wondered on the air why the United States was represented in the Olympics by Kristi Yamaguchi and Mi chelle Kwan and not "real Americans." During the 1998 Winter Olympics, Michelle Kwan's major rival for the gold medal was Tara Lipinski. When Kwan took a second place to Lipinski's gold medal performance, the Microsoft National Broadcasting Company's website announced that an "American beat Kwan." After several Asian Pacific Americans protested, the wording of the announcement was changed, but MSNBC issued no apology. [14]

More recently, the San Francisco 49ers set off a firestorm of controversy when the media learned and reproduced a disturbing segment of a training video designed to improve the cultural sensitivity of 49er players. While perhaps no harm was intended, the video could easily be seen as demeaning to women and gays, as well as depicting Asian Pacific Americans in a stereotypical fashion. To counteract the bad public relations resulting from the "outing" of the training video, 49er president John York presided over two town hall meetings, one of which took place in San Francisco's Chinatown's. While York apologized, Asian Pacific American community activists demanded that the team take positive steps including the implementation of a zero-tolerance policy regarding harassment and discrimination, as well as increased outreach to affected communities in the Bay Area. [15]

Yvonne Lee of the Asian and Pacific Islander American Health Forum asserted, "We're not asking [the 49ers] to write us a check and then we'll go on our merry way." "This isn't about money. They have a responsibility to know and support their neighbors, just like we've been supporting them. So we need to educate them about the different communities they serve, which will require an ongoing commitment from both sides." Lee hoped that the coalition of activists produced by the 49ers training tape would eventually form a partnership with the franchise that since 1946 has been an integral part of Bay Area community life. [16]

Less optimistic, Leon Chow of the Chinese Progressive Association expressed doubts whether the 49ers would institute any real transformation.. Chow admitted that a future boycott of the 49ers might be in the offing. Changes would have to take place to remove a boycott completely from the table: "I want to see how these changes are implemented and how they're enforced. I want to see the <anti-discrimination> language written into the multimillion dollar contracts that the players sign, not just in a handbook. Then I'll believe it." [17]

Consumer Culture

Several insightful scholars of American society have noted with ambivalence the development of a consumer culture in the nineteenth and twentieth centuries. During the seventeenth and eighteenth centuries, a producer's ethic fired economic development in America. People needed to work hard at the expense of personal enjoyment if they were to survive and hopefully thrive. There are all sorts of reasons, good and bad, for the successful development of capitalism in America, but clearly the willingness of numerous Americans to work hard, sacrifice personal comfort, and save for the future contributed invaluably to that development. [18]

Nevertheless, crafty entrepreneurs such as P.T. Barnum recognized before the Civil War that they could make money from commercializing leisure. Serious nineteenth century economic theorists complained that capitalism needed to overcome the problem of overproduction and under consumption. In other words, people needed to spend more. But what if they did not have the time or, more importantly, the inclination to spend? With the growth of industrial capitalism, technology freed significant numbers of Americans from ten to twelve hour workdays. A middle class with a certain amount of discretionary income emerged. Still, developing American capitalism needed entrepreneurs such as P.T. Barnum and Albert G. Spalding—entrepreneurs dead set on expanding the markets for circuses and baseball games.

American culture by the twentieth century, therefore, embraced consumerism--albeit with a great deal of trepidation and guilt. Baseball represented not merely something an American male might have played as a child. Rather, baseball meant also that he should spend an afternoon watching highly skilled, adult men play at a local baseball park, where he paid a chunk of his salary or wages on tickets, programs, popcorn, pennants, and hot dogs. Baseball became no longer a game, but a commercialized spectacle. Indeed, by the 1990s, when major leaguers went on a major strike all sorts of experts predicted the game's demise as if baseball could only exist as long as Barry Bonds or Roger Clemens got paid millions of dollars for playing it.

The emergence of a consumer culture has generated all sorts of possibilities for culturally diverse Americans. For one thing, the consumer culture creatively helped raise and reinforce hierarchies in the United States. As classical social theorists such as Max Weber, Antonio Gramsci, and C. Wright Mills asserted during the early and mid-1900s, people do not come out of their mothers' wombs craving inequality like milk. They might have to learn to accept inequalities as either good or as impossible to alter—as common sense. Of course, it becomes easier to accept inequalities if one happens to learn that his or her group reigns supreme over other groups. And if Americans wanted to know who was different and inferior to them, Madison Avenue and Hollywood furnished plenty of hard to resist advice.

Weber's concept of legitimation, Gramsci's concept of hegemony, as well as other perceptive theories connecting power to culture warns us that it is not simply a matter of many of us learning to accept inequalities. We also, more subtly, learn to ignore those inequalities or proclaim they no longer or never did exist despite powerful evidence to the contrary. Here, too, consumer culture's institutions can help convince us. How, for example, can sexism remain a prob lem in a country where "Xena the Warrior Princess" and "Buffy the Vampire Killer" reigned as popular culture icons as the twentieth-first century approached?

Consumer culture, however, does not simply delude us. Weber, Gramsci, Mills, C..L.R. James, Raymond Williams, and more recently Stuart Hall, Renato Rosaldo, and Lisa Lowe remind us of the contradictory relationships between culture and power. Consumer culture in America has enabled some members of aggrieved social groups to reconstruct themselves materially and culturally. The transformation of San Francisco's Chinatown into a "tourist trap" fed on the image of Chinese descended people as exotic others, but it also built bridges to non-Chinese Americans, who still may have thought that fortune cookies were invented by strange people, but perhaps now less threatening, potentially more knowable people.[19]

Near that Chinatown, Charlie Low established the first "all-Oriental" nightclub in the United States during the late 1930s. It was called "Forbidden City" and featured a cast of entertainers possessing Chinese, Japanese, and Hawaiian ancestries and, for years, it was often the place to go when visiting San Francisco during and after World War II. Low, it would seem, spent a lifetime trying to be both a "regular Joe" and a show business mogul. His nightclub performers crooned, jitterbugged, and, if women, wore very little. He bought a string of polo ponies and was said to be a good polo player. When he gave up his polo ponies, Low announced he was taking up golf. It is difficult to say how Low felt about it all when he died in the 1990s. Clearly, however, the rise of the consumer culture allowed him to knock down some stereotypes, while propping up others.[20]

Getting back to sports, we often hear that racism and nativism have become anomalies in the modern sporting world, which supposedly thrives on promoting merit, regardless of its racial and ethnic background. How can racial injustice reign when Tiger Woods is so wealthy and seems so powerful? Indeed, often racism and nativism are pronounced as bad for business, sports or advertising. If people did not understand that at one time, with few exceptions they do now. Still, more so than many of us care to admit, bigoted racial and ethnic conventions seem well rooted in the historical development of sports; especially commercialized sports—the kind of sports which helped construct the consumer culture. For instance, the late nineteenth and early twentieth century baseball promoters often expected black mascots to provide demeaning entertainment to white spectators. At the same time, the sporting press employed racial and ethnic stereotypes enthusiastically to enhance interest in commercialized sport.

Asian Pacific Americans have long been exploited as exotic novelties in commercialized sports. Certainly, we can say this about how Asian Pacific prizefighters in the late nineteenth and early twentieth centuries were marketed. An even more vivid case of how sports might have promoted Asian Pacific exoticization occurred when the Sacramento Solons and Oakland Oaks hired Nushida and Hong respectively. These athletes, to be sure, crossed cultural borders as they took the mound against Pacific Coast League batters. Nevertheless, the stereotype of Chinese and Japanese people as too exotic to excel in American professional sports shadowed Nushida and Hong. At the heart of the matter, one finds Pacific Coast League owners hoping that baseball fans would want to spend hard earned cash in the midst of the Great Depression to see Hong and Nushida do some rather unspectacular, although adept, pitching simply because the ballplayers' parents were born in Asia.

Race and ethnicity may not be exploited at the dawn of the twenty-first century so openly as a marketing strategy for commercialized sport. But the close ties between commercialized sport and manufacturers of athletic shoes combined with the knowledge that such highly expensive shoes have found a market among African American ghetto and other impoverished youth has been and remains troubling. Consequently, in recent decades the one sure place to see an African American male on television is an advertisement showing a black athlete jumping, running, or appearing physically intimidating.

The disturbing connection between the manufacturing of athletic shoes and sports apparel and equipment with the very real exploitation of workers of color in Asia and other parts of the world persists. At the same time, media criticism of this connection often, however, has targeted the frequently strained apologetics of individual athletes of color who receive a great deal of money from accused corporations such as Nike, while neglecting the greater responsibility of typically white corporate executives.

Nevertheless, journalist Bill Wong insisted that individual athletes such as Michael Chang must assume some responsibility for their corporate bed partners. Chang, Wong pointed out in the late 1990s, had become known in Hong Kong as "Marlboro's man," mainly because he played in several tobacco company sponsored tournaments in Hong Kong, Beijing, and Seoul. [21]

For good or ill, Asian Pacific American athletes have been used to plug various products. A lifetime of television commercial watching will likely reveal few, if any, Asian Pacific people playing street basketball, but Asian Pacific people ice skating might appear another matter. Kristi Yamaguchi, for example, seemed to have been dismissed by major advertisers after she won the 1994 gold medal. Media scholar Darrell Hamamoto attributed Yamaguchi's failure to win endorsements in the months after her Olympic triumph to racism. Indeed, anti-Japanese feelings spiraled upward in the United States about the time Yamaguchi won her gold medal. The Speaker of Japan's Lower House had just caused a firestorm in America when he condemned American workers as lazy. The owners of the Japanese corporation, Nintendo, had, moreover, provoked controversy in American sporting circles by trying to purchase the Seattle

Mariners. Much of the hostility Americans expressed towards the Japanese could have bled into public disinterest in a Japanese American commercial icon.[22]

Disagreeing she was burdened by a racial uniform, Yamaguchi claimed that the lack of endorsements trailing after her Olympic victory was her own choice. She wanted to prepare for the world championships and did not want to lose her focus. Lending some validity to her claim, advertisers began to find Yamaguchi an attractive person to pitch certain products in the mid and late 1990s. According to journalist Danielle Martin in 1996, "Kristi is one of the most successful athletes in the marketplace. She demonstrates that even in these oppressively ironic times the street value of sincerity is pretty high." Tod Boyd, a popular culture scholar, adds, "<Yamaguchi> has the look and is that wholesome person we want her to be. The marketeers show a little courage when they choose Kristi. They say to the public: The all-American image is not a white upper-class thing. It's not limited to class or color." Still, whether Yamaguchi likes it or not, she has often been viewed as an impressive representative of Asian Pacific Americans as model minority members. Advertisers who wish to display a "sensitivity" to racial differences have used Yamaguchi since she has been seen as hard working, wholesome, and non-threatening.[23]

The fact that a relative handful of Asian Pacific American athletes have become merchandisable icons troubles some commentators such as Bill Wong. During the 1998 Winter Olympiad, Wong conceded he rooted for Michelle Kwan, because she could "be a Chinese American star." Yet he also declared: "At the same time, I kick myself for having such wishes. Why should who we are need to be validated by network T.V. advertisers, and the American middle-class masses."[24]

Another journalist Philip Tajitsu Nash, has taken a more optimistic view of Asian Pacific American sports celebrities. In 2000, he wrote that Tiger Woods and Kristi Yamaguchi have emerged as important and positive role models for young Asian Pacific Americans. He observed, "Because of Kristi Yamaguchi and others, an Asian American who goes to a ice rink and says he wants to win a gold medal is not going to be laughed off the ice. Because of Tiger Woods, if I go to a golf course and sign up for a tournament, I won't be thought of as someone who could not possibly be a competitive player."[25]

Two Asian Pacific American young women, Christine Chen and Diana Wang, said much the same thing in response to watching Michelle Kwan compete for world titles in the late 1990s. Chen told the press, "My family is rooting behind Michelle Kwan because she represents not necessarily the American Dream, but the feeling that Chinese Americans can successfully assimilate in American society." For Wang, Kwan served as a valuable public role model. Christine Chen claimed, "Traditionally, Asian Americans have gone into engineering and science fields. But even if they're not thinking about going into ice skating, at least they'll learn the idea of 'Follow your dream.'"[26]

Moreover, for Chen, Kwan reinforced something akin to cultural citizenship. She and her Asian Pacific American friends gathered in front of the television to root for Kwan at the Nagano, Japan Winter Olympiad in 1998. As for as they were concerned, Kwan was skating for more than just Olympic gold but was skating for people like Chen, who declared, "Tiger Woods, Michelle Kwan, Kristi Yamaguchi or Michael Chang, they're sort of changing the picture of what America looks like, when it's usually white and black." Thanks to her appearances on Jay Leno's "Tonight" show and the cover of *Sports Illustrated*, it would appear that Kwan has assimilated. However, for Chen, Kwan "invokes her heritage by wearing a Chinese pendant and, for her short program a sequined costume that is vibrant red, a color that Chinese regard as lucky."[27]

Asian Pacific Americans do not just cheer on other Asian Pacific American athletes but nationals of various Asian Pacific countries such as China, Japan, and Korea, as well as the Pacific Islands.. Globally known athletes such as Ichiro Suzuki, Hideki Matsui, Yao Ming, Se Ri Pak, and Vijay Singh have demonstrated repeatedly that Asian Pacific people can inhabit the elite stratosphere of modern world sports. Sportswriter Tim Kawakami explains that regardless of Asian Pacific nationality, athletes such as Yao Ming and Nancy Kwan prove "<w>e have our own Iversons and McGwires and Roger Clemenses and Joe Montanas." While happy about Yao Ming dueling Shaquille O'Neal for rebounds and Ichiro Suzuki rapping out base hits with extraordinary consistency, some Asian Pacific Americans find that the presence of Asian Pacific superstars in American sports might be something of a double-edged sword. One told journalist Jeanne Chan in 2002, "It's good for the sports field, but it's not necessarily good for Asian Americans....He added that the presence of foreign players creates an obstacle when Asian American are lumped with foreigners....We want to say this land is lour land. We are no different."[28]

Conclusion

It seems few, if any, uncrossable racial and ethnic borders exist for Asian Pacific and other Americans to traverse in the world of sports. Through sports, Asian Pacific Americans have shown time and time again that they can overcome stereotypes. They can also assert their cultural citizenship--their right to claim both distinctiveness and American nationality--strongly and plainly. However, cultural borders endure and the border guards seem ever vigilant. Those of us who look at the Tiger Woods and Kristi Yamaguchis and optimistically argue that things have gotten better in recent years and naturally will get even better in the future have not been paying that much attention to the historical experiences of Asian Pacific Americans and other people of color in and beyond the ball park and arena.

Notes

1. Benedict Anderson, *Invented Communities: Reflections on the Origins and Spread of Nationalism,* (London: Verso, 1983); C..L. R. James, *Beyond a Boundary.* (New York: Pantheon Books, 1983).

2. James, *Beyond.*

3. *Ibid.*

4. Bulosan, *America in the Heart,* 102.

5. Smith, *Americans in Process.*

6. Jeffrey T. Sammons, *Beyond the Ring: The Role of Boxing in American Society.* (Urbana and Chicago: University of Illinois Press, 1988).

7. John Hoberman, *Darwin's Athletes: How Sport Has Damaged Black America and Preserved The Myth of Race,* (Boston: Houghton-Mifflin Company, 1997), 137.

8. Harry Edwards, *The Sociology of Sport.* (Homewood, Ill.: Dorsey Press., 1973) Richard Lapchick, *Fractured Focus: Sport as a Reflection of Society,* (Lexington, MA: D.C. Heath and Co, 1986); Hoberman, *Darwin's Athletes;* Gerald Early, "Performance and Reality: Race, Sports and the Modern World," *Nation,* August 10-17, 1998.

9. Brian Liou, "Tall Order," www.asianweek.com, November 25, 1999.

10. Takaki, *Strangers;* chapter 12; Chan, *Asian Americans: An Interpretive History,* (Boston: Twayne, 1991), 167-171.

11. *Ibid.*

12. Michael Messner, Darnell Hunt, Michelle Dunbar, Perry Chen, Joan Lapp, and Patti Miller, "Children and Sports Media," Amateur Athletic Foundation Los Angeles: 1999.

13. Roy Saigo, "Academe Needs More Leaders of Asian Pacific Heritage, " www.chronicle.com, April 23, 1999.

14. *Asian Week,* March 4, 1998-March 11, 1998.

15. Bill Picture, "Looking for a Change, not a 49ers Band-Aid," www.asianweek.com, July 8, 2005.

16. Ibid.

17. Ibid.

18. Warren I. Susman, *Culture as History: The Transformation of American Society in the Twentieth Century,* (New York: Pantheon Books, 1984), xx.

19. Max Weber, From Max Weber: Essays *in Sociology, Hans Gerth and C. Wright Mills,* (eds.), (New York: Oxford University Press, 1958), 78-99; Antonio Gramsci, *Selections From The Prison Notebooks,* Q. Hoare and G. Smith, (eds.) (New York: International Press, 1971); C. Wright Mills, Raymond Willliams, *Marxism and Literature,* (New York and London: Oxford University Press, 1977). Stuart Hall, "Gramsci's Relevance for the Study of Race and Ethnicity," *Journal of Communication Inquiry,* 10, (Summer, 1986); Rosaldo, *Culture and Truth;* Lisa Lowe, *Immigrant Acts: On Asian American Cultural Politics,* (Durham and London: Duke University Press, 1996).

20. *Chinese Press,* November 11, 1949, p. 7.

21. Bill Wong, "Marlboro Man: Michael Chang's Smoky Image Abroad, " *Asian Week*, May 30, 1997-June 4, 1997

22. Darrell Y. Hamamoto, *Monitored Peril;* Danielle Martin, "The Selling of Kristi Yamaguchi," *The West, San Jose Mercury*, April 26, 1996.

23. Morton, "Kristi Yamaguchi."

24. *Asian Week*, February 26, 1998-March 4, 1998.

25. *Ibid.*, September 7, 2000-September 13, 2000.

26. David Nakamura, "Chinese Americans Bask in Olympic Spotlight," *Washington Post*, February 20, 1998.

27. *Ibid.*

28. Jeanne Chan, "Knocking Stereotypes Out of the Park," www.aja.org, August 9, 2002.

Postscript: 2008

American athletes and coaches of Asian Pacific ancestry had an interesting and largely productive year in 2008. It is, of course, impossible to depict all they accomplished or tried to accomplish in a short postscript. However, we should take a look at the participation of relatively elite athletes and coaches in baseball, basketball, American football and soccer, golf, and the Olympics. We should, meanwhile, keep in mind that Americans of Asian Pacific ancestry continue to compete, with comparatively little recognition outside of their communities, in all sorts of sports and at all sorts of levels. Interestingly, since the main text of this edition was finished, I have become aware of notable athletes who possess some kind of Asian Pacific ancestry. The experiences of these athletes may not tell all that much except further point out how analytically bankrupt racial categories can be.

At the MLB level, Johnny Damon is no longer the only star of Asian Pacific ancestry. Injuries have plagued Damon's career with the New York Yankees. However, in 2008 he had a fine year, despite being put on the disabled list for the first time in his major league career. Across the continent, a young Tim Lincicum became one of the MLB's finest pitchers, while hurling for the San Francisco Giants. Possessing Filipino ancestry, Lincicum has been called a "freak," because of his ability to throw so hard while standing less than six feet and weighing less than 200 pounds. Less spectacular, perhaps, is that the Tampa Bay Rays shortstop, Jacob Bartlett, also can claim Filipino ancestry. Japanese American Kurt Suzuki, meanwhile, has become the regular catcher for the Oakland Athletics. And while in 2008, no one would confuse him with Johnny Bench, Suzuki has shown respectable batting and defensive skills. Indeed, he was probably the most consistent hitter on an admittedly not so good Athletic team. In Philadelphia, Shane Victorino has developed a favorite among the often surly Phillies' fans. A hustling, speedy outfielder, Victorino possesses indigenous Hawaiian ancestry, along with a rifle arm and a good batting eye. Aside from Lincicum, the San Francisco Giants have suited up the veteran hapa Dave Roberts in 2008 in addition to first baseman Travis Ishikawa and Pinoy pitcher Geno Espinelli, who showed potential as a southpaw reliever. [1]

MLB has finally named an Asian Pacific American as a field manager. Lenn Sakata left the San Francisco Giants organization for hopefully a better opportunity to advance himself in Japan. After coaching for the Chicago White Sox for a while, Donn Wakamatsu was considered a possibility to manage the Oakland Athletics in 2008. He did not get the job, but he did become the "bench coach" for new manager Bob Geren. In other words, Wakamatsu was second-in-command of the As. However, after the 2008 season, the Seattle Mariners named Wakamatsu as their field mangers. Yet as of this writing Kim Ng remains as the Dodgers' assistant General Manager.

Meanwhile, a Hawaiian team from Waipahu copped the Little League World Championship in 2008. This marked actually the second time in recent years that a Hawaiian nine won it all in Williamsport, Pennsylvania, the site of the Little League World Series. In 2005, the Ewa Beach squad made Hawai'i proud. Needless to say most of the players and coaches possessed Asian Pacific Islander ancestry.

Americans of Asian Pacific ancestry illuminated American football and soccer. One of the more interesting things I have learned is that feared New England Patriot linebacker Tedy Bruschi is part-Pinoy. He proudly points out that his middle name is Lacap, the maiden name of his mother, Pinay Juanita Lacap. Norm Chow is still not employed as a head coach of a major football program. The Tennessee Titans let him go as offensive coordinator, but he wound up on his feet, heading the UCLA offense. Harvey Unga proved that players of Pacific Islander ancestry can be excellent ball carriers. He carried the ball for over 1200 yards in 2007 for BYU and remained one of the nation's top running backs in 2008. At the University of Arizona quarterback Willie Tuitama was considered one of the best college quarterbacks in the West after fine 2007 and 2008 seasons. Americans of Asian Pacific ancestry illuminated American soccer in 2008. Possessing Hawaiian, Filipino, and Chinese ancestry, Natasha Kai helped the U.S. Women's team win the gold in the summer Olympiad. While Brian Ching did not make the men's Olympic team, he remains one of the best soccer players in the country in the fall of 2008.[2]

Basketball called upon the services of Asian Pacific American coaches in 2008. After Hall of Famer Pat Riley stepped down after several years of coaching the NBA's Miami Heat, his long-time assistant, Erik Spolestra, was named as his replacement. The son of a former NBA executive of European American background and Filipina mother, Spolestra played for the University of Portland before spending a couple of years as player-coach in Europe. He had worked with the Heat in a variety of capacities since 1995. At the NCAA level, Rex Walters was named to head up the once vaunted University of San Francisco program.[3]

The U.S. women's volleyball team took home a silver medal in the 2008 Olympiad. Robyn Ah Mow-Santos competed on that team. After graduating from UH Ah-Mow Santos played professionally in Switzerland. Former Stanford standout Logan Tom was also on the team. Tom had previously competed professionally in Russia. Lindsey Berg, a relative newcomer on the national stage, was one of the team's setters along with Ah-Mow Santos. Berg is a "hapa" Hawaiian. [4]

Perhaps surprisingly, the Asian Pacific American presence in ice hockey deserves note. Born in Korea and raised in Southern California and then Canada, Richard Park had a solid 2007-2008 year in the NHL for the New York Islanders. Julie Chiu suited up for the 2008 World Championship women's ice hockey team, as did Hawaiian born Jessica Kozumi. Providence College student Amber Yung, moreover, became a defender on the U.S. "Under -22 National Team." [5]

Aside from the athletes already mentioned, several Americans of Asian Pacific ancestry participated in the 2008 Olympiad. While overshadowed by Michael Phelps' achievements, Natalie Coughlin and Bryan Clay were probably the most notable. A University of California graduate possessing Filipino descent, Coughlin developed into one of the most dominant female swimmers in the world in the early 2000s. In 2008, she won the most medals of any woman in Olympic history. Moreover, she became the first woman to win the 100 meters backstroke in back-to-back Olympics. As for Bryan Clay, he only won the world decathlon, making him perhaps the world's greatest athlete. [6]

In golf, Tiger is still Tiger. An injury shortened his 2008 season, but he continued to rule as golf's greatest player—perhaps by far. Los Angeles born Anthony Kim emerged as one of the PGA's best young golfers in 2008. Meanwhile, Michelle Wie has yet to prove she can be the female Tiger. However, several golfers of Asian and Asian Pacific American background have stood out on the LPGA tour, among them UCLA grad Jane Park. [7]

Speaking of golf, Asian Pacific American communities throughout the nation were aroused by a LPGA edict issued in late summer. The LPGA had demanded that its players speak English on its future tours—a demand that seemed aimed at the wide number of Asian nationals not just competing but excelling on the tour. Asian Pacific American and other civil rights groups and activists in California took the lead. Moreover, Samuel Yee, a state assembly person from San Francisco and San Mateo Counties proved integral in organizing the opposition. As of early September, the LPGA had backed down from its edict. [8]

Notes

1. Joseph Pimental, "Filipino Fireballer: FilAm Baseball Player Espineli," *Asian Journal*, August 5, 2008.
2. Cynthia DeCastro, "NFL Hero is FilAm," Asian Journal, February 11, 2008; http://www.asianweek.com/2008/08/08/asian-americans-going-for-the-gold-in, September 5, 2008.
3. Lester Cavestany, "Fil-Am Erik Spolestra—New Miami Heat Head Coach, www.Filipinovoices.com, April 30, 2008.
4. http://www.asianweek.com/2008/08/08/asian-americans-going-for-the-gold-in, September 5, 2008.
5. http://www.usahockey.com//Template_Usahockey, September 5, 2008; http://friars.cstv.com/sports/w-hockey/spec-rel/070708aaa.html, September 5, 2008.
6. http://www.asianweek.com/2008/08/08/asian-americans-going-for-the-gold-in, September 5, 2008.
7. http://www.pgatour.com/players/02/97/18/
8. http://www.asianweek.com/2008/09/04/daily-dose-090408/

Selected Bibliography

Reports, Guides, Yearbooks, and Programs

Ahead in the Count: 130 Years of Women & Baseball: 1995 Colorado Silver Bullets Souvenir Program.

East-West Shrine Football Program, Kezar Stadium, San Francisco, December 19, 1951

La Torre. San Jose State College Yearbook. 1942.

___. 1957.

Nikkei Heritage, Diamonds in the Rough: Japanese Americans in Baseball. (Spring, 1997).

Pete Newell Challenge, Basketball Program, Oakland Coliseum Arena, December 29, 2000.

Recreation Commission of, City and County of Honolulu. ed. *A History of Recreation in Hawaii.* Honolulu, T.H.: 1936

San Francisco Giants Magazine. (no. 2: 1987).

San Jose CYS Basketball Invitational Program, San Jose, 2003.

San Jose State University vs. University of Pacific, Spartan Stadium, San Jose, November 7, 1987.

Stanford University vs. California State University, Fullerton, Baseball Program, Stanford University. February 2, 2002.

Stanford Women's Basketball Program, Maples Pavilion, Stanford University, January 28, 1999 and January 30, 1999.

Stanford University vs. San Jose State College, Football Program, Stanford Stadium, November 1, 1952

Stanford University vs. San Jose State College, Football Program, Stanford Stadium, November 13, 1952

Stanford University vs. San Jose State College, Football Program, Stanford Stadium, October 13, 1956.

Stanford University vs. San Jose State University, Football Program, Stanford Stadium, September 27, 1983.

Stanford University vs. Washington State University, Football Program, Stanford Stadium, October 20, 1984.

Stanford University vs. Arizona University, Football Program, Stanford Stadium, October 26, 1985.

Stanford University vs. San Jose State University, Football Program, Stanford Stadium, September 30, 1989.

Stanford University vs. Arizona University, Football Program, Stanford Stadium, October 17, 1992.

Stanford University vs. Washington State University, Football Program, Stanford Stadium, November 14, 1992.

Stanford University v. University of Southern California, Football Program, Stanford Stadium, October 15, 1994.

Stanford University vs. San Jose State University, Football Program, Stanford Stadium, September 30, 1996.

Stanford University vs. Oregon University, Football Program, Stanford Stadium, September 27, 1999.

Stanford University vs. University of California, Volleyball Program, Maples Pavilion, Stanford University, October 9, 1998.

United States Census Manuscripts. City and County of Honolulu, 1900.

___. City and County of Honolulu, 1920.

___. City and County of Honolulu, 1930.

___. City and County of Los Angeles, 1930.

___. City of Ogden and County of Weber, Utah, 1930.

___. County of Placer, California, 1930.

___. Ewa Plantation, Hawaii, 1920.

___. Hilo, Hawaii, 1910.

___. Wailuki, Maui, 1930.

United States Immigration Commission. *Reports of the Immigration Commission*: Immigrants *in Industries, Part 25, Japanese and Other Immigrant Races in the Pacific.* Government Printing Office: Washington, D.C., 1911.

University of California vs. Stanford University, Football Program, Memorial Stadium, Berkeley, California, November 24, 1934.

University of California v. University of Southern California, Football Program, Memorial Stadium, Berkeley, California, October 20, 1951

University of San Francisco vs. Marquette Football Program, Kezar Stadium, San Francisco, November 20, 1949.

Periodicals

1946 Illustrated Football Annual
American Golfer
Appleton Post-Crescent
Asian Student
Asian Weekly
Atlantic Monthly
Atlantic Constitution
Baseball Monthly
Bennington Evening Banner
Berkshire Evening Telegram
Bismarck Daily Tribune
Bridge
Bridgeport Telegram
California Chinese Press
Charleston Daily Mail
Chicago Daily Tribune
Chicago Defender
Chillicothe Constitution
Chinese Digest

Chinese Press
Chinese Students
Colliers
Coschocton Tribune
Daily Alta California
Daily Commonwealth
Daily Palo Alto
Daily Worker
Decatur Review
East/West
Elyria Evening Telegram
Fil-America Advocate
Filipinas
Fort Wayne News
Fort Wayne Sentinel
Frederick Post
Hawaii Herald
Hawaiian Gazette
Heart Mountain Sentinel
Helena Independent
Hokubei Mainichi
Honolulu Advertiser
Honolulu Star-Bulletin
Honolulu Weekly
Houston Chronicle
Indiana Evening Gazette
Indianapolis Daily Star
Little India
Korean Independence
Los Angeles Evening Express
Los Angeles Sentinel
Los Angeles Times
Los Gatos Times
Manzanar Free Press
Marion Star
Metro (San Jose, California)
Middletown Times Press
Mind and Body
Monitor
Nevada State Journal
Newport News
New York Age
New York Times
Nichi Bei Times
Nikkei Heritage
Nikkei Northwest

Oakland Tribune
Outlook
Oxnard Press-Courier
Pacific Citizen
Pacific Commercial Advertiser
Pacific Magazine and Islands Business
Philippine Daily Inquirer
Philippine News
Philippines Mail
Philippines Star Press
Placer Mountain Democrat
Playground
Portland Oregonian
Rafu Shimpo
Reno Evening Gazette
Rice Paper
Sacramento Bee
Salt Lake City Herald Republican
San Francisco Chronicle
San Francisco Evening Bulletin
San Francisco Examiner.
San Francisco News
San Jose Herald.
San Jose Mercury
San Jose Metro
Santa Ana Register
Scene
Seattle Post-Intelligencer
Spartan Daily
Sport
Sport Life
Sporting Life
Sporting News
Sports Illustrated
Sports Review Football Annual 1957
St. Joseph's Herald Press
Stanford Daily
Tennis
USGA and Turf Management
Utah Nippo
Volleyball Monthly
Washington Post
Waterloo Daily Courier
Waukeda Daily Freeman
Williamsport Grit
Yolk

Oral History

"An Olympian Oral History, Sammy Lee." interview by Dr. Margaret Costa, edited by Carmen Rivera, (Los Angeles: AAFLA, 1999).

Theses

Cariaga, Ramon R. *The Filipinos in Hawaii: A Survey of their Economic and Social Conditions Thesis.* University of Hawaii, 1936.
Kaulukukui, Thomas. "The Development of Competitive Athletics in the Schools of Hawaii," University of Hawaii, 1941.
Naku, Jr., Manuel Romero. "Filipino Service Center," MS Thesis, San Jose State University, 1974.

Books and Articles

Anderson, Benedict. *Invented Communities: Reflections on the Origins and Spread of Nationalism,.* London: Verso, 1983.
Anzaldua, Gloria. *Borderlands/La Frontera: The New Mestiza.* San Francisco: Spinsters/Aunt Lute, 1987.
Ardolino, Frank. "Jackie Robinson and the Honolulu Bears." *The National Pastime.* (no. 15, 1995).
___. "The Big Leaguers hit the Beach." *The National Pastime* (no. 16, 1996).
Bacho, Peter. "A Manong's Heart," in *Turning Shadows into Light.* edited by Mayumi Tsutakawa and Alan Chong Law. Seattle, WA: Young Pines Press, 1982.
Bailey, Beth. and David Farber. *First Strange Place: The Alchemy of Race and Sex in World War II Hawaii.* New York: The Free Press, 1992.
Bellah, Robert. *et. al. Habits of the Heart: Individualism and Commitment in American Life.* Berkeley and Los Angeles: University of California Press, 1985.
Blanchard, Kendall B. and Alyce Cheyska. *The Anthropology of Sport: An Introduction,* South Hadley, Massachusetts: Bergin and Garvey Publishers, Inc., 1985.
Bruce, Janet. *The Kansas City Monarchs: Champions of Black Baseball.* Lawrence: KS: University of Kansas Press, 1985.
Buck Elizabeth. *Paradise Remade: The Politics of Culture and History in Hawai'i.* Philadelphia: Temple University Press, 1993.
Bulosan, Carlos. *America is in The Heart.* Seattle: University of Washington Press, 1973.
Burrows, Edward. *Hawaiian Americans: An Account of the Mingling of Japanese, Chinese, and Polynesian People.* New York: Archon Books, 1970.
Cahn, Susan K. *Coming on Strong: Gender and Sexuality in Twentieth-Century Women's Sport.* New York: Free Press, 1994.
Catapusan, Benicio. *The Filipino Occupational and Recreational Activities in Los Angeles.* Saratoga, CA: R & E Research Associates, 1975.
Chan, Sucheng. *This Bittersweet Soil: The Chinese in California Agriculture, 1870-1910.* Berkeley and Los Angeles: University of California Press, 1986.
___. *Asian Americans: An Interpretive History.* Boston: Twayne, 1991.

Chatwin, Dean. *Wahine Ball: The Story of Hawai'i's Most Beloved Team.* Honolulu: Mutual Publishing, 1997.

Chinn, Thomas. Bridging the Pacific: San Francisco Chinatown and Its People. San Francisco: Chinese Historical Society, 1989.

Christagu, John. *The Origins of the Jump Shot: Eight Men Who Shook the World of the Basketball.* Lincoln, Nebraska: University of Nebraska Press, 1999.

Cisco, Dan. *Hawai'i Sports: History, Facts, & Statistics.* Honolulu: University of Hawai'i Press, 1999.

Cooper, Pamela. *American Marathon.* Syracuse: Syracuse University Press, 1998.

Cordova, Fred. *Filipinos: Forgotten Asian Americans.* .Dubuque, Iowa: Kendall/Hunt Publishing Company, 1983.

Drinnon, Richard. *Facing West: The Metaphysics of Indian Hating and Empire Building,* New York: Schocken Books, 1991.

Early, Gerald. "Performance and Reality: Race, Sports and the Modern World." *Nation,* August 10-17, 1998.

Edward, Harry. *The Sociology of Sport.* Homewood, Ill.: Dorsey Press, 1973.

Ellison, Ralph. *The Invisible Man.* New York: Random House, 1952.

Espiritu, Yen Le. *Filipino American Lives.* Philadelphia: Temple University Press, 1995.

Ethnic Studies Oral History Project. *Remembering Kakaako.* Honolulu: University of Hawaii, Manoa, 1978.

___. *Kalihi, Place of Transition.* Honolulu: University of Hawai'i, Manoa, 1984.

Feldman, Jay. "Baseball Behind Barbed Wire," *The National Pastime: A Review of Baseball History.* (no. 12, 1992).

Flores, William V and Rina Benmayor, (eds.). *Latino Cultural Citizenship: Claiming Identity Space and Rights.* Boston: Beacon Press, 1997.

Friedrich, Otto. *City of Nets, A Portrait of Hollywood in the 1940s.* New York: Harper & Row, 1986.

Friday, Chris . *Organizing Asian American Labor: The Pacific Coast Canned-Salmon Industry, 1870-1942.* Philadelphia: Temple University Press, 1994.

Gill, Bob. *Best in the West: The Rise and Fall of the Pacific Coast Football League, 1940-1948.* Pacific Football Research Association, 1988.

Gonzalves, Theodore S. "When the Walls Speak a Nation, "*Journal of Asian American Studies,* (February, 1998).

Gorn, Elliot. *The Manly Art: Bare-Knuckle Prize Fighting in America.* Ithaca, NY: Cornell University Press, 1986.

Gramsci, Antonio. *Selections From The Prison Notebooks.* Edited by Q. Hoare and G. Smith. New York: International Press, 1971.

Gregory, James N. *American Exodus: The Dust Bowl Migrations and Okie Culture in California.* New York and London: Oxford University Press, 1989.

Hagedorn, Jessica., ed. *Charlie Chan is Dead: An Anthology of Contemporary Asian American Fiction.* New York: Penguin Books, 1993.

Hall, Sandra Kimberley and Greg Ambrose. *Memories of Duke: The Legend Comes to Life.* Honolulu: The Bess Press, 1995.

Hall, Stuart. "Gramsci's Relevance for the Study of Race and Ethnicity." *Journal of Communication Inquiry.* (Summer, 1986.)

Hamamoto, Darrell. *Monitored Peril: Asian Americans and the Politics of TV Representation.* Minneapolis, Minnesota: University of Minnesota Press, 1994.

Hardy, Stephen. *How Boston Played: Sports, Recreation, and Community, 1865-1915.* Boston: Northeastern University Press, 1982.

Hoberman, John. *Darwin's Athletes: How Sport Has Damaged Black America and Preserved the Myth of Race.* Boston: Houghton-Mifflin Company, 1997.

Hollander, Zander Hollander and Alex Zachary. (eds.) *The Official NBA Encyclopedia.* New York: Villard Books, 1989.

Holway, John. *Voices from the Great Negro Baseball Leagues.* New York: Dodd, Mead, & Company, 1975.

Horowitz, Irving Louis. (ed.) *Power, Politics and People: The Collected Essays of C. Wright Mills.* New York: Oxford University Press, 1963.

Hosokawa, Bill. *Nisei: The Quiet Americans.* New York: William Morrow and Company, Inc., 1969.

Ichioka, Yuji. The *Issei: The World of First Generation Japanese Immigrants, 1885-1924.* New York: The Free Press, 1988.

Ishikawa, Yoshimi. *Strawberry Road: A Japanese Immigrant Discovers America.* Translated by Eve Zimmerman. Tokyo, New York and London: Kondansha International, 1991.

James, C. L. R. *Beyond a Boundary.* New York: Pantheon Books, 1983.

King, C. Richard. (ed.) *Native Americans in Sports.* Armonk NY: Sharpe Reference, 2004.

Kirsch, George, Othello Harris and Claire E. Notle, (eds.) *Encyclopedia of Ethnicity and Sports in the United States.* Westport, Connecticut: Greenwood Press, 2000.

Kitano, Harry. *Japanese Americans: The Evolution of a Subculture.* Englewood Cliffs, New Jersey: Prentice-Hall, 1976.

Klein, Allen. *Baseball on the Border.* Princeton, New Jersey: Princeton University Press, 1997.

Kodama-Nishimoto, Michi. *et. al. Hanahana: An Oral History Anthology of Hawaii.* Ethnic Studies Oral History Project, University of Hawaii, Manao, 1984.

Lai, William T. "Buck". *Championship Baseball From Little League to Big League.* New York Prentice Hall, 1954.

Lapchick, Richard *Fractured Focus: Sport as a Reflection of Society.* Lexington, MA: D.C. Heath and Co, 1986.

Lasker, Bruno. *Filipino Immigration.* Chicago: University of Chicago Press, 1931.

Lee, Marjorie. "Building a Community." *Linking Our Lives.* Los Angeles: Chinese Historical Society of Southern California, 1984.

Lee, Mary Paik. *Quiet Odyssey: A Pioneer Korean Woman in America.* Edited and introduction by Sucheng Chan. Seattle: University of Washington Press, 1990.

Leonard, Karen Isaksen. *Making Ethnic Choices: California's Punjabi Mexican Americans.* Philadelphia: Temple University Press, 1992.

Levine, Peter. *From Ellis Island to Ebbets Field: Sport and the American Jewish Experience.* New York: Oxford University Press, 1992.

Lewis, Michael. *Moneyball: The Art of Winning An Unfair Game.* New York: W.W. Norton, 2003.

London, Jack. *Learning Hawaiian Surfing: A Royal Sport at Waikiki Beach.* Honolulu: Boom Enterprises, 1983.

Lowe, Lisa. *Immigrant Acts: On Asian American Cultural Politics.* Durham and London: Duke University Press, 1996.

Lukes, Tim and Gary Okihiro. Japanese *Legacy: Farming and Community Life in California's Santa Clara Valley.* California History Center: Cupertino, CA, 1985.

Lum, Lydia. "Breaking Football's Color Barrier." *Black Issues in Higher Education.* April 15, 1999.

Lydon, Sandy. *Chinese Gold: The Chinese in the Monterey Bay Region.* Capitola, CA: Capitola Books, 1985.

Ma, Eve and Jeong Hui Ma. *The Chinese of Oakland: Unsung Builders.* Oakland Chinese History Research Committee, 1982.

Mandell, Richard D. *Sport: A Cultural History.* New York: Columbia University Press, 1984.

Marquesse, Mike. "Sport and Stereotype: From Role Model to Muhammad Ali." *Race and Class.* (April-June, 1995).

Mason, Tony. "Cricket," in *Encyclopedia of World Sport: From Ancient Times to the Present,* I (Santa Barbara, CA: ABC-CLIO, 1996.

Matsumoto, Valerie. *Farming the Home Place: A Japanese American Community in California, 1919-1982.* Ithaca, New York: Cornell University Press, 1993.

McCarthy, Bernie. "Squirmin Herman and the Whiz Kids," *College Football Historical Society.* vol. 22. 1987.

McCunn, Ruthanne Lum. *Chinese American Portraits: Personal Memories, 1828-1988.* San Francisco: *San Francisco Chronicle* Books, 1988.

Mears, Eliot. *Resident Orientals on the American Pacific Coast.* Chicago: University of Chicago Press, 1928.

Messner, Michael, Darnell Hunt, Michelle Dunbar, Perry Chen, Joan Lapp, and Patti Miller. "Children and Sports Media." Amateur Athletic Foundation Los Angeles: 1999.

Misawa, Steven. (ed.) *Beginnings*: Japanese *Americans in San Jose.* San Jose: Japanese American Community Senior Service, 1981.

Mochizuki, Ken. *Baseball Saved Us.* New York: Scholastic, Inc. 1993.

Nagata, Yoichi. "The First All-Asian Pitching Duel in Organized Baseball: Japan vs. China in the PCL." *Baseball Research Journal,* (no. 21).

___. and John Holway. "Japanese Baseball," in *Total Baseball.* Edited by John Thorn and Peter Palmer. New York Warner Books, 1989.

Nakagawa, Kerry Yo. *Through A Diamond: 100 Years of Japanese American Baseball.* San Francisco: Rudi Publishing Company, 2001.

Nelson, Lyle E. "A Real Upset." *College Football Historical Society.* (May, 1996).

Ng, Franklin. (ed.). *The Asian American Encyclopedia.* Toronto, Marchall Cavendish, 1995.

Nomura, Gail M. "Beyond the Playing Field: The Significance of Pre-World War II Japanese American Baseball in the Yakima Valley," in *Bearing Dreams, Shaping Visions: Asian Pacific American Perspectives.* Edited by Linda A. Revilla, Gail M. Nomura, Shawn Wong, and Shirley Hune. Pullman, Washington: Washington State University Press, 1993.

Odo Franklin and Kazubo Sinota. *A Pictorial History of the Japanese in Hawaii, 1885-1924.* Honolulu: Bishop Museum Press, 1985.

Odo, Frank. *No Sword to Bury: Japanese Americans in Hawai'i During World War II.* Philadelphia: Temple University Press, 2004.

Official Baseball Annual 1956, Rules, Teams, Photos. Wichita, KA: National Baseball Congress, 1956.

Oh, Sadaharu and David Faulkner. *A Zen Way of Baseball.* New York: Times Books, 1984.

Okamura, Jonathan. ed. *Japanese American Contemporary Experience in Hawai'i,* Honolulu: University of Hawai'i Press, 2002.

Okihiro, Gary. *Cane Fires: The Anti-Japanese Movement in Hawaii, 1865-1915.* Philadelphia, PA: Temple University Press, 1991.

___. *Storied Lives: Japanese American Students and World War II.* Seattle : University of Washington Press, 1999.

Omi, Michael Omi and Winant, Howard. *Racial Formation in the United States: From the 1960s to the 1990s.* 2nd Edition. London and New York: Routledge, 1994.

Osorio, Jonathan Kay Kamakawio'ole. *Dismembering Lāhui: A History of the Hawaiian Nation,* Honolulu: University of Hawai'i Press, 2002.

Peterson, Harold. *The Man Who Invented Baseball.* New York: Charles Scribner's and Sons, 1973.

Pope, S.W. *Patriotic Games: Sporting Traditions in the American Imagination, 1876-1926.* New York: Oxford University Press, 1997.

Regalado, Samuel O. "Sport and Community in California's Japanese American 'Yamato Colony' 1930-1945," *Journal of Sport History.* (Summer 1992).

___. "Incarcerated Sport: Nisei Women's Softball and Athletics during Japanese Internment," *Journal of Sport History.* (Fall, 2000).

Riess, Steven. *Touching Base: Professional Baseball and American Culture in the Progressive Era.* Westport, Connecticut: Greenwood Press, 1980.

Rosaldo, Renato. *Culture and Truth: The Remaking of Social Analysis.* Boston: Beacon Press, 1989.

Said, Edward. *Orientalism.* New York: Vintage Books, 1979.

Sakamaki George. "Japanese Athletes in Hawaii." *Bulletin of the Pan-Pacific Union,.* (August, 1931).

Saldivar, Jose David. *Border Matters: Remapping American Cultural Studies.* Berkeley: University of California Press, 1997.

Sammons, Jeffrey. *Beyond the Ring: The Role of Boxing in American Society.* Urbana, Ill.: University of Illinois Press, 1988.

Saxton, Alexander. *The Indispensable Enemy: Labor and the Anti-Chinese Movement in California.* Berkeley and Los Angeles: University of California Press, 1971.

See, Lisa. *On Gold Mountain.* New York: St. Martin's Press, 1995.

Seymour, Harold. *Baseball: The People's Game.* New York: Oxford University Press, 1990.

Siu, Paul P.C. *The Chinese Laundryman: A Study in Social Isolation.* New York: New York University Press, 1987.

Smith, William C. *Americans in Process: A Study of Our Citizens of Oriental Ancestry.* Ann Arbor, MI: Edwards Brothers, 1937.

Social Science Research Institute, University of Hawai'i, Manoa,. *Kalihi: Place of Transition.* Honolulu: Ethnic Studies Oral History Project, 1984.

Spalding, Albert G. *America's National Game*. Lincoln and London: University of Nebraska Press, 1992.

Spalding, John E. *Sacramento Senators and Solons: Baseball in California's Capital, 1886-1976*. Manhattan, KS: Ag Press, 1995.

Starr, Kevin. "The Sporting Life." *California History*. (Winter, 1984).

Strong, Edward K. *The Second Generation Japanese Problem*. New York: Arno Press, 1970.

Suehiro, Arthur. *Honolulu Stadium; Where Hawaii Played*. Honolulu: Watermark Publishing, 1995.

Sussman, Warren I. *Culture as History: The Transformation of American Society in the Twentieth Century*. New York: Pantheon Books, 1984.

Takahashi, Jere. *Nisei, Sansei: Shifting Japanese American Identities and Politics*. Philadelphia: Temple University Press, 1997.

Takaki, Ronald. *Pau Hana: Plantation Life and Labor in Hawai'i, 1835-1924*. Honolulu: University of Hawai'i Press, 1983.

___. *Strangers from a Different Shore: A History of Asian Americans*. Boston: Little Brown, 1989.

Trask, Haunani-Kay Trask. *From a Native Daughter: Colonialism & Sovereignty in Hawaii*. Monroe, Maine: Common Courage Press, 1993.

Tuan, Mia . *Forever Foreign or Honorary Whites: The Asian Ethnic Experience*. New Brunswick, New Jersey: Rutgers University Press, 1998.

Walsh, Peter. *Men of Steel: the Lives and Times of Boxing's Middleweight Champions*. London: Robson Books, LTD., 1992.

Weber, Max. From *Max Weber: Essays in Sociology*. Edited by Hans Gerth and C. Wright Mills. New York: Oxford University Press, 1958.

Welky, David B. "Viking Girls, Mermaids and Little Brown Men: U.S. Journalism and the 1932 Olympics." *Journal of Sport History*. (Spring, 1997).

White, Richard. *The Middle Ground: Indians, Empires, and Republics in the Great Lakes Region, 1650-1815*. New York: Cambridge University Press, 1991.

Wiebe, Robert. *Self-Rule: A Cultural History of American Democracy*. Chicago: University of Chicago Press, 1995.

Wiggins, David K. *Glory Bound: Black Athletes in a White America*. Syracuse: Syracuse University Press, 1997.

Williams, Raymond. *Marxism and Literature*. New York and London: Oxford University Press, 1977.

___. *Keywords: A Vocabulary of Culture and Society*. New York: Oxford University Press, 1983.

Wrynn, Alison M. "The Recreation and Leisure Pursuits of Japanese Americans in World War II Internment Camps," in *Ethnicity and Sport in North American History and Culture*. Edited by George Eisen and David K. Wiggins. Westport, CT: Greenwood Press, 1994.

Yee, George and Elise Yee, "The 1927 Chinese Ball Team." *Gam San Journal*. (December 1986).

Yu, Connie Young. *Chinatown San Jose, USA*. San Jose: Historical Museum Association, 1991.

Yung, Judy. *Unbound Feet: A Social History of Chinese Women in San Francisco*. Berkeley and Los Angeles: University of California Press, 1995.

___. *Unbound Voices: A Documentary History of Chinese Women in San Francisco.* Berkeley and Los Angeles: University of California Press, 1999.

Zia, Helen and Susan B. Fall. (eds.) *Notable Asian Americans.* Detroit: Gale Research, 1995.

Zieff, Susan. "From Badminton to the Bolero: Sport and Recreation in San Francisco's Chinatown." *Journal of Sport History.* (Spring, 2000).

Zingg, Paul J. And Mark D. Medeiros. *Runs, Hits, and an Era: The Pacific Coas League, 1903-1958.* Urbana, Illinois: University of Illinois Press, 1994.

Index

About the Author

Joel Franks received his BA and MA in History from San Jose State University and his PH.D. from the Program in Comparative Culture at the University of California, Irvine. Author of several publications, he presently teaches Asian American and American Studies at San Jose State University.